CONSTITUTIONALISM AND A RIGHT TO EFFECTIVE GOVERNMENT?

Nations around the world are facing various crises of ineffective government. Basic governmental functions – protecting rights, preventing violence, and promoting material well-being – are compromised, leading to declines in general welfare, in the enjoyment of rights, and even in democracy itself. This innovative collection, featuring analyses by leaders in the fields of constitutional law and politics, highlights the essential role of effective government in sustaining democratic constitutionalism. The book explores "effective government" as a right, principle, duty, and interest, situating questions of governance in debates about negative and positive constitutionalism. In addition to providing new conceptual approaches to the connections between rights and governance, the volume also provides novel insights into government institutions, including courts, legislatures, executives, and administrative bodies, as well as the media and political parties. This is an essential volume for anyone interested in constitutionalism, comparative law, governance, democracy, the rule of law, and rights.

Vicki C. Jackson is Laurence H. Tribe Professor of Constitutional Law at Harvard Law School. She has written widely on comparative and US constitutional law, in works including *Constitutional Engagement in a Transnational Era* (2010), *Comparative Constitutional Law* (with Mark Tushnet, 3d. ed. 2014), and *Defining the Field of Comparative Constitutional Law* (with Mark Tushnet, 2002).

Yasmin Dawood is the Canada Research Chair in Democracy, Constitutionalism, and Electoral Law, and Associate Professor at the Faculty of Law, University of Toronto. She also holds an appointment in the Department of Political Science. She has published widely on voting rights, comparative election law, and the theory and practice of democratic constitutionalism.

COMPARATIVE CONSTITUTIONAL LAW AND POLICY

Series Editors

Tom Ginsburg *University of Chicago*
Zachary Elkins *University of Texas at Austin*
Ran Hirschl *University of Toronto*

Comparative constitutional law is an intellectually vibrant field that encompasses an increasingly broad array of approaches and methodologies. This series collects analytically innovative and empirically grounded work from scholars of comparative constitutionalism across academic disciplines. Books in the series include theoretically informed studies of single constitutional jurisdictions, comparative studies of constitutional law and institutions, and edited collections of original essays that respond to challenging theoretical and empirical questions in the field.

Books in the Series

Constitutionalism and a Right to Effective Government?
Edited by Vicki C. Jackson and Yasmin Dawood
The Fall of the Arab Spring: Democracy's Challenges and Efforts to Reconstitute the Middle East
Tofigh Maboudi
Filtering Populist Claims to Fight Populism: The Italian Case in a Comparative Perspective
Giuseppe Martinico
Constitutionalism in Context
Edited by David S. Law
The New Fourth Branch: Institutions for Protecting Constitutional Democracy
Mark Tushnet
The Veil of Participation: Citizens and Political Parties in Constitution-Making Processes
Alexander Hudson
Towering Judges: A Comparative Study of Constitutional Judges
Edited by Rehan Abeyratne and Iddo Porat
The Constitution of Arbitration
Victor Ferreres Comella
Redrafting Constitutions in Democratic Orders: Theoretical and Comparative Perspectives
Edited by Gabriel L. Negretto
From Parchment to Practice: Implementing New Constitutions
Edited by Tom Ginsburg and Aziz Z. Huq
The Failure of Popular Constitution Making in Turkey: Regressing Towards Constitutional Autocracy
Edited by Felix Petersen and Zeynep Yanaşmayan
A Qualified Hope: The Indian Supreme Court and Progressive Social Change
Edited by Gerald N. Rosenberg, Sudhir Krishnaswamy, and Shishir Bail
Reconstructing Rights: Courts, Parties, and Equality Rights in India, South Africa, and the United States
Stephan Stohler
Constitutions in Times of Financial Crisis
Edited by Tom Ginsburg, Mark D. Rosen, and Georg Vanberg

Hybrid Constitutionalism: The Politics of Constitutional Review in the Chinese Special Administrative Regions
Eric C. Ip
Constitution-Making and Transnational Legal Order
Edited by Tom Ginsburg, Terence C. Halliday, and Gregory Shaffer
The Invisible Constitution in Comparative Perspective
Edited by Rosalind Dixon and Adrienne Stone
The Politico-Legal Dynamics of Judicial Review: A Comparative Analysis
Theunis Roux
Constitutional Courts in Asia: A Comparative Perspective
Edited by Albert H. Y. Chen and Andrew Harding
Judicial Review in Norway: A Bicentennial Debate
Anine Kierulf
Constituent Assemblies
Edited by Jon Elster, Roberto Gargarella, Vatsal Naresh, and Bjorn Erik Rasch
The DNA of Constitutional Justice in Latin America: Politics, Governance, and Judicial Design
Daniel M. Brinks and Abby Blass
The Adventures of the Constituent Power: Beyond Revolutions?
Andrew Arato
Canada in the World: Comparative Perspectives on the Canadian Constitution
Edited by Richard Albert and David R. Cameron
Constitutions, Religion and Politics in Asia: Indonesia, Malaysia and Sri Lanka
Dian A. H. Shah
Courts and Democracies in Asia
Po Jen Yap
Proportionality: New Frontiers, New Challenges
Edited by Vicki C. Jackson and Mark Tushnet
Constituents before Assembly: Participation, Deliberation, and Representation in the Crafting of New Constitutions
Todd A. Eisenstadt, A. Carl LeVan, and Tofigh Maboudi
Assessing Constitutional Performance
Edited by Tom Ginsburg and Aziz Huq
Buddhism, Politics and the Limits of Law: The Pyrrhic Constitutionalism of Sri Lanka
Benjamin Schonthal
Engaging with Social Rights: Procedure, Participation and Democracy in South Africa's Second Wave
Brian Ray
Constitutional Courts as Mediators: Armed Conflict, Civil-Military Relations, and the Rule of Law in Latin America
Julio Ríos-Figueroa
Perils of Judicial Self-Government in Transitional Societies
David Kosař
Making We the People: Democratic Constitutional Founding in Postwar Japan and South Korea
Chaihark Hahm and Sung Ho Kim
Radical Deprivation on Trial: The Impact of Judicial Activism on Socioeconomic Rights in the Global South
César Rodríguez-Garavito and Diana Rodríguez-Franco

Unstable Constitutionalism: Law and Politics in South Asia
Edited by Mark Tushnet and Madhav Khosla
Magna Carta and Its Modern Legacy
Edited by Robert Hazell and James Melton
Constitutions and Religious Freedom
Frank B. Cross
International Courts and the Performance of International Agreements: A General Theory with Evidence from the European Union
Clifford J. Carrubba and Matthew J. Gabel
Reputation and Judicial Tactics: A Theory of National and International Courts
Shai Dothan
Social Difference and Constitutionalism in Pan-Asia
Edited by Susan H. Williams
Constitutionalism in Asia in the Early Twenty-First Century
Edited by Albert H. Y. Chen
Constitutions in Authoritarian Regimes
Edited by Tom Ginsburg and Alberto Simpser
Presidential Legislation in India: The Law and Practice of Ordinances
Shubhankar Dam
Social and Political Foundations of Constitutions
Edited by Denis J. Galligan and Mila Versteeg
Consequential Courts: Judicial Roles in Global Perspective
Edited by Diana Kapiszewski, Gordon Silverstein, and Robert A. Kagan
Comparative Constitutional Design
Edited by Tom Ginsburg

Constitutionalism and a Right to Effective Government?

Edited by

VICKI C. JACKSON

Harvard Law School

YASMIN DAWOOD

University of Toronto

CAMBRIDGE
UNIVERSITY PRESS

CAMBRIDGE
UNIVERSITY PRESS

University Printing House, Cambridge CB2 8BS, United Kingdom

One Liberty Plaza, 20th Floor, New York, NY 10006, USA

477 Williamstown Road, Port Melbourne, VIC 3207, Australia

314–321, 3rd Floor, Plot 3, Splendor Forum, Jasola District Centre, New Delhi – 110025, India

103 Penang Road, #05–06/07, Visioncrest Commercial, Singapore 238467

Cambridge University Press is part of the University of Cambridge.

It furthers the University's mission by disseminating knowledge in the pursuit of education, learning, and research at the highest international levels of excellence.

www.cambridge.org
Information on this title: www.cambridge.org/9781009158534
DOI: 10.1017/9781009158541

First published 2022

A catalogue record for this publication is available from the British Library.

ISBN 978-1-009-15853-4 Hardback

For our children and grandchildren, may they grow to help human rights flourish and governments work well to represent, protect, and respect all human beings.

Contents

Tables

Contributors

N. W. Barber is Professor of Constitutional Law and Theory, Oxford University.

Manuel José Cepeda Espinosa is former Dean of the Universidad de Los Andes Law School and former President of the Constitutional Court of Colombia.

Yasmin Dawood is the Canada Research Chair in Democracy, Constitutionalism, and Electoral Law and Associate Professor of Law and Political Science, University of Toronto.

Vicki C. Jackson is Laurence H. Tribe Professor of Constitutional Law at Harvard Law School.

Tarunabh Khaitan is Professor of Public Law and Legal Theory at the Faculty of Law, Oxford; an Honorary Professorial Fellow at Melbourne Law School; and Head of Research at the Bonavero Institute of Human Rights, Oxford.

Madhav Khosla is Associate Professor of Law at Columbia Law School.

Jeff King is Professor of Law at the Faculty of Laws, University College London.

David Landau is Mason Ladd Professor and Associate Dean for International Programs, Florida State University College of Law.

David S. Law is the E. James Kelly, Jr., Class of 1965 Research Professor of Law and Courtesy Professor of Politics, University of Virginia and Honorary Professor of Law, University of Hong Kong.

Jane Mansbridge is Charles F. Adams Professor Emerita, Harvard Kennedy School.

Gillian E. Metzger is Harlan Fiske Stone Professor of Constitutional Law, Columbia Law School.

Martha Minow is 300th Anniversary University Professor, Harvard Law School.

Gerald L. Neuman is J. Sinclair Armstrong Professor of International, Foreign, and Comparative Law, Harvard Law School.

Guillermo Otálora Lozano is Adjunct Lecturer, Universidad de los Andes.

Richard H. Pildes is Sudler Family Professor of Constitutional Law, New York University School of Law.

Katharina Pistor is Edwin B. Parker Professor of Comparative Law at Columbia Law School and Director of Columbia Law School's Center on Global Legal Transformation (CGLT).

Daphna Renan is Peter B. Munroe and Mary J. Munroe Professor of Law, Harvard Law School.

Matthew C. Stephenson is Eli Goldston Professor of Law, Harvard Law School.

Mark Tushnet is William Nelson Cromwell Professor of Law Emeritus at Harvard Law School.

Katharine G. Young is Professor of Law and Associate Dean of the Faculty at Boston College Law School.

Acknowledgments

We owe more people more thanks for their help in thinking through these ideas than we can possibly list or remember. We are grateful to all with whom we have discussed this work. We are especially grateful to Dean John Manning of Harvard Law School and Deans Edward Iacobucci and Jutta Brunnée of the University of Toronto Faculty of Law for their support and encouragement. We also wish to thank Ran Hirschl and Tom Ginsburg, editors of the Comparative Constitutional Law and Policy series at Cambridge University Press, for their enthusiasm and insightful guidance, and an anonymous peer reviewer for valuable feedback which shaped, at an early stage, the contours of this book project. We are also very grateful to Richard Albert and Robert Schuetze for their helpful comments.

The ideas in this book were developed over a long period of time, and through conversations with many colleagues in the comparative constitutional law and human rights communities; they were discussed and debated at a May 2019 conference organized by Professor Vicki Jackson at Harvard Law School. For a rich, lively, and productive discussion, we thank all the participants at the conference, including Danielle Allen, Nicholas Barber, Elizabeth Bartholet, Manuel Cepeda, Tom Ginsburg, Tarun Khaitan, Madhav Khosla, Jeff King, David Landau, David Law, Jane Mansbridge, Gillian Metzger, Martha Minow, Gerald Neuman, Richard Pildes, Katharina Pistor, Sabeel Rahman, Daphna Renan, Matthew Stephenson, Mark Tushnet, Robin West, and Katharine Young. We extend our profound thanks as well to Oren Tamir for his always helpful insights, and to Chelsea McGovern, Liz Meyer, Daryl Muranaka, Megan O'Neil, and Benjamin Carignan for their invaluable administrative assistance with this book and the conference. Finally, we are enormously grateful to the editorial team at Cambridge University Press, including Matt Gallaway, Cameron Daddis, Jadyn Fauconier-Herry, and Becky Jackaman, as well as the team at Integra Software Services and freelance copy-editor Lori Heaford, for deftly steering this project to completion. We are also grateful to Arc Indexing for their assistance in preparing the index. A book like this is always a collective work, requiring both high-quality research and scholarship and high-quality editorial and administrative support. This book is fortunate to have had both.

PART I

Introduction

1

Constitutionalism and Effective Government

Rights, Institutions, and Values

Vicki C. Jackson and Yasmin Dawood

1.1 INTRODUCTION

In recent years, nations around the world have faced a veritable crisis of ineffective government. Basic governmental functions – preventing private violence, resolving disputes through lawful means, providing an infrastructure to enable people to meet their most elementary needs for shelter, nutrition, transportation, communication, education – go unmet. In some countries, these basic functions are met but longer-term governance issues languish, and government is perceived to be unresponsive in ways that some believe contribute to political backlashes, including those against minority groups. These failures in governance are also perceived to have contributed to a global upsurge in authoritarianism and a concomitant decline in democracy.[1]

Moreover, the basic freedoms protected in many democratic constitutions – freedom from state-sanctioned torture and from punishment or coercion without fair process; freedom of expression, of religion, of movement; freedom from invidious discrimination; enjoyment of property without arbitrary government interference; free exercise of the suffrage – cannot exist, in an organized society, without government effective enough to control itself and its agents and otherwise to secure the protection of those rights. If governments are "instituted to secure these rights" of "life, liberty and the pursuit of happiness," as was famously asserted in 1776[2] – that is, if a basic purpose of government is to protect rights – those governments must be effective enough to do so.

The goal of this collection is to raise the important question of whether effective government should not itself be understood as an aspect of liberal democratic constitutionalism.[3] This is a new (or at least insufficiently discussed) question in

[1] *Cf.* David E. Pozen & Kim Lane Scheppele, *Executive Underreach, in Pandemics and Otherwise*, 114 AM. J. INT'L L. 608, 615 (2020) ("[E]xecutive underreach may tend to foster executive overreach . . . .").

[2] Declaration of Independence (U.S. 1776).

[3] *Cf.* CARL J. FRIEDRICH, CONSTITUTIONAL GOVERNMENT AND DEMOCRACY 57 (4th ed. 1968) ("The popular antithesis between bureaucracy and democracy is an oratorical slogan which endangers the future of

the study of constitutionalism.[4] Many of the chapters in this volume argue, from different perspectives, that effective government should indeed be understood as a crucial component of democratic constitutionalism. Thus, a principal contribution of this collection is to situate the issue of effective government squarely within a positive conception of constitutionalism. A focus on effective government, we suggest, not only reconfigures the meaning of constitutionalism but also has profound consequences for a host of interconnected issues, including the nature of the state, the functioning of political institutions, democratic governance, the rule of law, and the protection of constitutional rights.

There is an array of conceptual approaches to effective government – as a right, an interest, a duty, and a principle – that the chapters in this collection shed light on. The collection also brings together questions typically treated separately within comparative constitutional law and public law more generally – for example, the role of courts, the roles of legislators and legislatures, and the role of political parties – to explore in each of these areas the significance of taking effective government seriously within democratic constitutionalism. In addition, the chapters offer reflections on political shifts, sociolegal changes, and transformations in media that serve as important contexts for constitutional governance. As such, the collection contributes to a constellation of scholarly literatures, including constitutional theory, comparative constitutional law, international human rights, constitutional design, political theory, and comparative politics.

It is our hope that this book will generate further scholarly research and conversation. To this end, we discuss in this introduction a number of preliminary conceptual issues and questions. Section 1.2 focuses on the connection between effective

democracy. For a constitutional system which cannot function effectively, which cannot act with dispatch and strength, cannot live.").

4 To be sure, this question has been discussed by some scholars. *See e.g.*, Vicki C. Jackson, *Pro-constitutional Representation: Comparing the Role Obligations of Judges and Elected Representatives in Constitutional Democracy*, 57 WM. & MARY L. REV. 1717, 1741 (2016) (arguing that "an important goal of the Constitution was to create an effective, working government"); N.W. BARBER, THE PRINCIPLES OF CONSTITUTIONALISM 1 (2018) (defining constitutionalism as a collection of principles that create "an effective and competent set of state institutions"); TURKULER ISIKSEL, EUROPE'S FUNCTIONAL CONSTITUTION: A THEORY OF CONSTITUTIONALISM BEYOND THE STATE 34 (2016) (arguing that effective government can serve as a normative justification of constitutional authority, in addition to the conventional justifications of collective self-government and individual rights); *see also, e.g.*, sources cited in notes 5–10, 17 *infra*. A related area of scholarship focuses on whether constitutional design is a causal determinant of democratic dysfunction, which we understand as a corollary concept of effective government. *See e.g.*, SANFORD LEVINSON, OUR UNDEMOCRATIC CONSTITUTION: WHERE THE CONSTITUTION GOES WRONG (AND HOW WE THE PEOPLE CAN CORRECT IT) (2006); SANFORD LEVINSON & JACK M. BALKIN, DEMOCRACY AND DYSFUNCTION (2019); Yasmin Dawood, *Democratic Dysfunction and Constitutional Design*, 94 B.U. L. REV. 913 (2014). We do not adopt any single definition for the terms "liberal democratic constitutionalism" and "effective government," recognizing that these are highly contested concepts; that said, we do not believe that "liberal constitutionalism" is inconsistent with an active positive state and we believe that "effective government" in constitutional democracies is not simply a positive concept measured by whatever goals the government has, but is normatively constrained.

government and constitutionalism, while Section 1.3 takes up four alternative conceptions of effective government – as a right, an interest, a duty, and a principle – and briefly explores the implications of each for constitutionalism. In addition to providing a description of each chapter in the collection, Section 1.4 further elaborates the normative and institutional dimensions of effective constitutional government. The conclusion in Section 1.5 summarizes the volume's principal scholarly contributions.

1.2 RECONCEPTUALIZING CONSTITUTIONALISM AND EFFECTIVE GOVERNMENT

A central objective of this volume is to reorient scholarly attention so that the predominant focus on negative constitutionalism is balanced by a deeper engagement with positive constitutionalism. Much of the scholarly literature, in the USA and elsewhere, is focused on rights, treating them as free-standing from government structures. And, in the USA and a number of other older common-law constitutional democracies, much of the literature is focused on *negative* aspects of constitutionalism, that is, on what the government should not do, rather than on more positive aspects, on what – as a constitutional matter – the government should do. The international human rights literatures, and literatures in those countries whose constitutions provide for positive rights associated with human well-being, do consider how to protect and implement those rights, but for the most part not within the broader framework raised by this book,[5] that is, of the overarching idea that constitutions must aim to produce governments that are at once effective and workable, and rights-protective.

Although US constitutionalism and the US Constitution itself are conventionally described as concerned only with "negative" rights, and sometimes as being committed to a highly "limited" view of the role of government, these understandings are increasingly being challenged. Scholars have shown positive conceptions of constitutionalism in the US states,[6] and others have begun to explore the positive obligations imposed by the federal Constitution and contemplated

[5] Some of the human rights literature acknowledges and explores the role of budgeting in making positive human rights effective, including, e.g., the need to consider resource mobilization as well as spending, or limitations on retrogression even for financial reasons, *see, e.g.*, Olivier de Schutter, *Public Budget Analysis for the Realisation of Economic, Social and Cultural Rights: Conceptual Framework and Practical Implementation*, *in* THE FUTURE OF ECONOMIC AND SOCIAL RIGHTS 527 (Katharine Young ed., 2019); Rodrigo Uprimny et al., *Bridging the Gap: The Evolving Doctrine on ESCR and "Maximum Available Resources," in id.* at 624, and in fulfilling positive constitutional rights, *see, e.g.*, Katharine Young, *Waiting for Rights: Progressive Realization and Lost Time, in id.*, but, so far as we are aware, not in the framework of a general obligation to have an effective and functioning government. *See also* STEPHEN HOLMES & CASS R. SUNSTEIN, THE COST OF RIGHTS: WHY LIBERTY DEPENDS ON TAXES (1999) (arguing that the protection of rights is dependent, in part, on their enforcement by government).

[6] *E.g.*, EMILY ZACKIN, LOOKING FOR RIGHTS IN ALL THE WRONG PLACES (2013) (showing, inter alia, how virtually all state constitutions require the provision of a free public education).

by its framers[7] – by its provisions for elected representatives (see Chapter 14 by Vicki C. Jackson),[8] by its "take care clause,"[9] by its Fourteenth Amendment guarantee of the "equal protection" of the laws.[10] To be sure, our invocation of positive constitutionalism as deserving of academic attention is not so much a new development as it is a return to a historic approach that situated governance at the core of constitutionalism. As various chapters (including Chapter 4 by Yasmin Dawood and Chapter 12 by Gillian E. Metzger) discuss, the eighteenth-century framers focused on both elected branches as securing effective governance; the framers of the "Second Founding,"[11] including the Fourteenth Amendment, focused on Congress's role in making effective the new guarantees of equal citizenship.[12] More generally, as argued in Chapter 2 by N. W. Barber, the very nature of a constitution contemplates government obligations to act to advance the people's well-being.[13]

We also raise questions about the supposed opposition between rights and government structures. As noted briefly already, the US Declaration of Independence sets forth a claimed relationship between government and rights. Its second paragraph begins: "We hold these truths to be self-evident, that all men are created equal, that they are endowed by their Creator with certain unalienable Rights, that among these are Life, Liberty and the pursuit of Happiness. – That to secure these rights, Governments are instituted among Men, deriving their just powers from the consent of the governed, ..." That is, governments are created to do certain important things – to protect rights, very broadly defined. Effective government without any rights protection is not desirable; but if governments are not effective enough, rights may not be able to be protected (as explored in Chapter 4 by Yasmin Dawood). Effective self-government must be compatible with both democracy (and rights to participate in self-government, as Katharina Pistor argues in Chapter 5) and human rights.

7 E.g., Sotirios Barber, *Fallacies of Negative Constitutionalism*, 75 FORDHAM L. REV. 651 (2006); SOTIRIOS A. BARBER & JAMES E. FLEMING, CONSTITUTIONAL INTERPRETATION: THE BASIC QUESTIONS ch. 4 (2007) (discussing the "Positive Constitutionalism of the Federalist").

8 *See also* Neil Siegel, *After the Trump Era: A Constitutional Role Morality for Presidents and Members of Congress*, 107 GEO. L. J. 109 (2018); William P. Marshall, *The Limits on Congress's Power to Do Nothing: A Preliminary Inquiry*, 93 IND. L. J. 159, 171 (2018).

9 Andrew Kent et al., *Faithful Execution and Article II*, 132 HARV. L. REV. 2111 (2019) (arguing that the US Constitution "imposes a duty of faithful execution on the President").

10 *See* Robin West, *Towards an Abolitionist Interpretation of the Fourteenth Amendment*, 94 W. VA. L. REV. 111 (1991); *see also* ROBIN WEST, CIVIL RIGHTS: RETHINKING THEIR NATURAL FOUNDATION (2019).

11 *See* ERIC FONER, THE SECOND FOUNDING: HOW THE CIVIL WAR AND RECONSTRUCTION REMADE THE CONSTITUTION (2019).

12 *See, e.g.*, FONER, *supra* note 11, at 85; GARETT EPPS, DEMOCRACY REBORN: THE FOURTEENTH AMENDMENT AND THE FIGHT FOR EQUAL RIGHTS IN POST-CIVIL WAR AMERICA 233 (2006). On the importance of reconstructing politics, and representation, to the drafters of the Fourteenth Amendment, see also Mark Graber, *Constructing Constitutional Politics: Thaddeus Stevens, John Bingham, and the Forgotten Fourteenth Amendment* (U. Md. Legal Studies Research Paper No. 2014–37), https://ssrn.com/abstract=2483355 (last visited Apr. 23, 2020).

13 *See also* BARBER, *supra* note 4.

These kinds of questions about the affirmative constitutional obligations of government have only begun to be discussed in the US literature on constitutions and constitutionalism, though for scholars writing about other constitutional systems the argument in Chapter 6 for what David S. Law calls a "post-liberal" reconceptualization may seem especially compelling. Gillian E. Metzger, in her 2017 Foreword to the *Harvard Law Review*,[14] briefly raised the possibility that constitutional government today requires a complex administrative state, an idea that she elaborates in Chapter 12, in part by explaining historically how the strands of positive versus more limited conceptions of the role of the state emerged in the twentieth century. In other countries, such as India and South Africa, the idea of positive obligations is often associated with specific human rights.

A focus on "effective government" not only leads to a reconceptualization of constitutionalism but also has important implications for constitutional structures, institutions, norms, and values. Do institutions such as courts have either the mandate or the competence to enhance state capacity? What kinds of normative obligations, if any, ought to guide the work of legislators and legislatures as they engage in governance? How should some of the challenges, such as corruption or a weak political party system, that stand in the way of effective government be addressed? What is the impact of large-scale transformations, such as the rise of social media, on political and social contexts within which constitutional governance takes place? As detailed in Section 1.4, the chapters explore a wide array of institutional and normative considerations that are raised by the question of whether constitutionalism does or ought to embrace a commitment to effective government.

To be sure, a threshold question is what is meant by "effective government." There are multiple meanings of effectiveness: As Gerald L. Neuman suggests in Chapter 8, it could be taken to mean effectiveness toward whatever goals those in power seek to advance and are able to embody in law, with potentially adverse consequences for both democracy and rights and raising dangers of autocracy and authoritarianism. One of the reasons why we think it urgently important to recognize the importance of effective government is because of the need to defend democratic constitutionalism from its illiberal, authoritarian critics, some of whom seek to galvanize populist pressures to depart from democratic constitutionalism.[15] Mindful of the dangers of nonnormative approaches to "effectiveness," we embrace a multilayered conception that assumes a commitment to democratic self-governance, as Katharina Pistor's Chapter 5 emphasizes, and human rights.

[14] Gillian E. Metzger, *1930s Redux: The Administrative State Under Siege*, 131 HARV. L. REV. 1 (2017).

[15] For discussion of the multiple causes for the rise of illiberal, authoritarian governments in former democracies, *see, e.g.*, WOJCIECH SADURSKI, POLAND'S CONSTITUTIONAL BREAKDOWN (2019); TOM GINSBURG & AZIZ HUQ, HOW TO SAVE A CONSTITUTIONAL DEMOCRACY (2018); CONSTITUTIONAL DEMOCRACY IN CRISIS? (Mark A. Graber et al. eds., 2018).

The concept of "government" is likewise conducive to multiple interpretations. First, there are some generic functions that governments should be expected to perform in order for individuals to be able to exercise their humanity in freedom. These include suppressing violence; promoting public health; promoting infrastructure for transportation, communication, and education; and facilitating an economy that affords opportunities for meaningful work. This is, perhaps, a somewhat minimalist understanding – but it is one too often not achieved in communities across the world. Second, there are functions very closely connected with sustaining democracy that governments should be expected to provide for – maintaining an electoral system that provides free, fair, and competitive elections, supported by inclusive voting processes and institutions, and freedoms of political expression including a free press. Finally, particular governments may have particular responsibilities due to allocations of jurisdiction in constitutions; so, in the United States, the national government has special responsibilities for foreign affairs and regulation of the national economy.[16]

1.3 EFFECTIVE GOVERNMENT AS A RIGHT, INTEREST, DUTY, OR PRINCIPLE?

Conceptualizing "effective government" as an essential part of democratic constitutionalism does not resolve how it might be understood in the analytical frameworks of constitutional law. It is important not to simply assume that a "right" to self-government should be defended and promoted. Alternative conceptualizations exist: there could be a "right" to effective (self-)government; a "duty" of effective government; a "principle" of effective government; or even a governmental "interest" in effective government. Their implications are overlapping but distinct.

So, should a "right to effective government" be understood as a necessary part of democratic constitutionalism? Constitutional theory, especially in the United States, has, with rare exceptions, accepted a conception of "rights" that turns on the ability of courts to secure their vindication and that is rooted in a "negative" conception of rights as requiring only that governments refrain from certain actions.[17] Recognizing a "right to effective governance" (as argued by David S. Law in Chapter 6) or to "effective self-governance" (as argued in Chapter 5 by

[16] *See* Jackson, *supra* note 4, at 1768.

[17] Although current US Supreme Court doctrine rejects arguments for recognizing positive rights based on the US Constitution, important efforts to ground a federal constitutional right to minimal welfare developed in the late 1960s and early 1970s (e.g., Frank I. Michelman, *Foreword: On Protecting the Poor through The Fourteenth Amendment*, 83 HARV. L. REV. 7 (1969): Frank I. Michelman, *In Pursuit of Constitutional Welfare Rights: One View of Rawls' Theory of Justice*, 121 U. PA. L. REV. 962 (1973)). Scholars have argued that the enforcement of positive rights is not necessarily different in principle than enforcement of "negative" rights. *See, e.g.*, Mark Tushnet, *State Action, Social Welfare Rights, and the Judicial Role: Some Comparative Observations*, 3 CHI. J. INT'L L. 435 (2002). New scholarship is exploring economic inequality and governance, *see, e.g.*, K. SABEEL RAHMAN, DEMOCRACY AGAINST DOMINATION (2016), and conceptions of constitutional citizenship entailing greater government efforts to promote

Katharina Pistor) would, then, challenge existing understandings in US constitutional theory.

Constitutional theory in some other countries where constitutions recognize judicially enforceable "positive" rights, for example to housing, health care, or nutrition, has grounded judicial imposition of positive obligations on government on these particular positive rights, but has not recognized a more general right to effective government. International human rights law may impose affirmative duties on states to "respect, protect and fulfill" specified human rights; "fulfilling" is understood to impose an affirmative obligation on states with respect to the designated human rights. However, recognizing a "right to effective government" or "self-governance" would challenge existing understandings in international law: Although scholars have articulated arguments for a "right to democratic governance" in international law,[18] the question of a right to *effective* self-government or self-governance is distinct. International human rights law prioritizes the individual (or group) that is the holder of a "right" – whether freedom of expression, freedom of religion, rights of cultural autonomy, rights to adequate food or shelter – and not the need for a working and effective government.

Recognizing a "right to effective self-governance" would thus be a marked shift. It would be grounded on a view of rights as dependent upon, rather than entirely oppositional to, government. As such, it could be criticized as tending to conflate "governance" and "rights" in ways that cut across existing understandings of the former as the realm of "politics" and the latter as the realm of "law"; it might be critiqued as thereby devaluing the role (rhetorical and conceptual) of rights in constitutionalism; and it might require reconceptualization of existing constitutional doctrines, for instance around "balancing" tests or "proportionality" review. As noted, US constitutional law, for example, often conceives of rights, per Ronald Dworkin,[19] as "trumps" fencing off an area from government regulation, or as a "shield" putting a thumb on the scale against government regulation absent a very strong degree of justification.[20] Other influential US approaches conceive of

economic equality, *see* William E. Forbath, *Constitutional Change and the Politics of History*, 108 YALE L. J. 1917 (1999); *see also* William E. Forbath, *The Distributive Constitution and Workers Rights*, 72 OHIO ST. L. REV. 1115 (2011). There is also important scholarship arguing that the Fourteenth Amendment's right to equal protection of the law should be understood to impose duties (including on legislators) to protect persons from private violence, *see* West, *supra* note 10; *see also* Robin West, *Unenumerated Duties*, 9 U. PA. J. CONST. L. 221 (2006). There are thus strands of US constitutional theory that point toward a more positive conception of the role of government, although they have not yet been conceptualized together as resting on or supporting a general right to effective government.

18 *See, e.g.*, Thomas Franck, *The Emerging Right to Democratic Governance*, 86 AM. J. INT'L L. 46 (1992); Vivien Hart, *Democratic Constitution Making*, 107 U.S. INST. PEACE 1 (2003).

19 *See* RONALD DWORKIN, TAKING RIGHTS SERIOUSLY (1977).

20 Frederick Schauer, A *Comment on the Structure of Rights*, 27 GA. L. REV. 415, 430 (1993); *cf.*, FREDERICK SCHAUER, FREE SPEECH: A PHILOSOPHICAL ENQUIRY 132–33 (1982) ("In all cases of balancing freedom of speech against the general public interest, . . . we do balance the interests, but with our thumbs on the free speech side of the scales.").

"rights" as excluding certain bases for action by the government, or as a "right against rules."[21] These concepts are primarily concerned with what government cannot do, rather than with what it must do; and they do not provide a ready conceptual apparatus to address the challenges of achieving basic levels of effective governance. Moreover, they focus primarily on courts as the forum for enforcement, rather than legislatures or executive offices.

International human rights law recognizes certain affirmative obligations on the part of states to respect, protect, and fulfill rights – but can these be inferred from liberal constitutions? For several of the writers in this collection, the answer is yes, but with cautions. A key question, noted earlier, is whether recognizing a right to effective governance would *undermine* the effectiveness of rights, both as a constraint on government and as a basis for improving governance in discrete areas. Dictators and tyrants might find comfort in being able to claim that their threats to eliminate checks and balances, or basic democratic institutions, are necessary to provide effective governance. This concern lends importance to Katharina Pistor's argument in Chapter 5, noted already, that what should be valorized is effective *self*-governance – with its emphasis on democracy (and the concomitant rights needed to preserve effective democracy). Constitutional democracy is valued primarily not for its efficiency but for its ability over the long haul to promote a reasonably just and decent society.

To be clear: If a "right to effective governance" came to be recognized, this would not necessarily imply that the right was judicially enforceable in any specific manner.[22] It is possible, moreover, to conceive of rights that depend on legislation for their implementation.[23] Indeed, there are constitutional traditions in the world that envision parliaments or legislatures as the primary vindicators of rights, as in Australia. But it might provide a stronger normative foundation for expecting and demanding positive actions from governments, actions that work to the benefit of many with respect to the kinds of public good that require collective action to sustain and that are foundational to maintaining a decent society. To be sure, there has been scholarly discussion of adjudication or implementation of "positive rights" in the areas of material sustenance and protection from violence by state actors or against protected groups, but these are rarely framed within a more general concern for the purposes of constitutionalism to enable effective governance – including the building and maintenance of roads and of communications infrastructure, and more generally providing protection against private violence.

[21] *See, e.g.*, Matthew D. Adler, *Rights Against Rules: The Moral Structure of American Constitutional Law*, 97 Mich. L. Rev. 1 (1998).

[22] Indeed, there are conceded rights violations in the USA that do not receive any judicial remedy. *See, e.g.*, Safford School Dist. v. Redding, 557 U.S. 364 (2009) (denying civil damages where a child was subject to an unlawful search of her underpants, because the government actors, though having violated her Fourth Amendment rights, had not acted inconsistently with "clearly established" law).

[23] *See, e.g.*, Grégoire Webber et al., Legislated Rights (2018).

A second, more specific conceptualization is to view effectiveness in governance as an "interest" or "government purpose," which could be relevant as a potential "justification" for government action that infringes on an area protected by rights.[24] This raises the question, then, as an alternative to a rights-based approach, of whether there is a strong constitutional *interest* – but no constitutional right – in effective government? An "interest" in effective government is a concept that can be invoked to defend or justify government action challenged as intruding on rights, or as an action that is ultra vires the particular government actor or organ. Would constitutional discourses benefit from a richer understanding of the significance of such interests? Would this require modifications of current understandings of whether administrative or financial considerations justify some government actions claimed to interfere with rights? The choice between a rights-based approach and one that relies on government interests is significant, at least in some jurisdictions. In US constitutional law, for instance, government interests are regarded as *optional*; even compelling government interests are, it turns out, ones that the government has a choice about whether to pursue.[25] It is the emphatic claim of the editors that effectiveness in government should not be optional; it is an essential element, indeed a precondition of successful constitutional democracy.

Still a third conceptualization of effective government is that it is a "duty" owed by members of the government – legislative, executive, and judicial – rather than an individually assertable right, and more than an "optional" interest. A "duty" to act so as to promote effective governance might capture the idea of a mandatory government interest. Such a duty might be justiciable, or it might not be, as is the case in some constitutions with "directive principles," establishing goals toward which government must work but which are stated to be nonjusticiable. In some systems there may be good reason to treat the duty as one established under the constitution that is enforceable only through political means, as Chapter 12 by Gillian E. Metzger, Chapter 14 by Vicki C. Jackson, and Tarunabh Khaitan's Chapter 15 might be understood to suggest. In this sense, a "duty" may be far less subject to judicial enforcement than a "right." But that some duties to protect certain positive rights may be subject to judicial enforcement, even without redressing any individual person's right (as in Government of the Republic of

24 *See, e.g.*, Newfoundland (Treasury Board) v. N.A.P.E. [2004] 3 SCR 381 (Sup. Ct. Canada) (upholding a provincial law that withdrew an agreed-upon plan to provide pay equity to discriminated-against female workers, because even though the law infringed the section 15 equality rights of these female workers, it was nonetheless justifiable under section 1 due to a severe financial crisis in the province).

25 *See* Vicki C. Jackson, Constitutional Engagement in a Transnational Era 220–23 (2010) (discussing US constitutional law on abortion, which treats the state's interest in protecting fetal life as optional, but also as compellingly supporting prohibitions of abortion after viability, and of affirmative action, which treats state's interests in diversity in educational setting as optional, but compelling when invoked); *cf.* Grutter v. Bollinger, 539 U.S. 306, 357–58 (2003) (Thomas, J., dissenting) (arguing that there cannot be a "compelling" interest in having an academically prestigious public law school because some states do not have any public law school at all).

South Africa v. Grootboom[26]), is implicit in Manuel José Cepeda Espinosa and Guillermo Otálora Lozano's Chapter 9, Mark Tushnet and Madhav Khosla's Chapter 10, and Chapter 11 by Katharine G. Young. Recognition of a constitutional duty may have particular resonance even within the political sphere.

Finally, effective government can be thought of as a principle or a value running through understandings of constitutional rights, duties, and structures. In the United States, effectiveness was (notoriously) dismissed as irrelevant to structural interpretation by Chief Justice Warren Burger;[27] but the better view is that expressed by Justice Robert Jackson, that the Constitution "contemplates that practice will integrate the dispersed powers into a workable government."[28] That is, a purpose of a constitution and thus of constitutionalism is to provide a suitable framework for the effective performance of government functions. But if effective government is both a precondition for and a purpose of constitutionalism, a perhaps more-embracing way to think of effective government is as a "principle" of constitutionalism that is both precondition and purpose.

1.4 EFFECTIVE CONSTITUTIONAL GOVERNMENT: NORMATIVE AND INSTITUTIONAL CONSIDERATIONS

The rest of this volume is organized into six further parts. Parts II and III explore basic questions about the nature of the state, of constitutionalism, and of the rule of law, shedding light on rights, interests, duties, and principles as analytical approaches to the relationship between effective government and constitutionalism. Parts IV–VII consider the connections between effective government and an array of institutions: courts; executive and administrative branches; legislatures; and political parties. Each of these institutions can be understood as playing an important role in governance and/or politics; each is constituted, defined, or regulated by laws emanating, in most instances, from the constitution of the state.[29] Parts IV–VII also address large-scale trends in politics, sociology, media, and corruption as important contexts for constitutionalism and governance. Cross-currents traverse these different sections.

The chapters in Part II, *What Are Constitutions For?*, radically reconceptualize the conventional accounts of constitutionalism. In Chapter 2, N. W. Barber argues that constitutionalism requires a positive, not simply a negative, conception of the

26 CCT11/00) [2000] ZACC 19; 2001 (1) SA 46; 2000 (11) BCLR 1169 (Oct. 4, 2000).

27 *See* I.N.S. v. Chadha, 462 U.S. 919, 944 (1983) ("Convenience and efficiency are not the primary objectives—or the hallmarks—of democratic government . . .").

28 Youngstown Sheet & Tube Co. v. Sawyer, 343 U.S. 579, 636 (1952).

29 Although political parties are not part of government as such, they have played key roles in facilitating democratic choices, as discussed in Chapter 17 by David Landau and Chapter 18 by Richard H. Pildes. Many of the world's constitutions refer explicitly to political parties, although the US Constitution does not. *See e.g.*, GERMAN BASIC LAW art. 21 ("Political parties").

state as existing to advance the well-being of its people, with ensuing consequences for constitutions. He questions, though, whether constitutional strategies of resolving contested questions, which may serve important purposes, are always essential to advancing this basic purpose. In some contexts, he argues, the accommodation of disagreement as a constitutional strategy, though cutting "against the normal approach of lawyers to constitutions," may actually better enable a form of constitutionalism that advances the well-being of the people of a state, by promoting what he calls a "stable disharmony" of accommodating divergent interests and goals. In Chapter 3, Jeff King, describing effective governance through regulation of private persons as the "poor cousin of constitutionalism," argues that the rule of law – the application of which to the state is often associated with basic premises of constitutionalism – is an idea that itself requires a positive and social component to what law does; in order to prevent a state of anarchy, positive measures by effective governments must be taken and maintained. He thus argues for a "regulatory conception of the rule of law, affirming the positive virtues of law and of the state," rather than viewing the growth of the state and its law as a vice.

In Chapter 4, Yasmin Dawood offers an analysis of the range of relationships between effective government and rights protection, noting not only that effective governance and rights protection can be mutually enforcing in some situations but also that effectiveness is not necessarily tied to democratic rights-protecting governance. With respect to democracies, she argues that effective government requires some degree of constitutionalism for its functioning; and, conversely, that constitutionalism is dependent, at least to some degree, on effective government to secure its protections. This duality is particularly evident with respect to the right to vote: a "basic requirement of effective government is to provide the right to vote and the institutions and processes needed for free and fair elections" and, conversely, "the right to vote, coupled with a fair electoral system, is indispensable for holding elected officials to account and thereby enhancing the effectiveness of government." In Chapter 5, Katharina Pistor argues, as noted earlier, that, rather than identifying a right to "effective government," the right should be conceptualized as a collective right to effective *self*-government; such a collective right, she suggests, is a predicate for constitutionalism, given the extent to which financial globalization has reconfigured state power. Her emphasis on "self-"government helpfully seeks to maintain a focus on sustaining democracy, and thereby helps vitiate some of the concerns that recognizing a right to effective government would undermine democracy.

If a basic function of constitutions is to secure working governments that respect and protect rights, does it necessarily make sense to conceptualize a "right to effective government" or "effective self-government"? Opening Part III, *Positive Rights and Rights to Effective Self-Government*, David S. Law argues affirmatively in Chapter 6 for recognizing a right to effective government. He characterizes such a right as an analytically useful bridge torward what he terms "post-liberal constitutionalism," appropriating elements of the rights orientation of liberal constitutionalism with an understanding of the government as a necessary actor in positively advancing the goals of society. In light of the "prospect that the premises of liberal theory about what people need and what the state must do are obsolete," he argues, a right to effective government should be recognized as "not just another post-liberal right but, rather, a condition to the fulfillment of other post-liberal [positive] rights . . . a right to have rights." In Chapter 7, Martha Minow also explores a more positive understanding of rights, asking when *inaction* by the government should be seen as the proximate cause of rights violation, and analyzing the range of positive measures that government would need to take in order fully to vindicate even classical liberal rights, such as freedom of the press. She argues that the First Amendment's presumption that "the press" exists "could support an obligation for affirmative governmental action – an obligation for government to undertake reforms and regulations to ensure the viability of a news ecosystem."

But Gerald L. Neuman takes issue in Chapter 8 with arguments for recognizing a general right to effective government. He recognizes that doing so might, if accepted, result in significant and useful legal change in the United States, overcoming cases like *DeShaney* v. *Winnebago County*,[30] which had rejected arguments that the Constitution obligates government to protect vulnerable persons from harm. But in much of the rest of the world, he argues, which has formally embraced positive human rights and obligations to act to protect and respect those rights, this conceptual move may do more harm than good, hobbling government by claims that existing (bad) laws be more fully enforced, or further empowering business interests to influence government through asserting claims to effective governance.

As the chapters in Parts II and III suggest, a "right" to effective government is a conceptualization that would in some respects conflate "governance" and "rights" in ways that cut across existing understandings; it would treat "rights" as in some respects dependent on governance, rather than simply as oppositional. Can such an approach be used as a normative basis for improving the capacities of the institutions of governance, including courts, to perform well their tasks of advancing social welfare and protecting the rights of individuals and groups? Or does a "right to effective government" distort any conceptual coherence around the idea of a "right"? Would it do too much harm to the foundational concept of a right and the utility of rights in advancing goals of justice?

The remainder of the volume casts light on these questions as it considers further institutional implications of treating effective government as an essential component of constitutionalism. In Part IV, *The Role of Courts in Building State Capacity*

[30] 489 U.S. 189 (1989) (rejecting a constitutional challenge to a state's failure to protect a child from an abusive parent). In addition to *DeShaney*, other US cases that might come out differently were more positive constitutional obligations recognized are United States v. Morrison, 529 U.S. 598 (2000) (rejecting the constitutionality of a key part of the federal Violence Against Women Act) and Castle Rock v. Gonzales, 545 U.S. 748 (2005) (rejecting a constitutional challenge to a police failure to enforce a judicial protective order that was followed by the murders of three children).

and Promoting Effective Self-Government While Protecting Rights, the contributors consider how a number of constitutional courts have given effect to requirements for positive government action to vindicate specific positive rights to housing, medical care, water, and food. These decisions for the most part are predicated upon the existence of a governmental structure. But if enforcing such rights requires a governance structure that does not in fact exist, can courts call such structures into existence?

A line of decisions in the Colombian Constitutional Court, dealing with an "unconstitutional state of affairs," discussed in Chapter 9 by Manuel José Cepeda Espinosa and Guillermo Otálora Lozano, suggests that this might indeed be possible: Where a widespread pattern of rights invasions exists by multiple parts of government, with many people affected, and there is a manifest insufficiency of public funds to meet the situation, use of the doctrine is justified to authorize courts to bring government agencies and funds together to improve the massive rights violations. Cepeda and Otálora suggest that judicially constrained doctrine can be developed that nonetheless permits courts to address serious problems of government ineffectiveness that adversely affect people's rights. Mark Tushnet and Madhav Khosla's Chapter 10 complicates this analysis by comparing the experiences of courts in Brazil, India, and South Africa in responding to problems of state capacity. They show that, depending on the nature of state incapacities, courts have some, albeit limited, ability to improve the effectiveness of state organs, and that courts in the Global South take very different approaches to this, including "giving existing bureaucracies incentives to modify their workings, directing decision-makers to consult more widely with 'outsiders,' and absorbing into themselves some tasks."

And Katharine G. Young, in Chapter 11 on the "new managerialism" in enforcing positive social and economic rights, examines courts' efforts to deal with "governments already strained by other political and economic trends, such as a rise of anti-establishment, noninstitutionally mediated populist politics or of pressures to outsource or privatize government" through new techniques including "more personalized managerialism, more insistent dialogue, and a more contentious experimentalism," as well as "open[ing] up complaints to a broader net of governmental actors and stakeholders." The result, she says, is "a form of governance that is highly reactive to litigation, and dependent on the premise that courts will not themselves be tainted by the features of dysfunction that they serve to guard against."

Most of the literature on positive rights has, understandably, focused on meeting discrete needs of discrete groups of persons, rather than on the larger idea of effective governance. But there may be strong conceptual rewards in exploring the implications of existing concepts in the realm of positive rights for broader questions of effective governance. And as the contributions in this part underscore, courts may themselves function so as to build the capacity of other organs of self-government, in the process of adjudicating positive right claims; that being said, the courts' role in managing both to enforce ambitious social welfare rights and to harness and improve the capacity of often-fragile state institutions may be a challenge.

Moving from courts to the execution and administration of the laws raises a number of questions addressed by contributions in Part V, *The Essential Roles of Executive and Administrative Constitutionalism*. In Chapter 12, Gillian E. Metzger analyzes two opposing phenomena – first, the centrality of effective governance to the basic structure and historical development of the US Constitution and second, the near-absence of the concept of effective governance in contemporary US constitutional discourse, theory, and doctrine. After a detailed explication of these two phenomena, and of why effective governance became decentered in US discourse, she argues that a constitutional account of effective governance needs to include a focus on both executive and legislative branches, to adopt a more robust understanding of constitutional duties, with a more systemic perspective, and, finally, to treat any systemic duty of effective governance as nonjusticiable. While she details reasons not to view a right to effective government as an individually justiciable right, she also argues that recognizing the constitutional character of this obligation is an important counterweight to the rhetoric of the purported constitutional illegitimacy of the administrative state.

Administration of the laws as a central component in both constitutionalism and effective self-government emerges not only in Metzger's contribution[31] but also in Daphna Renan's. In Chapter 13, she explores what she argues is the necessary duality in the role of the head of the government – as an individual person with human motives and as an institution with regularized procedures, needed for both effectiveness and accountability. These two different modes have different implications for, among other things, the continuity of executive orders, access to presidential papers, and immunity from criminal or civil process. More broadly, Renan's work points to the need for public law to recognize and manage both roles – a highly singular, individually focused conception and a more pluralistic conception of the presidency as a deliberative office acting over time.

Does effective constitutional government require an effective legislative branch with effective representation? This is a central question taken up in Part VI, *Legislatures, Representation, and Duties of Effective Self-Government*. In separate chapters, Vicki C. Jackson (Chapter 14) and Tarunabh Khaitan (Chapter 15) each urge attention to the normative expectations, derived from democratic constitutions, that should be articulated as standards for elected representatives to live up to in the course of their political work. For Vicki C. Jackson, in Chapter 14, normative obligations of elected representatives, obligations that include the willingness at times to compromise to enable the legislature to act, are derivable not only from general conceptions of the role of elected representatives (of, in Hanna Pitkin's

[31] *See also, e.g.*, Gilian E. Metzger, *Ordinary Administrative Law as Constitutional Common Law*, 110 COLUM. L. REV. 479 (2010); *The Constitutional Duty to Supervise*, 124 YALE L. J. 1836 (2015); and Metzger, *supra* note 14.

terms, "acting for" those represented) but also, in the United States, from specific constitutional requirements of a system in which representatives are chosen on terms of equality (either by population or by state), and representatives are obligated to work together in a body that must "assemble" and can act only through collective decision-making. Extending her prior work on pro-constitutional representation,[32] she argues that legislatures are central to democratic constitutionalism and must be able to work effectively to fulfill the goals of representation in a democracy; to this end, she urges more scholarly and public attention to legislators' normative duties.

For Tarunabh Khaitan in Chapter 15, the Indian Constitution's "directive principles," which are expressly declared to be nonjusticiable, serve a valuable function as a moral guide for legislators' substantive action within the framework of political constitutionalism.[33] Such "directive principles" might be understood not in terms of rights but, rather, in terms of state "duties" and government "interests" that may support action otherwise subject to challenge; they involve purposive, future-oriented, and nonjusticiable expressions of what he calls a "duty to govern well." Similarly, Jane Mansbridge, whose work on "deliberative negotiation" has influenced legal scholarship on the role of legislators,[34] argues in Chapter 16 for the necessity of reconceiving representation as recursive, "meaning mutually responsive and iterated communication between representatives and constituents." This idea is grounded in her claim that the need for government coercion has intensified in our increasingly interconnected and complex world; "[a]s our need for state coercion increases, we need more legitimacy for that coercion than we did in an era when it could make sense to say that a government is best which governs least." Her innovative idea of recursivity envisions a more ongoing form of deliberative feedback loops – not only between elected representatives and constituents but also between government administrators and those affected by regulation, and major organs of civil society and their constituents, as a way of deepening both legitimacy and effectiveness.

David Landau's Chapter 17 explains the adverse impacts on the effectiveness and democratic responsiveness of legislatures of a variety of political party systems, including systems with very weak political parties, or with a single dominant party,

32 *See* Jackson, *supra* note 4.

33 Thus, in India, one of the "directive principles" is titled "Equal justice and free legal aid" and states: "The State shall secure that the operation of the legal system promotes justice, on a basis of equal opportunity, and shall, in particular, provide free legal aid, by suitable legislation or schemes or in any other way, to ensure that opportunities for securing justice are not denied to any citizen by reason of economic or other disabilities." Courts sometimes rely on "directive principles" to interpret judicially enforceable constitutional provisions, *see, e.g.*, Vijayashri Sripati & Arun K. Thiruvengadam, *India: Constitutional Amendment Making the Right to Education a Fundamental Right*, 2 INT'L J. CONST. L. 148 (2004).

34 Mark E. Warren & Jane Mansbridge, with Andre Bachtiger et al., *Deliberative Negotiation*, *in* NEGOTIATING AGREEMENT IN POLITICS 86, 93 & n.21 (Jane Mansbridge & Cathie Jo Martin et al. eds., Report of the Am. Pol. Sci. Ass'n Task Force on Negotiating Agreement in Politics, 2013); *see generally* POLITICAL NEGOTIATION (Jane Mansbridge & Cathie Jo Martin eds., 2015).

and thereby forms a bridge between Part VI and our final Part VII, on *Politics, Sociology, Media, and Corruption as Contexts for Constitutionalism and Governance*. The impact of political parties on democracy has been much debated.[35] Landau's central concern is with the multiple ways in which political parties contribute to democratic erosion (ranging from too-strong, dominant parties to very weak, noninstitutionalized parties). Because there are so many variations, the challenges they present are not readily preventable through *ex ante* constitutional design, he argues; solutions all face challenges arising from the inevitability of trade-offs, endogeneity, and the necessary location of political parties in between government and society. He suggests focusing attention on electoral rules as a way of addressing concerns over the role of parties in democratic erosion.

The chapters in Part VII recognize, as do several prior contributions, the central role of political, social, and economic practices in sustaining – or eroding – democratic constitutionalism. Governance takes place through institutions but always in the context of a particular sociolegal culture. Legal scholars are just beginning to turn serious attention to the role of political parties in democratic constitutionalism; similarly, the role of corruption should receive more attention in comparative constitutional scholarship. In addition to David Landau's focus on different forms of dysfunctionalities in systems with different kinds of political parties, Richard H. Pildes' Chapter 18 raises even broader questions about the possibilities of effective and democratic self-governance. He argues that "political fragmentation is one of the major challenges and defining features of democracies today," contributing to a "dramatic decline in the effectiveness of government." In most democracies, he argues, political power is no longer "effectively controlled by, or contained within, the centralized, major institutions that had long been perceived to be the legitimate vehicles for organizing and exercising that authority." A principal cause of this fragmentation, he explains, is the communications revolution and the access and power made possible through social media. The stability of political parties is declining, as "disruptors" like French president Macron gain power through social media (and are then "disrupted" themselves). Such phenomena reflect "both the fragmentation of political authority and the resulting difficulty of sustaining legitimate authority." Together, Pildes' and Landau's work links legislatures and political parties as urgent objects of scholarly attention in exploring effective governance in constitutional democracies.

Finally, in Chapter 19, Matthew C. Stephenson explores corruption, which can be a significant challenge to both constitutionalism and effective governance as is noted in earlier chapters, including Chapter 11 by Katharine G. Young and Jane Mansbridge's Chapter 16. Corruption lowers confidence that democracy is a workable and good system; it may even contribute to the rise of demagogues.

[35] *See, e.g.*, Nancy L. Rosenblum, On the Side of the Angels: An Appreciation of Parties and Partisanship (2008) (assessing "antipartyism" and arguing for the benefits of partisanship).

Stephenson makes the intriguing and counterintuitive claim that *both* corruption and anti-corruption efforts can work against having effective government in a democratic constitutional system, making analysis of the particular forms of corruption and how best to combat them a task at once complex and vital to sustaining the rule of law and democratic constitutionalism. He also identifies elements of constitutional design that bear on controlling corruption, including, among other elements, provisions securing the independence of prosecution services, federal systems with parallel courts and prosecutors, direct anti-corruption provisions, and independent anti-corruption bodies.

1.5 CONCLUSION

The goal of this volume is to encourage scholars to take seriously the relationship between democratic constitutionalism and effective government. In situating governance at the core of constitutionalism, we have discussed various analytical frameworks for conceptualizing effective government within constitutional law. As we observed earlier, a "right to effective self-government" may be a "right" that is not justiciable but would inform evaluation of government policies challenged by conventional rights-holders. It might thus be better expressed as a "duty," or as a compulsory government "interest," or as a constitutional "principle." Moreover, a "right to effective self-government" may be uniquely well-situated for vindication by elected officials, or administrators, rather than judges. It may be valuable to articulate effective government as a constitutional obligation for democratically elected legislatures and executive officials to fulfill; if normative expectations are not expressed, they may be ignored.[36] As the various chapters suggest, there are multiple frameworks for conceptualizing the role of "effective government" in constitutional democracy. Our bottom-line view is that, however it is conceptualized, effective government is a precondition for sustaining democratic constitutionalism.

The chapters in this collection contribute to constitutional theory by fundamentally reconceptualizing an array of theoretical frameworks, while also reconsidering the basic function of institutions of government and politics, including courts, executive and administrative branches, legislatures, and political parties. The volume thus contributes to the constitutional design literature, which, though engaged with questions of the relationship of different structures toward producing politically stable democracies, and of the relationships between the design of constitutional review and outcomes, has not (for the most part)[37] focused on the role of legislative,

36 International human rights norms that lack effective judicial enforcement are still invoked to evaluate and motivate governmental conduct.

37 In addition to works cited *supra* notes 4–10, 17, exceptions – meaning works that focus in part on the kinds of issues that this book seeks to bring more attention to – include, e.g., studies of the effectiveness of parliamentary committees under the UK Human Rights Act, see Janet L. Hiebert, *Parliament and the Human Rights Act: Can the JCHR Help Facilitate a Culture of*

executive, and administrative (including civil service) branches, or the courts, in producing rights protection while providing government services.

Moreover, the collection draws attention to a significant gap in the literature on comparative constitutionalism, which has, for the most part, treated issues relating to the quality of government as "political" rather than constitutional questions. At a time of debate over the nature of the field of comparative constitutional law,[38] the volume brings together concerns traditionally associated with constitutionalism and concerns traditionally associated with the study of government. As such, it is an important entry into debates over different models of constitutionalism (e.g., authoritarian constitutionalism versus liberal democratic constitutionalism), suggesting that liberal democratic constitutionalism might best be understood or reconceptualized as including a positive component (as well as the more familiar negative constraints on government). Finally, this collection engages with the political science literature, which, while focused on state capacity and the centrality of institutions for the state's ability to provide public goods, has tended to pay less attention to the role of constitutions and constitutional law in enabling states to engage in effective governance. The interdisciplinary focus of this collection suggests the benefits of combining the skills and disciplinary orientations of academic lawyers and political scientists in analyzing the grave issues confronting the constitutional democracies of the world.

In sum, we hope that having these contributions in one volume provides an important set of perspectives, through different lenses, on the idea of effective government in constitutional theory and practice. These perspectives, we hope, have laid the groundwork for future scholarly research into constitutionalism and its relationships to the values and institutions of effective democratic government.

Rights?, 4 INT'L J. CONST. L. 1 (2006), or of fourth branch institutions, see MARK TUSHNET, THE NEW FOURTH BRANCH: INSTITUTIONS FOR PROTECTING CONSTITUTIONAL DEMOCRACY (2021); Charles Fombad, *The Diffusion of South African-Style Institutions? A Study in Comparative Constitutionalism*, *in* CONSTITUTIONAL TRIUMPHS, CONSTITUTIONAL DISAPPOINTMENTS: A CRITICAL ASSESSMENT OF THE 1996 SOUTH AFRICAN CONSTITUTION'S LOCAL AND INTERNATIONAL INFLUENCE 359 (Rosalind Dixon & Theunis Roux eds., 2018) (on South Africa's Chapter 9 institutions).

[38] Ran Hirschl has recently argued for calling the field "comparative constitutional studies," with an emphasis on causal relations proven through the methods of social science, and Theunis Roux has responded by arguing that comparative constitutional *law* is distinctive. *See* RAN HIRSCHL, COMPARATIVE MATTERS: THE RENAISSANCE OF COMPARATIVE CONSTITUTIONAL LAW (2014); Theunis Roux, *Comparative Constitutional Studies: Two Fields or One?* 13 ANN. REV. L. & SOC. SCI. 123 (2017).

PART II

What Are Constitutions For?

2

Resolution and Accommodation in the Good Constitution

N. W. Barber[*]

2.1 INTRODUCTION

Those who ask what counts as a good constitution normally mean to ask a different question; that is, they mean to ask what counts as a good state. Most people do not care whether the wording of the constitution is elegant or crude, whether its structure is clear or complex, or whether it was produced by an elected convention or is an accident of history, and, generally, they are right not to care: what matters is the state that the constitution has produced. When the state is succeeding in its primary task of advancing its people's well-being, the constitution is, by derivation, successful too.[1] But whilst the constitution is defined by its relationship to the state – the assemblage of rules which creates that institution – it remains an instrument in its own right, distinct from the state which it creates. This chapter asks whether there are features of the constitution that can render it, in itself, good, separately from the state it constitutes. An answer to this question would need to show that the constitution, as a bare set of rules, can play a part in helping the state achieve its primary task, distinct from the construction and operation of the constitutional institutions it instantiates. Though a range of answers to this question could be given, this chapter will examine two contenders. Each of these provides ways in which the constitution might, in itself, serve to moderate disagreement within the community and help unite people behind the state. First, the rules of the constitution may stand as *resolutions* of disagreement in society, articulating a conclusion reached by the state about a contested issue. Second, the rules may *accommodate* this disagreement, allowing those on each side of the argument to see their position contained within the constitution, thus enabling the state to span these positions. These are two contrasting constitutional techniques to deal with disagreement in society, and each makes use of the expressive function of constitutions: the constitution rule stands as an articulation of the state's position on an issue, and this articulation may,

[*] I am grateful to Tarunabh Khaitan, Julius Yam, and the editors for comments on an earlier draft.

[1] For an argument, this is the defining point of the state, *see* N.W. BARBER, THE CONSTITUTIONAL STATE (2010).

in itself, shape the way the state's people interact, both with each other and with the state.

Constitutional scholars tend to be drawn to one or other of these two approaches, depending, perhaps, on their temperament. Some see clarity and consistency as virtues, as qualities that we should expect a constitution to embody, whilst others see clarity and consistency as luxuries, potentially cutting against the inherently political nature of the state. However, although these two approaches to constitutions are contrasting, they are not contradictory. Each is seeking to advance what Dieter Grimm has called the 'integrative' function of the constitution, containing and regulating disagreement within the state.[2] As Grimm puts it, the constitution 'is expected to unify the society that it has constituted as a polity, regardless of the difference of opinions and conflicting interests that exist in all societies'.[3] To an extent, this is a necessary precondition of a state. If the state is radically unable to keep disagreement within the boundaries of the constitution, it will collapse into civil war, as people cease to accept its dispute-resolving processes and try to achieve their political ends outside of state institutions. The rules of the constitution, in themselves, can play a role in this integrative function, by standing as resolutions of disagreements or by seeking to accommodate them. Which of these two approaches is the right one to adopt will depend on the situation: sometimes constitutions should provide answers; sometimes they should leave questions open. This chapter will examine these two responses to the question of what makes a 'good' constitution, and close with some suggestions about how, in particular situations, we should choose between them.

2.2 CONSTITUTIONAL RULES AS RESOLUTIONS

Most arguments for the resolution of disputed issues in constitutions turn on the merits of the application of that resolution by institutions. Our primary concern is, for example, that the judiciary upholds a right or the executive provides a benefit. But there are least three groups of arguments which contend that, sometimes, there are inherent benefits in constitutions taking a position on these issues, benefits which are distinct from the value of the subsequent application of those rules. First, there are those arguments grounded in the value of the process by which these rules have been produced, with the constitution rule providing a memorialisation of the process of its production. Second, there are arguments grounded in the capacity of the constitution to resolve disputes just by deciding; once a decision is contained within the constitution, people may come to accept it for this reason. Finally, there are arguments grounded in the inherent value of some constitutional rules; there are, perhaps, some rules that all constitutions should

2 Dieter Grimm, Constitutionalism: Past, Present and Future (2016) (ch. 6, 'Integration by Constitution').

3 *Id.* at 144.

contain simply because they are declarations that all states should make, given a state's relationship with its people.

The first set of arguments, grounded in the value of the mode of production of constitutional rules, forms the basis of a recent case for a written constitution for the United Kingdom, advanced by Jeff King. King contends that constitutions should be seen, in part, as 'mission statements' which express the core values of a community, and contain commitments intended to guide the state towards the achievement of these goals.[4] For these 'mission statements' to be of value, they must be produced democratically, with communities acting as authors of their own constitutional order, making decisions about the structuring and ends of the state.[5] Over time, of course, the community changes, and for the mission statement to remain the mission statement of this group, the constitution must be rewritten, with each generation crafting its own constitution. Resting content with the constitution given by past generations or, worse still, with a constitution handed down from another state amounts to a failure to exercise democratic control over the rules that govern a people. For this reason, King's constitutions have a built-in obsolescence, expiring after a twenty-year period, forcing their communities to rewrite a constitution, presumably from scratch.[6] The very act of writing a constitution is, for King, of value; by so doing we ensure that the constitution is a democratic document, the expression of the will of the people.

The second set of arguments uses the expressive aspect of constitutions as a tool with which constitutions can shape behaviour outside of the normal operation of the law. Distinct from their role in directly guiding action, constitutional norms also serve as articulations of the values of the community and, by that act of articulation, can shift social norms within that group.[7] As Cass Sunstein has argued, these rules can amount to a statement of what is or is not acceptable within the community. So, for example, legislation in discrimination law often turns on the superficial aspects of discrimination – unequal pay, unfair exclusion from promotion, and so forth – but, whilst the focus of the legislation may be on the manifestation of discrimination, the aspirations of the law often go deeper. The law stands as a statement by the community that it is committed to equality, that people should not be treated differently because of their race or gender, and such a statement may, itself, help shift attitudes, conditioning what people say and think.[8] The shifting of attitudes serves to reduce disagreement within society, uniting people behind the constitution. Sunstein argues that, on occasion,

4 Jeff King, *Constitutions as Mission Statements*, *in* SOCIAL AND POLITICAL FOUNDATIONS OF CONSTITUTIONS 73 (Denis J. Galligan & Mila Versteeg eds., 2013). *See also* Kim Lane Scheppele, *Aspirational and Aversive Constitutionalism*, 1 INT'L J. CONST. L. 296 (2003); Michael Dorf, *The Aspirational Constitution*, 77 GEO. WASH. L. REV. 1631 (2009).

5 Jeff King, *The Democratic Case for a Written Constitution*, 72 CURRENT LEGAL PROBS. 1 (2019).

6 Here, King is echoing a claim by Thomas Jefferson: *see* Dorf, *supra* note 4, at 1631.

7 Cass Sunstein, *On the Expressive Function of Law*, 144 U. PA. L. REV. 2021 2031 (1996); *see also* RICHARD H. MCADAMS, THE EXPRESSIVE POWERS OF LAW: THEORIES AND LIMITS (2015), ch. 5.

8 MCADAMS, *supra* note 7, at 139–43.

putting an answer to a socially disputed question in the constitution can remove that issue from political debate, focussing attention on other, less divisive areas of political dispute. Controversially, Sunstein offers the legality of abortion as an example of how a constitutional rule can defuse political debate.[9] Making access to abortion a constitutionally protected right, taking the question of the legality of abortion out of the normal dispute-resolving processes of the constitution will result, claims Sunstein, in people turning their attention to areas in which it is more likely that progress towards agreement can be made. Through its inclusion of a resolution of the issue in the constitution, the state discourages disagreement over the issue by making it harder to change the law, and so reduces people's interest in the issue.

As regards the third set of arguments, inclusion of certain rules in the constitution may be of inherent value. In an important book, Alon Harel takes the expressive function of law a stage further, contending that there are certain rights which should be included in constitutional texts as an expression of the state's recognition of the duties it owes to its people.[10] Harel argues that these rights should be judicially enforceable, and emphasises the significance of judicial review, but also contends that the explicit recognition of these rights is, itself, important. Even if enshrining the right in the constitution does not render it better protected, Harel contends that the act of public recognition by the state is essential to the protection of freedom, embodying an acceptance by the state of its duties towards its people. Drawing on the work of republican political theory, Harel writes that it is only citizens whose rights are constitutionally entrenched who do not live 'at the mercy' of their legislatures; without such legal recognition, their freedom depends on the inclinations of legislators, who may, or may not, be inclined to honour their rights.[11] Here, the constitution acts as a sort of self-denying ordinance, heading off some disputes before they arise; the constitution embodies a repudiation by the state of its capacity to exercise its power in certain ways, and the repudiation is, in itself, valuable.

These three arguments identify value in having a rule within a constitution that embodies a decision on some dispute or other, whether that value comes from the constitution memorialising the process through which the decision was reached, from the bare fact of the constitution expressing a decision on a contested topic, or from the public repudiation of a potential capacity. In each case, inclusion of a rule in the constitution expresses a resolution to a dispute and, in so doing, may reduce disagreement within the state.

2.3 CONSTITUTIONAL RULES AS ACCOMMODATIONS

The second set of techniques for responding to disagreement is radically different: rather than seeking to provide resolution, these techniques seek to accommodate the

9 Cass Sunstein, *Constitutionalism and Secession*, 58 U. Chi. L. Rev. 633 (1991).

10 Alon Harel, Why Law Matters ch. 5 (2014).

11 *Id.* at 150–52.

disagreement. The use of accommodation as a constitutional strategy cuts against the normal approach of lawyers to constitutions. In their reasoning, most lawyers, including most academic lawyers, present constitutions as coherent: as grounded in a set of complementary values and, as a result, speaking in a single voice. This methodological commitment to coherence underpins and constrains most interpretations of constitutions and is particularly marked in judicial reasoning. Judges strive to show that their decisions square with constitutional values, claiming that these are decisions grounded in the constitution and not the judge's personal preferences. After all, admitting that there are multiple values within the constitution which are, sometimes, in tension would be to admit that the judge had a choice, that a range of decisions were available to him or her. But whilst the presumption of coherence is one that judges should normally adopt when deciding disputes, when we examine the constitution outside of the courts it is sometimes useful to put this presumption to one side and approach the constitution as a sociological entity, as an instrument that has been shaped by different groups of people over a long period of time. Gary Jacobsohn has developed an account of what he calls the 'disharmonic constitution' that nicely captures this aspect of constitutions.[12] The disharmonic constitution contains multiple constitutional identities within itself, different visions of what the constitution is and should become. Rather than a single mission statement, to use King's term, the constitution embodies multiple, competing statements. These different visions can provide different perspectives on particular constitutional rules, which are explicable in terms of these different constitutional identities, and thus support competing understandings of these rules within the constitution. For Jacobsohn, the principal merit of a disharmonic constitution is that it provides material for the development of the constitution, allowing for the creative interaction of various strands of identity.[13] But a further merit is that it allows people with radically different views about the content of the constitution to identify with that instrument; by meaning different things to different people, the disharmonic constitution advances the integrative aim of the constitution. Sometimes the disharmonies within the constitution are unstable, and quickly collapse, but sometimes they can persist, and embody long-lasting accommodations of rival constitutional ideologies. There are four constitutional features that can facilitate stable disharmony: the breadth of the constitution, its size permitting different constitutional ideologies to operate in different areas; the capacity of particular constitutional rules to bear different interpretations; the ability of constitutions to leave questions open; and, finally, the potential for inconsistent rules within constitutions.

First, the sheer size and complexity of constitutions allow those instruments to accommodate differing constitutional visions. The United Kingdom, with its unusually long constitutional history, provides many examples of this. For

[12] Gary Jeffrey Jacobsohn, Constitutional Identity 4 (2010).

[13] *Id.* at 102.

traditionalists, the United Kingdom is a monarchy, with a queen, an established church, bishops and hereditary peers in the legislature, and plenty of historical dressings – gothic buildings, robes, and crowns. For staunch democrats, the United Kingdom is the paradigmatic political constitution, with Parliament enjoying wide legislative power and the courts lacking the capacity to challenge its decisions, whilst for those who regard rights as the basis of the constitution there are the Human Rights Act 1998, the Equality Act 2010, alongside other statutes which can be invoked in courts against the state. The list could go on; there are multiple different ways of looking at the United Kingdom constitution, all of which can claim some support from different parts of that system. A recurrent trope of United Kingdom constitutional scholarship is that the UK constitution is one thing in the guise of another – a republic in the guise of a monarchy, a federation in the guise of a unitary state – but, perhaps, it would be better to say that it manages to be all of these things at once, with the element that predominates depending on the observer's ideological perspective.

These different constitutional identities can operate in distinct parts of the constitution, but they can also overlap, with a single rule forming part of both strands. Cass Sunstein has written of the value of incompletely theorised agreements within constitutions.[14] Where these are present, people agree with the inclusion of a rule, but disagree over the reasons underpinning it. Sometimes this disagreement will relate to competing visions of the constitution; a given rule could be grounded in either ideology. So, for example, in the United Kingdom courts cannot strike down statutes that run contrary to the Human Rights Act; they can only issue a 'declaration of incompatibility' that may then trigger a legislative reappraisal of the statute. For those who emphasise rights as at the core of the constitution, this is tantamount to striking down the statute – Parliament has never, to date, refused to alter a statute after such a declaration. Under this interpretation of the constitution, the purpose of the rule is to enable Parliament, an institution with differing strengths and capacities from those of the court, to make the changes needed to protect rights. For those who emphasise democracy, though, the rule exists to give Parliament the final decision about the significance and implications of individual rights; the purpose of the rule is to preserve the position of the legislature in the constitution. The same rule can form part of two different pictures of the UK constitution, and is capable of being accommodated within rival ideological accounts of the state. Whilst problems might arise further down the line, when disputes over the implications of the rule require resolution and the lack of an agreed purpose makes interpretation of the rule controversial, such disputes may be rare, and, most of the time, the two understandings of the rule can comfortably coexist.

[14] Cass Sunstein, *Incompletely Theorized Agreements*, 108 Harv. L. Rev. 1733 (1995); Hanna Lerner, Making Constitutions in Deeply Divided Societies 39–41 (2011).

Rules that rest upon incompletely theorised agreements appear to resolve disputes as their language seems clear and certain but their underlying purpose remains ambiguous. A more direct way of accommodating rival constitutional ideologies is to explicitly leave the question open, postponing its resolution to a later date.[15] The most notorious example of this is, of course, found in the American Constitution which included a twenty-year moratorium on the legality of the slave trade. The effect of this provision was to reassure those opposed to slavery that the issue could be addressed through constitutional institutions in the future, whilst also promising those who supported the practice that this would not occur in the short term. It is important to note that this provision did not leave open the question of slavery's legality – the Constitution accepted that it was lawful; it simply made clear that the issue would need to be reconsidered in the future, postponing the debate rather than resolving it. Tarun Khaitan has shown how the postponement of issues was skilfully used to help gain support for the Indian Constitution, through the device of directive principles.[16] Directive principles are constitutional statements that are not directly enforceable by the courts; they are aspirations, rather than justiciable rules. As Khaitan notes, this feature allows the setting of goals that can draw groups which support them into the constitution, whilst reassuring others that the implementation of these objectives can be debated at a later point: directive principles combine a commitment to a goal with a promise not to implement the goal without further deliberation within the constitutional institutions.

A final method by which disagreement may be accommodated rather than resolved is through the inclusion of inconsistent rules within the constitution. In particular, within a single constitutional order there may be multiple, inconsistent rules giving priority to rival sources of law, or identifying rival institutions as having the final say about the content of the legal order. I have written at length about inconsistencies of this type elsewhere.[17] Whilst they might seem pathological, embodying contradictions that would appear antithetical to the very idea of a legal order, they are far from uncommon, and frequently arise during constitutional ruptures, periods when new states emerge from the constitutional structures of an older constitutional order. So, for example, the Australian legal order started life as an offshoot of the imperial legal order, with the Imperial Parliament – Westminster – the highest law-making body in the system, and the Privy Council standing as the final court of appeal. As Australia's constitutional identity emerged during the twentieth century, this legal position became anachronistic, and, well before the Australia Acts, passed by the Australian and United Kingdom Parliaments, settled the issue, Australian judges had started to

[15] Rosalind Dixon & Tom Ginsburg, *Deciding Not to Decide: Deferral in Constitutional Design*, 9 INT'L J. CONST. L. 636 (2011).

[16] Tarunabh Khaitan, *Directive Principles and the Expressive Accommodation of Ideological Dissenters*, 16 INT'L J. CONST. L. 389 (2018); *see also* Tarunabh Khaitan, *Constitutional Directives: Morally-Committed Political Constitutionalism*, 82 MOD. L. REV. 603 (2019).

[17] BARBER, *supra* note 1, ch. 9; Nicholas W. Barber, *Legal Inconsistency and the Emergence of States*, *in* LAW AND THE NEW LOGICS (H. Patrick Glenn & Lionel D. Smith eds., 2016).

create constitutional space between Australia and the old imperial institutions.[18] Some Australian judges identified the constitutional basis of the Australian system as grounded in the Australian people, rather than in a statute passed by Westminster, and argued that Westminster's law-making power over Australia had expired.[19] However, others held to the view that Australia remained a subset of the British Empire, reliant on a UK statute for its constitution and subject to legislative decisions made in Westminster.[20] This inconsistency allowed two constitutional ideologies to coexist within the Australian order, one in which Australia was a sovereign state, the other in which Australia formed part of a larger imperial constitutional unit. This allowed Australian traditionalists to regard Australia as remaining part of the British Empire, and the more progressively minded to see Australia as an independent state. Similar inconsistencies can be found in other polities where there is disagreement over fundamental features of the constitution. Whilst such inconsistencies might seem to bring with them the risk of confusion or constitutional fragmentation, provided that the disagreement does not affect lower-level rules, they can prove long-lasting, with judges taking different views of the constitutional basis of the laws they apply.

2.4 CONCLUSION: RESOLUTION OR ACCOMMODATION?

These two groups of strategies for using the rules of constitutions to regulate and contain disagreement show that the rules of the constitution, in themselves, can help the state to achieve its objectives, distinct from the operation of the institutions instantiated by that instrument; the expressive function of constitutions can be, in itself, valuable. Sensible policymakers will consider strategies of resolution and accommodation when faced with disagreement, and will make use of both approaches, resolving some disputes whilst seeking to accommodate others. Perhaps the most important lesson to take from the preceding sections is that both strategies have roles to play in making constitutions work successfully. Though constitutional lawyers tend, by virtue of their training, to be attracted to the certainty offered by strategies of resolution, even when it is possible to write an answer to a dispute into the constitution accommodation may still be the better option. King's proposal for a regular and comprehensive rewrite of the constitution should be rejected for this reason, amongst others: it assumes that resolution is invariably better than accommodation, that people should be pushed towards resolving issues. As Hanna Lerner warns, debates during constitutional drafting can inflame foundational disagreements within society.[21] Recognising the value of accommodation

[18] Australia Act 1986 (Cth); Australia Act 1986 (UK).

[19] Bistricic v. Rokov (1976) 135 CLR 552, 565–67; Robinson v. Western Australia Museum (1978) 138 CLR 283; Kirmani v. Captain Cook Cruises Pty Ltd *(No. 1)* (1985) 159 CLR 351, 442.

[20] China Ocean Shipping Co. v. South Australia (1979) 145 CLR 172.

[21] LERNER, *supra* note 14, at 35–38.

requires us to acknowledge that, on occasion, it is better to avoid answering some questions than to resolve them.

The overarching question of which strategy should be used, resolution or accommodation, turns on questions relating to the political capital of the state, that is, the support that people have for the constitutional order, and the moral permissibility of compromise, that is, whether these are issues that it is permissible to avoid answering. These will largely turn on the particular issues raised by the area of dispute.

In terms of the costs of making a decision, both the need to make it and the timeliness of the decision must be evaluated. Sometimes, there are issues that have to be resolved there and then, and only one acceptable decision is open to the state. There are some options that states should never permit to remain open, issues which have to be resolved in a particular way because the state is a state; that is, its resolution is implied by its identity as a state. For example, the initial tolerance of slavery by the American Constitution was a mistaken accommodation. Given the evils of slavery, the fact that the practice cuts against the very purpose of the state, its legality is not a question that should ever have been allowed to remain open. Harel's comments about the importance of the state recognising limits on what it can legitimately authorise are significant here. Whilst we might be sceptical of Harel's claim that states need to memorialise these constraints in law, he is right to argue that there are certain moral limits on a state's authority that any decent state must recognise, and, moreover, that the recognition of these limits is an essential feature of a successful state. Permitting slavery to continue was a concession that the Founders should have realised was not open to the state to make, and being willing to consider compromising on this was, in itself, an assumption of a capacity that a state should renounce.

Conversely, there may be some questions that it is simply not necessary to answer. Where an issue does not make a difference to people's lives, it may be better to leave it open than to answer it; the costs of resolving it cannot be justified. For example, whether or not a constitution has a religious base, whether it is grounded in the will of God or the dictates of reason, is a question that people might have strong views over but which may not need resolution. Difficult questions about the place of religion within the state may arise lower down the constitutional order, and will need to be answered there, but the fundamental question about the basis of the constitution need not be addressed. For the constitution to pick a side on this debate risks alienating one group or other, reducing the capacity of that group, or those groups, to identify with the constitutional order; accommodation expends far less political capital than resolution.

Connectedly, the timeliness of the decision should be considered.[22] There are some issues which are likely to become easier to answer over time, where postponing their resolution is likely to reduce the eventual costs of addressing and answering

22 Dixon & Ginsburg, *supra* note 15, at 641–43.

them. For example, the grand question of whether the European Union is, or should be, a federal state, a confederation of states, or a mixture of these two constitutional forms has remained open for most of the EU's existence.[23] To resolve this question now would be costly, both in terms of the time spent debating the issue and, of course, in terms of the price paid by creating a losing side, a group whose vision of Europe has been excluded. It is likely that, over time, it will become clearer which constitutional model of Europe is preferred by those within the polity; the question will become less controversial and thus easier to answer. On the other hand, there are questions that are likely to become more controversial over time, making a push for early resolution favourable. For example, the question of the regularity of secession referendums in Scotland is unanswered. During the last independence referendum, there seemed to be broad agreement that the vote could be held once in a generation – but there was little clarity about how long a generation lasted or what, if any, exceptional circumstances might mean that an earlier vote could be held. Had the issue been addressed immediately after the 2014 referendum, when the political tensions over the question were at their lowest, it might have been possible to reach a decision that many, if not all, of the participants could accept. Now, in 2022, the question of whether Scotland is constitutionally entitled to hold a second referendum is a deeply controversial one, a question which presses for resolution but which is hard to resolve. The decision to allow different understandings of the required length of time between referendums to persist, to accommodate rather than resolve, was a mistake. Frustratingly, the timeliness of a constitution decision is often inversely related to the political will to resolve it: the pressure to make a decision is likely to be at its most intense when the issue is a focus of controversy, and thus hardest to resolve, whereas when passions cool, few outside a small group of constitutional lawyers are interested in the issue.

Finally, and most generally, as well as considering the costs of making a decision, the subsequent costs of it having been made should also be considered. As we have seen, both resolving and accommodating disagreement may, in some situations, benefit effective government in the state. Sometimes the inclusion of a rule resolving a dispute will act as a focus for identification with the state, a statement of a value around which people can unite. As King's depiction of constitutions as 'mission statements' reminds us, constitutional rules can express ideologies that people can rally behind, uniting people rather than dividing them. Sometimes, as Sunstein argues, resolving an issue can end or mitigate debate around it. But one example Sunstein gives, of abortion law in America, shows the hazards of confusing legal resolution with political resolution. By constitutionalising the right to abortion, the issue has been made legally more stable, with the law strongly resistant to change, but this may have made the politics around the issue more heated as the normal

[23] N.W. Barber, *The Two Europes*, *in* The Rise and Fall of the European Constitution (N.W. Barber et al. eds., 2019).

avenues for legal change have been closed. Recalling Khaitan's work on the Indian Constitution, making it clear to opponents of a rule that there is a plausible path to legal change, even if the rule they object to remains in effect, may encourage them to support constitutional structures rather than subvert them.

Constitutions are intertwined with states but have an existence distinct from them. Whilst the primary purpose of constitutional rules is to establish and regulate state institutions, these rules can possess a significance beyond their constitutive effect, standing as public statements of the state's approach to issues of controversy, seeking either to resolve these disputes or to accommodate them. Thus, the constitution, itself, can facilitate the integrative function of the state, helping to bolster the community's support for, and acceptance of, state institutions.

3

Effective Governance and the Social Dimension of the Rule of Law

Jeff King

3.1 INTRODUCTION

Assuming that effective governance refers to the state's regulatory powers over private natural and legal persons, it is fair to say that it has been the poor cousin of constitutionalism. Liberal constitutional thought has been largely preoccupied with the need to restrain executive power rather than to justify it.[1] That was true first of its focus on royal prerogative power, later of its antagonism toward rule by executive decree or legislation, and into the twentieth century of its uncertain aversion to regulation. Those theorists and public lawyers that resisted that narrative of 'constraint', predominantly on the social democratic left, would for the most part choose the language of *democracy* as their contrarian justificatory framework.[2] The contest has similarly played out across the twentieth century in British constitutional thought through an argument between parties who align themselves, roughly put, with one of two supposedly competing principles at the core of the British constitution: the sovereignty of Parliament and the rule of law.[3] None of the parties to that dispute are concerned to make the case for executive power per se. So too with critical, Marxist, and postmodern approaches to law and justice, which have been sceptical of judges and of the state, and offered some often inchoate conception of radical democracy as the alternative. Quite simply – few Anglo-American theorists were willing to make the case for the Leviathan.[4]

[1] I have elsewhere been concerned to challenge that view: J. King, *Constitutions as Mission Statements*, *in* THE SOCIAL AND POLITICAL FOUNDATIONS OF CONSTITUTIONS ch. 3 (Dennis J. Galligan & Mila Versteeg eds., 2013).

[2] Examples of American or US-based writers I take to be in this category are Alexander Bickel, John Hart Ely, Frank Michelman, Bruce Ackerman, Lawrence G. Sager, William Forbath, and Jeremy Waldron. In Europe this list would include Jürgen Habermas, J.A.G. Griffith, Richard Bellamy, and perhaps Dieter Grimm.

[3] While this oversimplifies the complexity of the various positions, an outline of this division of loyalties is explored in MARTIN LOUGHLIN, PUBLIC LAW AND POLITICAL THEORY (1992).

[4] As often noted, the situation in France and Germany was different, with well-developed ideas of the state and of its role as a social facilitator. In France this tradition is exemplified in the work of Leon Duguit and in Germany by a range of 'state law' theorists (*Staatsrechtlehrer*), both conservative and social democratic in disposition. On German legal theory and practice, *see* MICHAEL STOLLEIS,

Of course, not all constitutional thinkers avoided formulating a deep position on the functional virtues of executive power, or of government. The Federalist cause was plainly motivated by making the case for 'The Necessity of a Government at Least Equally Energetic with the One Proposed'.[5] Most New Deal luminaries would continue the Progressivist concern with the need for executive power in the form of regulation and redistribution.[6] In Britain, New Liberal philosophers would argue for a proactive state policy to secure real liberty to citizens,[7] with some historians now crediting the early British welfare state as a largely liberal bequest rather than Labour Party achievement.[8] Before them, John Stuart Mill would write a deep, if largely forgotten text which outlined the relationships among a functioning government, administration, and the representative chamber.[9] Nevertheless, in the United States, the New Deal vision of the state was largely overtaken by a liberal rights conception in the post-World War II period, one in which administrative expertise would lose its settled status and the administrative state would (again) come into repeated conflict with constitutional values.[10] Jerry Mashaw's *Bureaucratic Justice* (1986) and Cass Sunstein's *After the Rights Revolution* (1990) and *The Partial Constitution* (1994) stand out as compelling analyses and vindications of bureaucracy and regulation. But it is hard to discern whether they represented a constitutional status quo or a rearguard defence against a resurgent anti-administrativism that would become more potent in law, just as it

Public Law in Germany: A Historical Introduction from the 16th to the 21st Century ch.9, esp. 74–75 (Thomas Dunlop trans., 2017) ('They advocated a strong state that stood above societal conflicts and should also have a representative who stood above the parties. . . . [They] lamented that parties were invading the shaping of the public will outside parliament.').

5 The title of the Federalist No. 23. *See* James Madison, Alexander Hamilton & John Jay, The Federalist Papers (Isaac Kramnick ed., 1987) (1788); *see also* The Anti-Federalist Papers and the Constitutional Convention Debates (Ralph Ketcham ed., 1986).

6 I take James McCauley Landis, The Administrative Process (1938), to be one such study. For a relevant discussion of the New Deal luminaries along these lines, *see* J.O. Freedman, Crisis and Legitimacy: The Administrative Process and American Government (1978). In another, excellent book, K. Sabeel Rahman, Democracy Against Domination (2016), the focus of the confrontation is again between, as the title suggests, democracy and private forms of domination.

7 Peter Clarke, Liberals and Social Democrats (1978); Peter Weiler , The New Liberalism: Liberal Social Theory in Great Britain, 1889–1914 (1982). Such philosophers had an important influence on John Dewey: *see* Alan Ryan, John Dewey and the High Tide of American Liberalism 85–89 (1995) (on T.H. Green's impact on Dewey).

8 Chris Renwick, Bread for All: The Origins of the Welfare State (2017). Notably, William Beveridge and John Maynard Keynes were liberal politicians and scholars.

9 John Stuart Mill, Considerations on Representative Government esp. ch. XIV (1861). The other disciples of Jeremy Bentham, in fact, were energetic participants in the rapid expansion of administrative government in the Victorian period: Anthony Brundage, England's Prussian Minister: Edwin Chadwick and the Politics of Government Growth, 1832–54 (1988).

10 I am thinking here particularly of what is called regulatory ossification. *See* Jerry L. Mashaw & David L. Harfst, The Struggle for Auto-Safety (1990); Jerry L. Mashaw & David L. Harfst, *From Command and Control to Collaboration and Deference: The Transformation of Auto Safety*, 34 Yale J. on Regul. 167 (2017). Other examples would include the influence of public choice and constitutional economics.

had in politics.[11] And in Britain, while the welfare state and nationalisation would expand rapidly in the post-World War II period, scholars of the functionalist style of public law would lament the absence of any theory of the state (as opposed to well-developed accounts of the role of the state in public law to be found in Germany and France), as well as the domination of the legal system by an elitist and predominantly conservative bar and judiciary.[12] The functionalists' approach was distinguished by a fine-grained understanding of the administrative and political process, and how it related to a conception of public law outside the courts. Yet although Robson, Laski, and Jennings were each quite politically influential in their own day,[13] it was their Oxford-based intellectual enemy Albert Venn Dicey (1835–1922) and his Cambridge torchbearer William Wade (1918–2004) who would exert the dominant influence on public law thinking in the academy and at the bar in the mid to late twentieth century. The present-day successors to the functionalists, the self-styled political constitutionalists, focus their attention on opposition to judicial review and the legal constitution, basing their case on democratic arguments and the epistemic limits of rationalism rather than on grounded understandings of the functional advantages of administrative government. Thomas Poole's deep study of prerogative power stands as something of an exception in recent studies, but is chiefly theoretical and historical rather than empirical and current.[14]

3.2 A SOCIAL DIMENSION OF THE RULE OF LAW?

If executive power is the poor cousin of constitutionalism, it is, within that same liberal constitutional tradition, all but the enemy of the rule of law. As noted by the philosopher Judith Shklar, much of the writing about the rule of law appears like 'a football in a game between friends and enemies of free market liberalism'.[15] Lord Hailsham, an influential member of Prime Minister Margaret Thatcher's Cabinet

11 See Gillian E. Metzger, *Foreword: 1930s Redux: The Administrative State Under Siege*, 131 Harv. L. Rev. 1 (2017).

12 Martin Loughlin, *The Functional Style in Public Law*, 55 U. Toronto L. J. 361 (2005). That approach to public law included notable figures, all at the London School of Economics (LSE), such as William A. Robson (1895–1980), Harold J. Laski (1893–1950), Ivor Jennings (1903–65), Carol Harlow and Richard Rawlings (both still working), and was a potent influence on J.A.G. Griffith (1918–2010) and Martin Loughlin (still working). *See also* Janet McLean, Searching for the State in British Legal Thought (2012).

13 *See supra* note 12. William Robson cofounded the political journal *The Political Quarterly* along with notables such as G.B. Shaw and J.M. Keynes, and also co-authored a book published in 1925 with Clement Attlee, later post-World War II UK prime minister (of the Labour Party). Laski chaired the British Labour Party Conference in 1945–6 and sat on the Donoughmore Committee on Ministers' Powers which reported in 1932. Jennings was extensively involved in constitution-making around the British Empire.

14 Thomas Poole, Reasons of State: Law, Prerogative and Empire (2015).

15 Judith N. Shklar, *Political Theory and the Rule of Law*, *in* The Rule of Law: Ideal or Ideology? 6 (Alan C. Hutchinson & Patrick Monahan eds., 1987).

in the late 1970s, would expound a theory of limited government in a popular 1976 speech for the BBC entitled 'The Elective Dictatorship', later expanded into a book. 'As an alternative to regulation', Hailsham clarified of his theory, 'it propounds the rule of law.'[16] J.A.G. Griffith, the scholar of Parliament, left-wing firebrand, and founding editor of the British journal *Public Law*, would observe in a famous essay that '[t]he Rule of law is an invaluable concept for those who wish not to change the present set-up'.[17] The anti-regulatory conception of the rule of law elaborated systematically by Friedrich Hayek had a profound effect on political thinking in both the United States and Britain.[18] It amplified pre-existing hostility to the idea on the left, in particular because, as Hayek claimed to show with profound competence, in reality his ideas were merely a restatement of the classical liberal tradition. For Hayek, the rule of law and constitutionalism were largely two aspects of the same thing. As he argues in *The Constitution of Liberty*, '[t]he idea of a constitution … involves not only the idea of a hierarchy of authority or power but also that of a hierarchy of rules or laws, where those possessing a higher degree of generality and proceeding from superior authority control the contents of the more specific laws that are passed by a delegated authority'.[19]

This chapter outlines a project that responds to that tradition of constitutional thought and in particular as it relates to the rule of law concept.[20] The core argument in that project is that to fully respect the political ideal of the rule of law, an economically advanced society would *require* rather than substantially restrain extensive market regulation and a rudimentary welfare state. Accordingly, this chapter argues for a regulatory conception of the rule of law, affirming the positive virtues of law and of the state, rather than emphasising (but without denying) their vices. Insofar as constitutionalism concerns application of the rule of law to government, the argument is that constitutionalism itself requires a robust, positive conception of the need for effective governance.

3.3 THE ARGUMENT IN A NUTSHELL

More specifically, this conception argues for the following key propositions. First, the rule of law is best understood as a *regulatory* ideal that requires proactive legal regulation rather than as an ideal that favours governmental restraint. It can be contrasted with an ideal that is indifferent or silent about *whether* there is legal regulation, and is concerned only with what *form* any *given* legal regulation takes.

16 Lord Hailsham, The Dilemma of Democracy: Diagnosis and Prescription 13 (1978).

17 J.A.G. Griffith, *The Political Constitution*, 42 Mod. L. Rev. 1, 15 (1979).

18 Friedrich August Hayek, The Road to Serfdom (1944), The Constitution of Liberty (1960), and Law, Legislation and Liberty: A New Statement of the Liberal Principles of Justice and Political Economy (1982).

19 Hayek, The Constitution of Liberty, *supra* note 18, at 156.

20 For a more detailed working out of some of these ideas, see Jeff King, *The Rule of Law*, in The Cambridge Handbook of Constitutional Theory (R. Bellamy & J. King eds., forthcoming 2023).

And it is particularly to be contrasted with libertarian understandings, of the Hayekian variety. It also claims that such an account better answers two unanswered problems for the more restricted views – the problem of explaining the commitment to *anti-anarchy* in the rule of law ideal, and the problem of reconciling the rule of law and discretion that is exercised by public officials.

Second, the long-standing preoccupation with the regulation of *arbitrary power* in the rule of law tradition is best understood as a deep concern about the role of law in protecting freedom, and, more specifically, with addressing the use of *coercion* by public officials. This is evident in the genealogy of the idea across the eighteenth to the twentieth century, and explains its intimate though not analytically necessary relationship to social contract theory and democratic law-making. Consequently, those theories which derive the rule of law idea from an account of the essence of law or legality itself are mistaken, or at any rate misguided.

Third, the reasons justifying a liberal rule of law concern for the legal regulation of public coercion also justify such a concern to regulate (a) the use of *private coercion* such as sexual assault, domestic violence, robbery, paramilitary activity, and criminal racketeering, and (b) the resort to *private exploitation* in which persons are wronged and have no choice but to consent to the wrongdoing. This latter concern in particular can be called the social dimension of the rule of law. It does not entail a violation of any commitment to the principle of liberal neutrality.

Fourth, the social dimension of the rule of law is best understood as a state duty to legally regulate forms of non-consensual exploitation. Non-consensual exploitation involves transactions in which one person takes unfair advantage of another, and that other has no choice but to consent. Both unfair advantage and defect of consent in this sense are difficult to define, but that both are systemic social problems is undeniable. As unfair advantage and lack of consent are difficult to determine on a case-by-case basis, I do not argue that the social dimension of the rule of law should in the main be fulfilled by judges applying vague principles (such as a duty to avoid exploitation). Instead, such an ideal could be fulfilled only through the enactment of bespoke regulatory regimes in exploitative fields of social interaction. Such regimes must furnish frameworks grounding individual rights and duties that are enforceable in the courts and tribunals of the land. It is that last quality – the legal form of protection, and the detailed elaboration of rights and duties that it demands – that truly makes it appropriate as a rule of law conception. The rule of law demands a wide set of legalistic responses to exploitation, which sound in both legislation and adjudication.

All told, this regulatory conception of the rule of law accepts the traditional desiderata of the rule of law (i.e., clarity, prospectivity, adjudication, fair procedures, etc.), but argues that the ideal also imposes duties upon the state to regulate the private sphere to ensure that citizens are also not vulnerable to private domination and exploitation. That is the social dimension of the rule of law. The rule of law on the whole is a political value which requires the legal regulation of unfree interactions in the public and private sphere.

3.4 PLAUSIBILITY

The argument supporting these various propositions is further detailed in other work.[21] I choose here to focus on what have been communicated to me as the key points of disagreement. To many seasoned readers, and to the student of jurisprudence in particular, the argument is radical in two ways. First, it exacerbates a widely debated concern about how so-called substantive conceptions of the rule of law end up collapsing the rule of law into a 'complete social philosophy' in which the 'term lacks any useful function'.[22] Second, it not only denies the opposition between the rule of law and the welfare state that has characterised much of the discussion thus far; in the ultimate act of alchemy, it would actually make them bedfellows.

I am all too aware of these challenges. I had previously for some time adopted Joseph Raz's conception of the rule of law, and taught it emphatically as the correct approach. And, as a writer concerned with social rights and the welfare state, I am not only aware of but have written about the damaging role that rule of law rhetoric played in the establishment of the welfare and regulatory states in Britain and America.[23] These doubts have also been confronted consistently in various seminars at which the social dimension of the rule of law has been presented and argued for. The persistent line of up-front scepticism is that while my claims about the role of law in averting exploitation are accepted (or not denied), the link to the rule of law is seen as 'unnecessary', 'puzzling', or even 'troubling'. The rule of law could not be widely agreed on such a definition, and the argument looks like an attempt to smuggle social justice into the rule of law ideal. However, that scepticism has been consistently muted when those offering it are asked the following question: Is anarchy compatible with the rule of law? Most accept that, at least intuitively, it is not – at any rate not in a mildly complex community. The rule of law presupposes

[21] *See supra* note 20. Some of the thinking is detailed in Jeff King, *Martin Krygier and the Tempering of Power*, 11 HAGUE J. ON RULE L. 363 (2019).

[22] Joseph Raz, *The Rule of Law and Its Virtue*, 93 L. Q. REV. 195 (1977), *reprinted in* JOSEPH RAZ, THE AUTHORITY OF LAW ch. 11, at 211 (1979). A survey of disagreements between formal and substantive conceptions is found in the seminal discussion by Paul Craig, *Formal and Substantive Conceptions of the Rule of Law*, PUB. L. 467 (1997). *See also* Lord Bingham, *The Rule of Law*, 66 CAMBRIDGE L. J. 67 (2007); Evan Fox-Decent, *Is the Rule of Law Really Indifferent to Human Rights?*, 27 L. & PHIL. 533 (2008); Peter Rijpkema, *The Rule of Law Beyond Thick and Thin*, 32 L. & PHIL. 793 (2013); Julian Sempill, *Ruler's Sword, Citizen's Shield: The Rule of Law and the Constitution of Power*, 31 J. L. & POL. 333 (2016).

[23] JEFF KING, JUDGING SOCIAL RIGHTS esp. chs. 2, 6 (2012); Jeff King, *Social Rights as Capstone*, *in* THE FUTURE OF SOCIAL RIGHTS (Katharine Young ed., 2019). *See also* Christopher McCrudden & Jeff King, *The Dark Side of Nudging: The Ethics, Political Economy and Law of Libertarian Paternalism*, *in* CHOICE ARCHITECTURE IN DEMOCRACIES: EXPLORING THE LEGITIMACY OF NUDGING (Alexandra Kemmerer et al. eds., 2015).

law. But, the sceptics maintain, it is nothing so extravagant as what I propose. But then what is it? They might accept the basic kernel of insight in Lon Fuller's statement that 'law is the enterprise of subjecting human conduct to the governance of rules',[24] or perhaps Joseph Raz's unexplored (and fully ignored) claim that one of two foundational ideas underlying the rule of law is that 'people should be ruled by law and obey it'.[25] But neither of these theorists, nor those invoking their authority, fully developed the implications of these statements for a conception of the rule of law.

This is no minor oversight. If one accepts the idea that anarchy and the rule of law are incompatible, then much of the rest of my argument on the need for regulation is likely to follow. One will need to take some view on precisely what ought to be regulated by law under the rule of law ideal.[26] On no view does the rule of law require careful legal regulation of *all* human behaviour. Questions of taste, whether to marry or divorce, to believe or reject religion, and of what kind of association to attend or leave are matters that are in the main not (or no longer) minutely regulated by law in the way we expect many other social interactions to be. They are very unlike questions of interpersonal violence, or even of bullying and harassment. To simply declare that the rule of law requires law is insensitive to the need to delineate domains of behaviour to which the ideal applies.

For some, this argument may appear to conflate the idea of *what law should regulate*, on the one hand, with what *the rule of law is*, on the other. I reject any such contention because my argument is that the two ideas are intimately linked. The deeper and longer tradition of thinking about the rule of law situates it, as a normative ideal, within a political theory rather than as the product of a theory of the nature of law.[27] Such is evident in the tradition of rule of law thinking in the discourse of the Founding Fathers of the US Constitution as well as in the related ideas of John Locke,[28] in the work of Immanuel Kant (the intellectual originator of the German *Rechtsstaat* idea), and in much of the writing of the twentieth century, including that of Friedrich Hayek. These are theories that integrate the rule of law idea into a broader political theory that specifies a pre-eminent function for law and

24 Lon L. Fuller, The Morality of Law 106 (1964).

25 Raz, Authority of Law, *supra* note 22, at 213. For my critique of Raz's views, see King, *The Rule of Law*, *supra* note 20.

26 Some have denied this move. They argue that the argumentative case for (a) having the law and the state exist is of a different argumentative character than (b) the detailing of what law and the state should do. I deny that there is any meaningful reason to invoke this distinction when reasoning about the rule of law. The arguments in favour of a legal order and of the state necessarily carry over to the functions of the legal order and the state, and *especially so when both legal systems and the state can be profoundly oppressive*. I am grateful to discussions with Professor Christopher Essert (University of Toronto) and Richard Bellamy (University College London) for their contrary views on these points.

27 These arguments are detailed more fully in King, *The Rule of Law*, *supra* note 20.

28 The ideas of the Founding Fathers and of Locke in this connection are explored in Brian Z. Tamanaha, On the Rule of Law: History, Politics, Theory ch. 4 (2004). Also see the outstanding discussion in Sempill, *supra* note 22.

its essential role in constitutional government. But their views can hardly be described as instances of conflation or confusion, or, if so, then such would make the criticism a form of academic pedantry. Their visions have had a very long endurance and enormous impact on public policy.

That is not to say that the rule of law should not be, and in my account is not, distinctive in some ways from a broader account of justice. Arguing that the rule of law requires the legal regulation of exploitative and unfree transactions falls far short of requiring justice. It would leave much of health care, old age pensions, disability benefits, public health, climate protection, natural resources preservation, just parenting, and fair distribution of household work as something mostly not managed by rule of law ideals. That is so even though justice (in my view) imposes concrete and stringent duties in respect of these arrangements. The rule of law is concerned in particular with the role of legal regulation, whereas justice must address fairness in distribution as well as the protection of rights.

3.5 FORCE AND FREEDOM: ARBITRARINESS AND PRIVATE DOMINATION

Writers such as Locke, the Founding Fathers, Kant, Hayek, and the bulk of the users of the term presently, do in fact have an answer to what it is that the rule of law requires to be regulated by law: *arbitrary power*. The idea of non-arbitrariness remains central in the development of rule of law conceptions today.[29] I contend that when one digs more deeply into the nature of arbitrary power, this cashes out as a deep concern for liberty – that those in a position to infringe it be subject to legal regulation and not act on whim or caprice, or be unanswerable to anyone or anything. This concern was evident in claims like John Locke's that 'where-ever law ends, tyranny begins',[30] or Hayek's that 'protection against unpredictable interference … is the essential condition of individual freedom, and to secure it is the main function of law'.[31] It is also visible in the republican tradition that Philip Pettit identifies as taking the view that 'law is or can be creative of liberty'.[32] It is worked out most systematically in the work of Immanuel Kant, particularly the *Doctrine of Right* (*Rechtslehre*), in which he understood the juridical state, the *Rechtsstaat*, to be the juridical-institutional framework for giving effect to the axiom of external or 'innate' freedom (i.e., 'independence from

29 Useful examinations of the idea of arbitrariness are found in Gerald Postema, *Fidelity in Law's Commonwealth*, *in* Private Law and the Rule of Law (Lisa M. Austin & Dennis Klimchuk eds., 2014), and especially in Sempill, *supra* note 22, at 366ff. Various essays by Martin Krygier explore the idea in both a theoretical and a contextual way.

30 John Locke, Second Treatise of Government s.202 (1980) (1689).

31 Hayek, The Constitution of Liberty, *supra* note 18, at 141.

32 Philip Pettit, Republicanism: A Theory of Freedom and Government 37 (1997). Pettit's own conception of the rule of law is a narrow, formal one. Non-domination in his account was something for the constitution and political obligation to care for. A properly functioning legal system was an important part of it. Domination in his scheme is broader than non-consensual exploitation, my subject.

being constrained by another's choice').[33] That deep and historical concern for liberty, and its opposition to unconstrained or arbitrary power, explains the natural extension of the rule of law to entail the idea that people deserve legal protection of their basic rights.[34]

Now, in that classical liberal and republican tradition, the 'arbitrary power' consistently recognised was the power of the state to use coercive force over its subjects. That, among other reasons, explains why it became an anti-regulatory ideal. That focus on arbitrary *state power* has come into question, however.[35] Robin West, to take one example, detects a distinct failure in most formal rule of law treatments (and in Waldron's account in particular). She argues that these accounts 'ignore the ways in which the law expresses the will of the state to protect weaker parties harmed not by the state but by stronger private entities'.[36] As Martin Krygier (a perceptive critic of post-communist authoritarianism) so aptly noted of her observation, 'West's point is true of every society, including my own (and yours), where the state is relatively effective and all the more so of many conflictual, postconflict, transitional, and failed states, where the miseries from which the rule of law would be a deliverance are closer to those imagined by Hobbes than to those understood by Locke.'[37] It is increasingly common to recognise the problem of private arbitrary power in discussions of the rule of law.[38] The most obvious instances include the private use of force, such as domestic violence, sexual harassment, extortion, or criminal racketeering. I would not only contend but assert as intuitively compelling that a state that fails to take action against such activities fails in the rule of law, whether or not, and perhaps especially if, it fails to proscribe such activities altogether. To relate such claims to the idea that arbitrary power must be

33 Immanuel Kant, *The Doctrine of Right, within* THE METAPHYSICS OF MORALS, *in* THE CAMBRIDGE EDITION OF THE WORKS OF IMMANUEL KANT: PRACTICAL PHILOSOPHY 393 (Mary J. Gregor trans. & ed., 1996) (1797). *See also* B. SHARON BYRD & JOACHIM HRUSCHKA, KANT'S DOCTRINE OF RIGHT: A COMMENTARY (2010); ARTHUR RIPSTEIN, FORCE AND FREEDOM: KANT'S LEGAL AND POLITICAL PHILOSOPHY ch. 2 (2009).

34 The four leading indices of the rule of law, and the working definitions of the United Nations, the Venice Commission of Democracy through Law, the German Federal Constitutional Court, and the view of the late Lord Bingham, Britain's pre-eminent judge, all accept the protection of rights as among the rule of law desiderata. Raz's view to the contrary, shared widely among legal philosophers, is starkly juxtaposed.

35 I show that the concern with private power was evident in the theories of Immanuel Kant, Robert von Mohl, John Locke, and others. *See* Jeff King, Order and Liberty (June 2021) (unpublished manuscript, on file with author).

36 Robin West, *The Limits of Process, in* GETTING TO THE RULE OF LAW: NOMOS L 32, 35 (James Flemming ed., 2011). *See also id.* at 47 (saying that Waldron's idealised conception of the rule of law 'does not contain even a hint of a reference to law's protective function').

37 Martin Krygier, *Four Puzzles About the Rule of Law: Why? What? Where? And Who Cares?, in* GETTING TO THE RULE OF LAW: NOMOS L, *supra* note 36, 64 at 89.

38 *See, e.g.*, PRIVATE LAW AND THE RULE OF LAW, *supra* note 29; FRANK LOVETT, A REPUBLIC OF LAW (2016); Timothy Endicott, *The Reason of the Law*, 48 AM. J. JURIS. 83, 84–85 (2003) ('If the clear, open, general, prospective, coherent, and stable rules do not control the use of violence between persons, there is no justification for saying that the community attains the rule of law.').

regulated by law requires only recognising that private as well as public arbitrariness counts – hardly a radical shift.

Nevertheless, accepting the plausibility of extending the rule of law idea in this way can have radical implications. One will have difficulty showing that there is a relevant moral difference, internal to the reasoning about the scope of the rule of law, between the private use of coercion and the private use of non-consensual exploitation. As I argue elsewhere, non-consensual exploitation occurs in a transaction between persons in which one person *takes unfair advantage of another* (paradigmatically, where a person requests, of a person in a situation of vulnerability, either a gross material inequality of exchange or that they sacrifice some fundamental aspect of personal dignity) *and* there is *a defect of consent* (arising from existential needs or mental incapacity).[39] In cases of both private coercion and private non-consensual exploitation, the chance of persons being wronged without their consent is so significant that there is a very strong prima facie case for careful legal regulation and protection. Both involve a power of one person over another that can be and historically has been the occasion for predatory behaviour. Indeed, philosophers such as Alan Wood and Joel Feinberg simply refer to such non-consensual exploitation as 'coercion', with the latter referring to the idea of 'coercive offers'.[40]

Protest as one might about the ambiguity of this definition, the fact is that the control of exploitation of this sort was a real motivation behind enormously important changes in law and society across the world in the late nineteenth and especially the twentieth century.[41] In my argument, respect for the rule of law would require the legal regulation of both public and private coercion and non-consensual exploitation. If this line of argument is accepted, then the social dimension of the rule of law is recognised. The case for market regulation, including in labour and landlord–tenant relations, as well as in consumer protection and of course family affairs, is supported and indeed required by the rule of law ideal. The provision of at least a rudimentary system of social security rights as insurance against exploitation follows demonstrably from that duty.[42]

39 King, *The Rule of Law*, *supra* note 20. Notably, consensual exploitation is much broader.

40 Joel Feinberg, Harmless Wrongdoing: The Moral Limits of the Criminal Law 177ff (1988) (ch. 31, 'Exploitation With and Without Harm'), and The moral Limits of the Criminal Law Volume 3: Harm to Self (1989) (ch. 24, 'Failure of Consent: Coercive Offers'); Allen Wood, The Free Development of Each: Studies on Freedom, Right, and Ethics in Classical German Philosophy ch. 12 (2014).

41 T.H. Marshall, Citizenship and Social Class, and Other Essays (1950); E.P. Hennock, The Origins of the Welfare State in England and Germany: Social Policies Compared, 1850–1914 (2007); The Development of Welfare States in Europe and America (Peter Flora & Arnold J. Heidenheimer eds., 1981); *see also* Patrick S. Atiyah, The Rise and Fall of Freedom of Contract (1979); Stolleis, *supra* note 4, at ch. 15.

42 In this line of argument, *see* Elizabeth Anderson, Private Government: How Employers Rule Our Lives (and Why We Don't Talk About It) (2017).

3.6 METHODOLOGY

A scepticism remains. Granted that there is widespread disagreement about the meaning of the rule of law, and that the understanding on offer here is likely to deepen rather than resolve disagreement, would it not be wiser simply to stipulate to some thin definition?[43] Having done so, we might then defend such a definition in instrumental terms. Under such a strategy, a narrow understanding of the rule of law has the advantage of widespread acceptance and fit, and there is little doubt that it identifies something (consistency, predictability, and fairness of the legal system) that is very important on any view. It would also serve to meet what Jeremy Waldron has called the 'separation thesis', namely, that '[w]e are better off arguing for the Rule of Law in the respects in which the Rule of Law's concerns cannot be duplicated under the auspices of any other ideal'.[44]

I see two problems with this line of argument. The first is that the rule of law is a political ideal, and it makes little sense to stipulate to the meaning of a normative ideal. For the ideal to be compelling as a ground for political obligation, it must be normatively generative in a way that a stipulation cannot be. The rule of law ideal does specify institutional arrangements, to be sure, but so too with the ideas of democracy (legislatures and voting systems), human rights (courts and remedies), and distributive justice (tax and bureaucracy). It also sets out a standard for the reform of such institutions. It is also true that other normative ideals may cover the same field, and hence there is overlap between the conception of the rule of law I put forward and justice, human rights, and liberty. However, that is also true of many political values such as dignity, equality, liberty, distributive justice, democracy, well-being, and the suite of constitutional values such as the separation of powers, human rights, representation, and so on.[45] Provided each value picks out something distinct and worthy of independent analysis, there is no reason to insist on complete reductionism.

At any rate, were it the case that the best way to reason about the rule of law is to just stipulate to a 'useful' definition and argue for its instrumental benefits, then we would have reason to stipulate to the social dimension of the rule of law as well. It would correct a tendency in international development, and in libertarian national politics, to use a widely accepted value to advance an anti-regulatory agenda.[46]

43 I have encountered this in several seminars and it is the approach taken in LOVETT, *supra* note 38, an outstanding book.

44 JEREMY WALDRON, THE RULE OF LAW AND THE MEASURE OF PROPERTY 75 (2012); *see id.* at chs. 1 and 2; *see also id.* at 13–14 (providing a detailed defence of the separation thesis).

45 The relationship between these foundational concepts in constitutional theory is the subject of the large volume, THE CAMBRIDGE HANDBOOK OF CONSTITUTIONAL THEORY, *supra* note 20. The editors divide the field into *values* (which are of intrinsic worth), *modalities* (which are instrumental for achieving values, but are processual in nature), and *institutions* (including the state, judicial review, electoral systems, central banks, and much more). Continuity among the three is a significant theme in the book.

46 UGO MATTEI & LAURA NADER, PLUNDER: WHEN THE RULE OF LAW IS ILLEGAL (2008).

The reaction to the neo-liberal usage of rule of law discourse cannot be to reject the idea altogether, as Marxists and sometimes socialists would encourage. Anyone who has spent any time in a country where the rule of law is lacking, in the sense that *people in power can do what they want*, will know that this is a terrible idea and that legality is essential for security, freedom, and dignity, as much as it is for democracy.[47]

It is also unpersuasive to deny fully that the thin conception of the rule of law is in some way hostile to a robust welfare and regulatory state. The requirements of clarity and that discretionary power be subject to meaningful judicial control are both challenged by the rise of the welfare and regulatory state. Raz was prepared to accept some of Hayek's arguments that the two were or were arguably incompatible. He felt that these arguments demonstrated little because '[c]onflict between the rule of law and other values is just what is to be expected'.[48] He identifies the 'assumption of overriding importance' as one of the major fallacies of the rule of law.[49] Yet Raz's way out of the superficial incompatibility between a major constitutional and political principle, and one of the most important and pervasive institutions of the modern state, is no way out at all. It is a political necessity to explain how the rule of law and the welfare and regulatory state are to be reconciled and rendered consistent – each represents political fundamentals in the liberal democratic state. Attempts at such reconciliation have generated important institutional reforms (e.g. the greater legal 'structuring' of discretion). And the inability to reconcile them on some levels can encourage us to revise our conceptions of the one (e.g. that the clarity requirement should be strict, or that common law courts are necessary for adjudication) or the other (e.g. that efficiency should exclude benefits adjudication, or that legal rights have any place in the modern welfare state). The social dimension of the rule of law sees regulation as, to an important extent, the fulfilment of rule of law virtues and duties. Administrative discretion, like the police power generally, becomes (when properly directed) a part of the rule of law apparatus of the state. The executive branch more generally – which must of necessity articulate the manifold standards of goods and services regulation and social policy delivery – becomes more of an agent of the rule of law, rather than its principal antagonist.

Furthermore, and from a different direction, a thin conception of the rule of law that is concerned solely with regularity and consistency is liable to abuse by public authorities advocating rule-by-law, or 'law and order', sometimes called 'authoritarian rule of law'.[50] This conception emphasises obedience to state law and regularity,

47 The work of Martin Krygier on the rule of law is especially alive to this problem, as well as to the protective function of the rule of law that I aim to expound.

48 Raz, *supra* note 22, at 228.

49 *Id.* at 210.

50 Jothie Rathja, Authoritarian Rule of Law: Legislation, Discourse and Legitimacy in Singapore (2012); Carl Minzer, *How China's Leaders Will Rule on the Law*, ChinaFile (Oct. 15, 2014), http://www.chinafile.com/reporting-opinion/viewpoint/how-chinas-leaders-will-rule-law. *Cf.* Nick Cheesman, *Law and Order as Asymmetrical Opposite to the Rule of Law*, 6 Hague J. Rule L. 96 (2014).

but is silent on the aims of legal regulation, of liberty, and of democracy. Here, too, a thin conception of the rule of law has given rhetorical support to bad politics.

All told, were we expected to defend a definition of the 'rule of law' as a matter of stipulating to a definition for instrumental reasons, then it seems clear that the scholarly concern over good semantic housekeeping about extravagant substantive theories is overwhelmed by two concrete social practices (libertarian and authoritarian) in which the wrong kind of rule of law conception is promoting harmful forms of government. It is nevertheless my view that we do not define the rule of law in anything resembling this type of approach. It is a value with a history and appeal, and I aim to show, in this project, that both tend in the long run to recognise the social dimension of the rule of law.

3.7 CONCLUSION

Constitutionalism is sometimes thought of as the application of the rule of law to government itself. This chapter has introduced a necessarily complex argument that the rule of law must be understood to have a social dimension, requiring contemporary government to engage in regulation to prevent and redress private coercion and exploitation, in addition to the dimension that requires the restraint of government's own abuse of power. This follows from a recognition that the antithesis of the rule of law is not only *tyranny* but also *anarchy*. Effective governance is as necessary to prevent the latter as effective restraint on governance is to prevent the former.

4

Effective Government and the Two Faces of Constitutionalism

Yasmin Dawood *

4.1 INTRODUCTION

In recent years, nations around the world have fallen prey to what might be described as a crisis of ineffective government. Basic governmental functions and services, such as ensuring education, health care, and a strong economy, are deeply compromised. Not only does ineffective governance undermine the general welfare, it can also pave the way for authoritarian regimes to take hold in erstwhile democracies. In their bid for power, autocratic leaders have often capitalized on citizens' disenchantment with governance failures. In response to the rise of authoritarianism in democratic nations, considerable scholarly attention has been paid to the relationship between constitutionalist structures and democratic sustainability.[1]

Yet what is the connection, if any, between constitutionalism and effective government? Effective government can be thought of as government that works, while constitutionalism refers to government that is constrained by law. The following puzzle arises: Certain governments are effective but they guarantee little in the way of rights and freedom (for instance, authoritarian regimes with robust economies and potent military capacities), while other governments protect rights but are lacking in efficacy (for instance, democracies with weak economies and negligible public services). To shed light on this puzzle, this chapter explores, in a preliminary fashion, the following interconnected questions: Does the concept of constitutionalism contain within it a commitment to effective government? Does effective government require constitutionalism for its functioning, and, conversely, does constitutionalism depend upon effective government to secure its protections?

To address these questions, this chapter begins by reconsidering the meaning of constitutionalism. As discussed in Section 4.2, constitutionalism is conventionally understood as government limited by law through such mechanisms as rights. Yet

* Many thanks to Vicki Jackson, Evan Fox-Decent, Turkuler Isiksel, Mariah Zeisberg, and participants at the 2019 Harvard Law School Workshop on Effective Governance and the 2021 McGill Conference on Constitutionalism and the Free Society for very helpful comments and conversations.

[1] *See* CONSTITUTIONAL DEMOCRACY IN CRISIS? (Mark A. Graber et al. eds., 2018); TOM GINSBURG & AZIZ Z. HUQ, HOW TO SAVE A CONSTITUTIONAL DEMOCRACY (2018).

constitutionalism arguably has a second function, which is to establish the institutions and processes that are required for effective government. Drawing on the political thought of the founding era of the US Constitution, Section 4.2 shows that constitutionalism not only applies legal constraints to the power of government through law; it also defines and establishes the institutions through which such power is generated and wielded. A focus on the two faces of constitutionalism – power-generating and power-limiting – sheds fresh light on the relationship between effective government and constitutionalism.

Although constitutionalism and effective government are conceptually linked, the relationship between these two concepts is highly complex. To capture this complexity, Section 4.3 offers a typology consisting of four possibilities: (a) effective government and rights; (b) effective government without rights; (c) ineffective government with rights; and (d) effective government versus rights. As a caveat, this typology is not comprehensive; instead, it presents a partial sketch of the main possibilities.[2] While it focuses primarily on the connection between effective government and constitutional rights, it also considers the role of constitutionalist structures more generally.

A few observations can be drawn from this preliminary analysis, as discussed in Section 4.4. In authoritarian regimes, effective government is usually dependent upon constitutionalism in its power-generating sense, but often takes place in the absence of constitutionalism in its power-limiting sense. By contrast, in democratic nations, rights can help to protect, and indeed may be indispensable for, effective government. At the same time, a minimum level of effective government is required to secure rights. The right to vote provides a useful illustration of this duality. In democracies, a basic requirement of effective government is to provide the right to vote and the institutions and processes needed for free and fair elections. By the same token, the availability of regular, open, and competitive elections, supported by electoral and participatory rights, can strengthen the accountability and functioning of democratic government.

Taken together, these observations suggest, at least with respect to democracies, that constitutionalism is dependent to some degree on effective government to secure its protections, and, conversely, that effective government requires constitutionalism, to some degree, for its functioning. However, it is important to note, as argued in Section 4.4, that the availability of constitutionalist structures is not wholly determinative of the effectiveness of democratic government. Instead, it is the *interaction* of various factors – constitutional, political, institutional, and civic – taken together that produces effective government. To put it another way, constitutionalism is a minimally necessary but not sufficient condition for effective democratic governance.

2 For instance, the typology sets aside the obviously unhappy case of an ineffective government that does not respect rights.

To be sure, a threshold question is how to define "effective government." The word "effective" means "successful in producing a desired or intended result." A minimalist approach would identify certain markers of effective government, such as a robust economy, little or no poverty, widespread education, full employment, and access to social services. On this minimalist account, "effective government" means that the government is successful in meeting the needs of society by appropriately managing public resources and public affairs.

This minimalist approach to effective government can be contrasted with a thicker conception that would include key democratic ideals such as citizen participation, responsiveness to constituents, deliberation, and compromise with political opponents.[3] On this view, government cannot possibly be "effective" unless it is democratically responsive to citizens. As Katherina Pistor observes, we can distinguish effective governance from effective *self*-governance.[4] For the purposes of this chapter, I examine effective government in both authoritarian regimes and democracies; this examination, however, should not be construed as an endorsement of effective government irrespective of the larger context. As a normative matter, I support a thicker conception of effective government, one that ties governance to democratic values and principles.

The remainder of the chapter is organized in four sections. Section 4.2 sets out the two faces of constitutionalism. Section 4.3 offers a typology to capture the complex relationship between effective government and the two faces of constitutionalism. Section 4.4 analyzes the interdependence of effective government and constitutionalism, and sets out the interactional account described above. The conclusion in Section 4.5 summarizes the main findings.

4.2 THE TWO FACES OF CONSTITUTIONALISM

The standard view of constitutionalism is that it provides a limit to governmental power based on law. Constitutionalism can be defined as a "determination to bring ... government under control and to place limits on the exercise of its power."[5] More specifically, constitutionalism "is the antithesis of arbitrary rule; its opposite is despotic government, the government of will instead of law."[6] The constitutionalist mechanisms of legal constraint take various forms. The constraints can be found in rights, such as the right to free speech, the right to due process, and the right to equal protection of the law. Additional constitutionalist structures

3 *See* Carole Pateman, Participation and Democratic Theory (1970); Jane Mansbridge, Beyond Adversary Democracy (1980); Amy Gutmann & Dennis Thompson, The Spirit of Compromise: Why Governing Demands It and Campaigning Undermines It (2012).

4 *See* Chapter 5, this volume.

5 M.J.C. Vile, Constitutionalism and the Separation of Powers 2 (1998); Stephen M. Griffin, American Constitutionalism: From Theory to Politics 6 (1996) ("the basic idea of American constitutionalism is conducting government under the provisions of a fundamental law").

6 Charles Howard McIlwain, Constitutionalism Ancient and Modern 21 (1947).

include the separation of powers, federalism, bicameralism, judicial review, and rule-of-law constraints on various institutions and processes.[7] These mechanisms – singly and collectively – are said to reduce the ability of the government to abuse power.[8]

Constitutionalism also implies that these constraints are entrenched such that a government cannot on a whim alter or expunge the limitations on its powers. This entrenchment is usually secured through an amending formula that requires more than a simple majority to effectuate constitutional change. In addition, constitutionalism encompasses various nonjusticiable norms or conventions that limit the exercise of government power. These conventions amount to political rather than legal limitations.[9]

For the Framers, constitutionalist mechanisms were the answer to the problem of tyranny.[10] The abuse of power by the government could be minimized through a host of structures, including federalism, bicameralism, and the separation of powers. According to Madison, federalism protected against unjust legislation for "[n]o law or resolution can now be passed without the concurrence, first, of a majority of the people, and then of a majority of the states."[11] The dependence of the national government on the state legislatures for the appointment of senators would guard against the power of the national government.[12] Likewise, bicameralism was indispensable for a republican government. A divided legislative power would protect the people against the danger of concentrated governmental power.[13]

Madison was influenced by Montesquieu's assertion that the separation of powers was essential for the preservation of liberty: "When legislative power is united with executive power in a single person or in a single body of the magistracy, there is no liberty .... Nor is there liberty if the power of judging is not separate from the legislative power and from executive power."[14] By dividing the government's power into three functions – legislative, executive, and judicial – and by instituting checks and balances among the three branches, the risk of an abuse of power by the state is lessened. Judicial review, for instance, enables courts to invalidate those legislative

7 W.J. Waluchow, *Constitutionalism*, *in* STANFORD ENCYCLOPEDIA OF PHILOSOPHY (2001).

8 Yasmin Dawood, *The Antidomination Model and the Judicial Oversight of Democracy*, 96 GEO. L. J. 1411 (2008) (discussing the illegitimate exercise of power).

9 Conventions serve "a normative function within constitutional politics, leading political actors to better realize constitutional ends." Keith E. Whittington, *The Status of Unwritten Constitutional Conventions in the United States*, 5 U. ILL. L. REV. 1847, 1853 (2013). The classic account of constitutional conventions in the United Kingdom is A.V. DICEY, INTRODUCTION TO THE STUDY OF THE LAW OF THE CONSTITUTION (8th ed. 1915).

10 *See* THE FEDERALIST PAPERS (Clinton Rossiter ed., 1999) [hereinafter THE FEDERALIST] NO. 51, at 291 (James Madison).

11 THE FEDERALIST NO. 62, at 346 (James Madison).

12 *See* THE FEDERALIST NO. 62, at 345 (James Madison).

13 *See* THE FEDERALIST NO. 51, at 290 (James Madison).

14 CHARLES LOUIS DE SECONDAT, Baron de Montesquieu, THE SPIRIT OF THE LAWS 157 (Anne Cohler et al. eds., 1989).

and executive rules and actions that violate the constitution. The threat to liberty by arbitrary state coercion is a central theme of republican theories of government.[15]

A constitution, however, does not only place limits on governmental power; it also establishes the institutions through which the government's power is generated and exercised. Constitutional provisions empower various entities of the state to perform the functions of governance; in other words, as Madison put it, "the constitution is a bill of powers."[16] The Constitution produces certain relations of power among various institutions and agents as it brings them into being. The idea that a constitution has a power-generating function tends to get less attention than its power-limiting function. Yet it is arguably the very purpose of a constitution to establish a government that works. The debates among the drafters of the US Constitution, for instance, were concerned in large measure with establishing a government that would govern well. Madison's tyranny-minimizing understanding of democratic government did not mean that he was unconcerned with the public good, for the objective of the political system was "the happiness of the people."[17]

The general proposition that the purpose of a constitution is to enable a democratic form of government has received support in recent years.[18] As Cass Sunstein observes, "the central goal of a constitution is to create the preconditions for a well-functioning democratic order, one in which citizens are genuinely able to govern themselves."[19] According to Christopher Eisgruber, the US Constitution is "a practical device that launches and maintains a sophisticated set of institutions which, in combination, are well-suited to implement self-government."[20] In some sense, then, a constitution can be viewed as a precommitment strategy on how to create, structure, and continually reproduce a democratic system.[21]

While the establishment of a *democratic* government is not necessarily the same thing as the establishment of an *effective* government, the usual assumption is that the constitution, if designed correctly, would result in a "well-functioning democratic order"[22] that is "well-suited to implement self-government."[23] For Vicki Jackson, "an important goal of the Constitution was to create an effective, working government."[24]

15 Philip Pettit, Republicanism: A Theory of Freedom and Government 171 (1997).
16 James Madison, Speech in the House of Representatives (June 8, 1789), *in* The Papers of James Madison (William T. Hutchinson et al. eds., 1962–1991), at 12:205.
17 The Federalist No. 62, at 348 (James Madison).
18 *See* Stephen Breyer, *Madison Lecture: Our Democratic Constitution*, 77 N.Y.U. L. Rev. 245, 247 (2002); Robert A. Dahl, How Democratic Is the American Constitution? 3 (2001).
19 Cass R. Sunstein, Designing Democracy: What Constitutions Do 6 (2001).
20 Christopher L. Eisgruber, Constitutional Self-Government 3 (2001).
21 I have taken the concept of "pre-commitment" from Stephen Holmes, *Precommitment and the Paradox of Democracy*, *in* Constitutionalism and Democracy 215 (Jon Elster & Rune Slagstad eds., 1988).
22 Sunstein, *supra* note 19, at 6.
23 Eisgruber, *supra* note 20, at 3.
24 Vicki C. Jackson, *Pro-constitutional Representation: Comparing the Role Obligations of Judges and Elected Representatives in Constitutional Democracy*, 57 Wm. & Mary L. Rev. 1717, 1741 (2016).

According to N. W. Barber, constitutionalism is best understood as a collection of principles that create "an effective and competent set of state institutions."[25] Turkuler Isiksel has argued that the European Union (EU) instantiates a novel model of constitutional authority, one that is based on the logic of effective government.[26] In contrast to democratic or liberal modes of constitutionalism, the EU follows a "functional" mode of constitutionalism that "relies heavily on a claim to effective government, and only incidentally on other political values."[27] Although her focus is the EU, she posits that effective government can serve as a normative justification of constitutional authority as a general matter.[28] For instance, the Framers of the US Constitution "were motivated as much by the imperative of making government *effective* as they were by the principles of popular sovereignty and individual liberty."[29] It is worth noting that Isiksel's concern is primarily normative, focusing on the justification of constitutional authority rather than on the elaboration of a causal or explanatory paradigm.[30] She thus argues for a tripartite approach to constitutional legitimacy which treats three principles – collective self-rule, individual rights, and effective government – as the basis of justified authority.[31]

A related area of scholarship focuses on whether constitutional design is a causal determinant of democratic dysfunction, which we can understand as a corollary concept of effective government.[32] The constitutional dimension of effective government is also germane to debates over positive rights and positive constitutionalism.[33] Notions of effectiveness or efficiency are relevant as well to the justification of constitutionalist structures such as the separation of powers.[34] While this brief overview cannot do justice to these areas of scholarly inquiry, the main idea is that constitutionalism encompasses both the creation and the limitation

Likewise, a pro-constitutional representative is one that would actively promote "a working and democratic constitutional government." *Id.* at 1718.

25 N.W. Barber, The Principles of Constitutionalism 1, 11–18 (2018). These principles are sovereignty, the separation of powers, the rule of law, civil society, democracy, and subsidiarity.

26 Turkuler Isiksel, Europe's Functional Constitution: A Theory of Constitutionalism Beyond the State (2016).

27 *Id.* at 32–33.

28 *Id.* at 34.

29 *Id.* at 48.

30 *Id.* at 45.

31 *Id.* at 32, 40–41.

32 Sanford Levinson's work on the democratic dysfunction created by certain features of the US Constitution best exemplifies this area of scholarship. *See* Sanford Levinson, Our Undemocratic Constitution: Where the Constitution Goes Wrong (and How We the People Can Correct It) (2006).

33 For an analysis of weaker and stronger versions of positive constitutionalism, see Adrienne Stone & Lael K. Weiss, *Positive and Negative Constitutionalism and the Limits of Universalism: A Review Essay*, Oxford J. Legal Stud. (Apr. 29, 2021), https://doi.org/10.1093/ojls/gqab012.

34 *See e.g.*, Geoffrey Sigalet, On Comity and Contestation: Republicanism and the Separation of Powers (May 2021) (unpublished manuscript, on file with author) (arguing that we ought to take greater account of "efficiency" rationales for having independent courts decide cases involving fundamental rights instead of focusing exclusively on "contestatory liberty-oriented" accounts of judicial review).

of power, and, as such, is concerned not only with constraints on power but also with governance itself.

4.3 EFFECTIVE GOVERNMENT AND CONSTITUTIONAL RIGHTS AND STRUCTURES: A TYPOLOGY

The relationship between effective government and the two faces of constitutionalism – power-generating and power-limiting – is complex. This section focuses in particular on the relationship between effective government and rights. Rights are a subset of constitutionalism, and in certain circumstances rights can serve as a shorthand for constitutionalism as a whole. Yet in other cases, as described later in this section, rights do not necessarily appear together with other constitutionalist structures. This section briefly explores the following four possibilities: (a) effective government and rights (Section 4.3.1); (b) effective government without rights (Section 4.3.2); (c) ineffective government with rights (Section 4.3.3); and (d) effective government versus rights (Section 4.3.4). This section also considers the relationship between effective government and constitutionalist structures more generally.

4.3.1 *Effective Government and Rights*

There are good reasons to think that effective government and rights are mutually reinforcing. Rights, and other constitutionalist mechanisms, can foster effective government by providing a check against various phenomena, such as corruption and the abuse of power, that can undermine good governance. Conversely, effective government can protect rights. This protection can take place in both a positive and a negative sense.[35] In terms of negative rights, a well-functioning government has the capacity to act in such a way as to not violate people's rights. With respect to positive rights, for instance social and economic rights,[36] an effective government can furnish not only the positive rights in question but also the conditions under which such rights can flourish.[37]

The interdependence of effective government and rights is perhaps best illustrated by the right to vote. Elsewhere I suggest that the right to vote amounts to a "structural right" because its existence depends upon on an entire infrastructure of political institutions.[38]

[35] *But see* David S. Law & Mila Versteeg, *Sham Constitutions*, 101 CALIF. L. REV. 863, 872, 880 (2013) (arguing that constitutional rights are not necessarily upheld in practice). Constitutional compliance is weakest with respect to positive socioeconomic rights. *Id.* at 872, 916.

[36] KATHARINE G. YOUNG, CONSTITUTING ECONOMIC AND SOCIAL RIGHTS 6 (2012).

[37] To be well-functioning in the modern era, governments are dependent on the administrative state. *See* Gillian E. Metzger, *Foreword: 1930s Redux: The Administrative State Under Siege*, 131 HARV. L. REV. 1, 7 (2017) (arguing that features of the administrative state such as an expert civil service "are essential for the accountable, constrained, and effective exercise of executive power").

[38] The discussion on structural rights is drawn from Yasmin Dawood, *Electoral Fairness and the Law of Democracy: A Structural Rights Approach to Judicial Review*, 62 U. TORONTO L. J. 499, 501 (2012).

Structural rights are individual rights that take into account the broader institutional framework within which rights are defined, held, and exercised.[39] Structural rights theory holds that the participation of individuals is key (hence the emphasis on rights) but that individuals participate within an institutional framework that is constituted by relations of power (hence the emphasis on structure).[40] Rights do not exist in a vacuum but are instead exercised within a particular political, institutional, and societal context.[41] While structural rights theory can be applied to many kinds of rights, it has particular salience for democratic rights.

The upshot of this analysis is that some level of governmental effectiveness is required not only for the enforcement of rights but also for the very existence of those rights, such as the right to vote, that are structural in nature. The right to vote, while held by individuals, presupposes the existence of a wide array of institutions and actors, including elections, candidates, political parties, constituencies, candidates, legislatures, and so forth. A basic requirement of effective democratic governance is to protect the right to vote, and the associated institutions and processes, in particular free and fair elections, that render such a right meaningful. By the same token, the right to vote, coupled with a fair electoral system, is indispensable for holding elected officials to account and thereby enhancing the effectiveness of government. In this way, effective government and constitutionalism can be interdependent and mutually reinforcing.

4.3.2 *Effective Government Without Rights*

Authoritarian regimes can have effective government, understood in its minimal sense as the provision of the needs of society by appropriately managing public resources and public affairs. As an illustration of this point, consider authoritarian regimes such as China and Russia. The existence of these regimes suggests that it is possible to have effective government without a traditional rights system or other power-limiting constitutionalist mechanisms. At the same time, authoritarian

39 *Id.* Democratic rights inevitably have a structural dimension because an individual's exercise of his or her rights takes place within an existing organization of social and political power. By contrast, other individual rights, such as the right to liberty, necessarily inhere in individuals and are not dependent upon the existence of a prior institutional framework. *Id.*

40 Structural rights theory should be distinguished from Richard Pildes's influential account of the "structural conception of rights." See Richard H. Pildes, *Why Rights Are Not Trumps: Social Meanings, Expressive Harms, and Constitutionalism*, 27 J. LEGAL STUD. 725 (1998). Under Pildes's structural conception, rights are linguistic tools that constrain the kind of reasons and justifications that governments can act upon. Rather than focusing solely on the interests of the rights-bearer, a structural conception of rights is concerned in addition with the legitimate scope of state authority and the realization of common goods. *Id.* at 731–33. For a discussion of the "structural" political markets approach to election law, *see* Samuel Issacharoff & Richard H. Pildes, *Politics as Markets: Partisan Lockups of the Democratic Process*, 50 STAN. L. REV. 643 (1998).

41 Yasmin Dawood, *Democracy and the Right to Vote: Rethinking Democratic Rights Under the Charter*, 51 Osgoode Hall L. J. 251, 244 (2013).

regimes can display constitutionalism in the power-generating sense. That is to say, these regimes have the institutions and structures of governance. Indeed, it could be argued that every regime has a constitution to enable basic governance and policy development.[42] Constitutions have multiple functions: they act as coordination devices by structuring and settling expectations and by reducing uncertainty;[43] they enable the management of conflict;[44] and they allow for the control of agents, the provision of information, and the organization of official action.[45] While authoritarian regimes have constitutionalism in the power-generating sense, they typically lack constitutionalism in the power-limiting sense.

In addition to full-blown authoritarian regimes, there exists an array of hybrid regimes.[46] Democratic erosion usually involves a shift to a competitive authoritarian regime in which electoral competition, rights, and the rule of law are weakened.[47] In competitive authoritarian regimes, elections may take place, but opposition candidates and parties face significant hurdles.[48] Elected autocrats often take advantage of the tools of constitutionalism in order to subvert democracy.[49] For instance, incumbent leaders can deploy the mechanisms of constitutional change to entrench themselves in power and reduce the efficacy of institutional checks.[50] The state cooptation of public and private entities such as the courts and the media likewise involves the use of constitutional mechanisms.[51] Hybrid regimes have constitutionalism in the power-generating sense, but they

42 Mark Tushnet, *Authoritarian Constitutionalism*, 100 CORNELL L. REV. 391, 421 (2015).

43 Whittington, *supra* note 9, at 1862.

44 SAMUEL ISSACHAROFF, FRAGILE DEMOCRACIES: CONTESTED POWER IN THE ERA OF CONSTITUTIONAL COURTS 10 (2015) (arguing that "the use of constitutionalism, and the accompanying institution of constitutional courts, has emerged as a primary means of managing conflict in the difficult national settings of so many of the world's democracies and of so doing in the service of state building").

45 Tom Ginsburg & Alberto Simpser, *Introduction: Constitutions in Authoritarian Regimes*, *in* CONSTITUTIONS IN AUTHORITARIAN REGIMES 1–8 (Tom Ginsburg & Alberto Simpser eds., 2014).

46 STEVEN LEVITSKY & LUCAN WAY, COMPETITIVE AUTHORITARIANISM: HYBRID REGIMES AFTER THE COLD WAR 5 (2010) (defining competitive authoritarian regimes as "civilian regimes in which formal democratic institutions exist and are widely viewed as the primary means of gaining power, but in which incumbents' abuse of the state places them at a significant advantage vis-à-vis their opponents"); ELECTORAL AUTHORITARIANISM: THE DYNAMICS OF UNFREE COMPETITION (Andreas Schedler ed., 2006); Tushnet, *supra* note 42, at 396 (distinguishing absolute constitutionalism, mere rule-of-law constitutionalism, and authoritarian constitutionalism).

47 GINSBURG & HUQ, *supra* note 1, at 44. For an appraisal of the literature on democratic decline, *see* Tom Gerald Daly, *Democratic Decay: Conceptualising an Emerging Research Field*, HAGUE J. ON RULE L. (2019).

48 STEVEN LEVITSKY & DANIEL ZIBLATT, HOW DEMOCRACIES DIE 1–10, 97–109 (2018).

49 *Id.*

50 David Landau, *Abusive Constitutionalism*, 47 UC DAVIS L. REV. 189, 191 (2013); Kim Lane Scheppele, *Autocratic Legalism*, 85 U. CHI. L. REV. 545, 548 (2018) (defining "autocratic legalism" as the phenomenon that occurs when "electoral mandates plus constitutional and legal change are used in the service of an illiberal agenda"). Scheppele argues that legalistic autocrats use the tools of democracy against constitutionalism, thereby undercutting liberalism. *Id.* at 557.

51 Landau, *supra* note 50, at 212.

have different degrees of constitutionalism in the power-limiting sense. The main point, though, is that it is possible to have effective government in the absence of power-limiting constitutionalism.

4.3.3 *Ineffective Government With Rights*

Governmental effectiveness exists on a spectrum. An ineffective government is not necessarily synonymous with a failed government. Countries with ineffective governments may have weak economies, high levels of unemployment, and an insufficient provision of social services. A system with an ineffective government may nonetheless have a rights-protection regime. That being said, the failures in governance could reach such a point that the protection of rights becomes impossible. For this reason, it can be argued that rights protection depends upon some minimal level of effective government.[52]

4.3.4 *Effective Government versus Rights*

While rights and effective government can be mutually reinforcing, the protection of certain rights can, counterintuitively, undermine the effectiveness of government. The right to free speech, while indispensable to democracy, raises various challenges for its effective functioning. For instance, social media provides citizens with a voice, but it also has the capacity to foster echo chambers, create bias, and exacerbate polarization.[53] Various actors, including foreign governments, have used social media to influence elections by targeting citizens with fake news.[54]

Likewise, speech-protective campaign finance rules in the United States have accentuated the disproportionate political influence of the wealthy.[55] Congress has become dependent on a tiny minority of the population, the so-called donor class, which funds the bulk of American politics.[56] Empirical research shows that elected representatives are more responsive to the preferences of the affluent as compared to the preferences of most citizens.[57] The outsized political power of the wealthy has

52 Stephen Holmes & Cass R. Sunstein, The Cost of Rights: Why Liberty Depends on Taxes (1999).

53 Cass Sunstein, Republic: Divided Democracy in the Age of Social Media (2017).

54 For a discussion of current challenges, *see* Yasmin Dawood, *Combatting Foreign Election Interference: Canada's Electoral Ecosystem Approach to Disinformation and Cyber Threats*, 20 Election L. J. 10 (2021).

55 For a review of the literature, *see* Yasmin Dawood, *Campaign Finance and American Democracy*, 18 Am. Rev. Pol. Sci. 1 (2015).

56 Spencer Overton, *The Donor Class: Campaign Finance, Democracy, and Participation*, 153 U. Pa. L. Rev. (2004); Lawrence Lessig, Republic, Lost: How Money Corrupts Congress—and a Plan to Stop It 110 (2011).

57 Larry Bartels, Unequal Democracy: The Political Economy of the New Gilded Age (2008); Martin Gilens, Affluence and Influence: Economic Inequality and Political Power in America (2012); Nicholas Stephanopoulos, *Aligning Campaign Finance Law*, 101 Va. L. Rev. 1425 (2015).

arguably distorted policy-making in Congress.[58] Although this distortion is not necessarily the equivalent of ineffective governance, it does create a climate in which the provision of basic social services is undermined.

That being said, there is no doubt that the positive contributions of the freedom of speech vastly outweigh any negative consequences. But the problems posed by the distorting power of wealth and social media present real threats to effective government. In this way, the protection of rights does not necessarily reinforce and may in certain circumstances undermine effective government.

4.4 THE INTERDEPENDENCE OF EFFECTIVE GOVERNMENT AND CONSTITUTIONALISM

A few observations can be drawn from the analysis in Section 4.3. First, the relationship between effective government and constitutionalism is deeply contextual and contingent on the particular constellation of political institutions and actors in a given jurisdiction. Different nations have different combinations of the two faces of constitutionalism. In authoritarian regimes, effective government is dependent on power-generating constitutionalism but usually takes place without power-limiting constitutionalism. Hybrid regimes likewise rely on power-generating constitutionalism, but they have different degrees of power-limiting constitutionalism.

With respect to democratic nations, rights can help to protect, and indeed may be indispensable for, effective government. At the same time, a minimum level of effective government is required to secure rights. The right to vote provides a useful illustration of the interdependence of effective government and constitutionalism. An effective government is required to protect the right to vote, and to provide the institutional infrastructure, including free and fair elections, that is needed to exercise the franchise in a meaningful way. By the same token, the right to vote, and the institutions and processes of a fair electoral system, can serve to enhance the accountability and effectiveness of government.

A preliminary observation, then, at least with respect to democracies, is that constitutionalism is dependent to some degree on effective government to secure its protections, and, conversely, that effective government is dependent to some degree on constitutionalism for its functioning. It is important to observe, however, that while the availability of constitutionalist structures is an important factor, it is not wholly determinative of the effectiveness of democratic government.[59] As the example of the United States illustrates, the fact that the level of dysfunction in governance fluctuates over time suggests that the structural features of the

[58] LESSIG, *supra* note 56, at 110. For a discussion of the role of the regulatory state in combating economic domination, *see* K. SABEEL RAHMAN, DEMOCRACY AGAINST DOMINATION (2017).

[59] This discussion is drawn from Yasmin Dawood, *Democratic Dysfunction and Constitutional Design*, 94 B.U. L. REV. 913, 914–15 (2014).

Constitution are not solely responsible.[60] Effective government is also the product of the choices made over time by political parties, elected officials, administrative officials, and government actors.[61] For this reason, I suggest that while constitutional mechanisms are necessary for effective government, they are not sufficient on their own to guarantee it.

Instead, it is the *interaction* of various factors – constitutional, political, institutional, and civic – that ultimately produces either effective or dysfunctional governance.[62] An interactional approach takes into account the ebbs and flows of effectiveness and dysfunction. At some points in time, the relevant factors generate too great a constraint on governmental action, thereby producing dysfunction. In the United States, for instance, these factors include constitutional structures such as multiple veto points, political factors such as the increasingly partisan divide between Republicans and Democrats, institutional factors such as the filibuster, and civic factors such as the rise in hyperpolarization and the decline in compromise.[63] At other moments, by contrast, these factors are better aligned, thereby producing effective government.[64]

4.5 CONCLUSION

This chapter set out to address, in a preliminary fashion, the following questions: Does the concept of constitutionalism contain within it a commitment to effective government? Does effective government require constitutionalism for its functioning, and, conversely, does constitutionalism depend upon effective government to secure its protections? To address these questions, this chapter first explored the meaning of constitutionalism. It argued that there are two faces of constitutionalism – power-limiting and power-generating. The conventional power-limiting view of constitutionalism holds that the power of the state is limited by law through a host of constitutionalist structures and norms, such as the separation of powers, federalism, judicial review, rights, and rule-of-law principles. However, constitutionalism has a second, power-generating function, which is to establish the institutions and

60 Sanford Levinson argues that the US Constitution is responsible for producing a dysfunctional government. Levinson, *supra* note 32, at 9. Constitutional features, such as multiple veto points, the Senate's unequal representation, and the absence of a mechanism for removing incompetent presidents, contribute to dysfunctional governance. *Id.* at 38, 49, 59, 79.

61 Thomas E. Mann & Norman J. Ornstein, The Broken Branch: How Congress Is Failing America and How to Get It Back on Track 11–12, 44 (2006); Nelson W. Polsby, How Congress Evolves: Social Bases of Institutional Change (2005); Richard H. Pildes, *Why the Center Does Not Hold: The Causes of Hyperpolarized Democracy in America*, 99 Calif. L. Rev. 273 (2011); Mark Tushnet, *Constitutional Hardball*, 37 John Marshall L. Rev. 523 (2004).

62 Yasmin Dawood, *The Fragility of Constitutional Democracy*, 77 Md. L. Rev. 192, 196 (2017).

63 *Id.*

64 David R. Mayhew, Divided We Govern: Party Control, Lawmaking, and Investigations 1946–2002 (2d ed. 2005); Daryl J. Levinson and Richard H. Pildes, *Separation of Parties, Not Powers*, 119 Harv. L. Rev. 2311, 2313 (2006).

processes of government that are required for effective government. On this view, the concept of constitutionalism contains within it a commitment to setting up a government that works. Constitutionalism not only limits power; it also enables its creation.

Although constitutionalism and effective government are conceptually linked, the relationship between these two concepts is complex in practice. This chapter has shown that political systems around the world have different combinations of the two faces of constitutionalism. The case of authoritarian regimes shows that while effective government requires constitutionalism in its power-generating sense, it can take place without constitutionalism in its power-limiting sense. By contrast, an analysis of democratic regimes suggests that rights and effective government can be mutually reinforcing in a positive direction. Rights can help to protect effective government but, at the same time, a minimum level of effective government is required to secure rights.

These observations suggest that, at least with respect to democracies, effective government requires constitutionalism for its functioning, and, conversely, that constitutionalism is dependent, at least to some degree, on effective government to secure its protections. This chapter has also suggested, with respect to democratic systems, that the design of the constitutional framework, while important, does not on its own result in effective government. Other factors, in particular the actions and choices of political actors and institutions, can have a dramatic impact on the functioning of government. In sum, constitutionalism and effective government are conceptually linked, and often interdependent in practice, raising important implications for democratic functioning and sustainability.

5

The Right to Effective Self-Government

Katharina Pistor

5.1 INTRODUCTION

Protecting individual rights is a core feature of democratic constitutionalism. The centralization of the means of coercion gave rise to the Hobbesian dilemma, the fear that this enormous power might be abused unless it be effectively controlled. In addition to dividing power among different branches of government or sharing it between the federation and its units, constitutions have fortified individual rights with judicial review and enforcement mechanisms against the executive branch to rein in state power.

Proposing a *collective* right to effective *self-government* sits oddly with a vision that pitches free individuals against an all-powerful state. Such a right can, however, be justified on two interrelated grounds. First, in the absence of effective protection by a state, individual civil and political rights remain empty declarations. Stateless people, Hannah Arendt has taught us, are the most vulnerable; they have no legal rights and no way of seeking protection as a matter of right.[1] Second, individual rights are always exercised in relation to others and thus bounded by their own individual rights. By protecting individual *self-authorship*, democratic constitutions create the conditions for a plurality of interests, each with a legitimate claim for prioritization and protection, which have to be brought into some kind of agreement with one another.[2] This is the purpose of democratic government. It is a difficult and in many ways an impossible task, but it is the very foundation of democratic constitutionalism.[3] Approximating the normative aspirations of collective self-government requires that the government is neither beholden to a particular

[1] Hannah Arendt, The Origins of Totalitarianism part II, ch. 5 (titled "The Decline of the Nation-State and the End of the Rights of Man") (Schocken ed. 2004).

[2] For the concept of democratic self-authorship, *see* Hanoch Dagan & Avihay Dorfman, *The Human Right to Private Property*, 18 Theoretical Inq. L. 391 (2017).

[3] *See also* Jean L. Cohen, *Rethinking Human Rights, Democracy, and Sovereignty in the Age of Globalization*, 36 Pol. Theory (2008) (insisting that sovereignty, vested in a demos bound by constitutional rules, is critical for the realization of human rights, viewed as distinct from sovereignty); Jean L. Cohen, Globalization and Sovereignty: Rethinking Legality, Legitimacy and Constitutionalism (2012).

group nor bound by legal constraints that would commit its policies and resources to special, rather than the plurality of, interests and needs.[4]

Sadly, governments are often captured by powerful interest groups, become corrupted, or operate inefficiently as they fail to reconcile competing interests and hide behind the walls of bureaucracies. These phenomena are well recognized in the literature.[5] However, government can also be emasculated by law: by domestic and/or international legal constraints that constrain the autonomy that governments need to create the conditions for their citizens to realize their capabilities, that is, to live the lives they have reason to value.[6] In fact, as I argue later, expansive property and investor protections have allowed special private interests to hijack the legal system and at times to subvert government agendas.

This chapter argues that private law has increasingly eroded democratic constitutionalism or collective self-government. Recognizing a collective right to govern oneself by and through law does not place collective interests over and above individual rights; rather, it is meant to ensure that individual rights are not eroding the capacity for self-government.

My argument proceeds in three steps. First, I will explain the relation between power and law. Second, I will show how state power has been configured to privilege specific individual rights that have been encoded in law at the expense of collective self-government. Third, I will offer some thoughts on protecting a collective right to self-government in domestic and international law.

5.2 POWER AND LAW

The rise of modern nation-states is closely associated with the centralization of the means of coercion.[7] Self-governance by clans and communities, including feuds and other mechanisms of self-help, gave way to centralization of the means of coercion to ensure internal and external peace. In what became part of an emergent state, the delegation of law enforcement to abstract institutions was a transformative moment in social ordering.[8] Importantly, the transformation of the organization of the means of coercion did not end there. Rather, the organization of what is best

4 For the purpose of this chapter I am agnostic about what form democracy should take. For a thoughtful critique of elected representative as well as direct democracies, which she contrasts with "open" democracy, see HÉLÈNE LANDEMORE, OPEN DEMOCRACY: REINVENTING POPULAR RULE FOR THE TWENTY-FIRST CENTURY (2020).

5 *See also* George J. Stigler, *The Theory of Economic Regulation*, 2 BELL J. ECON. & MGMT. SCI. 3 (1971); Michael E. Levine & Jennifer L. Forrence, *Regulatory Capture, Public Interest, and the Public Agenda: Toward a Synthesis*, 6 J. L., ECON. & ORG. 167 (1990).

6 On the concept of capabilities, *see* Amartya Sen, *Human Rights and Capabilities*, 6 J. HUM. DEV. 151 (2005); MARTHA NUSSBAUM, CREATING CAPABILITIES: THE HUMAN DEVELOPMENT APPROACH (2011).

7 MAX WEBER, ECONOMY AND SOCIETY (Guenther Roth & Claus Wittich eds., 1978).

8 *See* Geoffrey M. Hodgson, *On the Institutional Foundations of Law: The Insufficiency of Custom and Private Ordering*, 43 J. ECON. ISSUES 143 (2009) (arguing that the suppression of self-help was a central feature of this transformation).

conceived of as society's collective means of coercion is a continuous process. It involves not only agencies of the state itself (the executive, legislature, judiciary, etc.) but private actors with lawyers by their sides. If we conceive of the centralized means of coercion as a social resource, the legal system can be described as the way in which access to and use of this resource have been institutionalized. This institutionalization varies from place to place and changes over time. It can be more or less centralized, give more power to individual or to collective rights, or grant access to it primarily through public or private agents.

This depiction of the state and its laws differs from more conventional accounts that consider the state to be a "neutral arbiter," the main task of which is to enforce the rules of the game, in particular the formal institutions that constrain human behavior while leaving informal institutions largely to self-governance.[9] This conventional account personifies the state as a unitary actor. Moreover, it assumes that institutions (the rules of the game) are fixed with human agents as the players in this social game abiding by their constraints. Yet, as every lawyer knows, law is not static; new rules as well as new rights are created all the time; and legal change is not the exclusive prerogative of legislatures but results from the interplay among private lawyering, the occasional litigation, and even less frequently from legislative or regulatory intervention. Pushing the interpretative boundaries of the law or extending well-recognized legal protections to new interests or assets is a central part of this game, for which the winnings are often outcome determinative.[10]

When recognizing a claim by one person against another as legally enforceable, the legal system confers power on the claim holder. This legal empowerment is not identical with the asset itself. A piece of land is not property; property rights to it are created only by zoning, titling, and allocating title to an owner. And, contrary to the widely held assumption, the decision as to which rights or interests shall be recognized as property rights is not necessarily made by legislatures or bestowed on private actors by way of delegation.[11] First-generation property rights tend to be the legal *ex post* recognition of de facto claims. Further, property rights are created continuously by grafting the legal attributes that confer power over assets onto different objects, claims or ideas, from land all the way to credit derivatives. These legal coding processes, which occur primarily in the offices of private attorneys, will be challenged from time to time in a court of law. Official recognition affirms their status but is not a precondition for the exercise of priority rights over others. Put differently, property rights are the product not of creationism but of accretion.

9 *See* Douglass Cecil North, Institutions, Institutional Change, and Economic Performance (1990), whose views have deeply informed the new institutional economics.

10 On the incompleteness of law, *see* Katharina Pistor & Chenggang Xu, *Incomplete Law*, 35 J. Int'l L. & Pol. 931 (2003). On the legal coding of capital, *see* Katharina Pistor, The Code of Capital: How the Law Creates Wealth and Inequality (2019).

11 This, however, is how Morris Cohen has depicted the empowerment of private agents, who can then use their powers over others. *See* Morris Cohen, *Sovereignty and Property*, 13 Cornell L. Rev. 8 (1927).

This largely decentralized process of coding private interests as legal entitlements can be traced to the age of feudalism.[12] Importantly, it did not change fundamentally with the advent of constitutional democracy, certainly in common law jurisdictions, which explicitly endorse a bottom-up law-making process. However, civil law jurisdictions, such as Germany and France, also leave substantial room for private autonomy. France sought to make a clean break with the past by denying judges the power to make law after the French Revolution. Still, the open-ended language of the civil code and similar codifications, along with the need to adapt a code dating back to 1804 to the changes brought about by the industrial and digital revolutions, left judges with more de facto power to adapt old law to new circumstances than is often recognized.

Indeed, the adaptability of law to a changing environment is critical for a dynamic market economy. That, however, should not prevent us from recognizing the tension between the private rights of some and the quest for self-government by constitutional democracies. One might argue that private legal rights frequently receive a democratic imprimatur by courts, if and when challenged. Yet, many legal innovations are never vetted in court. Private law is policed not by state but by other private agents who often face resource constraints. Regulators may impose restrictions, but private law itself is often used to arbitrage around regulatory constraints.

The possibility of harnessing the centralized means of coercion by legally protecting private interests creates a powerful first mover advantage. The challenge for democracies is to strike a proper balance between outsourcing law-making to private agents and protecting the capacity for self-government. This balancing task is easier within a single, unitary system. It becomes more difficult in federal systems paired with the power of private actors to pick and choose the legal rules that best suit their needs. On the positive side, competition helps guard against the abuse of centralized power and facilitates the adaptation of law to changing norms and circumstances. However, competition can also result in a race to the bottom in which the most resourceful players shop for the most lenient rules. If they are allowed to carry these rules with them and enforce them in other jurisdictions, notwithstanding that these may have different norms, they can escape democratic control. Taking regulatory arbitrage to the transnational setting further amplifies this problem. When states allow private parties to pick and choose from a menu of different legal systems, selecting the one that best suits their needs along with the assurance that the state will enforce their selected rules, states effectively hand over control of the rules of the game to powerful private parties at the expense of other constituencies whose interests they ought to protect.

5.3 THE SUBORDINATION OF SELF-GOVERNMENT TO PRIVATE RIGHTS

In most Western legal systems, the antidote to private legal power is administrative or regulatory power. In many instances this may be the only way to ensure that the

[12] Bernard Rudden, *Things as Things and Things as Wealth*, 14 OXFORD J. LEGAL STUD. 81 (1994).

interests of weaker parties, who lack resources or face collective action problems, are adequately protected. The downside of this approach is that it allows powerful private parties to successfully portray themselves as victims of state overreach. They fight back by claiming greater autonomy in their private rights and interests. Particularly within the transnational realm, they have been able to fortify these rights in law along three dimensions: private autonomy, investor protection, and the legal protection of creditors in sovereign debt contracts.

5.3.1 *Private Autonomy*

Private autonomy is a powerful claim that has been used to expand the ability of some to self-govern by picking and choosing the law of jurisdictions that protect their interests better than others. In the postwar era, Hayek has been most closely associated with the argument that there was law before the state and that people are quite capable of governing themselves in a bottom-up fashion.[13] Legal academics, especially those in the law and economics tradition, have hailed "order without law" and "opting out of the legal system" as evidence that free people can govern themselves freely without the need for state tutelage.[14] This argument misses the major social achievement of pooling the means of coercion to overcome internal strife and unite previously fragmented societies. The real question, thus, is not whether groups can self-govern – they have always been able to so – but how to balance competing interests so as to ensure that all may avail themselves of the centralized means of coercion to protect their individual or group-specific rights.

Contract law is built around the notion of private autonomy. Private parties may order their relations with one another as they wish, as long as they do not impose burdens on others without their consent. If they wish to ensure that their contracts will be enforceable in a court of law, they must comply with the basic requirements of contract *law* stipulating what constitutes a contract.[15] *Consent* and *compliance* with *de minimis* legal requirements for enforceability are two principles that can help define the proper boundaries of private autonomy within a broader social order that is replete with diverse and often competing interests.

To state the obvious, if every member of society were allowed to choose the law by which he or she wished to be governed, self-government would be impossible. Eliminating choice of law is also not an option, especially in a world of transnational economic activities supported by mostly national law. Furthermore, it would also eliminate a powerful constraint on the potential for abusing the legal monopoly that

[13] Friedrich A. Hayek, Law, Legislation and Liberty: Rules and Order § 1 (1973).

[14] Lisa Bernstein, *Opting Out of the Legal System: Extralegal Contractual Relations in the Diamond Industry*, 21 J. Legal Stud. 115 (1992); *see also* Robert C. Ellickson, Order without Law: How Neighbors Settle Disputes (1991).

[15] Melvin Eisenberg, *The Emergence of Dynamic Contract Law*, 88 Calif. L. Rev. 1743 (2000) (arguing that this is ultimately for the legislature to decide).

states enjoy. The solution to this dilemma is not binary (i.e., choice or no choice); it is about finding the right balance between the desire for choice and the quest for self-government. Deliberation and compromise tend to be slow and cumbersome and rarely lead to optimal results. Decrying this process as inefficient and allowing well-resourced players to opt out of and into legal orders they prefer at their own behest, however, defies self-government.

And yet, this is the direction of the evolution of choice of law rules, especially the ones facilitating trade and finance.[16] How far the disassembly of national legal systems has progressed is suggested by the following quote of a legal practitioner:

> [A] few years ago, I was unable to complete a transaction for a short-term secured loan by a Canadian bank to a Canadian life insurance company after a week of trying to piece together the legal advice necessary to do the deal. The security for the loan was to be bonds of a foreign issuer that had been deposited into Cedel (now Clearstream) in Luxembourg. The physical certificates were actually being held in safekeeping in the Cayman Islands, for tax reasons, and could not be moved. The bonds were owned not by the Canadian life company directly, but by its French subsidiary, which had its chief executive offices in Paris. Five law firms struggled for a week to figure out how to put together the chain of opinions that would be necessary to assure the lender that the loan was fully secured by the bonds, and could not do it. Because we were unable to advise the client as to the nature and extent of the risks involved, it could not price the transaction appropriately or get internal approval to proceed.[17]

The problem arose from two interrelated factors: First, financial market developments dispensed with paper as the embodiment of legal rights and enabled the practice of holding financial interests indirectly through intermediaries. Eliminating paper implies that financial assets no longer have a *physical location*, the critical connecting factor for invoking the property laws of the jurisdiction where they are located. Second, even if individual countries adapted their law to take account of indirect holdings, financial assets that were held indirectly outside their borders were left in unchartered waters. The solution to this conundrum was a new choice-of-law rule that transformed a property rule (location) into a contractual one (choice of parties). The Hague "PRIMA" convention (prima stands for the place of the relevant intermediary approach) says that the location of the intermediary who is managing the account where the assets are held determines the applicable law. With the expansion of the free choice of law for corporate charters under the incorporation theory, this means effectively that financial asset–holders can shop for the property law that shall govern these assets.

16 Horatia Muir Watt, *"Party Autonomy" in International Contracts: From the Makings of a Myth to the Requirements of Global Governance*, 6 Eur. Rev. Cont. L. 250 (2010).

17 Bradley Crawford, *The Hague "PRIMA" Convention: Choice of Law to Govern Recognition of Dispositions of Book-Based Securities in Cross Border Transactions*, 38 Can. Bus. L. J. 157, 163 (2003).

At a deeper level, the example reveals the interests of the financial sector to have legal certainty to price any asset even when it conflicts with the claim to self-government, including the ability to tax and to define the basic rules of property and collateral law that apply to financial assets traded within that government's jurisdiction. It may well be the case that, in a world in which the bulk of assets are intangible, a conflict-of-law rule that relies on physical location is no longer workable. But it does not follow that free choice is the only alternative.

The reliance on choice-of-law rules for global markets has divided the world into a handful of rule-makers and the rest as rule-takers. Most globally traded assets do not bear the imprint of a myriad legal systems. The global financial system is far more parochial: The vast majority of globally traded financial assets are issued under the laws of England and the state of New York.[18] This is true even for sovereign debt of many emerging markets that choose to issue it under foreign law (see later). Further, most large financial intermediaries have selected London and New York City as the base for their global business, and their lawyers and most global law firms are located there as well. This puts these two jurisdictions in the position of rule-makers for the globe and all other countries that recognize and enforce the laws of these two jurisdictions in the role of rule-takers. Being a rule-maker is, from the perspective of self-government, clearly preferable to that of rule-taker. Yet, defending this role over time tends to skew law-making to serve the interests of finance, giving it undue weight over the interests of other constituencies.

For rule-takers, the situation is even more dire. They expose their domestic constituencies to risks that are created elsewhere and which they are often ill-equipped to control. Public regulation to guard against the risk emanating from certain financial assets or intermediaries remains an option, but it comes at a cost. Furthermore, regulation is always a catch-up battle with the more agile and resourceful private sector, and, when regulators are not familiar with the legal rules that were used to code these assets in the first place, regulation is likely to be even less effective. Last but not least, attempts to regulate global capital risks losing out in the competition for attracting it. Coordination among states is therefore critical, but the rule-makers, which are also the home jurisdictions for the most powerful financial players, have little interest in reining in finance, especially when they can capture much of the upside while sharing the downside risk with others.

5.3.2 *Expanding Property Rights of Foreign Investors*

Another mechanism for protecting private against collective interests is to bind the hands of sovereign states in their relation to foreign investors. This has been accomplished by a network of more than 3,000 bilateral investment treaties that states have entered into with one another. A cornerstone of these treaties is an investor-state

[18] For details, *see* PISTOR (2019), *supra* note 10, ch. 6 "A Code for the Globe."

dispute settlement (ISDS) mechanism: It allows a foreign investor to sue a host state where it has invested for damages should that state have infringed its investments.[19] Disputes will be resolved not in court but by an arbitration tribunal located outside the territory of this state.[20]

There is no requirement to dispute the case in the host state's domestic court system at all. In contrast, victims of human rights abuses have access to regional human rights tribunals only after exhausting domestic remedies. The outside arbiters exercise extensive powers of interpretation, because bilateral investment treaties are couched in general terms. What counts as an "investment" and what amounts to "unfair and inequitable treatment" is left for them to decide. The arbiters are bound only by the treaty and not by the host state's law, not even its constitution. The explanation is that the 1967 Vienna Convention on the Law of Treaties stipulates that the violation of domestic law cannot be used for justifying the violation of the international law that a country is bound by.[21] This convention, of course, predates the rise of international law for empowering private actors and the proliferation of ISDSs, and it has never been updated to account for developments that empower private parties to hold sovereign states liable.

The foreign investor rights enshrined in bilateral investment treaties (BITs) put governments in a bind. Legislation aimed at enhancing social justice or environmental protection can potentially give rise to liability claims by foreign investors. The mere threat of liability may cause governments to discipline themselves. Further, there is no tribunal or mechanism that might resolve conflicts between the interests of foreign investors and those of the citizens of the state whose actions foreign investors constrain. It is not uncommon for "the state" to be held liable to a foreign investor as well as to its citizens, a result that is clearly at odds with an understanding of collective self-government where the state is not the principal but an agent – an agent of its citizens.[22]

5.3.3 *Sovereign Debt*

Sovereign debt is another example of how (private) law can help subordinate the state to private interests. Sovereign debt contracts are contracts of a special kind. Contract theorists have been bewildered by the willingness of private financiers to contract with a sovereign – given that a sovereign by definition has the power to

19 Tomas Mach, *On the Particular Nature of Bit-Based Investment Protection Regimes and the Direct Rights of Claimants in Investment Protection Arbitration*, Prague Y.B. Compar. L. 95 (2009).

20 Oona Hathaway & Scott J. Shapiro, *Outcasting: Enforcement in Domestic and International Law*, 121 Yale L. J. 252 (2011). *See also* David Schneiderman, *Investment Rules and the New Constitutionalism*, 25 L. & Soc. Inq. 757 (2006).

21 *See* Mach, *supra* note 19, at 101.

22 Arbiters on these tribunals are more likely to be recruited from commercial practice than the public realm. *See* Anthea Roberts, *Clash of Paradigms: Actors and Analogies Shaping the Investment Treaty System*, 107 Am. J. Int'l L. 45 (2013).

renege on the contract without facing sanctions.[23] Yet, private financiers have funded sovereign states for centuries – and have been able to benefit from this, notwithstanding occasional defaults.[24]

Several reasons account for this. First, sovereign borrowers are repeat players; they do not go anywhere and they will never be liquidated. While the threat of liquidation may serve as a deterrent against default for willful defaulters, it reassures creditors that some portion of the payment will be forthcoming eventually. Second, while most sovereign borrowers prefer to borrow in their own currency and under their own laws, not all do. Some countries have relinquished their own currency and therefore will have to pay their debt in one they themselves have no control over. Others have been pushed to accept having to repay their obligations in foreign currency or even issuing their sovereign debt under foreign law. This has the effect of depriving a sovereign of the power to lower the debt burden by issuing more money or to adopt a new law that alters the legal basis for the outstanding debt contract. It binds their hands and makes them look and behave more like a corporation than a sovereign.[25] Third, the sovereign issuer's preferences are not necessarily outcome determinative for how debt contracts are classified. US courts hold that sovereigns that waive the sovereign immunity in private bond contracts, which they regularly do, can be sued by private parties in a US court – a shift from absolute to restrictive sovereign immunity, which was codified by the Foreign Sovereign Immunities Act in 1976.[26] Fourth, even in cases where sovereign states issue debt in their own currency and under their own laws, they rarely default for fear that their own default would have major repercussions for others in their economy. The threat of other domestic actors being held hostage by excluding them from access to international debt markets is a powerful tool for ensuring compliance, no matter what the circumstances and the capacity of the government to manage its debt.[27]

5.4 PROTECTING THE RIGHT TO DEMOCRATIC SELF-GOVERNMENT

As the previous examples suggest, democratic self-government can and has been curtailed in the name of individual property rights and contractual commitments. The legal devices for protecting individual rights have been extended beyond the

23 Mitu Gulati & George G. Triantis, *Contracts Without Law: Sovereign Versus Corporate Debt*, 75 U. Cin. L. Rev. 977 (2007).

24 Jeremy Roos, Why Not Default? The Political Economy of Sovereign Debt (2019).

25 *See also* Julian Schumacher et al., *What Explains Sovereign Debt Litigation*, 58 J. L. & Econ. 585 (2015) (providing data confirming the rise of litigation over sovereign debt contracts).

26 For a careful analysis of the evolution of the restrictive sovereign immunity doctrine, *see* W. Mark C. Weidemaier, *Sovereign Immunity and Sovereign Debt*, 2014 U. Ill. L. Rev. 67 (2014) (arguing that "[t]he shift from the absolute to the restrictive theory of sovereign immunity was nothing short of a doctrinal revolution," *id.*, at 111).

27 *See* Roos, *supra* note 24.

domestic legal systems that created them with choice-of-law rules and international law also playing a part. There may be good reasons for protecting individual claims in many instances. However, it is worth remembering that individual rights are derived from a common source: a legal system that is backed by the centralized means of coercion. This is a social, not private good, a resource the value of which depends on a shared commitment to the rule of law. The legitimacy of this legal order is threatened by harnessing state power primarily for the benefit of private interests without regard to how they might affect others.

The problem is not individual rights, including property rights as such, but the claim that these rights are often treated as absolute and unbounded, and paired with demands for their full and relentless enforcement. If we accept that there are heterogeneous preferences and respect that every person should have the right to live the life that he or she has reason to value, as the capabilities approach suggests,[28] no one's rights can be fully optimized. At best, different rights can be brought into congruence, such that most are protected to the greatest extent possible given the legitimate countervailing interests of others. In the absence of a single price mechanism to resolve conflicts that inevitably arise, a single equilibrium is beyond reach. This leaves us with the messy job of balancing competing interests. Setting the parameters for this balancing act is what effective self-governing is all about. Not only should they prevail internally but they should also apply in relation to outsiders when they seek access to law and the centralized means of coercion.

How these principles might be used to bring into better alignment individual rights with the collective right to self-government will have to await future research. For now, a few rough sketches have to suffice.

Regarding private autonomy, the right to collective self-government will not eliminate choice of law. However, it will subject the enforcement of whatever legal system is chosen to a balancing test when seeking enforcement in a given jurisdiction. The greater legal uncertainty that comes with such a "check and balance" should be understood as part of the cost that actors face when they opt for foreign rather than domestic law.

Further, foreign investors should not be treated worse than domestic investors, but neither should they benefit from stronger protections than domestic ones. The risk of future legal change is part of the risk of doing business anywhere. As long as future change is not arbitrary and directed primarily against foreign investors, they should not be able to challenge it. Changing the composition or holding arbitral tribunals might also help to bring more public-mindedness to an adjudication process that is largely dominated by commercial interests.

Lastly, realizing collective self-government might be most difficult in the case of sovereign debt, the third example used earlier to show how law can be used to constrain self-government. Many less developed countries have learned valuable

[28] *See supra* note 6.

lessons from issuing debt in foreign currencies and under foreign law, and they now prefer to issue their debt under domestic law and/or in local currency, even if this increases the costs of finance. Still, this does not eliminate the additional problem that their own default might result in cutting off private actors from global debt markets. Ensuring that they issue most of their debt in local currency would mitigate some of this risk.

Before concluding, I would like to address a major objection that will undoubtedly be raised against this proposal. Given that international law respects state sovereignty, what is the added value of a collective right to self-government? My answer to this objection is twofold: First, the right to self-government can be asserted not only internationally but also domestically. It limits the extent to which private rights can be enforced without regard to the effects this might have on the ability to engage in meaningful self-government. Many might fear that this collective right could be used to trample private rights. My hope is that it would be used just as any of the other fundamental constitutional principles that radiate and shape the interpretation of the constitution, as do the principles of democracy, federalism, the rule of law, and social welfare in the German constitution, for example.[29] Second, in the international realm, sovereignty has been curtailed with the help of investment and trade treaties that empower private actors against sovereign states. Here, too, insistence on the ability to engage in collective self-government would serve as a counterweight.

As this chapter suggests, claiming a right to collective self-government is only the beginning of a discussion about how to realize it, and solutions will vary according to context. Insisting on such a right is meant to shift the debate, not end it.

[29] These principles are protected against amendments and have been used by the German Constitutional Court to interpret domestic law as well as international law commitments.

PART III

Positive Rights and Rights to Effective Self-Government

6

Post-Liberal Constitutionalism and the Right to Effective Government

David S. Law[*]

We, the democrats of the world, need to reassess our political achievements and redefine our political responsibilities. ... The political antidote to Communism is effective democratic government. ... This can be achieved not by giving the underprivileged alms or opiates but by practical measures which recognize the human rights of all citizens and raise the standard of living at all levels of society.

—William O. Douglas, *Democracy Charts Its Course*, 1 U. FL. L. REV. 133 (1948)

Autocrats think that democracy can't compete in the 21st century with autocracies. ... We have to prove democracy still works, that our government still works, and that we can deliver for our people.

—President Biden, Address to a Joint Session of Congress, Apr. 28, 2021

6.1 INTRODUCTION

Notwithstanding the efforts that have been made to pluralize the concept, constitutionalism continues to be identified closely with, and for many remains synonymous with, classical liberal thought.[1] The eighteenth-century notion that constitutionalism is mainly about restraining the Leviathan refuses to die. The continuing strength of the association between constitutionalism and this particular strain of liberalism does not preclude movement to a post-liberal (or post-neoliberal) understanding of constitutionalism. It does suggest, however, that post-liberal constitutionalism is more likely to stick if it assumes at least some of the trappings of old-school liberal constitutionalism. The best way to transform the language of liberal constitutionalism, in other words, is to speak some version of the language of liberal

* Thanks are due to Lorraine Wu for her usual superb research assistance, and to the editors for their close reading and thoughtful suggestions.

1 *See* Albert H.Y. Chen, *Constitutions and Constitutionalism: China*, *in* CONSTITUTIONALISM IN CONTEXT 61, 61, 68–69 (David S. Law ed., 2022).

constitutionalism. This is why the idea of a "right to effective government" (hereinafter, REG) suggests itself as an ideal vehicle for this kind of evolutionary development: it appropriates elements of liberal constitutionalism and puts a decidedly post-liberal twist on them. The result looks reassuringly familiar yet is fundamentally different – a wolf in sheep's clothing.

There are a number of reasons why REG is profoundly post-liberal. First, at a normative level, REG inverts the ideological premises of liberal constitutionalism. The viability of a right to effective government turns on first-order principles and beliefs about the nature and purpose of the state or, more simply, the ideology of the state that are difficult to reconcile with liberalism. From a liberal perspective, the state is a necessary evil (the state that governs best, governs least), and we should be skeptical of or even hostile to the very idea of collective goals (the individual comes first; only individuals, not imaginary collectivities, have goals; the idea of collective goals is a dangerous fiction).[2] And from this perspective, it becomes difficult to argue for a right to effective government. A state that cannot tie its own shoelaces, the governmental equivalent of the Keystone Cops, becomes affirmatively desirable. But if the state has any legitimate end(s) – any affirmative raison d'être beyond mere escape from the Hobbesian state of nature[3] – then a constitutional imperative of effective government seems inescapable. If there is an end, there must be a means, and the means is the state. Ineffective government means that the government is failing to fulfill the purpose for its existence, the very reasons for which it was constituted.

Second, at a practical level, REG is not just another post-liberal right but, rather, a condition to the fulfillment of other post-liberal rights. Hannah Arendt famously described citizenship as "the right to have rights."[4] Much the same could be said of REG. No less than citizenship, REG is a master right: it is a right to have rights, in several senses. A government incapable of acting effectively is a government incapable of fulfilling a right to health, or a right to education, or a right to a healthy environment, and so on. Effective government is, in other words, a necessary precondition to the fulfillment of positive rights.

It is tempting from a liberal perspective to look down on post-liberal rights, and thus also on REG, as secondary or inferior to liberal rights – perhaps because they lack a centuries-old pedigree, or they are difficult to enforce, or they are simply too

2 Broad-brush generalizations of this type about "liberal political theory" can of course be treacherous. Rousseau's notion of the "general will," for example, celebrates the idea of a collective good, Jean-Jacques Rousseau, The Social Contract 63–64 (Christopher Betts trans., 1994) (1762), but it does not mesh well with the individualistic mainstream of Anglo-American liberal thought, which is the focus here. *See, e.g.*, Colin Bird, The Myth of Liberal Individualism 11–12, 105 (1999) (noting the often-made criticism that Rousseau's concept of the "general will" paved the way for "totalitarian collectivism"); David R. Hiley, *The Individual and the General Will: Rousseau Reconsidered*, 7 Hist. Phil. Q. 159, 160 (1990) (describing various lines of criticism frequently leveled against the concept of the "general will").

3 Thomas Hobbes, Leviathan 183–90 (1968) (1651).

4 Hannah Arendt, The Origins of Totalitarianism 296 (1973) (1958).

expensive in a world of pressing scarcity to be taken seriously as rights. But that would be a mistake. Some things are first-order needs, meaning that they are ordinally superior (or, as Rawls might say, lexically prior[5]) to other needs. And most of those things – for most people, most of the time – are probably not negative liberties. They are more likely to be the stuff of post-liberal rights.[6] Are you going to feed your children freedom of speech? Will you put a roof over their heads with freedom of religion? When a floundering government proves incapable of protecting your family from a raging pandemic, what consolation is the freedom to assemble in large numbers and infect one another? To them, shall we say: let them eat negative liberty?

We need REG, and the post-liberal constitutionalism that REG makes possible, for a variety of reasons. Among other things, liberal constitutional discourse has done little to articulate a positive vision of how public officials ought to behave. Nor does it have much to say about the problem of private power, which in practice can be at least as threatening to human flourishing and liberty as public power. Perhaps most troubling, however, is the prospect that the premises of liberal theory about what people need and what the state must do are obsolete.

In the liberal constitutional narrative, the state is perpetually typecast as the villain, ever anxious to encroach upon the liberty of upstanding republican citizens and grudgingly tolerated only as part of some Faustian bargain. Amidst the increasing interdependence of contemporary society, however, the state is not merely or even primarily a threat to our liberty but rather the means of our survival. The romantic ideal of the self-sufficient yeoman farmer is dead and gone. Our survival today requires more than that we simply leave each other alone and refrain from a perpetual war of all against all.[7] Our ability to act on the problems and threats that face us, or even to meet the challenges of everyday living, is increasingly dependent upon coordination, cooperation, and collective effort. For better or for worse, the state is the linchpin of all of these things. Subtract the state from a complex, diversified, post-industrial economy populated with hedge fund managers and pet stylists and constitutional law professors, and the result is social collapse. Without effective government, nothing is safe: not life, or limb, or anything else.

The practice of constitutionalism must reflect this reality. Twenty-first-century life demands twenty-first-century constitutionalism. And, in this age, liberal fears of government that can do too much compete with growing post-liberal fears that government cannot do enough. Climate change, mass population displacement, killer viruses: time and again, the early twenty-first century has been gripped by crises

5 John Rawls, A Theory of Justice 302 (1971).

6 *See* David S. Law & Chien-Chih Lin, *Constitutional Inertia and Regime Pluralism in East Asia*, *in* Constitutional Democracy in Crisis? 423, 431–33 (Mark Graber et al. eds., 2018) (arguing that regime longevity depends first and foremost upon the regime's ability to satisfy first-order needs, which are likely to be primarily material).

7 Hobbes, *supra* note 3, at 185–88, 196.

that cater to post-liberal fears of ineffective government, not liberal fears of overreaching government. Crises of this sort do not play to the perceived strengths of unreconstructed liberal constitutionalism. If anything, they play instead into the hands of dictators and despots keen to convince the world that authoritarianism provides the strong, decisive leadership needed to get things done – unlike that bickering, undisciplined, self-defeating, weak form of government known as democracy.[8] To survive and thrive, constitutional democracy must demonstrate its capacity not just for limited government but also for effective government.

What make REG so promising as a bridge between liberal and post-liberal constitutionalism are the ways in which it resonates with and reinterprets core elements of the existing liberal tradition, even as it challenges that tradition. REG involves several moves that draw upon, yet put a twist on, liberal constitutionalism.

1. REG employs the language of rights yet defies easy categorization as a right.
2. REG simultaneously affirms a liberal understanding of rights and a post-liberal rights culture.
3. REG adds a post-liberal layer to the idea of checks and balances.
4. REG acts as a bridge between liberal "rights talk" and post-liberal "role talk."

6.2 BEYOND LIBERAL AND POST-LIBERAL RIGHTS TALK

One way in which REG feels at least superficially like a familiar move within the existing framework of constitutionalism is that it employs the language of rights. However, it does so in a way that defies the usual liberal as well as post-liberal categories of rights. It is obviously not a traditional liberal right, in the sense of imposing some restriction upon government. Yet it is not a conventional post-liberal right either. Rather, REG defies the conceptual distinctions that organize both liberal and post-liberal rights talk. Specifically, REG scrambles the core analytical distinctions that define rights talk and delineate among different species of rights, namely: (a) the distinction between *liberal* and *post-liberal* rights; (b) the distinction between *substantive* and *procedural* rights; and (c) the distinction between constitutional *rights* and constitutional *structure*.

Volumes have been written about the differences between various species or generations of rights, which correspond to the distinction between liberal and post-liberal rights. Liberal or negative rights are shields; post-liberal or positive rights are entitlements. Negative or "first-generation" rights guarantee freedom from the state;

[8] For an example of how such crises can feed flattering stereotypes about authoritarianism and dictatorship, consider the twisted alchemy by which the COVID-19 pandemic became an opportunity for the Chinese Communist Party to loudly claim credit for "swift and decisive" and even "miraculous" action – even though it was that very same regime that had bungled and covered up the initial outbreak at devastating cost to all of humanity. Xin He, *The State Advances, the People Retreat: China's Political and Legal Responses to COVID-19*, VERFASSUNGSBLOG (May 4, 2021), https://perma.cc/GN3V-3RUW.

positive or "second-generation" rights guarantee goodies from the state; "third-generation" rights are group rights. These devices share little in common beyond one thing: they are claims against the state expressed as imperatives. Hemmed in on all sides by these imperatives, the state is akin to a beast of burden that is simultaneously restrained (by negative rights) and overtaxed (by positive rights). Our attitudes toward the beast are ambivalent, if not schizophrenic. We view it simultaneously as an oppressor, a necessary evil, the repository of our hopes and dreams, and the means of our deliverance from want and fear. This ambivalence is reflected in the heterogeneity of the claims that have crystallized as "rights."

Where does REG fit in the existing scheme of liberal and post-liberal rights? For the most part, it does not. At first glance, it might seem to belong in the post-liberal category of positive rights: REG is a claim or entitlement to something – namely, effective government. But the "thing" to which REG entitles us is not analogous to the kind of "thing" that positive rights (or second-generation rights, or third-generation rights) ordinarily entail. Second-generation rights are rights to tangible things, the necessities of life – food, education, housing, health care, clean air, and water. Third-generation rights of a collective nature, though harder to summarize, nevertheless involve relatively familiar things such as protection against discrimination, language rights, religious rights, associational rights, and so on. The claims all involve some variation on the same basic formula: the government must perform (or not perform) certain acts upon people, or it must give certain things to people. Thus, we already know what a lawsuit involving second-generation rights or third-generation rights looks like, what kind of relief such a lawsuit might seek, and how a court might award it.[9]

REG does not comply with this basic formula. It is not about forcing the state to perform (or not perform) certain acts upon people, or to give certain things to people. Instead, REG might be understood as promising a minimally competent and proactive state that is not paralyzed by obstruction and dysfunction. It prescribes a mode of behavior for politicians and a way of ordering political institutions. In other words, it implicates both governmental *process* and governmental *structure*. Enforcement as traditionally understood thus becomes difficult to envision. Who would sue whom, and for what? Is judicial enforcement even apposite?

Given its concern with governmental process, one might try to assimilate REG into conventional rights talk by classifying it as a procedural right, but this is not an easy move to make either. What makes a procedural right merely a "procedural" right is that it guarantees only that the state will follow certain procedures, not that it will reach certain outcomes. In other words, the concept of a procedural right assumes that procedure can be distinguished from, and guaranteed independent of, substance. Not so for REG. The idea of a right to effective government implies

[9] *See, e.g.*, Julieta Rossi & Daniel M. Brinks, *Social and Economic Rights: Argentina*, *in* CONSTITUTIONALISM IN CONTEXT, *supra* note 1.

that the adequacy and correctness of governmental processes are to be judged by the *effectiveness* of government. Practical outcomes can, of course, be relevant to the scope of procedural rights.[10] It would be going too far, however, to say that liberal constitutionalism recognizes the existence of sweeping procedural rights on consequentialist grounds, instead of relying on deontological talk of notions like basic fairness or fundamental justice rooted in some combination of moral intuition and time-honored tradition.

The challenge of conceptualizing REG is not simply that it resists assignment to a particular category of rights (substantive or procedural, positive or negative, liberal or post-liberal). Rather, it resists characterization as a right altogether. Second- and third-generation rights may be post-liberal, but they at least conform to the traditional dichotomy between constitutional *rights* and constitutional *structure*. A positive right is ultimately just a right to have the government do the best job that it can of providing some basic good. It does not necessarily require that the government be reformed in order to provide that good more effectively. From a positive rights perspective, the structure of government is an afterthought, or merely a means to an end. To be sure, it is a well-documented weakness of positive rights that the government may simply be incapable of fulfilling them. From time to time, courts have tinkered with institutional structure in the name of rights enforcement and implementation. But structural reform incidental to the fulfillment of specific rights is inherently piecemeal. There is no guarantee that incidental reform will lead to effective government. On the contrary, it may even contribute to dysfunction by diverting attention and resources away from fundamental challenges and systemic reform to narrow problems and ad hoc solutions.

REG, by contrast, effectively collapses the traditional rights/structure distinction. A right to effective government cannot help but regulate institutional structure because institutional structure determines the prospects for effective government. It is a basic insight of political science that institutions shape the range of possible outcomes.[11] Gridlock is a product of institutional design; so too is effective government. A right to effective government is therefore, at its core, a license and indeed an obligation to dive deep into institutional structure. In this manner, REG turns the structure of government into an end in and of itself rather than simply a means to the end. It blurs the distinction between rights and claims, on the one hand, and

[10] *See, e.g.*, Mathews v. Eldridge, 424 U.S. 319, 321 (1976) (factoring "risk of an erroneous deprivation" and "probable value" of additional procedural safeguards into the determination of due process requirements).

[11] For example, a core lesson of the public choice literature is that, under conditions of even moderate disagreement – which is inescapable in any society of even moderate diversity – it is impossible to speak of pre-institutional outcomes (meaning outcomes that don't depend on the institutional configuration). *See, e.g.*, William H. Riker, Liberalism Against Populism: A Confrontation between the Theory of Democracy and the Theory of Social Choice 189–92 (1982) (explaining that the outcome of collective choice is frequently endogenous to the institutional structure for making choices, and thus casting doubt on the existence of a unique and determinate "popular will").

structures and outcomes, on the other, which from an empirical perspective is entirely justified. At the conceptual level, however, it is a radical move. Consequently, even the vocabulary of conventional post-liberal constitutionalism is inadequate, and some new term beyond "positive" or "negative" right (or first-, second-, third-generation right) is required. We might call it a "structural right" or an "institutional right." Any neologism we might fashion, however, would involve some kind of oxymoron and highlight the fact that REG cannot be assimilated into the basic analytical categories of liberal constitutionalism; instead, it transgresses against them.

6.3 LIBERAL RIGHTS AND POST-LIBERAL RIGHTS CULTURE

There is some incoherence, if not contradiction, at the heart of liberal constitutionalism's approach to the concept of rights. On the one hand, constitutional rights are supposed to be categorical; otherwise, what is the point of calling them "rights" instead of "interests" or "goals"? The whole point of framing certain claims as rights is to establish that they are not supposed to be shrugged off for the sake of convenience or expediency. On the other hand, the idea that government may intrude on established constitutional rights is utterly ubiquitous among liberal constitutional democracies. The liberal constitutional tradition recognizes a variety of situations in which the government may act decisively and at the expense of enumerated negative rights. Governmental infringements on well-established liberal constitutional rights – invasions of privacy, restrictions on expression or freedom of movement, and so forth – can be justified by "compelling governmental interests" in emergencies and other situations where life and limb are at stake. If and when these infringements are not authorized by the constitutional text, they are simply authorized by the courts.

A weakness in the conceptual framework of liberal constitutionalism is its lack of a coherent account as to how this state of affairs is acceptable and can be reconciled with the concept of rights. Liberal constitutionalism has a meager repertoire of stock responses. One response is to write some limitation into the definition of the right itself: explicit yet vague limitation clauses of some kind have become the rule rather than the exception. Still, this move isn't always available; thus, for example, those in the Hugo Black mold might point to the absolute, unconditional text of the First Amendment.[12]

Another response is to say, in effect, that unacceptable harms result from the recognition of absolute rights. Absolutist Hugo Black-type arguments are framed as unrealistic or naïve, rather than wrong in some normative or logical sense. We are asked to accept that considerations of practicality and "compelling governmental interests" can and must trump rights. For liberal rights-lovers, this does not feel

[12] Hugo L. Black, *The Bill of Rights*, 35 N.Y.U. L. Rev. 865, 867, 874 (1960).

especially satisfying: it is not a desirable state of affairs but rather a necessary evil, at best something to be endured.

Proportionality-type analysis is essentially a concession to this effect, combined with an effort to soften the blow by putting a wrapper of analytical structure and thus procedural rigor around a mushy core of balancing analysis. As long as some vestigial sense of rights-as-trumps lingers – and we have the continuing hegemony of liberal constitutionalism to thank for that – this response cannot help but feel disappointing or even embarrassing. Trying to counter a rights argument with balancing analysis and practical considerations – even when dressed up as proportionality analysis – feels like a very lopsided contest, or a comparison of apples and oranges.

A third response is to find, or acknowledge, that there exist conflicting rights. The one thing that can limit a right, without doing any violence to the categorical logic of rights, is another right. From the liberal perspective, such situations are supposed to be at least somewhat exceptional: if for every right there is a countervailing or conflicting right, then rights cancel each other out and become inconsequential. However, a defining characteristic of modern rights culture – which reflects the empirical realities of both "rights creep"[13] and "rights inflation"[14] – is the ubiquity of conflicting rights.

In a world of second-string and even esoteric rights,[15] the idea of a right to effective government would seem not only legitimate but overdue. The language of rights may do a better job of capturing the importance of our interest in effective government than the language we use now. Talk of "compelling governmental interests" can obscure what is really at stake – namely, the urgent needs of actual people who are depending upon the government's ability to act effectively. This kind of talk implies, inaccurately, that the rights of actual people are on one side of the balance, while nothing more than the interests of some amorphous abstraction called the "state" or the "government" is on the other. In reality, there are often "rights-level" arguments on both sides of the equation. From this perspective, REG is merely an articulation or reframing of what we already know: people are entitled to the protection and aid of their government, and the more vulnerable they are, the stronger their claim to this protection and aid. A government incapable of acting effectively on behalf of those who need its help is a government in dereliction of its constitutional responsibilities.

Ironically, it may be more faithful to the liberal concept of rights-as-trumps to recognize competing rights everywhere, than to maintain that rights can be

[13] David S. Law & Mila Versteeg, *The Evolution and Ideology of Global Constitutionalism*, 99 Calif. L. Rev. 1163, 1194–98 (2011) (documenting the empirical and global tendency of constitutions to contain a growing number of rights over time).

[14] Kai Möller, The Global Model of Constitutional Rights 3 (2012) (noting the "increasing protection of relatively trivial interests as (prima facie) rights," a trend that is "sometimes pejoratively called 'rights inflation'").

[15] *See* Law & Versteeg, *supra* note 13, at 1220–21 (identifying and contrasting "generic" and "esoteric" rights).

balanced away by anything other than competing rights. It is safe to insist that rights are trumps as long as everyone holds a trump card.

6.4 A POST-LIBERAL CONCEPTION OF CHECKS AND BALANCES

On its face, REG lacks any obvious connection to the practice of checks and balances in the traditional liberal sense. Liberal constitutionalism is concerned with ensuring that state institutions are limited, through both explicit restrictions (enumerated powers, rights) and competitive forces (checks and balances). REG would seem to prescribe the opposite: the idea is not to have government institutions limit each other but rather to guarantee the efficacy of the government as a whole.

The problem with the traditional liberal understanding of checks and balances is that state power is not the only concentration of power upon which some check is required. The lived experience of liberal democracy underlines the dangers posed by unchecked concentrations of *private* power.[16] Plutocrats and corporations wield as weapons the constitutional rights that were intended to protect (presumably weak or defenseless) individuals from the Leviathan of the state. Property rights and speech rights support control of the mass media and the monetization of access to public office; freedom of contract provides the basis for the reallocation of economic surplus from labor to capital.

Political reporting tracks the machinations of the Koch brothers and the Sheldon Adelsons of the world, and for good reason.[17] Their economic power, not only unchecked but amplified by the constitutional framework that restrains public power, gives them the power to sway elections. Those on the other side of these agglomerations of power are left to place their hope in the existence of countervailing plutocrats: a Bloomberg for every Koch, a Soros for every Adelson. In other words, we are left to hope that fortune delivers checks and balances on the oligarchy from within the oligarchy itself. Moreover, these private Leviathans are increasingly overtaking and transcending the state: these concentrations of private power are increasingly transnational in character and thus beyond the reach of any particular state.[18]

The domain of politics (the public Leviathan) is a potential counterbalance to plutocracy (the private Leviathan) because it is the domain in which persons are, at least in some formal sense, guaranteed equality (one person, one vote). By design, however, the restraints imposed on the state by liberal constitutionalism render this

16 *See, e.g.*, K. Sabeel Rahman, Democracy Against Domination 1–30 (2017) (discussing the need for reform of government institutions to enable democracy to withstand "economic domination").

17 *See, e.g.*, Jane Mayer, Dark Money: The Hidden History of the Billionaires behind the Rise of the Radical Right 370–409 (2016) (discussing the efforts of Sheldon Adelson and the Koch brothers during the 2016 US presidential campaign); Russell Berman, *A Guide to the Billionaires Bankrolling the GOP Candidates*, Atlantic (Apr. 24, 2015), https://perma.cc/BRF6-Y9NP.

18 *See, e.g.*, David Schneiderman, Constitutionalizing Economic Globalization: Investment Rules and Democracy's Promise (2008).

a lopsided contest and place a heavy hand on the scales in favor of the private over the public. The primary justification for this emphasis on the restraint of public power is the state's monopoly on the legitimate use of force. But, as a practical matter, one might question whether "mere" economic power of the type wielded by private actors is in practice less coercive or less threatening than the type of force that liberal constitutionalism aims to restrain. What experience teaches us, in other words, is that there is a need for checks and balances not only among institutions of public power but also between public and private power.

A right to effective government is nothing less than a right to a government capable of making and asserting decisions on the part of the demos against oligarchs and plutocrats. Without effective government, there is no balance. Post-liberal constitutionalism can simultaneously enshrine and extend the concept of checks and balances by acknowledging the full range of forces that need to be checked and balanced. Coercion of the individual can come from the private sphere as well as the public sphere. Post-liberal constitutionalism can and should liberate the concept of checks and balances from the public/private distinction. A contest of Leviathans is a form of checks and balances. Effective government can serve as an antidote or counterweight to unaccountable concentrations of nonstate power.

6.5 FROM "RIGHTS TALK" TO "ROLE TALK"

The notion that men are not angels, and that institutions must be designed accordingly,[19] is a staple of Anglo-American liberal thought and liberal constitutionalism alike. Perhaps the most powerful and enduring insight of the American constitutional experience – one that ensures the continuing influence of the US Constitution at the level of design philosophy – concerns its assumptions about human nature, and specifically the notion that constitutional design should anticipate and ideally harness behavior that is less than virtuous. Ambition must be made to counteract ambition:[20] it is a brilliant idea, brilliantly expressed. But it is also an idea that goes only so far.

An effective scheme of government will seek to harness norms as well as incentives. March and Olsen usefully divide explanations of human behavior into the logic of anticipated consequences and the logic of appropriateness.[21] Different disciplines place different emphasis on these modes of explanation. Some tend to think that people can be relied upon to act in ways that reflect calculations of self-interest (the logic of anticipated consequences at work), and that it is unwise, if not naïve, to place much faith in human virtue. Others tend to reject this view as not just

[19] Federalist No. 51 (Madison).

[20] *Id.*

[21] James G. March & Johan P. Olsen, *The Institutional Dynamics of International Political Orders*, 52 Int'l Orgs. 943, 949 (1998).

morally impoverished but also descriptively inadequate, and to insist that norms and ideals can and do shape political behavior (the logic of appropriateness).

Of course, both points of view are true, which means that we should prefer a two-pronged approach to institutional design that deploys norms as well as incentives. There is both room and need for some version of small-r republican or civic virtue. No constitutional structure can get all the incentives right, all the time. Thus, at a minimum, it is necessary to supplement stereotypically liberal constitutional design with the articulation and promotion of norms of political behavior.

But this is historically not a strength of our constitutional discourse, which is instead marked by the Madisonian emphasis on self-interest, self-aggrandizement, competition, checks and balances, and so on. Anglo-American liberal constitutionalism overwhelmingly speaks the language of entitlements and prohibitions (in the forms of rights and powers), not norms and ethics. The normative vocabulary for describing how public officials ought to act is meager by comparison. On the one hand, we have the concept of corruption, which is relatively hard-edged and unforgiving but narrowly defined. On the other hand, we have the concepts of statesmanlike behavior and good faith, but what else? Moreover, these latter concepts are mushy and lack definition, much less enforcement. Thus, for example, when the Senate Majority Leader vows publicly that "the single most important thing we want to achieve is for President Obama to be a one-term president,"[22] what basis do we have for condemning such behavior? Or are we resigned to the notion that this kind of behavior merely falls under the category of partisanship, an unfortunate but unremarkable occurrence?

A right to effective government would certainly clarify that it is wrong to engage in the politics of obstruction and destruction. If anything, the problem may be that a mere "right" is not broad enough to plug the hole. What is needed, perhaps, is the analogue of citizenship, but for officials rather than citizens – some concept that defines the role of officials the way that citizenship does for citizens.

It is a truism that citizenship encompasses duties and obligations as well as rights, but it may be helpful to spell out why this is so. In a well-functioning political order – as in any other institution – everyone has a role to play. An institution is, at the most basic level, a set of people playing a set of roles. The state is no exception. Institutions, including states, cannot function if people lack the tools to perform their roles. Nor can institutions function, however, if people are free to use those tools in any way that they wish, for any purpose that they wish. Hence, responsibility without power is undesirable, but so too is power without responsibility.

Citizenship is the name we give to the bundle of rights and duties that defines a citizen's role within the institution of the state. To speak of good citizens is to speak of people who play the role that they must play in order to bring the state to fruition.

22 Major Garrett, *Top GOP Priority: Make Obama a One-Term President*, National Journal, Oct. 23, 2010, at 29 (quoting then-Senate Majority Leader Mitch McConnell).

There must exist a corresponding bundle of rights and duties that defines the role of the official.[23] But what do we call it, and what does it contain? If *citizenship* is the bundle of capabilities and responsibilities that defines the role of the *citizen* in a functioning constitutional and political order, what is the analogous concept for officialdom? If civic virtue prescribes the proper conduct of upstanding citizens, what is the corresponding concept that prescribes the proper conduct of upstanding officials?

The content of such a concept would take some effort to elaborate and presumably would vary to some extent with the role of the particular official in question.[24] But surely its core content would obligate state officials to govern effectively, and thus to refrain from undermining, obstructing, or destroying the very institution that they exist to serve. A right to effective government is, in other words, at least partly a right to leadership, in the fullest sense of the word. Of course, we should not be so naïve as to place our faith in virtuous leaders. But we still have every right to demand virtue of our leaders in the first place, and to demand it with every means at our disposal. Indeed, it is not just our right but our responsibility to express our demands. If we are to grouse about the behavior of our leaders, the onus is on us to make clear how we would like them to behave instead. We cannot expect leaders who meet our expectations until we first articulate our expectations.

[23] *See, e.g.*, Suzanne Dovi, The Good Representative 78–81, 90–92 (2007) (identifying "fair-mindedness," "critical trust-building," and "good gatekeeping" as three core virtues of democratic representatives); Vicki C. Jackson, *Pro-constitutional Representation*, 57 Wm. & Mary L. Rev. 1717, 1737–78 (2016).

[24] For example, one promising approach might be, following Hanna Pitkin, to unpack the concept of representation and find within it component obligations "to work with others, to find compromises, to determine what is most intensely important and what is less so in order to be able to make deals and facilitate governance." Vicki C. Jackson, *Legislatures and Effective Government: Raising Expectations for Representatives, in* Constitutionalism and a Right to Effective Government? 184 (Vicki C. Jackson & Yasmin Dawood eds., 2022). The more precise the prescriptions, however, the more likely it becomes that the prescriptive framework contemplates a particular type of official (such as an elected member of a multimember legislative body whose colleagues are all elected by different constituencies). It is not immediately obvious to what extent such an analysis could be generalized to other types of official (e.g., those who lay claim to representing the whole rather than merely the parts), or if the applicable norms of conduct might need to vary accordingly.

7

Does the First Amendment Forbid, Permit, or Require Government Support of News Industries?

*Martha Minow**

7.1 INTRODUCTION

Does the First Amendment forbid reforms to save and improve newsgathering, production, and distribution? All features of the news ecosystem are currently under threat, but some interpretations suggest that the First Amendment either forbids relevant government action or has no relevance. Debates about potential reforms of the businesses and structures wreaking havoc on news and information in the United States often hit a roadblock: the assumption that the First Amendment bars government from playing a role in media systems and news industries.[1] Victor Pickard calls this "First Amendment fundamentalism."[2] We can understand why internet tech platforms invoke the First Amendment against any regulation and measures requiring them to pay for news posted on their sites but gathered by others.

* Thanks to Vicki Jackson for her encouragement and comments; to Jeremy Dang, Ben Horton, and Sejal Singh for research; and to Mira Singer, Joe Singer, Elliot Schrage, and Newton Minow for invaluable help.

1 Challenges to news industries are explored in MARTHA MINOW, SAVING THE NEWS: WHY THE CONSTITUTION CALLS FOR GOVERNMENT ACTION TO PRESERVE FREEDOM OF SPEECH (2021); and Martha Minow, *The Changing Ecosystem of News*, 64 LOY. L. REV. 499 (2018). As ad revenues rapidly shift to internet platforms, newspapers and broadcasters shed staff, shrink coverage, or close, leaving many communities with no local news reporting. Mathew Ingram, *Google and Facebook Account for Nearly All Growth in Digital Ads*, FORTUNE (Apr. 26, 2017), https://in.news.yahoo.com/google-facebook-account-nearly-growth-214226495.html; Henri Gendreau, *Don't Stop the Presses! When Local News Struggles, Democracy Withers*, WIRED (Nov. 30, 2017), https://www.wired.com/story/dont-stop-the-presses-why-big-tech-should-subsidize-real-journalism/; Clara Hendrickson, *Local Journalism in Crisis: Why America Must Revive Its Local Newsrooms*, BROOKINGS INST. (Nov. 12, 2019), https://www.brookings.edu/research/local-journalism-in-crisis-why-america-must-revive-its-local-newsrooms/; Amy Mitchell et al., *State of the News Media 2016*, PEW RES. CTR. (June 15, 2016), https://assets.pewresearch.org/wp-content/uploads/sites/13/2016/06/30143308/state-of-the-news-media-report-2016-final.pdf.

2 VICTOR PICKARD, DEMOCRACY WITHOUT JOURNALISM? CONFRONTING THE MISINFORMATION SOCIETY (2019).

Avoiding regulation makes their work easier and their bottom line richer. But the First Amendment is not such a bar.

Two types of effort to improve the ecosystem of news are permitted and may even be required by the First Amendment. The first type would tackle forces undermining the viability of private news organizations. A particular target is dominant digital platform companies, currently immunized against liabilities and enabling posting of materials reported and written by others without payment or reinvestment in new content as responsible players; legal reforms would impose duties and limits commensurate with the functions and powers of the tech giants. A second type would support, amplify, and sustain a variety of public interest news sources at the local, regional, and national level. Both approaches could help realize the meaning of the First Amendment – as endorsed by the Supreme Court – which includes protection of access to information that Americans need to be safe, productive, and self-governing.

Both kinds of reform not only are compatible with the First Amendment but also amplify prior efforts accepted within US law. Legislative and regulatory enactments permitted by the courts demonstrate ongoing government involvement with media and news industries. Nothing in the Constitution forecloses government action to regulate concentrated economic power, levy general taxes, invest revenues in public and private media, enforce intellectual property rights, require disclosure about who is financing particular communications, or strengthen public and private investments in the news functions presupposed by democratic governance.

The First Amendment constrains Congress from "*abridging*" the freedom of the press and the freedom of speech, but it does not block actions to strengthen these freedoms. To sustain freedom of the press, courts need to pursue new approaches. So do Congress, the states, and private actors. The global nature of contemporary information gathering and distribution means that more than one nation governs digital platforms. Preserving a role for the United States in the emerging regulations of US-based internet platforms and ensuring the viability of US constitutional democracy should hold significance as First Amendment doctrine develops.

7.2 HISTORICAL DEVELOPMENT

The Constitution's drafters and early national leaders offer explicit and emphatic statements of the ideals represented by the First Amendment.[3] Nonetheless, the First Amendment's protection for speech and the press produced too little judicial enforcement in the nation's first 120 years.[4] Because the First Amendment expresses

[3] Sam Lebovic, Free Speech and Unfree News: The Paradox of Press Freedom in America 9–10 (2016).

[4] *Id.* at 2–10, 32–44. During the early Republic, printers often exercised wide latitude but also faced prior restraints without legal limits. Christopher B. Daly, Covering America: A Narrative history of a Nation's Journalism 46–58 (2012).

a limit on Congress, state and local governments seemed beyond its reach.[5] Yet that changed with the enactment of the Fourteenth Amendment, whose clause protecting life, liberty, and property from deprivations by state governments gave rise to judicial interpretations applying some of the federal Bill of Rights to the states.

Between 1917 and the 1930s, active campaigns by fledgling civil liberties initiatives pushed back against wartime and other restrictions on speech and in the press. Labor and civil liberties groups challenged government suppression of speech, overcame reluctance to turn to the judiciary, and convinced a minority of justices on the Supreme Court.[6] Dissents by Justices Oliver Wendell Holmes, Jr. and Louis Brandeis pushed against punishments for anti-war publications and other forms of dissenting speech.[7] Their dissents ultimately convinced the Court's majority. The federal courts gained a critical role in assessing the regulation of speech.

New technologies prompted new interpretations. Courts ruled that First Amendment rights extend to broadcasters,[8] but broadcasters need government licenses made subject to government oversight guided by the standards "public interest, convenience, and necessity."[9] In its decision in *Red Lion Co.* v. *Federal Communications Commission*, the Supreme Court upheld a governmental policy applied to licensed broadcasters; the Fairness Doctrine required political balance.[10] The Court relied on the scarcity of broadcast frequencies and the legitimate claims of possible users, justifying regulation.

The Fairness Doctrine partially echoed an ideal of journalism first advanced by Founding Father Benjamin Franklin. He defended the service afforded to the public by the printer-editors who would be expected to open their pages to contrasting points of view, much as a ship captain or coach operator transports individuals who hold different views.[11] The Fairness Doctrine analogously required broadcasters to provide a platform for a reasonably balanced set of competing views.[12] But the predicate of scarcity faded with the rise of first cable and then the Internet, which expanded expression outlets. The federal government retired the Fairness Doctrine officially in 2011 after it faded from use in the late 1980s.[13]

5 Barron v. Baltimore, 32 U.S. (7 Pet.) 243 (1833).

6 Laura Weinrib, The Taming of Free Speech: America's Civil Liberties Compromise (2016).

7 *See* Abrams v. United States, 250 U.S.616, 624 (1919) (Holmes, J., dissenting); Debs v. United States, 249 U.S. 211 (1919); Gitlow v. New York, 268 U.S. 652, 672 (1925) (Holmes, J., dissenting); Whitney v. California, 274 U.S. 257, 372 (1927) (Brandeis, J., concurring).

8 *See* Red Lion Broad. Co. v. FCC, 395 U.S. 367, 369, 400–01 (1969).

9 Communications Act of 1934, 47 U.S.C. § 151 (amended to cover television and newer technologies).

10 Red Lion Broadcasting Co. v. FCC, 395 U.S. 367, 400 (1969).

11 Daly, *supra* note 4, at 25–26 (citing Benjamin Franklin, Writings, pp. 44–47).

12 Dan Fletcher, *A Brief History of: The Fairness Doctrine*, Time (Feb. 20, 2009), http://content.time.com/time/nation/article/0,8599,1880786,00.html.

13 Brooks Boliek, *FCC Finally Kills Off Fairness Doctrine*, Politico (Aug. 22, 2011), https://www.politico.com/story/2011/08/fcc-finally-kills-off-fairness-doctrine-061851.

Regulation persists nonetheless. Protection of children and of decency has been the focus of lawful regulation of cable and internet communications.[14] Congressional effort to protect children from sexually explicit speech on the Internet met with three rounds of litigation, two Supreme Court decisions, and ultimately left in place an appellate court's suspension of the law.[15] The Federal Communications Commission (FCC) still limits obscenity, indecency, and profanity during certain broadcasting hours.[16] Also the government requires broadcasters and cable operators to name their sponsors because listeners are entitled to know by whom they are being persuaded. The courts often acknowledge not just the rights of speakers but also the rights of listeners. Government should ensure that listeners have choices and knowledge relevant to those choices.[17]

7.3 EMERGENCE OF THE LIBERTARIAN – "WEAPONIZED" – FIRST AMENDMENT

Since the 1980s, corporate and anti-union advocates have used the First Amendment to challenge regulations of speech – and they have had some successes. The Supreme Court in 2018 ruled that government employees who are represented by a labor union but do not belong to that union cannot be required to pay a fee to cover the union's costs to negotiate a contract governing all employees.[18] Overturning a precedent of forty years at the foundation of labor-management negotiation, the Court also deployed what can be called a "libertarian" First Amendment in order to undermine economic regulation. In dissent, Justice Elena Kagan argued that the majority "weaponized the First Amendment, in a way that unleashes judges, now and in the future, to intervene in economic and regulatory policy."[19]

Currently, some members of the Supreme Court seem to be using the Constitution to enact a particular theory – elevating individual freedom over government regulation as the Court did once before, in *Lochner* v. *New York* and its progeny.[20] But that

[14] Denver Area Educational Telecommunications Consortium v. FCC, 518 U.S. 727 (1996) (Breyer, J., plurality opinion); United States v. Playboy Entertainment Group, 529 U.S. 803 (2000).

[15] *See* Ashcroft v. American Civil Liberties Union, 535 U.S. 564 (2002) (Ashcroft I); Ashcroft v. American Civil Liberties Union II, 542 U.S. 656 (2004) (Ashcroft II); Am. Civil Liberties Union v. Gonzales, 478 F. Supp. 2d 775 (E.D. Pa. 2007), aff'd Am. Civil Liberties Union v. Mukasey, 534 F.3d 181 (3d Cir. 2008), cert. denied, Mukasey v. Am. Civil Liberties Union, 555 U.S. 1137 (2009).

[16] FCC, CONSUMER GUIDE: OBSCENE, INDECENT AND PROFANE BROADCASTS (2017), https://transition.fcc.gov/cgb/consumerfacts/obscene.pdf.

[17] Red Lion Broadcasting Co. v. FCC, 395 U.S. 367, 390 (1969). See James Grimmelmann, *Listeners' Choices*, 90 COLO. L. REV. 365, 377–79, 200–401 (2019).

[18] Janus v. AFSCME, 138 S.Ct. 2448 (2018).

[19] *Id.* at 2501 (Kagan, J., dissenting).

[20] Amy Kapczynski, *The Lochnerized First Amendment and the FDA: Toward a More Democratic Political Economy*, 118(7) COLUM. L. REV. F. (2018), https://columbialawreview.org/content/the-lochnerized-first-amendment-and-the-fda-toward-a-more-democratic-political-economy/;
Robert Post & Amanda Shanor, *Adam Smith's First Amendment*, 128 HARV. L. REV. F. 165 (2015), https://harvardlawreview.org/2015/03/adam-smiths-first-amendment/.

proved a failed experiment; the Court reversed course in the face of the Great Depression and recognized that government is always regulating – whether to protect or limit freedom, to protect or limit property. Hence, the legal question is whether it does so with reason.

New aggressive uses of the First Amendment have antecedents in cases rejecting employee and consumer protections: during the 1930s and 1940s and again in the 1970s, the courts at times interpreted the First Amendment to reject local taxes on door-to-door peddling.[21] But these limited precedents have long been identified with the failed and rejected approach of the *Lochner* Court, substituting the judgment of judges for democratically enacted economic regulations.[22] Historians compare that *Lochner* era with present efforts to push libertarian suspicion of economic regulations.[23]

Businesses and trade groups now use the First Amendment and its recent application to "commercial speech."[24] Corporate organizations regularly challenge regulations of consumer, business, and securities trading practices. After an empirical examination, Professor John Coates concluded that "[n]early half of First Amendment legal challenges now benefit business corporations and trade groups, rather than other kinds of organizations or individuals."[25] At risk now are governmentally required factual disclosures and other measures meant to assist consumers and citizens.[26]

If emerging judicial construction of the First Amendment were to cast in doubt government regulation of news and media, that would undermine the Constitution's presumption of a viable press, supporting an informed citizenry. The Constitution is not "a suicide pact."[27] Courts restricting governmental regulation and subsidies of media and technology would also contradict long-standing American practices.

21 *See* Jeremy Kessler, *The Early Years of First Amendment Lochnerism*, 116 Colum. L. Rev. 1915 (2016) (describing these cases).

22 Douglas v. City of Jeanette, 319 U.S. 157, 179, 181–82 (Jackson, J., concurring in part and dissenting in part).

23 Weinrib, *supra* note 6; Kessler, *supra* note 21.

24 *See* Bigelow v. Virginia 421 U.S. 8091 (1975); Virginia State Board of Pharmacy v. Virginia Citizens Consumer Council, Inc. 425 U.S. 748 (1976).

25 John C. Coates, IV, *Corporate Speech & the First Amendment: History, Data, and Implications*, 30 Const. Commentary 223, 224 (2015). Business managers tackle regulations "in their personal interests at the expense of shareholders, consumers, and employees, and to degrade the rule of law by rendering law less predictable, general and clear," with long-term risks to the Republican form of government and to economic growth. *Id.*

26 *Compare* National Institute of Family and Life Advocates v. Becerra, 585 U.S. ___ (2018), 138 S. Ct. 2361 (2018) (striking down the provisions of a California requirement of certain notices given to reproductive health patients as compelled speech) *with* Zauderer v. Office of Disciplinary Counsel, 471 U.S. 626, 651 (1985).

27 The phrase has been attributed to President Abraham Lincoln, used in a dissenting opinion by Justice Robert Jackson, and associated with reflections by Thomas Jefferson. Terminiello v. City of Chicago, 337 U.S. 1, 37 (1949) (Jackson, J., dissenting); Letter from Thomas Jefferson to John B. Colvin (Sept. 20, 1810), in 11 The Works of Thomas Jefferson 146 (Paul Leicester Ford ed., Fed. ed. 1905).

7.4 GOVERNMENT-SHAPED AND SUPPORTED COMMUNICATION CHANNELS SINCE THE FOUNDING

Government from the start of the United States assisted the distribution of news and development of media gathering and distributing news. Congress in 1792 exercised its constitutional authority to create a postal service meant to aid communications and distribution of news.[28] Through discounted rates and by authorizing free exchange of publications among newspapers and publishers, the postal system underwrote distribution of newspapers, books, letters, and pamphlets even to remote villages.[29]

The federal government financed the first telegraph line in the United States. This enabled the telegraph to transmit news of the 1844 presidential convention. The federal and state governments provided use of public lands to support a transcontinental telegraph. Later, the federal government distributed licenses to operate radio and television frequencies and established public service criteria for licensees. It still enables private commercial interests to build business on the public airwaves while charging only nominal fees.[30]

Public broadcasting started as educational radio using portions of the airwaves allocated by the government to noncommercial stations in the 1950s.[31] Congress then adopted the All Channels Act in 1962, requiring manufacturers to include VHS tuners which opened room for increased variety of broadcasting channels, including ones for public educational broadcasting. National public television launched in 1967 with a nonprofit organization serving as a buffer between local stations and the federal government.[32] Federal financing of public radio, television, and web-based media, always a modest part of the annual budget, incentivized and amplified private donations with tax deductible treatment.[33] Even when auctioned off to private bidders for rights to create wireless networks for mobile devices, slices of the spectrum are public resources granted for private use and private gain.[34]

28 Richard R. John, Spreading the News: The American Postal System from Franklin to Morse 25, 191 (1992); Richard B. Kielbowicz, News in the Mail: The Press, post Office, and Public Information, 1700–1860s 31–56, 141–55 (1989).

29 Paul Starr, The Creation of the Media: Political Origins of Modern Communications 48 (2004).

30 Tom Hazlett, *Ronald Coase and the Radio Spectrum*, Fin. Times, Dec. 15, 2009, https://www.ft.com/content/bfffd9fa-e9e2-11de-ae43-00144feab49a.

31 *The History of Public Broadcasting*, UNC Sch. of Gov't (Oct. 21, 2013), https://onlinempa.unc.edu/history-of-public-broadcasting.

32 Karen Everhart, Mike Janssen & Steve Behrens, *Time-Line: The History of Public Broadcasting in the U.S.*, Current, https://current.org/timeline-the-history-of-public-broadcasting-in-the-u-s/ (last visited Mar. 18, 2021). Federal, state, and local governments fund 14 percent of NPR's budget. *See Public Radio Finances*, NPR, https://www.npr.org/about-npr/178660742/public-radio-finances (last visited Mar. 18, 2021); *Overview and History*, NPR, https://www.npr.org/about-npr/192827079/overview-and-history (last visited Mar. 18, 2021); *CPB FAQ*, Corp. for Pub. Broadcasting (Mar. 18, 2021), https://www.cpb.org/faq#2-1.

33 Lee Banville, *The Story of US Public Media*, SwissInfo (Feb. 6, 2018), https://www.swissinfo.ch/eng/npr–pbs-and-cpb_the-story-of-us-public-media/43877508.

34 *See* Thomas W. Hazlett, David Porter & Vernon Smith, *Radio Spectrum and the Disruptive Clarity of Ronald Coase*, 54(4) J. L. & Econ. S125–165 (2011).

Federal dollars covered at least 50 percent of research and development investment in the United States between 1951 and 1978, including research very substantially contributing to developing telecommunications and the Internet.[35] Government vision, direction, and financing have played critical roles in telecommunications technology development.[36] A prime example is that Google's basic algorithm was developed with a National Science Foundation grant.[37]

The federal government subsidized research into computer networking that became ARPANET, the precursor of the Internet.[38] The federal government also guaranteed consumers the right to use modems on their phone lines, prevented telephone companies from undermining the emerging computer network market, and required phone companies to share their lines with competing broadband services operating through phone lines.[39] After Congress overhauled telecommunications law in 1996, the FCC required phone companies to share their lines with competitors who wanted to provide DSL service – a kind of broadband internet access that works through phone networks. Congress promotes speech on the Internet, but also sets some guard-rails.[40]

Antitrust enforcement has promoted competition among news, media, and telecommunications organizations in services and in ownership, while protecting private investors in the United States from interests elsewhere.[41] Federal policies pursued universal service and steered private industries toward that goal.[42] Even when federal antitrust policies permit concentration of ownership and consolidation in media, they shape choices available to consumers.[43] While private enterprise has supplied crucial elements of news and media, federal antitrust policies and regulation have played powerful and essential roles in the nation's news ecosystem.

35 Jeff Madrick, *Innovation: The Government Was Crucial After All*, N.Y. Rev. (Apr. 14, 2014), https://www.nybooks.com/articles/2014/04/24/innovation-government-was-crucial-after-all/.

36 Mariana Mazzucato, The Entrepreneurial State: Debunking Public vs. Private Sector Myths (2014).

37 *Id.*

38 *ARPANET*, Def. Advanced Res. Projects Agency, https://www.darpa.mil/about-us/timeline/arpanet (last visited Mar. 18, 2021).

39 Timothy Lee, *Network Neutrality, Explained*, VOX (May 21, 2015, 5:07 PM), https://www.vox.com/2015/2/26/18073512/network-neutrality.

40 *See CDA 230: Legislative History*, Electronic Freedom Found., https://www.eff.org/issues/cda230/legislative-history (last visited Dec. 31, 2018).

41 Starr, *supra* note 29 at 186, 224, 393, 401.

42 *See* Christopher H. Sterling et al., Shaping American Telecommunications: A History of Technology, Policy, and Economics 270–79 (2005).

43 *See* Pickard, *supra* note 2; Robert W. McChesney, Telecommunications, Mass Media and Democracy: The Battle for the Control of U.S. Broadcasting 1928–35 (1993); Eugene E. Leach, *Tuning Out Education*, ch. 1, Current (Jan. 14, 1983), https://current.org/1983/01/tuning-out-education/.

7.5 CONSTITUTIONALITY OF GOVERNMENT EFFORTS TO SAVE THE NEWS

Certain institutions and practices are necessary for democracy to proceed.[44] Recent experiments with fledgling and failing democracies underscore this lesson.[45] Ensuring reliable circulation of robust news turns out to be crucial. In the USA, the private sector, the public, and indeed the government should not sit idly by and watch the industries providing news collapse.[46] Past government efforts assisting media have been compatible with the First Amendment and could be expanded now. The First Amendment coexists with antitrust, tax law, and government subsidies, disclosure requirements, consumer protection, as well as with intellectual property and libel and defamation laws.

Laws against defamation have coexisted with the First Amendment from the start.[47] They persist even with some adjustments for breathing room for journalists who make errors.[48] Government enforcement of truth-in-advertising and corporate disclosures has not contravened the First Amendment, nor should it in the future.[49] Similarly, governmental protections of intellectual property are permitted despite tensions with the First Amendment.[50]

Digital companies give users abilities to share without payment journalism produced by other companies. The digital companies then harvest and sell users' data without reinvesting in the apparatus necessary for investigating and reporting news. Why should not the government require online platforms to pay for the news that they or their users post?

Congress and the executive branch can and should promote competition and guard against the negative effects of concentrated ownership and power in the media.[51] In 1945, the Supreme Court approved antitrust enforcement to prevent exclusion of new actors from cooperative newsgathering efforts despite the assertion of a defense of the First Amendment.[52] The Court has reasoned that the First Amendment "acts as a sword as well as a shield" and "imposes obligations on the

44 Linda A. Klein, *A Free Press Is Necessary for a Strong Democracy*, ABA J. (May 1, 2017), https://www.abajournal.com/magazine/article/free_press_linda_klein.

45 *See* Marc Morjé Howard, The Weakness of Civil Society in Post-Communist Europe (2003).

46 *Editorial: Local Newspapers Are Dying: If Local News Goes Out of Business, the Damage to Our Democracy Will Be Severe and Irreversible*, L.A. Times, May 24, 2020, https://www.latimes.com/opinion/story/2020-05-24/local-newspapers-dying-ways-to-save-them.

47 *See* People v. Croswell, 3 Johns. Cas. 337, 393 (N.Y. Sup. Ct. 1804).

48 *See* N.Y. Times Co. v. Sullivan, 376 U.S. 254 (1964); United States v. Alvarez, 567 U.S.709 (2012).

49 *See generally* Bolger v. Youngs Drug Prods. Corp., 463 U.S. 60 (1983); Cent. Hudson Gas & Elec. Corp. v. Pub. Serv. Comm'n, 447 U.S. 557 (1980); Friedman v. Rogers, 440 U.S. 1 (1979); Gene Quinn, *Does the First Amendment Protect False and Misleading Speech?*, IPWATCHDOG (Feb. 9, 2012), https://www.ipwatchdog.com/2012/02/09/does-the-first-amendment-protect-false-and-misleading-speech/.

50 David L. Langue and H. Jefferson Powell, No Law: Intellectual Property in the Image of an Absolute First Amendment (2008).

51 *See* Sherman Antitrust Act of 1890, 15 U.S.C. §§ 1–7; the Federal Trade Commission Act, 14 U.S.C. § 45; and the Clayton Antitrust Act, 15 U.S.C. §§ 1227, 29 U.S.C. §§ 52–53.

52 Associated Press v. United States, 326 U.S. 1 (1945).

owners of the press in addition to protecting the press from government regulation."[53] In *Turner Broadcasting System, Inc.* v. *FCC*, the Court upheld a "must-carry" requirement despite objections that it was a penalty and would risk suppressing information.[54]

Government authority to challenge concentrated ownership and control of media exists to advance the public's receipt of information. That authority should be exercised to tackle concentration of control over the Internet and its supporting infrastructure. The federal government's own involvement in developing and funding the Internet carries grounds or obligations for government action to improve reliable access to material enabling competing views and authentication of messages and sources.[55] Just as parts of telecommunication have been treated as a public utility – subject to regulation because of dealings in a necessity of human life – the Internet and dominant internet tech companies could be treated as public utilities, subject to regulation.[56]

Another permissible policy would tax tech platform companies. They have disrupted the news industry by taking advertising dollars and permitting posting of news stories without compensation. The government may impose taxes on press or media, but may not do so in ways that regulate content, or that single out the press or a subgroup of the press for differential treatment.[57] A tax that falls more heavily on some rather than other forms of media can be upheld if it does not discriminate on the basis of ideas and instead is a general tax, not one selecting a narrow group to bear the burden.[58] New policies could go further and provide exemption from sales taxes for newspapers, magazines, and direct satellite broadcasting but not cable or internet platform companies. Treating different media differently is not a constitutional problem unless it implicates discrimination on the basis of ideas and views. Revenues from taxes on the digital companies could be reserved to subsidize news enterprises.

General taxpayer dollars already support public broadcasting and could do much more. That would mirror Great Britain, Japan, and other democratic nations.[59]

53 Miami Herald Publishing v. Knight Newspapers, 418 U.S. 241, 251 (1974).

54 Turner Broadcasting System, Inc. v. Federal Communications Commission (II), 520 U.S. 180 (1997); see C. Edwin Baker, *Turner Broadcasting: Content-based Regulation of Persons and Presses*, 1994 Sup. Ct. Rev. 57, 114 (discussing Turner Broadcasting v. FCC, 512 U.S. 622 (1994)).

55 Although secondary to freedom of expression, the right of access to information is an important part of the First Amendment and its commitments. *See* Bd. of Ed., Island Trees Union Free Sch. Dist. No. 26 v. Pico, 457 U.S. 853 (1982); Va. State Bd. of Pharmacy v. Va. Citizens Consumers Council, Inc., 425 U.S. 748 (1976); Stanley v. Georgia, 394 U.S. 557 (1969); Lamont v. Postmaster Gen., 381 U.S. 301, 308–09 (1965) (Brennan, J., concurring); Martin v. City of Struthers, 319 U.S. 141 (1943); April Dawkins, *Access to Information: A Universal Human Right*, Off. Intell. Freedom Blog (Apr. 8, 2017), https://www.oif.ala.org/oif/?p=8797.

56 See Packingham v. North Carolina, 582 U.S.___ (2017), 137 S. Ct. 1730 (2017); Susan Crawford, Captive Audience: The Telecom Industry and Monopoly in the New Gilded Age (2013).

57 Minneapolis Star & Tribune Co. v. Minnesota Comm'r of Revenue, 460 U.S. 575 (1983); Grosjean v. American Press Co., 297 U.S. 233 (1936).

58 Leathers v. Medlock, 499 U.S. 439 (1991).

59 *Media Today: Japan, South Africa, United States: Financing, Import, Export*, Penn. St. U. (Apr. 28, 2014), https://sites.psu.edu/yokuokimasu/2014/04/28/financing-import-export/.

With the challenges facing news gathering and distribution, especially in local communities, public support for public and nonprofit media should no longer be treated as optional. Instead, it must be secured and expanded.

Expanding direct public subsidies to news media would help effectuate First Amendment values. The Supreme Court has concluded that a public subsidy is compatible with the First Amendment even if its scope is vague because when the government acts as a patron rather than as a sovereign, the consequences of its decisions are less significant constitutionally.[60] Public-serving media – whether public or private – need mechanisms to insulate public support from the whims of particular political moments as well as reliance on multiple revenue sources.[61] Granting public media the flexibility to generate funding through underwriting by private sources would require policy changes; so does adjusting the Copyright Act's treatment of public media to reflect new distribution platforms.[62] Neither scholarly treatments nor the judicial doctrinal analyses prevent government from subsidizing media and leaving the editorial and content decisions to those who manage the subsidized entity. Indeed, the First Amendment forbids viewpoint discrimination in the use of public funds for student journalism and also disallows a ban on editorials by publicly funded broadcasters.[63]

7.6 CONSTITUTIONAL ARGUMENTS FOR THE AFFIRMATIVE DEMANDS OF THE FIRST AMENDMENT

Because the Constitution depends on informed and active members to make democracy work, it should compel development of the institutional context for democratic self-governance. If the economy collapses, the government takes action.[64] Government action always carries risks and needs to comport with constitutional guarantees, but government inaction can also jeopardize constitutional guarantees. If the basic mechanisms for collecting votes become vulnerable to hacking, the government should act.[65] And if the infrastructure for gathering,

60 National Endowment for the Arts v. Finley, 524 U.S. 569 (1998). *But see* Owen Fiss, *State Activism and State Censorship*, 100 YALE L. J. 2087 (1991) (equating viewpoint-based denial of funding with government censorship of the arts).

61 *See Losing the News: The Decimation of Local Journalism and the Search for Solutions*, PEN AMERICA (Nov. 20, 2019), https://pen.org/wp-content/uploads/2019/12/Losing-the-News-The-Decimation-of-Local-Journalism-and-the-Search-for-Solutions-Report.pdf.

62 Blair Levin, *Public Media at 50: What's Next for the Information Commons?*, KNIGHT FOUND. (2017), https://knightfoundation.org/public-media-white-paper-2017-levin/.

63 Rosenberger v. Rector and Visitors of University of Virginia, 515 U.S. 819 (1995); Federal Communications Commission v. League of Women Voters of California, 468 U.S. 364 (1984).

64 *See Bush: Bailout Necessary to Deal with Crisis*, CNN (Sept. 25, 2008, 8:09 PM), http://www.cnn.com/2008/POLITICS/09/24/bush.bailout/index.html; *see also* Josh Zumbrun, *Financial Crisis, Regulatory Agenda Shaped Obama's Economic Legacy*, WALL ST. J., Jan. 18, 2017, https://www.wsj.com/articles/financial-crisis-regulatory-agenda-shaped-obamas-economic-legacy-1484762499.

65 Michael Waldman, *The First Step to Hack-Proofing Our Elections*, BRENNAN CTR. (Feb. 15, 2018), https://www.brennancenter.org/analysis/first-step-hack-proofing-our-elections.

reporting, and distributing news is absent in many communities, readers and viewers are overwhelmed by distractions designed to take their attention, and no recourse is available through the usual accountability mechanisms.[66] Affirmative government steps may even be required by the Constitution as part of the public's right to access information and to become informed enough to participate in democratic self-governance. The First Amendment presumes the existence of the press and that presumption itself could support an obligation for affirmative governmental action – an obligation for government to undertake reforms and regulations to ensure the viability of a news ecosystem.[67]

To work effectively, democracy needs: (1) an arena where participants can engage in self-governance; (2) institutions enabling individuals to learn about social needs and personal desires, to deliberate, to express their views, and to select representatives to do the work of governing; and (3) the kind of information that enables people to act to advance their own and society's interests.[68] Federal action is necessary to overcome, in particular, local news deserts. The loss of reporting about local government, health and safety, and other conditions puts local residents at genuine risk. Local journalism holds local governments accountable; without it, residents cannot engage meaningfully in self-governance.[69] Robust public options are needed when private ones fail to meet human needs and lack competition and obligations.[70]

The current architecture of online communications enables anonymous and bot-initiated messages to fill the algorithms, determining what news individuals get. Challenges that include foreign interference, election tampering, and mass manipulation might even justify summoning the broad federal powers available to protect national security and the integrity of elections.

First Amendment freedoms and the crucial watchdog function of news hinge not only on the viability of news-producing enterprises. They also depend on redressing damaging decisions made by powerful internet companies, whose algorithms are invisible to those affected and whose systems have been demonstrably manipulated by treacherous schemers and enemies of the nation. To sustain freedom of the press and enable the people, courts need to pursue new approaches. So does Congress. The constitutional values of the First Amendment are central to understanding the need for both Congress and the courts to deal with these dangers. This need is

66 Tim Wu, The Attention Merchants: The Epic Scramble to Get Inside Our Heads (2016).

67 Cf. Gillian Metzger, *The Constitutional Duty to Supervise*, 124 Yale L. J. 1836 (2015); Gillian E. Metzger, *The Supreme Court 2016 Term – Foreword: 1930s Redux: The Administrative State Under Siege*, 131 Harv. L. Rev. 1 (2017). For other works developing the idea of affirmative constitutional duties, *see* David P. Currie, *Positive and Negative Constitutional Rights*, 53 U. Chi. L. Rev. 864, 886–87 (1986); Susan Bandes, *The Negative Constitution: A Critique*, 88 Mich. L. Rev. 2271 (1990); Michael J. Gerhardt, *The Ripple Effects of Slaughter-House: A Critique of a Negative Rights View of the Constitution*, 43 Vand. L. Rev. 409 (1990).

68 K. Sabeel Rahman, Democracy Against Domination 114 (2017).

69 Hendrickson, *supra* note 1.

70 *See* Ganesh Sitaraman & Anne L. Alstott, The Public Option: How to Expand Freedom, Increase Opportunity, and Promote Equality 224–27 (2019).

underscored by the ways in which government has contributed to the conditions creating these very dangers.

The affirmative duty on the federal government to take action to protect the generation, production, and distribution of news involves a moral and constitutional push for legislation and law enforcement. The duty should also bring hard looks at the development of First Amendment interpretations to make sure that they do not produce unnecessary barriers to government actions essential to revitalize the news business.

Government action, in specific ways, shapes the Internet and media. The complex ecosystem of contemporary media did not spring solely from private decisions, investments, or market strategies; it has been shaped, supported, and promoted by specific government policies and actions. The Constitution is implicated because the democracy it establishes depends on a citizenry informed by news in ways that are currently in severe jeopardy. The First Amendment should not only limit governments but steer them to protect the right of readers and listeners to gain access to information as well as the right of speakers and the press to express themselves. The First Amendment is more than a bar against government action. It has never prevented all government action bearing on speech. Now, its values face existential threats unless more concerted action to protect the public and democracy proceeds.

8

The "Right to Effective Governance" and the Human Rights Baseline

Gerald L. Neuman

8.1 INTRODUCTION

What is the added value – or disvalue – of a "right to effective governance"? That question is phrased in relative terms, and needs a baseline. If the baseline is the United States Constitution, then suffice it to say that the US Constitution is notoriously an eighteenth-century constitution with a few later additions, and that it includes rather few "positive rights" (meaning affirmative rights to government action, as opposed to negative rights to government forbearance). Assuming that the "right to effective governance" is defined in a manner that actually requires the government to do something, and especially if the right is enforceable by private persons, then it would add a great deal to the requirements of the US Constitution. (Whether the result would be a net benefit is a different question.)

Rather than comparing with the US Constitution, I will proceed from a different baseline, obligations under international human rights law. To make the comparison more concrete, consider the obligations from the treaties that are part of the "International Bill of Rights," the International Covenant on Civil and Political Rights (ICCPR) and the International Covenant on Economic, Social and Cultural Rights (ICESCR), either as set forth in their text or as construed by the relevant monitoring bodies, the Human Rights Committee and the Committee on Economic, Social and Cultural Rights.[1]

[1] *See* Helen Keller & Daniel Moeckli, *Introduction*, *in* THE HUMAN RIGHTS COVENANTS AT 50: THEIR PAST, PRESENT, AND FUTURE 1 (Daniel Moeckli & Helen Keller eds., 2018). The "International Bill of Rights" consists of these two treaties plus the nonbinding Universal Declaration of Human Rights that preceded them.

The United States is a party to the International Covenant on Civil and Political Rights (ICCPR), and not to the International Covenant on Economic, Social and Cultural Rights (ICESCR), but the vast majority of states are parties to both, and the focus need not be on the added value in the United States. Strictly speaking, the two Committees' interpretations of their respective Covenants are "authoritative" but not binding. *See* Geir Ulfstein, *Individual Complaints*, *in* UN HUMAN RIGHTS

Briefly put, the Covenants already require effective enforcement of human rights, within certain limits. Depending on how it is defined, a broader "right to effective governance" could still have added content in comparison with this human rights baseline. The concern expressed here is that the *net* added value of a broad or generic private "right to effective governance" would be negative, partly because of its excessive field of application, and partly because of who could and would enforce it.

8.2 "EFFECTIVE GOVERNANCE"

To make a relative evaluation of a right to effective governance, one would also need some clarity about what "effective governance" means in this context. Beyond its basic thrust, the term covers a wide range of meanings.

Substantively, governance could be "effective" in the value-neutral sense that the policies adopted generally achieve their intended outcomes. Instead, governance could be "effective" from the perspective of a designated set of substantive goals, in generally achieving those goals. They might be economic goals, human-rights-oriented goals, or any other kind of selected goals.

Procedurally, a requirement of effective governance might be understood as being satisfied by any method of governance that produces the right outcomes. Instead it might be shorthand for the use of a particular set of procedural methods that are expected to achieve outcomes, or as requiring the use of procedural methods that comply with chosen side constraints.

"Effective governance" may be related to but distinct from "good governance," another term with multiple meanings, initially promoted by the World Bank as a criterion for development aid, and subsequently adopted in other international contexts and in constitutions of developing countries.[2] The World Bank emphasized "nonpolitical" features supportive of economic development, and its Worldwide Governance Indicators identify six factors: voice and accountability; political stability and absence of violence; government effectiveness; regulatory quality; rule of law; and control of corruption.[3] Other organizations have adapted the concept of "good governance" to different normative settings, adding criteria informed by democracy or by human rights.[4]

TREATY BODIES: LAW AND LEGITIMACY 73, 92–100 (Helen Keller & Geir Ulfstein eds., 2012) (discussing the legal effect of treaty body rulings).

2 *See* Edith Brown Weiss & Ahila Sornarajah, *Good Governance*, *in* MAX PLANCK ENCYCLOPEDIA OF PUBLIC INTERNATIONAL LAW (online ed.) (Rüdiger Wolfrum ed., 2013); Paul Faustin Kihwelo, *The Human Rights Commission in Tanzania: An Idea Takes Shape*, 2 E. AFR. J. HUM. RTS. & DEMOCRACY 46, 50 (2004) (describing the origin of the Commission for Human Rights and Good Governance in a 2000 constitutional amendment).

3 *See* M.A. Thomas, *What Do the Worldwide Governance Indicators Measure?*, 22 EUR. J. DEV. RSCH. 31, 33 (2010). "Government effectiveness" involves "the quality of public services, the quality of the civil service and the degree of its independence from political pressures, the quality of policy formulation and implementation, and the credibility of the government's commitment to such policies."

4 Weiss & Sornarajah, *supra* note 2.

At the United Nations, the advisory Committee of Experts on Public Administration drafted a set of "Principles of effective governance for sustainable development," that is, designed in relation to the implementation of the 2030 Agenda for Sustainable Development, which were then approved by the Economic and Social Council in 2018. The eleven principles are grouped under three headings – Effectiveness (Competence, Sound policymaking, and Collaboration), Accountability (Integrity, Transparency, and Independent oversight), and the human-rights-infused Inclusiveness (Leaving no one behind, Non-discrimination, Participation, Subsidiarity, and Intergenerational equity).[5]

A constitutional "right to effective governance" could be drafted by copying one of these models, or a portion thereof, and framing it as a right rather than as an objective obligation. Or the drafters could simply state the right in general terms and leave the specification to future interpretation, and possibly to evolution with new professional trends in public administration.

8.3 EFFECTIVE HUMAN RIGHTS

The human rights baseline already includes requirements for government action directed at ensuring the enjoyment of human rights. Looking first to civil and political rights, Article 2 ICCPR sets out the general undertakings of states in relation to ICCPR rights, in three paragraphs. First, states undertake both to respect the rights and to ensure them to individuals, and furthermore to do so without various kinds of discrimination. Second, states undertake to adopt such legislative or other measures as are necessary to give effect to the rights, to the extent that they have not already done so. Third, states undertake to ensure that persons who suffer violation of the rights will have an effective remedy, determined by judicial, administrative, or legislative authorities, with encouragement to develop judicial remedies. Thus, even for the more traditional civil and political rights, states are expressly obliged by the text to do more than just avoid violating them – states are to implement them and give them effect, and to provide effective remedies when violations occur.

Moreover, the civil and political rights are not solely rights in relation to the action of the state. For example, Article 17 ICCPR provides that no one shall be subject to unlawful attacks on his honour and reputation, and requires the protection of the law against such attacks; the *travaux préparatoires* of the ICCPR (roughly speaking, the legislative history) demonstrate that this provision addressed private defamation as well as defamation by the state.[6] Article 20 ICCPR requires legal prohibition of certain categories of private hate speech. Article 24 ICCPR guarantees every child

5 *See* Committee of Experts on Public Administration, Report on the Seventeenth Session (Apr. 23–27, 2018), UN Doc. E/2018/44 (2018), para. 31; Philippe Destatte, *Some "New" Governance Models for Europe and the United States*, 3(6) Cadmus 73 (2019).

6 *See* Manfred Nowak, U.N. Covenant on Civil and Political Rights: CCPR Commentary 379–82 (2d ed. 2005).

the necessary measures of protection "on the part of his family, society and the State." Article 26 ICCPR requires the state to prohibit discrimination and to guarantee effective protection against discrimination, and again the *travaux* demonstrate that protection against private discrimination was intended.[7]

More generally, the Human Rights Committee has interpreted many of the rights in the ICCPR as having effect as between private parties, in the manner of *Drittwirkung*,[8] and requiring the state to implement them in that context as well. The Human Rights Committee's General Comment No. 31 on Article 2, summarizing its jurisprudence as of 2004, explains that

> the positive obligations on States parties to ensure Covenant rights will only be fully discharged if individuals are protected by the State, not just against violations of Covenant rights by its agents, but also against acts committed by private persons or entities that would impair the enjoyment of Covenant *rights insofar as they are amenable to application between private persons or entities*.[9]

Thus, the rights address public violence and private violence, public deprivation of liberty and private deprivation of liberty, but only the state conducts criminal proceedings, and criminal procedure rights apply only in state proceedings. Every child shall be registered immediately after birth (Article 24(2) ICCPR), and the state must maintain a system of registration, but the Covenant does not also require private registration systems. The right to vote applies in public elections, and should be protected against certain forms of private coercion or intimidation, but it does not apply to the governance of private entities.

In short, unlike William Rehnquist's view of the Fourteenth Amendment in *DeShaney* v. *Winnebago County*,[10] the purpose of the ICCPR is both to protect the people from the state and to ensure that the state protects them from each other.

The obligations under the ICCPR remain obligations of states – private actors would not "violate" the treaty, but rather the state would violate the treaty if it made inadequate efforts to ensure the enjoyment of the rights. In particular, General Comment No. 31 continues: "[A] failure to ensure Covenant rights as required by article 2 would give rise to violations by States parties of those rights, as a result of States parties' permitting or failing to take appropriate measures or to exercise due diligence to prevent, punish, investigate or redress the harm caused by such acts by

7 *Id.* at 632–34.

8 The term *Drittwirkung*, derived from modern German constitutional law, means "third party effect," and describes how fundamental rights applicable vis-à-vis the state have consequences for the legal relations between private parties. *See* Andrew Clapham, Human Rights Obligations of Non-state Actors 521–23 (2006).

9 Human Rights Committee, General Comment No. 31: The Nature of the General Legal Obligation Imposed on States Parties by the Covenant, para. 8 (2004), reprinted in Compilation of General Comments and General Recommendations Adopted by Human Rights Treaty Bodies, UN Doc. HRI/GEN/1/Rev. 9 (Vol. I) (2008) (emphasis added).

10 DeShaney v. Winnebago County Department of Social Services, 489 U.S. 189 (1989) (Rehnquist, C.J.).

private persons or entities."[11] The state is subject to a standard of care, often described as due diligence, rather than strict liability when it comes to private abuses.

What is true of the ICCPR, where the rights are often phrased in negative terms, is even more true of the ICESCR, where the rights are mostly phrased in terms of steps that states must take to ensure their full realization.[12] The text of Article 12 ICESCR on the right to health expressly includes not only rights to medical services but taking steps for "the improvement of all aspects of environmental and industrial hygiene," and "the prevention . . . of epidemic, endemic, occupational and other diseases"; the employment-related aspects of this right overlap with the right in Article 7 ICESCR to "just and favorable conditions of work which ensure . . . safe and healthy working conditions." Even within a model of progressive realization, these are rights to the existence of regulation and the operation of an administrative state. As interpreted by the Committee on Economic, Social and Cultural Rights in its General Comment No. 14 of 2000, the right to health entails immediately binding core obligations that concern several dimensions of the right, but also the obligation

> to adopt and implement a national public health strategy and plan of action, on the basis of epidemiological evidence, addressing the health concerns of the whole population; the strategy and plan of action shall be devised, and periodically reviewed, on the basis of a participatory and transparent process; they shall include methods, such as right to health indicators and benchmarks, by which progress can be closely monitored; the process by which the strategy and plan of action are devised, as well as their contents, shall give particular attention to all vulnerable or marginalized groups.[13]

If we extrapolate from these examples, as many experts think we should, then human rights generate a deeply ramifying set of affirmative obligations, aimed at achieving their effective protection against a broad range of public, private, and perhaps nonhuman risks, along with procedural and participatory requirements to safeguard the quality of the decision-making and the dignity of the stakeholders.

On this understanding, a large portion of the content of the "right to effective governance" is already covered by state obligations under the two Covenants.

8.4 ADDITIONAL CONTENT

What remains for a constitutional "right to effective governance" to guarantee? First, rather than a broad and concise pronouncement of the right, there might be

[11] General Comment No. 31, *supra* note 9, at para. 8.

[12] ICESCR art. 2(1) ("Each State Party . . . undertakes to take steps . . . to the maximum of its available resources, with a view to achieving progressively the full realization of the rights recognized . . .").

[13] Committee on Economic, Social and Cultural Rights, General Comment No. 14: The Right to the Highest Attainable Standard of Health (art. 12), para. 43 (2000), reprinted in Compilation of General Comments and General Recommendations Adopted by Human Rights Treaty Bodies, UN Doc. HRI/GEN/1/Rev. 9 (Vol. I) (2008).

a detailed specification of the means of governance to which rights-holders are entitled. That specification might include more elements than the human rights treaties and their monitoring bodies have identified, or it may be more closely adapted to the social and institutional arrangements of the particular state. The specification might also depart from the human rights vision of effective implementation – for example, some might think that effective governance requires cost–benefit analysis of a kind that human rights bodies reprehend, with less attention to requirements of nondiscrimination and less priority for the most disadvantaged.

Second, the substantive scope of the "right to effective governance" might include areas of the policy space that are not (yet) reached by obligations under the two Covenants.[14] That might include certain aspects of property law that are addressed by regional human rights treaties protecting civil and political rights but are not addressed by the ICCPR because the right to property was omitted in its drafting. Another possible area involves corruption. In the past, the Human Rights Committee tended to view corruption that took place within the content of particular rights, such as judicial corruption, police corruption, prison corruption, and so on, as part of its monitoring mandate, but not legislative corruption in general;[15] the Committee on Economic, Social and Cultural Rights has addressed large-scale corruption that diverts funds from spending on economic and social rights.[16] More recently, as international attention to corruption has grown, the Human Rights Committee has increased the breadth of its interest in the issue.[17] Nonetheless, a "right to effective governance" might permit a fuller examination of corruption or a different approach to corruption than the one the treaty monitors call for.

[14] Admittedly, there is an inflationary tendency in human rights advocacy, and in the interpretations of some human rights institutions, to turn every policy question into a human rights issue (analogously to what Alexis de Tocqueville said about the courts in the United States). Not only can everything that serves human interests potentially be linked to a positive or negative civil, political, economic, social, or culture right, but even matters that are framed independently of human interests, such as the protection of the environment for its own sake, or the inviolability of sacred beings, things, and places, can be associated with an individual or collective right of a person or a people. If we accept that tendency, then it may be impossible for the scope of a "right to effective governance" to exceed the scope of what human rights law requires. But this chapter will assume, notwithstanding contrary evidence, a more modest scope for human rights law. Even on that assumption, broad areas of law are not immune from human rights constraint when they involve cross-cutting issues such as discrimination. Human rights law may have little to say about corporate governance structure as a topic on its own, but human rights bodies are interested in the representation of women in positions of power within corporations, and in labor relations.

[15] *See* Anne Peters, *Corruption as a Violation of International Human Rights*, 29 Eur. J. Int'l L. 1251, 1256–57 (2018).

[16] Committee on Economic, Social and Cultural Rights, General Comment No. 24 (2017) on State Obligations under the International Covenant on Economic, Social and Cultural Rights in the Context of Business Activities, UN Doc. E/C.12/GC/24 (2017), para. 20.

[17] Peters, *supra* note 15, at 1284; Human Rights Committee, Concluding Observations on the Third Periodic Report of Bosnia and Herzegovina, para. 11, UN Doc. CCPR/C/BIH/CO/3 (2017) ("The Committee is concerned at reports of widespread corruption and impunity among public officials that obstructs effective participation in public life . . .").

Third, the ICCPR protects the rights of individuals, not the rights of corporations as legal persons, unlike the European Convention on Human Rights.[18] So if the "right to effective governance" is possessed by corporations, that may be a significant dimension of its value added (or some would say its value subtracted, as in *Citizens United* v. *Federal Election Commission*[19]).

Fourth, I should observe that I have been discussing the substantive reach of the norms, rather than the procedures for asserting them. The Covenants, like some other human rights treaties, set up monitoring processes that review a state's overall performance without waiting for individual cases to be brought by particular victims, in addition to more court-like case-based procedures.[20] If we consider a constitutional "right to effective governance" accompanied by enforcement mechanisms, and specifically judicial (or constitutional court) mechanisms, the breadth of that right might require expanded notions of standing that are not limited to alleged victims of past and imminent future violations.

8.5 NET VALUE?

Assuming that the "right to effective governance" does add coverage beyond what the obligation to effectively ensure the enjoyment of human rights already covers, would that entail disadvantages (putting aside the standard objections to judicial activism)? There are several grounds for concern.

One issue relates to the full absorption of the domestic policy space into the "right to effective governance." This may mean that beneficiaries of bad legislation and bad regulation have rights to insist on the effective enforcement of the laws as written. Once untethered from human rights, the "right to effective governance" may be drained of normative content. In other terminology, it may involve a thin Anglo-American-style concept of the rule of law rather than a thick German-style concept of the rule of law;[21] or it may resemble the World Bank's 1990s notion of good governance rather than the later models that merge in more human rights and environmental constraints. Enforcement of bad policies has troubling consequences both because the policies are bad and because their enforcement competes for resources with the enforcement of good policies. In conflicts between bad laws and human rights, the constitutional "right to effective governance" may add weight

18 Human Rights Committee, General Comment No. 31, *supra* note 9, para. 9 ("The beneficiaries of the rights recognized by the Covenant are individuals."); Dean Spielmann, *Companies in the Strasbourg Courtroom*, 5 CAMBRIDGE J. INT'L & COMPAR. L. 404 (2016).

19 558 U.S. 310 (2010) (overruling prior precedent and invalidating a prohibition against corporations spending their funds to advocate the election or defeat of a candidate).

20 *See* Gerald L. Neuman, *Giving Meaning and Effect to Human Rights: The Contributions of Human Rights Committee Members*, *in* THE HUMAN RIGHTS COVENANTS AT 50: THEIR PAST, PRESENT, AND FUTURE 31 (Daniel Moeckli & Helen Keller eds., 2018).

21 *See* Gerald L. Neuman, *The U.S. Constitutional Conception of the Rule of Law and the Rechtsstaatsprinzip of the Grundgesetz*, *in* DAS GRUNDGESETZ IM PROZESS EUROPÄISCHER UND GLOBALER VERFASSUNGSENTWICKLUNG 253 (Ulrich Battis et al. eds., 2000).

in the balance in favor of the bad laws. Even if it did not, and human rights always prevailed where they conflicted directly with bad laws, the competition for resources would limit the state's ability to ensure enjoyment of human rights.

Another concern relates to questions of standing and court access. Who is empowered to complain of noncompliance with the "right to effective governance," and how early in the period before their own material circumstances are specifically affected? The more the right can be asserted generally by citizens, the more it may become a tool for ideological plaintiffs to redirect government policy.

Next, who will have the resources and incentives to bring such complaints, and how will that determine which laws get effectively enforced? The "right to effective governance" sounds like a comprehensive right to wholesale effective governance, but if it is going to be litigated, it will presumably be litigated retail. A court will examine a particular law, or a particular group of interrelated laws, and perhaps only as they affect the litigants before it. Studies have shown the tendency of individualized constitutional litigation over social rights to disproportionately assist middle- and upper-class groups rather than those in greater need.[22]

And, once again, do corporations also hold the "right to effective governance"? In comparative constitutional terms rather than human rights law terms, it seems likely that an abstractly worded version of the right would be interpreted as including them. That interpretation would also skew the consequences of recognizing the right. Corporations, more than human beings, have the money and the incentives and the expertise and the opportunities as "repeat players" to make long-term strategic use of litigation as a means to shape the legal environment that affects them.[23]

For these reasons, I am concerned that adding a "right to effective governance," compared to the baseline provided in theory by human rights law, could be a net detriment rather than a net benefit.

[22] *See* David Landau, *The Reality of Social Rights Enforcement*, 53 HARV. J. INT'L L. 190 (2012).

[23] *See* MARC GALANTER, WHY THE HAVES COME OUT AHEAD: THE CLASSIC ESSAY AND NEW OBSERVATIONS (Shauhin A. Talesh ed. 2014).

PART IV

The Role of Courts in Building State Capacity and Promoting Effective Self-Government While Protecting Rights

9

The Unconstitutional State of Affairs Doctrine

Manuel José Cepeda Espinosa and Guillermo Otálora Lozano

9.1 INTRODUCTION

Constitutional adjudication routinely works against the backdrop of the assumption of a functioning government. Courts dispose of individual cases by declaring a specific violation and issuing a specific remedy. They do not go beyond the individual case because, by design, the political branches – legislatures and executive branches – are supposed to protect, respect, and ensure basic rights in most cases that do not reach the courts.

However, this is not the case with massive and structural violations of rights. In peaceful times, massive violations of rights are usually not a product of malfeasance or bad faith; they are the result of precarious institutional capacity and dysfunctional policies, political processes, or systems of government. In other words, they are the consequence of specific instances of a lack of effective governance.

The Colombian doctrine of "unconstitutional state of affairs" addresses the problem of a lack of effective government in specific institutions, with regard to sectors of the population or with regard to discrete policy domains. In Colombian constitutional law, an unconstitutional state of affairs is a situation in which rights are violated in a widespread and recurrent fashion, and these violations are caused by structural governmental failures due to omissions, actions, or both, usually involving several state organs.[1] The doctrine does not judge administrative or legislative acts; it judges a factual situation. As part of a larger trend of transformative constitutionalism,[2] it aims at closing the gap between what the Constitution promises and how individuals actually live.

The purpose of the unconstitutional state of affairs is to protect the violated fundamental rights and to give governmental organs time to overcome the structural causes of said state. The aim is not to reach a situation of zero violations. An

[1] Corte Constitucional [C.C.] [Constitutional Court], May 8, 2017, Sentencia T-302/17, https://www.corteconstitucional.gov.co/relatoria/2017/t-302-17.htm (Colom.).

[2] *See* Transformative Constitutionalism in Latin America (Armin von Bogdandy et al. eds., 2017).

unconstitutional state of affairs may be lifted, in part or in whole, by the Court whenever the structural causes are solved and the factual situation has changed in a significant way.

The Colombian Constitutional Court has jurisdiction to exercise both concrete and abstract review.[3] The unconstitutional state of affairs doctrine is used in the context of concrete review, via *acción de tutela* in which the Court may adopt orders beyond the specific case, in order to overcome a widespread factual situation that is contrary to the Constitution.

The declaration of an unconstitutional state of affairs usually includes the issuance of structural orders issued by the Constitutional Court to be implemented over several years. Since Decision T-025 of 2004 declared a state of unconstitutional affairs to protect internally displaced persons (IDPs), the Court has retained jurisdiction and adopted a follow-up mechanism to monitor the implementation of the orders. Monitoring is done by the Court or a delegated regional tribunal, with the cooperation of autonomous public control bodies (Ombudsman, Comptroller General, and *Procurador* General) and third parties (civil society organizations).

During the follow-up, the Court requests periodic reports to be presented by the responsible state agencies and discussed in public hearings with the participation of civil society organizations. The Court can issue additional orders that affect the discretion of the government if the measures fail to protect rights in a manner that is effective and at a reasonable pace, usually set by the Court after an initial proposal by the responsible state agencies.

In its inception, the doctrine was seen as a threshold requirement in order to issue structural remedies. Nowadays, the Court issues structural orders without the need to declare an unconstitutional state of affairs.[4]

However, such a declaration still serves an important expressive purpose, as an instrument that mobilizes state agencies and civil society organizations to focus on a pressing problem and that heightens the transformative function of the 1991 Constitution in the Colombian context.[5]

In this chapter, we trace the evolution of the unconstitutional state of affairs doctrine in Colombian case law, by dividing it in three stages: the early cases, the 2004 IDPs decision, and the later cases. All cases were decided unanimously. Then, we offer a reflection on how the doctrine of unconstitutional state of affairs has served to promote an effective government, by improving governmental processes

[3] On the jurisdiction and procedures of the Constitutional Court, *see* Manuel José Cepeda Espinosa & David Landau, Colombian Constitutional Law: Leading Cases 1–48 (2017).

[4] On the Colombian model of structural injunctions, *see* David Landau, *The Colombian Model of Structural Socio-economic Rights Remedies: Lessons from and for Comparative Experience*, *in* Constitutionalism: Old Dilemmas, New Insights, Proceedings from the XIII Academic Conference of the Colombian Constitutional Court 258–76 (Alejandro Linares Cantillo ed., 2021).

[5] On contextualized functionalism, *see* Vicki Jackson, *Methodological Challenges in Comparative Constitutional Law*, 28 Penn. St. Int'l L. Rev. 319–26 (2010).

and policies in order to better protect and ensure the effective enjoyment of fundamental rights.

9.2 EVOLUTION OF THE DOCTRINE

9.2.1 *The Early Cases*

The best-known case relating to the unconstitutional state of affairs doctrine is Decision T-025 of 2004, in which the Court protected the rights of millions of IDPs. However, the doctrine itself began to be used by the Court seven years earlier.

The term "unconstitutional state of affairs" was first used in a 1997 case relating to the enrollment of public-school teachers in a social security fund that had been created around a decade before.[6] The Court noted that only 21 percent of teachers in the country had been enrolled, due to a lack of funds for the municipalities that employed them, which itself stemmed from an unequal distribution of funds from the central government. Unenrolled teachers did not have access to public health care and did not have pension plans. The Court analyzed the general situation of the lack of enrollment and noted that the two individual cases under consideration were an expression of "a general problem which affects a substantial number of teachers in the country and the causes of which are related to the disordered and irrational implementation of educational policy." The Court labeled this a "state of affairs of a general character," and later in the judgment called it a "manifestly unconstitutional state of affairs."

In this first case, the Court did not go beyond informing the government of this state of affairs and notifying several agencies. However, the case signified a leap in the Court's view of its own role. The Court consciously ventured beyond the individual cases and diagnosed a widespread policy problem that was causing a widespread violation of rights. The Court made an explicit effort to justify this novel form of approaching constitutional cases, under the heading of "harmonious collaboration," a mandate contained in Article 113 of the Constitution of Colombia. Article 113 first enunciates the principle of separation of powers, and immediately thereafter mandates all branches of public power to "collaborate harmoniously" toward the achievement of the goals of the state.[7]

The Court framed its declaration of an unconstitutional state of affairs as a way of "collaborating" with the government by putting it on notice of the situation, and as a means to forestall the filing of subsequent constitutional complaints in similar cases:

> The Constitutional Court has the duty to collaborate harmoniously with the remaining organs of the state for the realization of their goals. In the same manner as the competent authority must be notified of the commission of a crime, there is

[6] C.C., Sentencia SU-559/97, Nov. 6, 1997, https://www.corteconstitucional.gov.co/relatoria/1997/SU559-97.htm (Colom.).

[7] *See* David Landau, *Political Institutions and Judicial Role in Comparative Constitutional Law*, 51 Harv. Int'l L. J. 319, 347 (2010).

> no reason why it [the competent authority] should not also be notified that a given state of affairs violates the Constitution. The duty to collaborate becomes imperative if a timely administrative action can avoid the excessive use of the tutela action. The resources of the administration of justice are scarce. If, a call for authorities to perform their constitutional obligations contributes to reduce the number of constitutional complaints, which would otherwise be unavoidably presented, such action is then also a legitimate means through which the Court can fulfill its function of guarding the integrity of the Constitution and the effectiveness of its mandates. If the unconstitutional state of affairs has a direct relation with the violation of fundamental rights, itself verified in a tutela proceeding by the Constitutional Court, the notification may be accompanied by a specific or a general order for the authorities to do or to abstain from an action. In this event, the notification and the order are part of the array of remedies that the Court can use, when reviewing a judgment, to reestablish the breached fundamental order.[8]

Thus, while in this case the Court only entered a general declaration of an unconstitutional state of affairs, its reasoning laid the groundwork for subsequent experiments with more ambitious remedies. In this first case, the Court, apparently self-conscious about the possibilities of broadening its remedial powers, was only comfortable with sounding an alarm for political branches to act, in a way like the weak remedies well-known in other jurisdictions.[9]

The second case in which the doctrine was used is Decision T-068 of 1998, in which the Court decided an individual case relating to the delay of an administrative agency in resolving applications for retirement pensions. The Court noted that more than 30,000 constitutional complaints had been lodged against the same agency, and held that this circumstance pointed to a "structural problem of administrative inefficiency." The Court additionally noted that the *tutela* complaint had, in practice, become a requirement for pension requests to be resolved by the agency. The Court therefore concluded that "the situation in the respondent agency has led to an unconstitutional state of affairs [which] ... crowds the judicial system ...." In this second case, the Court declared the unconstitutional state of affairs, and called on the government to "correct the failures in organization and procedure" that led to the case backlog. The Court also requested the Inspector General (Procurador General de la Nación), the Comptroller General, and the Ombudsman to supervise the implementation of this order and report back to the Court. Here, while the remedy was still very open-ended, the Court experimented with an albeit weak reporting mechanism.

During this period, the Court issued three more rulings declaring an unconstitutional state of affairs,[10] and a fourth one in which the Court stated for the record that

8 *See supra* note 6.

9 *See* Mark Tushnet, Weak Courts, Strong Rights: Judicial Review and Social Welfare Rights in Comparative Constitutional Law 237–44 (2008).

10 C.C., Oct. 20, 1998 Sentencia T-590/98, https://www.corteconstitucional.gov.co/relatoria/1998/t-590-98.htm (Colom.); C.C., May 26, 1998 Sentencia SU-250/98, https://www.corteconstitucional.gov.co/

it would have declared an unconstitutional state of affairs and issued structural remedies had it not been for Congress approving a law aimed at solving the dire administrative situation of some departments in which pensions were not being paid.[11]

The most notable decision in this period is Decision T-153 of 1998, in which the Court declared an unconstitutional state of affairs with regard to prison overcrowding.[12] The Court outlined what would become the main requirements of the declaration of an unconstitutional state of affairs:

> . . . [T]his Court has used the concept of unconstitutional state of affairs in order to remedy situations of violation of fundamental rights that have a general character – in that they affect a multitude of persons –, and the causes of which are of a structural nature – that is, that given their regularity, they are not originated exclusively in the respondent authority, and therefore, their solution demands the joint action of several agencies. In these conditions, given that thousands of people are in a similar situation, and if each and every one of them used the tutela complaint, they would unnecessarily overcrowd the judicial system, it is advisable to issue orders to the competent authorities so that they exercise their competencies to eliminate this unconstitutional state of affairs.
>
> Colombian prisons are characterized by overcrowding, serious deficiencies in public services, dominance of violence, extortion and corruption, and lack of opportunities and means for rehabilitation of inmates. The Ombudsman's Office is correct in stating that prisons have become mere warehouses of persons. This situation coincides completely with the definition of an unconstitutional state of affairs.[13]

In another passage, the Court justified its intervention as a protection of a political minority. The Court stressed that prison inmates are "outcasts" and are not an "interest group that can make its voice heard." According to the Court,

> the constitutional judge is bound to take up the cause of forgotten minorities, that is, those groups that hardly have any access to political organs. For this reason, the Constitutional Court is called to act in situations like this, by calling attention on the unconstitutional state of affairs present in the Colombian penitentiary system which demands measures from different branches and organs of political power, with a view to solving the state of affairs prevailing in Colombian prisons.[14]

The Court ordered government authorities to design a plan within three months and to implement it within the next four years, in order to overcome this

relatoria/1998/SU250-98.htm (Colom.); C.C., Apr. 28, 1998, Sentencia T-153/98, https://www.corteconstitucional.gov.co/relatoria/1998/t-153-98.htm (Colom.).

11 C.C., Feb. 2, 2000, Sentencia SU-090/00, https://www.corteconstitucional.gov.co/relatoria/2000/SU090-00.htm (Colom.).

12 *See* César Rodríguez-Garavito, *Beyond the Courtroom: The Impact of Judicial Activism on Socioeconomic Rights in Latin America*, 89 TEX. L. REV. 1669 (2011).

13 C.C., Sentencia T-153/98, *supra* note 10.

14 *Id.*

unconstitutional state of affairs. The decision led to the construction of new prisons and other specific measures, but did not solve overcrowding.[15]

However, Decision T-153 of 1998 is a foundational precedent for the application of the unconstitutional state of affairs doctrine. It laid down the two main features of an unconstitutional state of affairs – the massive violation of rights due to structural causes – and outlined a basic case for its political legitimacy – the protection of "forgotten minorities."

The early cases showed the Court's experimentation with remedies. It started by just informing the government. Then it added a general order to correct failures. By mid-1998, the orders involved a policy, plan, or program, as well as a delay to design or implement it (see Table 9.1). The main lesson learned from these decisions has been the need for a robust follow-up mechanism, which was first implemented in the IDPs case of 2004.

9.2.2 *The IDPs Case*

The largest state of unconstitutional affairs – in both the range of issues considered and the number of people protected – was declared in 2004 (Decision T-025) to protect all IDPs in the country,[16] millions at the time, as well as future IDPs, whose number reached more than 7 million in 2016 when the peace agreement with the Revolutionary Armed Forces of Colombia (FARC) was signed. The Court decided to join all the IDP *tutela* cases and asked the government to explain why access to humanitarian aid, housing, education, health, among other services, and rights was so scant. The government explained that the budget was insufficient and that the responsible administrative agencies were overburdened. The Court concluded that several fundamental rights – from freedom of residence and movement to access to humanitarian aid, health services, land, housing, and education – of all IDPs were being violated in a massive, protracted, and reiterated manner. Each case was just a manifestation of structural failures. The structural problem was caused, according to the Court, by the deep gap that existed between what the law promised to the IDPs, on the one hand, and the scant financial resources allocated to protect and assist IDPs, as well as the state's precarious institutional capacity to implement public policies, on the other.

15 *See* Rodríguez-Garavito, *supra* note 12. *See also* LIBARDO JOSÉ ARIZA & MANUEL ITURRALDE, LOS MUROS DE LA INFAMIA. PRISIONES EN COLOMBIA Y AMÉRICA LATINA 63 (2011).

16 C.C., Jan. 22, 2004, Sentencia T-025/04 (Judge Manuel José Cepeda Espinosa, unanimous), https://www.corteconstitucional.gov.co/relatoria/2004/t-025-04.htm (Colom.). On this decision, its follow-up and effects, *see* CÉSAR RODRÍGUEZ GARAVITO & DIANA RODRÍGUEZ FRANCO, CORTES Y CAMBIO SOCIAL. CÓMO LA CORTE CONSTITUCIONAL TRANSFORMÓ EL DESPLAZAMIENTO FORZADO EN COLOMBIA (2010). *See also* JUDICIAL PROTECTION OF INTERNALLY DISPLACED PERSONS: THE COLOMBIAN EXPERIENCE (Rodolfo Arango Rivadeneira ed., 2009).

TABLE 9.1 *Declarations of unconstitutional states of affairs by the Colombian Constitutional Court prior to 2004*

Decision	Judge	Subject	Did the Court issue orders beyond the concrete case?	Did the Court establish a reporting or follow-up mechanism?
SU-559/97	Eduardo Cifuentes	Very low enrollment of municipal public school teachers in compulsory social security plan.	No.	No.
T-068/98	Alejandro Martínez	Heavy backlog in decisions on application for public pension.	Yes. Called on the government to "correct failures in organization and procedure."	No. But the Court called on independent institutions to monitor compliance and report back to the Court.
T-153/98	Eduardo Cifuentes	Prison overcrowding.	Yes. Ordered the government to design a plan for prison building and refurbishment within three months, and to implement it within four years. Also ordered the suspension of a contract for the renovation of a prison, and ordered the separation of convicted prisoners from persons in pretrial detention.	No.
SU-250/98	Alejandro Martínez	No merit selection of notaries, even	Yes. Ordered the government to	No.

(continued)

TABLE 9.1 *(continued)*

Decision	Judge	Subject	Did the Court issue orders beyond the concrete case?	Did the Court establish a reporting or follow-up mechanism?
		though the 1991 Constitution ordered all notaries to be appointed by merit.	carry out a competitive examination for notaries within six months.	
T-590/98	Alejandro Martínez	Threats against the lives of human rights defenders.	Yes. Ordered all state authorities to "cease this situation," requested independent institutions to prioritize protection of the right to life of human rights defenders, called on all residents of Colombia to defend human rights "as a foundation of peaceful coexistence."	No.

In this decision, the Court summarized the conditions for the declaration of an unconstitutional state of affairs, as follows:

> Among the factors assessed by the Court to define whether there is an unconstitutional state of affairs, the following should be noted: (i) the massive and widespread violation of several constitutional rights that affects a significant number of people; (ii) the prolonged omission of the authorities in fulfilling their obligations to guarantee the rights; (iii) the adoption of unconstitutional practices (i.e. the refusal of public servants to protect a right already protected by the Constitutional Court unless a judge orders them to do so) such as requiring individuals to present Tutela petitions as part of the (bureaucratic) procedure to protect the violated right[17]; (iv)

17 Some public entities refused to grant a social benefit to petitioners entitled to it unless the petitioner had previously secured an order from the *tutela* judge confirming that the petitioner is entitled to

> the non-issuance of legislative, administrative or budgetary measures necessary to avoid the violation of rights; (v) the existence of a social problem whose solution involves the intervention of several entities, requires the adoption of a complex and coordinated set of actions and requires a level of resources that requires an important additional budgetary effort; (vi) if all the people affected by the same problem resorted to Tutela to obtain the protection of their rights, there would be greater judicial congestion.

The Court protected the fundamental rights of each individual that filed a *tutela* complaint and ordered the responsible agency to act to protect their fundamental rights. But it also issued a number of complex structural orders aimed at overcoming the unconstitutional state of affairs and therefore protecting the rights of all IDPs.[18] Moreover, for the first time the Court retained jurisdiction after issuing the judgment and adopted a robust follow-up mechanism. As opposed to Decision T-068/98, in which the Court simply asked for reports on compliance with its order, in T-025/04 the Court analyzed the reports and then continued issuing specific orders to different state institutions after the judgment.

The remedies were designed taking into account the complexity of the context and the functions of the political branches. For example, the Court did not order additional spending on IDPs. Instead, it ordered the government itself to estimate such increase and, within a one-year period given by the Court, to decide either to regress in the protection of IDPs' rights due to lack of money or to abide by its legal promises apportioning gradually each following year more public resources to ensure for IDPs the effective enjoyment of their rights. The government chose to increase the budget, and it did so significantly year after year. Moreover, nongovernmental organizations (NGOs) friendly to the cause of IDPs were invited by the Court to propose to the government how to solve IDPs' problems in successive hearings held by the Court over several years.

A large number of structural orders, in addition to individual orders for the benefit of the petitioners, were issued – far too many orders to be reproduced here (nearly forty in all). The orders adopted as the case developed became more specific and included orders to adopt programs to protect distinctly vulnerable groups of IDPs, such as children, women, persons with disabilities, ethnic groups, among others, with tighter time frames, in the event of initial noncompliance.[19]

Although the Court promoted a gradual approach to solving the structural problems, it did not accept paralysis. The Court required the government to adopt explicit timetables to measure progress as well as result indicators to assess whether

receive the social benefit. The *tutela* judgment thus became an additional document to be attached to the petition.

[18] In this sense, the Court followed a "two track" approach, combining both simple and complex remedies. *See* David Landau, *Choosing between Simple and Complex Remedies in Socio-economic Rights Cases*, 69 U. Toronto L. J. 105 (2019).

[19] See the Court's summary of follow-up decisions in https://www.corteconstitucional.gov.co/T-025-04/autos.php.

the progress in fact ensured the effective enjoyment of rights for an increasing number of IDPs.

The impact of this decision went beyond the political upheaval it generated. The government significantly increased the budget, adopted specific policies to protect IDPs responsive to the differential needs of the most vulnerable, established clear responsibilities in several agencies and improved coordination among them, adopted result indicators of the effective enjoyment of rights by IDPs, and reported periodically to the Court. Despite the progress achieved on several fronts, IDP-rights organizations have requested the Court to maintain the declaration of an unconstitutional state of affairs since they consider that lifting the state would lead the government to regress and most IDPs still do not effectively enjoy their rights. This decision also promoted greater civic engagement and empowered civil society organizations to participate in constructive public policy discussions with the government. This decision had the effect of prompting greater public deliberation, rather than judicially foreclosing the discussion. Here, as in other cases, the Court initiated a dialogue within constitutional parameters, but did not impose a final word on complex issues of public policy. The impact of the Court's approach extended beyond the courts: Even Congress approved a statute to protect victims of the armed conflict (Law 1448 of 2011) and to create additional agencies with better institutional capacity to govern effectively. The 2016 Peace Agreement with FARC guerrilla incorporates the concepts developed by the Court to protect all victims of the internal armed conflict, not only IDPs.

The IDPs case follow-up is still ongoing. The Court created a special three-judge chamber in charge of follow-up, with the support of a team of clerks.

The IDPs decision, along with its multiple follow-up orders, is a pivotal case in the Court's practice regarding unconstitutional states of affairs and, more broadly, structural decisions. The magnitudes were as huge as the IDPs problem. The agencies involved comprised not only half the ministerial cabinet and several administrative agencies but also policies in fields that had been previously unexplored. The decision also displayed a number of features that were largely absent from the pre-2004 court decisions, including a closer diagnosis of the multiple policy problems and their possible solutions, the empowering of civil society organizations that supported IDPs, and the design of more detailed remedies with differential timelines and beneficiaries. While the remedies themselves allowed the government to choose among different courses of action, they were also much more detailed and greater in number. In order to be responsive not only to the conditions of IDPs but also to the challenges faced by the state, the Court adopted a mix of weak, hard, and intermediate remedies.

The remedies themselves, by delving into a greater level of detail, reflected a more serious engagement by the Court with the complexities of the situation and with the difficulties in designing and implementing an effective policy. The remedies in this case were more narrowly directed toward solving specific policy problems than they were aimed at merely denouncing a worrisome situation. They were more responsive to the needs of IDPs, differentiating among vulnerable groups.

Additionally, the declaration of an unconstitutional state of affairs was turned into an operative concept. Whereas the pre-2004 decisions used the unconstitutional state of affairs doctrine as a call for action, Decision T-025 used it as a prerequisite for the issuance of structural remedies, with measurable targets, explicit delays, clear responsibilities, and explicit governmental accountability to IDPs, as well as result indicators on whether the situation had improved. Thus, the Court's follow-up procedures tied its retention of jurisdiction to the overcoming of the unconstitutional state of affairs, indicating that as long as this state of affairs continued, the Court would continue to monitor the situation and issue follow-up orders.

9.2.3 *After the IDPs Case*

Since the IDPs case, the Court has declared four states of unconstitutional affairs (while refusing to declare others requested by parties).[20] All adopted a follow-up mechanism.

In 2013, the Court declared an unconstitutional state of affairs with regard to the administrative backlog in Colombia's pension administrator, Colpensiones. This was a peculiar case in that the request for the declaration came from Colpensiones itself, a new governmental agency that inherited, in a poorly designed transition, the backlog, administrative chaos, and incomplete information from the Institute of Social Security, which had to be liquidated. The Court issued orders directed at ensuring that pensions were recognized and paid but also alleviating the administrative burden on Colpensiones by suspending deadlines and allowing it to catch up on backlogged work. Notably, it excluded contempt of court proceedings for non-timely compliance with previous *tutela* orders for a period of time, since the director of Colpensiones could solve the problems in a more effective way outside of jail.[21]

This decision differed from prior strategies in that, instead of combining simple and complex remedies, the Court opted for issuing a structural decision and suspending the execution of specific orders imparted by *tutela* judges while the administrative agency attempted to overcome the chaotic situation generated by the transition. Moreover, the delays were short and the follow-up focused on result indicators designed by Colpensiones itself. After two years, Colpensiones managed to solve the administrative structural problems and the Court lifted the state of unconstitutional affairs.[22]

20 After this chapter was written and as it was in final edit, the Constitutional Court announced the declaration of a new unconstitutional state of affairs related to the implementation of the security guarantees for former guerrilla fighters included in the Peace Agreement between the Government of Colombia and FARC. C.C., Jan. 27, 2022, Sentencia SU-020/22. See the press release at https://www.corteconstitucional.gov.co/comunicados/Comunicado%20No.%2001%20Enero%2027%20de%202022.pdf.

21 C.C., June 5, 2013, Auto A-110/13, https://www.corteconstitucional.gov.co/relatoria/autos/2013/a110-13.htm (Colom.).

22 C.C., Dec. 18, 2015, Sentencia T-774/15, https://www.corteconstitucional.gov.co/relatoria/2015/t-774-15.htm (Colom.).

In 2013 and 2015, the Court issued two different decisions relating to prison conditions. Decision T-388 of 2013 declared an unconstitutional state of affairs. In addition to factors cited in earlier decisions, the Court also explained that "(iii) the system has institutionalized clearly unconstitutional practices in its daily functioning; [and] (iv) there is a clear absence of legislative, administrative and budgetary measures that are urgently required."[23]

The Court issued individual orders to protect the petitioners and structural orders to overcome the unconstitutional state of affairs. The Court focused on six prisons at which the government was ordered to ensure "dignified and humane conditions of subsistence" for prison inmates, including reasonable meal times and bath times, sanitation conditions, availability of medical services, and supply of mattresses, pillows, and blankets; it would also have to create work and study spaces. The government was also ordered to observe a rule of "decreasing equilibrium," according to which new inmates should be allowed in the prison only if levels of occupation in the prison were not increased. The Court observed that "all measures are open to institutional dialogue, and the court has the possibility of adjusting the remedies, as far as [is] required to obtain the effective enjoyment of rights."

The Court did not retain jurisdiction to monitor compliance with its decision, entrusting this to the lower instance courts that decided the initial *tutela* complaints, but this changed later.

In 2015, the Court issued another decision on the same subject: Decision T-762.[24] In this new judgment, the Court reiterated the existence of the unconstitutional state of affairs previously declared in Decision T-388/13, but also declared that "Colombian criminal justice policy has been reactive, populist, non-reflexive, volatile, incoherent and subordinated to security policy," and that "the past management of criminal justice policy in this country has contributed to maintaining the massive violation of fundamental rights of persons deprived of liberty and currently impedes the rehabilitating goal of punishment." Thus, while Decision T-388/13 focused on conditions in specific prisons, Decision T-762/15 broadened the scope of its declaration to include the dysfunctionalities of criminal justice policy.

The Court then issued individual orders and a number of structural orders. The new structural orders dealt with more detailed aspects of the crisis, such as the deficiencies of information systems or the lack of real rehabilitation programs, and

[23] C.C., June 28, 2013, Sentencia T-388/13, https://www.corteconstitucional.gov.co/relatoria/2013/t-388-13.htm (Colom.) (also referring to other factors, including that "(i) the constitutional rights of detained persons are violated in a widespread and generalized manner; (ii) the obligations to respect, protect and ensure, derived from said rights, have been breached for a long time; ... (v) the solution of structural problems requires the intervention of several authorities, which must carry out complex and coordinated actions; and[,] finally, (vi) if all persons deprived of their liberty who are subject to this same state of affairs presented tutela complaints (or other means to defend their rights), like the petitioners did in the complaints that were consolidated in this case, the judicial system would be further congested").

[24] C.C., Dec. 16, 2015, Sentencia T-762/15, https://www.corteconstitucional.gov.co/relatoria/2015/t-762-15.htm (Colom.).

also turned the spotlight on the phenomenon known as "punitive populism," in which Congress reacts to individual news of crime by toughening criminal laws and aggravating the situation in Colombia's prisons. The Court retained jurisdiction in this case, but delegated close monitoring to the Ombudsman's Office, which would itself have to report back to the Court.

In a later decision, the Court instituted a special chamber to monitor compliance with both prison decisions, which itself has continued to issue follow-up orders, including orders on how to design indicators to report progress.[25]

The most recent decision declaring an unconstitutional state of affairs is Decision T-302/17, in which the Court protected the rights to water, food, and health of the children of the Wayuu community, which lives in the Guajira Department, the deserted northernmost region of Colombia.[26] The Court stated that a

> generalized, unreasonable and disproportionate violation of the fundamental rights of children of an indigenous ethnic group, caused by the structural failures of national and territorial entities, configures an unconstitutional state of affairs that must be overcome in a coordinated and articulated manner by all State entities, especially if the dignified existence of girls and boys is seriously compromised as well as their harmonious and integral development (due to lack of water, food and health), thus compromising the very existence of the indigenous people.

The Court issued structural orders, but it delegated the follow-up to the District Tribunal of the Guajira Department. It ordered the responsible agencies

> to set up a Special Mechanism for Monitoring and Evaluation of Public Policies to overcome the unconstitutional state of affairs . . . aimed at: . . . (ii) fulfilling the four conditions established in operative paragraph ten [mainly, achieve the minimum levels set in the basic result indicators of child nutrition] . . . (iii) meet the minimum constitutional objectives established in operative paragraph four of this judgment [mainly, eight objectives to be reached gradually concerning access to clean water, food, health, and dialogue with the indigenous authorities].

Like the IDPs case, in this decision the Court set out the goals to be achieved, but left the choice of means to the government. Unlike the IDPs case, monitoring was left to the lower court which had decided the *tutela* complaint in the first place. A notable difference between this case and other previous cases was that the lower courts had already issued structural remedies in their decisions on the *tutela* complaint. The District Tribunal had ordered the president to design and implement a plan to ensure access to water, food, and health services, and the Supreme Court of Justice had added an order for the president to fix "clear and detailed deadlines." The Constitutional Court's decision, unlike in previous cases in which

[25] C.C., Feb. 22, 2018, Auto 121/18, https://www.corteconstitucional.gov.co/relatoria/autos/2018/a121-18.htm (Colom.).

[26] C.C., May 8, 2017, Sentencia T-302/17, *supra* note 1.

lower courts had either denied the petitions or adopted only individual remedies, was built on the work of the lower courts. This is perhaps the reason why the Court decided to trust the District Tribunal to monitor compliance with the decision.

After this decision, the Court decided subsequent cases relating to the situation of the Wayuu community in which individual remedies were denied, because the Court had already declared an unconstitutional state of affairs and adopted structural remedies.[27]

In this third stage, the Court built upon the experience of the 2004 IDPs case (see Table 9.2). First, the unconstitutional state of affairs served as a tool with which to scrutinize specific problems of ineffective government. Perhaps the largest difference between the pre-2004 and the post-2004 cases is that newer cases include thorough and well-informed assessments of the situation and of existing policies. These assessments have, in turn, promoted public deliberation, both inside and outside government, about the characteristics of the problem and the ways to address it. They have also allowed the Court and the government agencies to focus on specific subsets of policy and institutional capacity problems.

TABLE 9.2 *Declarations of unconstitutional states of affairs by the Colombian Constitutional Court after 2004*

Decision	Judge	Subject	Did the Court issue orders beyond the concrete case?	Did the Court establish a follow-up mechanism?
A-110/13	Luis Ernesto Vargas	Backlog in processing pension applications.	Yes.	Yes, by the Court itself.
T-388/13	María Victoria Calle	Prison conditions.	Yes.	Yes. First it delegated monitoring to the Ombudsman. Then, a special chamber at the Constitutional Court was formed.
T-762/15	Gloria Stella Ortiz	Prison conditions and criminal justice policy.	Yes.	
T-302/17	Aquiles Arrieta	Famine of Indigenous children in a deserted region.	Yes.	Yes. Lower court close to the Indigenous community.

27 C.C., Aug. 31, 2018, Sentencia T-359/18, https://www.corteconstitucional.gov.co/relatoria/2018/t-359-18.htm (Colom.); C.C., Sentencia T-415/18, Oct. 10, 2018, https://www.corteconstitucional.gov.co/relatoria/2018/t-415-18.htm (Colom.).

Second, the newer cases include a larger battery of structural remedies, which follow the greater level of detail of the Court's assessments. Thus, instead of a general order calling on the government to solve a situation, the Court can issue a number of more specific orders relating to the different aspects of the problem, as was done in the IDPs case.

Third, the newer cases have experimented with other ways of monitoring compliance, without creating a large infrastructure within the Court, including entrusting monitoring to lower courts, but retaining jurisdiction.

9.3 PROMOTING – NOT REPLACING – AN EFFECTIVE GOVERNMENT

There have been only ten declarations of states of unconstitutional affairs in the history of the Colombian Constitutional Court – out of more than 20,000 judgments issued since the Court began its work in 1992. The follow-up, when retained by the Court, generates a heavy burden for the institution. Nevertheless, the impact of the doctrine has been significant.

The unconstitutional state of affairs doctrine has served to shift the attention of state agencies toward large groups of persons, generally extremely vulnerable and marginalized. By issuing large-scale, even countrywide remedies in some cases, the Court has extended judicial protection to persons who would not have realistically been able to access the Court in individual cases.[28] Moreover, the doctrine has led to better diagnosis of the structural causes and to more specific and responsive policies. In some cases, the structural problem was solved. In others, thousands or millions of Colombians not only felt protected but received effective state attention and benefits that allow them to enjoy their rights, even though the structural causes are still unsolved and the follow-up continues.

The unconstitutional state of affairs doctrine primarily seeks to address extreme cases of executive dysfunction, which lead to massive and recurrent violations of rights. The Court's cases have addressed inadequate assessments of serious problems, precarious administrative capacities, insufficient funding, as well as issues similar to both "blind spots" and "burdens of inertia."[29] These blockages, however, have occurred and been addressed mostly in administrative agencies and not in the legislative process: most decisions summarized in this chapter did not require the adoption of new legislation, merely the proper implementation of existing legislative mandates.

These cases (see Table 9.3) show that democratic government may exist and still be unable or unwilling to address specific policy problems, thus disproportionately affecting the rights of large portions of the population. A government may be ineffective, for instance, by underfunding programs that are vital for the effective enjoyment of rights (prison cases and IDPs case), by lacking a responsive policy through which to

[28] *See* David Landau, *The Reality of Social Rights Enforcement*, 53 HARV. INT'L L. J. 190 (2012).

[29] *See* Rosalind Dixon, *Creating Dialogue about Socioeconomic Rights: Strong-Form versus Weak-Form Judicial Review Revisited*, 5 INT'L J. CONST. L. 391 (2007).

TABLE 9.3 *Declarations by the Court, along with the dysfunctionalities addressed*

Case	Dysfunctionalities addressed
SU-559/97 (low social security enrollment of teachers)	Poorly designed system for allocation of funds to subnational units
T-068/98 (backlog in pension processing)	Administrative indifference and excessive red tape
T-153/98 (prison overcrowding)	Political inattention and lack of funding
SU-250/98 (no merit selection of notaries)	Lack of administrative processes for executing the law
T-590/98 (threats against human rights defenders)	Political inattention to the problem and precarious administrative capacity
T-025/04 (IDPs)	Precarious administrative capacities, lack of policies, lack of relevant information, absence of a clear characterization of the problem, and insufficient funding
A-110/13 (chaos in administrative transition)	New administrative entity overwhelmed
T-388/13 (prison conditions)	Political inattention, lack of funding, and incoherence in criminal policy
T-762/15 (criminal policy)	
T-302/17 (famine affecting Wayuu children)	Lack of policy and lack of relevant information

address a pressing problem (IDPs case and Wayuu case), or simply by not implementing a long-standing legislative mandate (1998 notaries case). In turn, the remedies adopted by the Court in the unconstitutional state of affairs cases have promoted key aspects of an effective government, including fact-based assessments, rational planning, policy evaluation and adjustment, and public participation, among others.[30]

9.4 CONCLUSIONS

Although problems still remain, the unconstitutional state of affairs cases have gradually improved the quality of Colombian public administration in specific policy domains, which in turn has enabled state authorities to better protect and ensure fundamental rights.

The unconstitutional state of affairs doctrine has not been seriously questioned in Colombia. Although some constitutional lawyers and scholars have expressed misgivings about separation of powers, the political branches have actively embraced the role of the Constitutional Court in the unconstitutional state of affairs cases, and the Congress has even declined to pass legislation aimed at curtailing the power of

[30] On the function of structural remedies, *see* Guillermo Otálora Lozano, *Commandeering the Institutions: The Legitimacy of Structural Judicial Remedies in Comparative Perspective*, 12 VIENNA J. INT'L CONST. L. 387 (2019).

the Court to protect rights beyond the specific case. The doctrine, and, more broadly, the power of courts to issue structural remedies, is now an accepted part of Colombian constitutional law.

The unconstitutional state of affairs doctrine has been an exceptional tool enabling the Colombian Constitutional Court to address the failure of government agencies in securing fundamental rights for specific populations or in specific policy domains. The declaration of an unconstitutional state of affairs can trigger new policy discussions, which, in turn, can promote focused public deliberation, empower participation, and strengthen administrative processes relating to the design, implementation, and evaluation of public policies.

10

Courts and Effective Governance

Mark Tushnet and Madhav Khosla[*]

10.1 INTRODUCTION: THE IMPORTANCE OF GOVERNMENT CAPACITY

Governments are put in place to carry out policies. Effective governance means that they have the capacity to implement those policies. As Samuel Huntington observed, "[t]he most important political distinction among countries concerns not their form of government but their degree of government."[1] For our purposes, state capacity is the ability of a government-in-place to develop and implement policies that its leaders believe will improve national well-being. The capacity to govern includes having the required material resources, the personnel for whatever is necessary to deliver the policies to their beneficiaries, and a bureaucratic organization that enables high-level officials to implement policies.

How does state capacity feature in constitutional adjudication? And how can courts contribute to effective governance? Of course, they can interpret constitutions and statutes to authorize government officials to use whatever capacity they have to implement their chosen policies. At the constitutional level they can ensure that governments implement their policies in a manner that does as little as reasonably possible to impair constitutional interests.

Do courts engage the question of state capacity? In doing so, can courts further a government's capacity? This chapter suggests that the answer is "Sometimes." Several case studies sketch some mechanisms by which courts negotiate the question of state capacity – and, in some cases and particular ways, help increase state capacity. They include giving existing bureaucracies incentives to modify their workings, directing decision-makers to consult more widely with "outsiders," and absorbing into themselves some tasks and thereby addressing the lack of state capacity to perform those tasks.

[*] This chapter is adapted from *Courts, Constitutionalism, and State Capacity: A Preliminary Inquiry*, American Journal of Comparative Law (forthcoming).

[1] Samuel P. Huntington, Political Order in Changing Societies 1 (1968).

This chapter considers case studies from Brazil, South Africa, and India. The cases capture how judiciaries can encourage the government to confront specific institutional realities; how they can force the government to adopt better informed policies; and how they can themselves absorb functions that are being underperformed by other institutions. We explore how the institutional role that courts play will, in an important sense, be shaped by the context in which they operate not only in terms of power relations and public opinion but also in terms of what can and cannot be achieved at the level of capacity. Our emphasis on building state capacity also speaks to the traditional concern in constitutional law for limiting state power. Abuses of power do not occur only in strong states, where the machinery of government can be used in a systematic and organized fashion to limit civil-political liberties. They occur in weak states as well, where the form of abuse involves agents acting independently in an environment where the state is unable to rein in its agents. An important dynamic exists between creating the state and preventing the misuse of power.

10.2 BRAZIL: INCREASING BUREAUCRATIC CAPACITY THROUGH STRONG INCENTIVES

Brazil's 1988 Constitution, like many post-1945 constitutions, contains a right to "health."[2] City, state, and national governments administer the delivery of health care, both by operating facilities themselves and by contracting with private providers for that delivery.[3] The Ministry of Health maintains a list of medications that will be provided to Brazilians who demonstrate a need for them.[4] The list, periodically updated, includes many medications, but not those the Ministry regards as experimental or whose benefits, the Ministry determines, have not been adequately established.

A Brazilian whose request for a specific medication (supported only by a doctor's prescription) has been denied can seek judicial review of the denial.[5] The complainant can argue, for example, that the Ministry mistakenly defined the medication as experimental, or that its identification of the permitted dosage of an approved medication is inconsistent with sound medical judgment. Or, in a constitutional register, the complainant can assert that the medication, though experimental, is necessary to protect the patient's constitutional right to health: the patient's life is at risk, all approved medications have failed to treat the patient's condition, and there is

2 Constituicao Federal [C.F.] [Constitution] arts. 6, 196 (Braz.).

3 According to Hoffman and Bentes, this is done "through more than seventy different payment modalities." Florian F. Hoffman & Fernando R.N.M. Bentes, *Accountability for Social and Economic Rights in Brazil*, *in* Courting Social Justice 100, 107 (Varun Gauri & David M. Brinks eds., 2008).

4 *Id.* at 127 (referring to the "*Consenso*, or list of approved medications and procedures").

5 *See* Octávio Luis Motta Ferraz, Health as a Human Right: The Politics and Judicialization of Health in Brazil 238–51 (2020).

some reason to believe that the medication might cure or at least alleviate the medical condition.

In such cases, Brazilian courts have historically regularly granted the patients' pleas, finding that denying the medication would violate the constitutional right to health. Success rates have been reported as being between 80 and 90 percent.[6] In such instances, many of the medications were quite expensive precisely because they were experimental or had not yet been shown to be effective.[7]

The result of such litigation has been predictable: large financial burdens on health ministry budgets. "More than half of the Brazilian Unified Health Care System (SUS) budget in 2010," it has been observed, "was spent on pharmaceuticals and hospital procedures."[8] These right-to-medication cases clearly affected – or distorted – the allocation of resources, both within the health budget and across budget categories.

Responding to the burgeoning right-to-medication cases, the Brazilian Supreme Federal Court, the nation's highest court for constitutional matters, convened a public audience or hearing in 2009. The Court "provided guidelines" for the courts to use in right-to-medication cases, then updated them in 2019: "[F]or benefits not already offered by the Brazilian health care system ..., the courts should distinguish cases where the medication/treatment was simply not considered by the legislative or executive branch from cases in which the government has considered the possibility and decided not to offer the medication/treatment."[9] The Court held that the government could not be required to provide "experimental drugs" whose efficacy and safety had not been proven. But, the Court noted, the government would be required to supply a medication that had been registered abroad if their registration in the Brazilian list of medications had been requested but not approved within a reasonable period (apparently, within one year). The Court further held that actions of this sort would need to be filed against the national health ministry rather than local ones.[10]

These guidelines can and do have powerful effects within the health bureaucracy. The national health ministry can reduce its costs by updating the list of approved medications because, having done so, it can negotiate with the drugs' manufacturers for discounts that would be unavailable were it to pay for the medications as result of

[6] Ana Paula de Barcellos, *Sanitation Rights, Public Law Litigation, and Inequality: A Case Study from Brazil*, 16 Health & Hum. Rts. J. 35, 36 (2014); Hoffman & Bentes, *supra* note 3, at 119.

[7] *See* Motta Ferraz, *supra* note 5, at 130–31 (reporting that "in 2012, 18 drugs and in 2016, ten drugs generated approximately 85% of the total costs of judicialization," and that in 2016, the 10 most expensive medications were awarded to 995 patients at a per capita cost of approximately USD 300,000).

[8] de Barcellos, *supra* note 6, at 36.

[9] Mariana Mota Prado, *The Debatable Role of Courts in Brazil's Health Care System: Does Litigation Harm or Help?*, 41 J. L. Med. & Ethics 124, 131 (2013).

[10] *Id.* at 131. The 2019 decision is described in Ingo Wolfgang Sarlet & Mariana Filchtiner Figueiredo, *Health as an Enforceable Positive Right: The Brazilian Supreme Federal Court's Case Law on the Access to Medicines*, 102 KritV (2019), DOI: 10.5771/2193-7869-2019-2-117.

litigation. Hoffmann and Bentes suggest that this occurs because "[o]nce a certain litigation density [that is, a significant volume of litigation dealing with a single medication] has been reached, public authorities tend to seek cover by including the medication in the SUS list . . . ."[11] Further, and in contrast to earlier times, when the authorities address themselves to the inclusion of a new medication or procedure on the approved list and offer reasoned justifications for refusing to do so, any litigation that ensues is transformed from the domain of constitutional to administrative law.

Rather than issuing structural injunctions that give the courts a continuing role in overseeing health ministries, the Brazilian approach may build state capacity more effectively. Structural injunctions attempt to reform state bureaucracies coercively, raising the possibility of bureaucratic resistance. Perhaps worse, structural relief does not give bureaucracies strong incentives to overcome the problems of incompetence, inertia, or even corruption that give rise to problems generating litigation. What is notable in the Brazilian case is the use of incentives to improve capacity. Judicial decisions giving bureaucracies incentives to increase their capacity are not a magic bullet. Hoffmann and Bentes have observed, for example, that the "one stop" shopping mechanism basically failed because the "stocking with medicines was delayed and insufficient."[12] Where capacity is absent because of incompetence or corruption, judicial remedies of any sort are likely to fail, and remedies that shift responsibility from the incompetent or corrupt institutions to other ones might be more promising. However, where capacity is absent because of bureaucratic inertia, a small-ish coercive shove may be able to help improve outcomes.

10.3 SOUTH AFRICA: ENABLING CAPACITY THROUGH PLANNING AND CITIZEN ENGAGEMENT

The 1996 South African Constitution's recognition of socioeconomic rights signaled a major moment in modern constitutionalism. The early years of scholarship on socioeconomic rights in South Africa were primarily focused on three cases: *Soobramoney*, *Grootboom*, and *Treatment Action Campaign*. These cases were seen by global commentators as offering a new model of judicial review – a model that had demonstrated the prospect of "weak-form" judicial review.

These initial cases are typically contrasted with more recent decisions of the South African Constitutional Court, which are viewed as "weaken[ing] the potential of socio-economic rights litigation to produce substantial benefits for poor people."[13] The particular charge has been that the Court has moved away from developing substantive commitments, and instead narrowly focuses on procedural

[11] Hoffman & Bentes, *supra* note 3, at 137.

[12] *Id.* at 131.

[13] Stuart Wilson & Jackie Dugard, *Constitutional Jurisprudence: The First and Second Waves*, *in* Socio-economic Rights in South Africa: Symbols or Substance? 35, 37 (Malcolm Langford et al. eds., 2014).

considerations. We consider the nature of the "second wave" of socioeconomic rights adjudication in South Africa by turning to two decisions: *Olivia Road*[14] and *Blue Moonlight*.[15]

In *Olivia Road*, hundreds of residents in Johannesburg challenged a mass-eviction program. The program was part of a plan to redevelop the city in ambitious ways, but it was noticeably silent on the problem of relocating persons who would be evicted. Here, the questions were whether the housing program was sustainable given Section 26 of the Constitution; whether the eviction of persons who had no real alternative shelter could be ordered; and what, if any, restrictions and safeguards might be placed upon such an order for eviction. In an interim order, the Constitutional Court declared that the state and the applicants must "engage with each other meaningfully . . . in an effort to resolve the differences and difficulties aired in this application" as per the constitutional and legal framework involved.[16] Subsequently, an agreement was reached on certain issues whereas others remained to be determined.

A central feature of the reasonableness requirement under provisions like Section 26, the Court observed, was that state action must be *implemented* reasonably. That is, the right in Section 26 was not only substantive in the guarantee that it provided but also procedural. Yet, the Court noted, no effort had been made to engage with the persons evicted prior to their removal. Engagement between both parties, the Court felt, might enable a kind of participation, allowing each group to better understand the objectives and constraints of the other. Importantly, the Court did not read any specific substantive requirement into Section 26. It stated that, depending on the situation, it might be "reasonable to make permanent housing available" or equally "to provide no housing at all."[17] What mattered was "the response of the municipality in the engagement process."[18] Requiring the government to engage meaningfully with the residents requires the government to *create* a new, though in each case ad hoc, institution for engaging the residents. The remedy, that is, helped to expand state capacity.

The general sense has been that the substantive rights which the Court's first wave promised have given way to a purely procedural set of guarantees, which have been relatively uninterested in the real freedom that people enjoy.[19] Brian Ray's book, *Engaging with Social Rights*, provides a somewhat different analysis.[20] The *Blue Moonlight* case plays a major role in Ray's study.[21] There the Court was faced with

14 Occupants of 51 Olivia Road, Berea Township v. City of Johannesburg [2008] ZACC 1.

15 City of Johannesburg Metropolitan Municipality v. Blue Moonlight Properties 39 (Pty) Ltd [2011] ZACC 33.

16 *See Olivia Road*, *supra* note 14, at ¶ 5 (excerpting the interim order).

17 *Id.* at ¶ 18.

18 *Id.*

19 *See* Paul O'Connell, *The Death of Socio-economic Rights*, 74 Mod. L. Rev. 532 (2011); Marius Pieterse, *Procedural Relief, Constitutional Citizenship and Socio-economic Rights as Legitimate Expectations*, 28 S. Afr. J. on Hum. Rts. 359 (2012); Wilson & Dugard, *Constitutional Jurisprudence*, *supra* note 13.

20 Brian Ray, Engaging with Social Rights: Procedure, Participation, and Democracy in South Africa's Second Wave (2016).

21 City of Johannesburg Metropolitan Municipality v. Blue Moonlight Properties 2012 (2) BCLR 150 (2011).

the problem of unlawful occupants on private property, and with having to determine the state's obligation to provide housing to the occupants if they were to be evicted. The Court noted that, though *it* could not impose impossible requirements on the state, neither could the state hide under the cover of resource constraints and the like if its budgeting and program-setting were the outcome of failing to understand its constitutional obligations. It further noted that all levels of government were to be involved in eviction cases of the kind, and proceeded to strike down the differentiation between different kinds of occupants (those that had been relocated by the Johannesburg government itself and those that private owners had evicted) in the state's housing policy.

It might be possible to see such a ruling in purely "procedural" terms, but it would hardly be accurate to view the outcome as one that did not significantly alter the rights of homeless persons. Ray's key point is that the Court's second wave reveals a "recharacterization of social rights as tools to enforce democratic accountability."[22] The turn to participation is, for Ray, a defining feature of the Court's orientation in recent years.

Ray's analysis might be carried further. It is worth regarding the "second wave" decisions not only as enabling democratic accountability, which he rightly does, but also as enabling state capacity. A crucial feature in the Constitutional Court's decisions was the recognition that bureaucrats and politicians often have their own agendas that displace the agendas of constituents. This is illustrated in several ways, whether one considers the participation requirements outlined in *Olivia Road* or the scrutiny of budgetary rationales in *Blue Moonlight*. The Court recognized that there are forms of institutional functioning that reveal shortfalls, and that attention to such shortfalls can allow the state to function better. This sensibility was reinforced by other features of the Court's decisions, such as the focus on different levels of government and the emphasis on coordination across state departments and tiers.

As per the Court, a valid program that fulfills the state's constitutional obligation is one that can be implemented. And an implementable program is one that is sensitive to the capacity question. The logic of this position should now be clear: for the state to be effective, it needs to understand how best to work with its own limitations; and understanding that will allow the state to move beyond those limitations. In other words, attention to the problem of capacity will allow the state to develop a more effective program.

10.4 INDIA: ABSORBING WEAK CAPACITY

The criminal justice system is a domain where weak state capacity is often most powerfully revealed. India is no exception to this. With its reality of weak governance, legal reform measures in the domain of criminal justice cannot escape the

[22] RAY, *supra* note 20, at 185.

problem of state capacity. Here we focus on one specific and unique feature of the Indian criminal justice system: its provision for *anticipatory bail*. Under the scheme of anticipatory bail, an individual can be granted bail before he or she is arrested, based on a worry about being arrested; with an order for anticipatory bail in hand, a person who is arrested must be released at the moment of arrest.[23] To compensate for gaps in state capacity, Indian courts have generously interpreted the anticipatory bail mechanism, and thereby sought to absorb the problem of weak capacity.

To better understand the idea of a pre-arrest bail mechanism where courts review claims from both parties, one must turn to the Forty-First Report of the Law Commission of India, submitted in 1969.[24] The Report observed: "The necessity for granting anticipatory bail arises mainly because sometimes influential persons try to implicate their rivals in false causes for the purpose of disgracing them or for other purposes by getting them detained in jail for some days." The Report proceeded to note that false cases of this kind had only increased with greater political competition. Moreover, there was an additional reason for anticipatory bail outside of false cases: "where there are reasonable grounds for holding that a person accused of an offence is not likely to abscond, or otherwise misuse his liberty while on bail, there seems to be no justification to require him to first submit to custody, remain in prison for some days and then apply for bail."[25]

The Report recommended allowing persons who had "a reasonable apprehension" of being arrested to apply to a court, which "may, in its discretion, direct that in the event of his arrest, he shall be released on bail."[26] Four years later, Section 438 of the Code of Criminal Procedure, 1973, enacted such a provision. The section listed factors that might be considered in determining whether a direction should be issued as well as conditions that might be specified in case a direction was issued.

With "false" cases, the weakness in the criminal justice system was the independence and integrity of the police. The police as an institution was not immune from powerful social and political forces, and it lacked the mechanisms to guard against individual officers being influenced. In other cases, the weakness was the judicial system, which resulted in arrested individuals lying in prison for some days, thereby offsetting the very point of bail. Anticipatory bail could respond to these weaknesses.

Initially, the Supreme Court declared that the power to grant anticipatory bail was "somewhat extraordinary in character" and was to be exercised "only in exceptional cases."[27] In time, however, the Court adopted a more liberal view.[28] The core difference between ordinary bail and anticipatory bail, the

23 See Section 438, Code of Criminal Procedure, 1973. *See* Vikramaditya S. Khanna & Kartikey Mahajan, *Anticipatory Bail in India: Addressing Misuse of the Criminal Justice Process?, in* Comparative Criminal Procedure 119 (Jacqueline E. Ross & Stephen C. Thaman eds., 2016).

24 Law Commission of India, Ministry of Law, Government of India, Forty-First Report (1969).

25 *Id.* at 321.

26 *Id.*

27 Balchand Jain v. State of Madhya Pradesh (1976) 4 SCC 572, 576.

28 Gurbaksh Singh Sibbia v. State of Punjab (1980) 2 SCC 565.

Court noted, "is that whereas the former is granted after arrest and therefore means release from the custody of the police, the latter is granted in anticipation of arrest and is therefore effective at the very moment of arrest."[29] The latter was "insurance against police custody."[30] The Court felt that, although police officials had no real incentive to abuse the arrest process for ordinary crimes and criminals, the situation was different when it came to cases that emerged from political rivalries and contests:

> Attended upon such investigations, when the police are not free agents within their sphere of duty, is a great amount of inconvenience, harassment and humiliation. That can even take the form of parading of a respectable person in handcuffs, apparently on way to a court of justice. The foul deed is done when an adversary is exposed to social ridicule and obloquy, no matter when and whether a conviction is secured or is at all possible. It is in order to meet such situations, though not limited to these contingencies, that the power to grant anticipatory bail was introduced into the Code of 1973.[31]

The jurisprudence around anticipatory bail proceeded alongside increased judicial attention toward the abuse of police powers in India. In 1978, the Supreme Court recognized that India faced major criminal law enforcement challenges, with increasing crime proceeding alongside increasing state abuse.[32] Subsequently, in *D. K. Basu*, the Supreme Court confronted the reality of persons being subject to violence and death while in police custody.[33]

The concern for weak state capacity with regard to the police – manifest in cases involving abuse and corruption – thus played a major role in cementing the Supreme Court's broadly liberal attitude toward anticipatory bail and in its checking of police investigative and interrogation practices. Over the past decade, the Court has cautioned against limiting anticipatory bail to a narrow set of exceptional cases, expressed concern over police violence, and highlighted the severity of the state's power to arrest individuals.[34]

The use of anticipatory bail in India has been the source of considerable legal doctrine. Within a broadly liberal approach, courts have considered how specific factual circumstances should shape the exercise of this power and what conditions should be imposed alongside anticipatory bail orders.[35] What remains striking, however, is the stable reality that deeper changes with regard to police reform are nowhere to be seen. The problems of false and unnecessary arrests, the lack of

29 *Id.* at 575.

30 *Id.*

31 *Id.* at 575.

32 Nandini Satpathy v. P.L. Dani (1978) 2 SCC 424, 433, 457–58.

33 D. K. Basu v. State of W.B. (1997) 1 SCC 416.

34 *See* Savitri Agarwal v. State of Maharashtra (2009) 8 SCC 325; Siddharam Satlingappa Mhetre v. State of Maharashtra (2011) 1 SCC 694; Arnesh Kumar v. State of Bihar (2014) 8 SCC 273; People's Union of Civil Liberties v. State of Maharashtra (2014) 10 SCC 635; Bhadresh Bipinbhai Sheth v. State of Gujarat (2016) 1 SCC 152.

35 *See Siddharam Satlingappa Mhetre, supra* note 34.

standards and guidelines and checks with regard to police behavior, and the colonial structure of the police force, and so forth, remain by and large unchanged. As weak state capacity is taken to be a permanent feature of the system, the judicial approach has been to absorb the problem of weak state capacity through a liberal approach toward anticipatory bail.

10.5 CONCLUSION: NEGOTIATING CAPACITY

Our case studies demonstrate the explanatory importance of state capacity. Constitutional doctrine is not only forged out of first principles that address the ideal limits of state power; it also emerges from an understanding of what states are capable of doing. Courts, we have shown, do address, often indirectly but sometimes directly, the question of state capacity in countries where capacity is a real concern. And, in certain cases, courts can contribute to the building of state capacity in important if limited ways. But how precisely should courts act while addressing the problem of weak capacity? In this concluding section, we shift focus from an explanatory analysis of how the problem of state capacity features in constitutional doctrine to a prescriptive assessment of how courts should negotiate gaps in capacity. The idealized model that we conceptualize sees courts as playing a role in building the state – in promoting capacity – in other branches where such capacity does not exist, but then involves courts receding and occupying a restrained posture when capacity does improve. Courts begin as capacity builders but then retreat into the background once other institutions begin to possess greater capacity.

The precise intervention that courts make in improving capacity will necessarily involve some degree of experimentation. In conceiving of a judicial role in building the state, it is worth recalling Michael C. Dorf and Charles F. Sabel's effort to shift the focus in democratic governance from first principles to a more pragmatist orientation.[36] In their vision, institutions should take an experimental approach toward public policy. Courts perform their role by framing their review in the context of what experimentation reveals. Such an approach, as Dorf and Sabel have noted, can provide for new kinds of citizen engagement, and can allow reform to proceed in useful and constructive ways. At the heart of the democratic experimentalist project has been the insight that the solution to a number of public policy problems can be determined only through practice. This fact seems to be especially true of a problem such as weak state capacity, which is deep-seated and systemic, and implicates a range of actors.

Courts might well approach the problem of weak state capacity with strategies envisioned by democratic experimentalism, such as "learning by monitoring." It is difficult to determine *ex ante* what kinds of judicial intervention are likely to

[36] Michael C. Dorf & Charles F. Sabel, A *Constitution of Democratic Experimentalism*, 98 Colum. L. Rev. 267 (1998).

promote capacity building. Courts will have to issue directions and grant remedies based on specific institutional realities – within, of course, what is legitimate and required within the applicable legal framework. Because judicial interventions that address capacity will be targeted and limited, they will not result in wholesale changes, but they can provide meaningful change in small ways, which may in turn lead to larger changes. A judicial engagement of this kind is related to what is now regarded as *dialogic judicial review*.[37] As scholars of comparative constitutional law have shown over the past decade, global practices are no longer exclusively explained by the strong form of judicial review that characterizes American constitutionalism. The idea of a judicial dialogue moves beyond a conflictual framing of the relationship between the legislature and the judiciary. The interpretive moves performed by both branches are part of a conversation, one in which the popular branches of government can deliberate based on constitutional considerations that courts bring to light.

Because judicial efforts at building state capacity will have budgetary implications in more direct ways than others, because they will involve upsetting established bureaucratic practices and institutional inertia, and because there is no single path to an increase in state capacity, judicial intervention may encourage lawmakers and bureaucrats to increase capacity in different ways from those the courts had initially envisaged. Here, to adapt the idealized form of dialogic judicial review, courts may help to bring the question of capacity to the attention of the legislature and prompt it to act in a way that can build the state.[38] The kind of experimentalist, dialogic model that we have in mind is partly driven by the reality of state capacity. Countries with weak state capacity manage to do *some* things remarkably well, and limited, targeted, and engaged judicial interventions that can grapple with the workings of capacity on the ground are likely to be most effective in improving capacity.

The case studies we have presented suggest certain strengths and weaknesses of this stylized model, and of the general ability of courts to address weak capacity in other institutions. In the Brazilian case, we see the potential of an iterative exchange, as the government's response to bureaucratic failures was directly engendered by litigation. Similarly, in the South African social rights cases, by the use of "engagement" remedies, the state was made more responsive, and it was made to improve its capacity to address specific concerns in the process of exercising its power.

The Indian case study offers an example of the role that courts can play in building the state, though it also reveals concerns and considerations that need factoring in. It is easy to understand the Indian judiciary's efforts given the genuine concerns over police abuse. Here the courts engaged in a kind of second-best constitutionalism. In the absence of any thoroughgoing attempt at police reform, they tried to address the worst outcomes generated by a weak and compromised

37 *See* Mark Tushnet, *Dialogic Judicial Review*, 61 Ark. L. Rev. 205 (2008).

38 *See id.* at 212.

police force. Yet, understandable as the judiciary's approach has been, it is worth noting that the absorption of state capacity in this fashion can create costs and perverse consequences, and it might even further weaken state capacity over the long run. The overall legitimacy of the criminal justice system is to an extent undermined, as false and unnecessary arrests are now seen as part of the system.

This can have important on-the-ground implications. The provision of anticipatory bail might only increase false and unnecessary arrests as the police know that the stakes of such errors are limited. Of course, the benefits may be equally limited, but the very fact that this matter is now viewed in such terms rather than through correcting the exercise of the arrest power already captures how much is lost. And, as is only to be expected, though anticipatory bail is a response to specific abuses, it can also itself be a source of abuse. In countries like India, courts are thus faced with a genuine dilemma. They lack the power to reform the criminal justice system in any serious way, and yet they recognize that denying the weak capacities of the system – such as by limiting anticipatory bail to a few isolated instances – is to ignore the social reality on the ground. The approach that the courts have taken toward anticipatory bail illustrates their effort to internalize the social reality into legal rules in the hope that, until systemic changes occur, the law can be at least somewhat responsive to the weaknesses of the system in which it operates, but it remains an open question as to whether this will only make the system weaker over the long run.

Even if courts can find ways to negotiate the problem of state capacity and interact with other branches of government, be cognizant of concerns such as perverse consequences, and attend to both creating and limiting the state, one worry might be an increased involvement by the judiciary in political decision-making and policy-related questions. Yet, our framework might not result in the aggrandizement of judicial power as courts are – in the final analysis – like other institutions, equally subject to capacity-related constraints. The model that we propose does not involve courts playing a very different role from the one they already occupy. Moreover, as our case studies show, courts are already engaged in matters involving social rights, bureaucratic decision-making, criminal justice, and more.

In conclusion, the case studies from Brazil, South Africa, and India – three prominent constitutional democracies where state capacity is a real worry – show that the problem of state capacity does inform the approach of courts, and a better understanding of this problem and how courts should act is crucial for understanding the theory and practice of constitutionalism in weak states. An appreciation of the judicial role in building the state allows us to better grasp the complex role that courts play in much of the developing world, and it enables us to better understand the challenge that constitutionalism faces in at once creating and limiting state power.

11

The New Managerialism

Courts, Positive Duties, and Economic and Social Rights

Katharine G. Young[*]

11.1 INTRODUCTION

The constitutional entrenchment of economic and social rights often requires courts to intervene directly in the administration of government. Such rights – to access goods, services, and programs such as social security, education, and health care – are now present in more than two-thirds of the world's constitutions.[1] Newer constitutional amendments extend such rights to housing, land, water, and a clean environment, implicating a wide array of government actions or omissions. Moreover, despite the conventional wisdom that such rights should not be enforced by courts, and should be entrenched at most as directive principles or other statements of aspiration, the duties for government that such rights create are increasingly justiciable.[2] For better or worse, courts have become central in enforcing both negative and positive duties, in complaints arising from such matters as medical treatment denials, evictions, education outcomes, pollution levels, or food distribution schemes.[3]

The scholarly response to these trends has mostly been focused on two adverse and largely opposing consequences: the judicial usurpation of the elected branches, or the judicial abdication of the enforcement role. In both versions, the constitutional entrenchment of economic and social rights portends further pressure on

* With thanks to Danie Brand, Yasmin Dawood, Vicki Jackson, and the participants of the Workshop on Constitutionalism and Effective Governance, Harvard Law School, May 2–3, 2019.

1 Textual counts include Courtney Jung, Ran Hirschl & Evan Rosevear, *Economic and Social Rights in National Constitutions*, 62 AM. J. COMPAR. L. 4, 1043–98 (2014).

2 Evan Rosevear, Ran Hirschl & Courtney Jung, *Justiciable and Aspirational Economic and Social Rights in National Constitutions*, *in* THE FUTURE OF ECONOMIC AND SOCIAL RIGHTS (Katharine G. Young ed., 2019).

3 For a range of such examples, *see* THE FUTURE OF ECONOMIC AND SOCIAL RIGHTS (Katharine G. Young ed., 2019). *See also* ADAM CHLTON & MILA VERSTEEG, HOW CONSTITUTIONAL RIGHTS MATTER ch. 7 (2020); Daniel Brinks et al., *Social Rights Constitutionalism: Negotiating the Tension Between the Universal and the Particular*, 11 ANN. REV. L. & SOC. SCI. 289 (2015).

governments already strained by other political and economic trends, such as a rise of anti-establishment, noninstitutionally mediated populist politics or of pressures to outsource or privatize government duties.[4] And yet the judicial practice of enforcement, particularly in the Global South, has been far more complex than such criticisms assume. From South Africa, India, and Colombia (as the most noted examples),[5] as well as other prominent jurisdictions, close analysis of particular periods and trends in jurisprudence indicate a varied repertoire of judicial enforcement, and a similarly assorted range of governmental responses. Within this variety, the muted enforcement of housing rights in the *Grootboom* case of South Africa has provided perhaps the most canonical example.[6]

This chapter magnifies this detail, in demarcating the trends of enforcement in South Africa over the last ten years. These trends suggest a heightened managerialism in enforcing positive duties, where courts directly manage and supervise the remediation of a rights complaint. Emerging forms of managerialism involve an increasing personalization of governmental responsibility, a broadening of duty-holders and stakeholders, and a rising urgency in responding to the government intransigence, incompetence, or inertia that have led to findings of unconstitutionality. In particular, the chapter updates a past typology of judicial review of economic and social rights complaints, in which a "catalytic" court embraces different forms of review, by accessing postures of managerialism, dialogue, deference, supremacy, or experiment in order to "catalyze" government (and broader public) action.[7] That typology, which sought to unsettle a simple opposition between "weak" or "strong" courts in economic and social rights cases,[8] confirmed the dynamism between those positions. In this analysis, the predicted trend that "weaker" stances become "strong" over time is observed, with both courts and other governmental actors – in particular the executive – as cocreators of the dynamic. Section 11.2 examines an increasing tendency of the courts to interpret rights, apply standards,

4 *See, e.g.*, Constitutional Democracy in Crisis? (Mark Graber, Sanford Levinson & Mark Tushnet eds., 2019). While this chapter was written prior to the COVID-19 pandemic, and does not deal with the significant changes wrought by it, the connection between government failures in this area, and earlier retrenchments of economic and social rights, was explicitly drawn in the UN Committee on Economic, Social and Cultural Rights statement: Committee on Economic, Social and Cultural Rights (CESCR), *Statement on the Coronavirus Disease (COVID-19) Pandemic and Economic, Social and Cultural Rights* para. 4 (2020).

5 E.g., Cesar Rodriguez & Diana Rodriguez-Franco, Radical Deprivation on Trial: The Impact of Judicial Activism on Socioeconomic Rights in the Global South (2015). Argentina, Brazil, Costa Rica, Latvia, Nepal, and even the US state constitutions provide interesting parallels, all beyond the scope of the present chapter. *See generally* The Future of Economic and Social Rights, *supra* note 3.

6 Katharine G. Young, *The Canons of Social and Economic Rights*, *in* Global Canons in an Age of Uncertainty: Debating Foundational Texts of Constitutional Democracy and Human Rights (Sujit Choudhry, Michaela Hailbronner & Mattias Kumm eds., forthcoming), https://papers.ssrn.com/sol3/papers.cfm?abstract_id=3818966.

7 Katharine G. Young, Constituting Economic and Social Rights (2012).

8 Mark Tushnet, Weak Courts, Strong Rights: Judicial Review and Social Welfare Rights in Comparative Constitutional Law (2008).

and order remedies through a theory of effective public administration. Sections 11.3–11.5 examine the evolving repertoire of managerial, dialogic, and experimental review, identifying a more personalized and urgent setting in which courts pursue the goals of effective, democratically responsive government through constitutional rights. Section 11.6 concludes.

11.2 POSITIVE DUTIES AND SOUTH AFRICAN CONSTITUTIONALISM

Due in part to its post-apartheid Constitution and the caliber of its first Constitutional Court, South African constitutionalism has become an influential model for economic and social rights enforcement, although examples from India in the 1980s–1990s and Colombia in the early 2000s are also familiar entry-points. In South Africa, economic and social rights are entrenched in the following textual formulation:

1. Everyone has the right to have access to [healthcare services, including reproductive health care; sufficient food and water; social security ... adequate housing ... a basic education].
2. The state must take reasonable legislative and other measures, within its available resources, to achieve the progressive realisation of each of these rights.[9]

Section 7 also sets out the government's duties to "respect, protect, promote and fulfil" the rights in the Bill of Rights, Section 36 confirms that rights may be limited "only in terms of law of general application to the extent that the limitation is reasonable and justifiable," and Section 39 mandates that courts interpreting rights consider international law and permits them to consider foreign law.

These textual guarantees have been interpreted to emphasize government accountability for rights-realization, rather than individual entitlement.[10] For example, the South African Constitutional Court has emphasized the government's duties to "take reasonable measures" to progressively realize these guarantees (i.e., it has emphasized subsection 2, above), in place of any self-standing notion of rights' essential or "core" content.[11] The Court has provided a theory of "reasonableness" in government action, injecting a heightened rights-responsiveness to traditional administrative law principles.[12] It has also been active in promoting remedial discretion, and the need

9 *See, e.g.*, S. Afr. Const., §§ 26, 27, 29.

10 For analysis, *see* David Bilchitz, *Towards a Defensible Relationship between the Content of Socio-economic Rights and the Separation of Powers: Conflation or Separation?*, *in* The Evolution of the Separation of Powers: Between the Global North and the Global South57 (David Bilchitz & David Landau eds., 2018).

11 *E.g.* Government of the Republic of South Africa v. Grootboom [2000] ZACC 19; 2001 (1) SA 46 (CC).

12 Sandra Liebenberg, Socio-economic Rights: Adjudication under a Transformative Constitution (2010); *see also* Katharine G. Young, *Proportionality, Reasonableness and Economic and Social Rights*, *in* Proportionality: New Frontiers, New Challenges (Vicki C. Jackson & Mark Tushnet eds., 2017).

to innovate with effective remedies.[13] Such remedies include, as will be discussed, reading in, reading down, severance of words, the limiting and retrospective effect of the declaration of invalidity, or a suspension of the declaration of invalidity, the use of interdicts, and the modification of the common law.[14]

A notable recent trend is the Court's recourse to constitutional text in order to substantiate the standard of reasonableness. For example, the South African Constitutional Court has reiterated the basic principles of public administration – section 195(1) – in successful economic and social rights claims. That detailed section requires that, for every sphere of government:

a. A high standard of professional ethics must be promoted and maintained.
b. Efficient, economic and effective use of resources must be promoted.
c. Public administration must be development-oriented.
d. Services must be provided impartially, fairly, equitably and without bias.
e. People's needs must be responded to, and the public must be encouraged to participate in policy-making.
f. Public administration must be accountable. . . .
[and g. transparent and h. actively instructed and i. representative]

This section is included alongside broader objects and duties of government, and rule of law principles.[15] These overarching governance principles are themselves nonjusticiable. Yet their appearance in the reasoning and the orders of recent cases has created, according to local advocate Nikki Stein, "a feedback loop, in terms of which the values and principles of good governance can be used to realize socio-economic rights, and litigation to advance socio-economic rights can be used to build and strengthen the principles set out in s 195."[16] This is a very different picture from the formal and static separation of "rights" and "structural principles" in broader constitutional analysis. Of course, these developments are not restricted to economic and social rights enforcement – the South African Constitutional Court has ordered a response to other failures of constitutional duty, such as its order that the parliament

[13] E.g., Fose v. Minister of Safety and Security, 1997 (3) SA 786 (CC), paras. 18–19, 69 (interpreting the Interim Constitution) ("In our context an appropriate remedy must mean an effective remedy"). See also S. Afr. Const., §§ 38 and 172(1)(b), which provides that the Constitutional Court may make any order which is just and equitable.

[14] See summary, Georgina Jephson & Osmond Mngomezulu, *Constitutional Litigation Procedure*, *in* Public Interest Litigation (Jason Brickhill ed., 2018) 135, 149.

[15] E.g., S. Afr. Const., § 4 (constitutional principle of cooperative government); § 41 (cooperative government among organs of state); § 100 (justifying national intervention to assume responsibilities when necessary for essential national standards etc.); § 152 (stating the objects of local government and requiring municipalities to strive to achieve these objects); § 153(a) (providing that a municipality must "structure and manage its administration and budgeting and planning processes to give priority to the basic needs of the community, and to promote the social and economic development of the community"); § 154 (national and provincial governments to support municipalities); § 156 (authorizing municipalities to carry out their functions).

[16] Nikki Stein, *A Better Life for All: Using Socio-economic Rights Litigation to Enforce the Principles Governing Public Administration* 34 S. Afr. J. Hum. Rts. 91, 98–99 (2018).

had failed its constitutional duty to hold the president accountable for corruption proceedings – an act that arguably brought an end to Jacob Zuma's nine-year presidency (2009–18).[17] Courts have been frustrated – or perhaps emboldened – by several egregious government lapses, and the economic and social rights jurisprudence should be read as part of these broader developments. Moreover, these juridical developments must be understood against a complex backdrop of what we might call post-liberal constitutional ambition. An increasing concern among constitutional and wider commentators has been the gap between a "politics of accountability" and a "politics of capability."[18] For this reason, it is worth revisiting the model of catalytic courts that attempted to tie accountability to capability.

My 2010 typology suggested that judicial enforcement occupied a range of distinctive positions, from managerialism (such as command-and-control style structural injunctions), to dialogue (such as suspended declarations), to experimentalism (such as participatory remedies), to more supremacist or deferential measures, depending upon the government's failure of duty.[19] The remainder of this chapter explores the trends toward new forms of managerialism, dialogue, and experimentalism in South Africa.

11.3 MANAGERIALISM: PERSONALIZING OR BROADENING RESPONSIBILITY

Judicial managerialism refers to the courts' supervision of both the rights' substantive content and the duty required of government when shortfalls are identified. This occurs, for example, when courts issue structured and/or mandatory forms of relief that require continuing, day-to-day control and raise the prospect of contempt proceedings against government officials if compliance is not achieved. The classic example is the structural injunction, and the US template is, of course, *Brown II* and its progeny, when the court was involved in the management of desegregation through school registrations, busing, etc. (prison reform is another obvious precursor in the USA).[20] In South Africa, lower

[17] Heinz Klug, *State Capture or Institutional Resilience: Is There a Crisis of Constitutional Democracy in South Africa?*, *in* CONSTITUTIONAL DEMOCRACY IN CRISIS? 295, 308 (Mark A. Graber, Sanford Levinson & Mark Tushnet eds., 2018) (describing a series of Constitutional Court cases that held the president – and parliament – accountable to the Constitution).

[18] On the connection between these and the robust response to social security rights enforcement, *see* Stuart Woolman, *A Politics of Accountability: How South Africa's Judicial Recognition of the Binding Legal Effect of the Public Protector's Recommendations Had a Catalysing Effect That Brought Down a President*, 8 CONST. CT. REV. 155 (2018).

[19] Katharine G. Young, *A Typology of Economic and Social Rights Adjudication: Exploring the Catalytic Function of Judicial Review*, 8 INT'L J. CONST. L. 385 (2010); YOUNG, *supra* note 7, at 142–66. This short paper is thus helpfully read alongside the earlier typology.

[20] *E.g.*, Brown v. Board of Education 349 U.S. 294 (1955) (Brown II) (ordering schools to integrate "with all deliberate speed"). Such actions have been theorized in the USA by, among others, Abram Chayes, Alexander Bickel, Owen Fiss, Judith Resnik, Malcolm Feeley, and Ed Rubin.

courts have enthusiastically followed this path.[21] An influential model prescribes such relief when government actors are "intransigent, incompetent or inattentive."[22] Orders to address incompetency – or government incapacity or ineffectiveness – sometimes recall bankruptcy reorganization.[23] Increasingly, courts call on managerialism when previous declaratory orders have not been complied with (as predicted by Mark Tushnet and others).[24] Below, I highlight a new and increasingly complex repertoire of managerial responses that have arisen in complaints in relation to the constitutional rights to social security, education, and housing.

11.3.1 *Personalizing Responsibility*

One notable trend is the use of cost orders (often awarded, in South Africa, against the losing party), as personal to the responsible government official. For example, after a series of cases involving the failure to respect the right to social assistance, the Constitutional Court ordered the responsible minister to pay 20 percent of the costs of the complainants, with the rest apportioned to the department and the agency.[25] Noting that "it is a novel matter to hold a cabinet minister personally responsible for the costs of litigation,"[26] the Constitutional Court also directed the court's registrar to forward the judgment and a commissioned report to the National Director of Public Prosecutions, to consider whether the minister had lied under oath and, if so, whether she should be prosecuted for perjury.[27] Citing section 195 of the Constitution, the

21 In the famous *Grootboom* case, for example, the lower court had ordered the municipal government to promptly provide tents, latrines, etc., to repair the government's failure to protect the rights of housing of children; the Constitutional Court, in a now common move, reversed the order and issued a declaration only (see Section 11.4).

22 Kent Roach & Geoff Budlender, *Mandatory Relief and Supervisory Jurisdiction: When Is It Appropriate, Just and Equitable?*, 122 S. Afr. L. J. 325 (2005).

23 For a useful assessment of some predictable parallels, following Abram Chayes, *see* William H. Simon, Kathleen G. Noonan & Jonathan C. Lipson, *Reforming Institutions: The Judicial Function in Bankruptcy and Public Law Litigation*, 94 Ind. L. J. 491, 538 (2019) (endorsing these parallels on the theory that "courts can induce reforms in both bankruptcy and [public law litigation] because they are removed from the causes of system failure and the political and market pathologies that often prevent extra-judicial reform").

24 Tushnet, *supra* note 8. *See, e.g.*, Malcolm Langford, *Housing Rights Litigation: Grootboom and Beyond, in* Socio-economic Rights in South Africa: Symbols or Substance? 187 (Malcolm Langford et al. eds., 2014).

25 Black Sash Trust v. Minister of Social Development [2018] ZACC 36; 2018 (12) BCLR 1472 (CC) (Black Sash III). There are parallels with the High Court holding President Zuma personally responsible for legal costs for his application to prevent the Public Protector from "finalizing and releasing" her report on state capture; see Klug, *supra* note 17, at 306. After the completion of this chapter, in February 2021, Zuma refused to appear before the Commission on State Capture, defying a court order; the issue of contempt is currently before Constitutional Court.

26 *Black Sash III* [2018] ZACC 36, at para. 16. See also Gauteng Gambling Board and Another v. MEC for Economic Development, Gauteng Provincial Government (620/2012) [2013] ZASCA 67; 2013 (5) SA 24, at para. 54 (SCA) ("It is time for courts to seriously consider holding officials who behave in the high-handed manner described above, personally liable for costs incurred. This might have a sobering effect on truant public office bearers").

27 *Id.* at para. 1 (Minister Dlamini).

Constitutional Court affirmed the basic values and principles governing public administration and the seriousness of the minister's lapse, and her use of her position "as Minister of the Department to place herself between constitutionally enshrined rights and those entitled to them."[28] When the Court later faced the question of holding the Public Protector to a personal cost order, the majority emphasized how the common-law tests of bad faith and gross negligence are "infused" by constitutional obligations.[29] This consideration outweighed any potential threat of personal costs to her independence,[30] including in her handling of powerful and well-resourced persons or office holders, and the majority also allowed the punitive cost order to stand.

11.3.2 *Personal Joinder and Inquiry*

The enormity of these lapses in the coordination of social assistance had led to other remedial innovations. The government department – and its minister – had left the payment system for social grants in limbo for a period of five years, after an earlier declaration of the unconstitutionality of the initial contracts. This inaction risked disrupting the payment of social grants affecting some 17 million South Africans. Before issuing the personal costs order described already, the Constitutional Court ordered the minister to provide reasons why she should not be ordered to pay the cost of the application.[31] When her returning affidavit stated facts that conflicted with those given by members of the department, the Constitutional Court joined her in her personal capacity,[32] and appointed a referee to conduct a fact-finding inquiry.[33] The results of this inquiry, which determined that she had sought to mislead the court, were made public.

11.3.3 *Control of State Assets*

Similar frustration has been expressed by lower courts enforcing the right to a basic education. In one case, when the relevant education department had not reimbursed schools for the payment of teachers' salaries, despite an order to do so, the court was asked to declare the salaries as public debts under state liability legislation.

28 *Id.* at para. 12 (citing § 195 and the Public Administration Management Act 11 of 2014 (pending proclamation of commencement)). The Court also noted: "The Department of Social Development … is as much responsible for the realisation of rights outlined in the Constitution as this Court").

29 Public Protector v. South African Reserve Bank [2019] ZACC 29; 2019 (6) SA 253 (CC) para. 154 (refusing to set aside an order to pay 15 percent of the South African Reserve Bank's costs). The High Court had found that the Public Protector, Ms. Busisiwe Mkhwebane, abused her office in issuing reports on the Reserve Bank, which had caused severe harm to the South African economy.

30 Id. *Cf.* para. 6 (Mogoeng CJ dissent, emphasizing the "chilling effect" of personal cost orders).

31 Black Sash Trust v. Minister of Social Development [2017] ZACC 8; 2017 (3) SA 335 (CC) (Black Sash I), para. 76.

32 Black Sash Trust v. Minister of Social Development [2017] ZACC 20; 2017 (9) BCLR 1089 (CC) (Black Sash II) para. 24.

33 Order dated Aug. 2, 2017.

Attorneys then took steps to attach state property – the motor vehicles used by the minister of education and her director general – and have this property sold at sales in execution to realize the moneys owed.[34] The salaries were immediately paid.[35] A corollary can be found in High Court orders directing the auctioning of municipal vehicles to settle debt, including debt owed to water service providers.[36] At the same time, the latter disputes have resulted in court orders preventing water service providers from restricting their bulk water supply below certain levels, when they had threatened to do so in order to enforce payments from financially strapped municipalities (later placed in administration).[37]

11.3.4 *Joinder of State Actors*

In other litigation involving evictions and the right to adequate housing, initial suits that have ostensibly not involved state actors have resulted in their joinder, or other orders of information and reports. Where private landowners have sought to evict occupiers from private land, the Constitutional Court has requested, in reviewing whether the eviction is just or equitable, information from local municipal authorities. Because of the constitutional duty to provide temporary accommodation to those threatened with homelessness, which applies to those occupying public land, or private land, and to those residing in a contractual relationship of tenancy, the municipal authority has been deemed implicated and the courts have relied on both sections 26 and 152.[38] Indeed, a rule of practice has developed so that the relevant local authority *must* be joined as a party in any large-scale eviction, in order to provide information about foreseeable disruption, and possibilities for providing alternative accommodation.[39]

11.3.5 *Supervision of Timing*

As well as issuing dates for when each step must be complied with, in classic structural mode, the Constitutional Court has also sequenced each step to avoid a rights violation. For example, in another evictions case, the date of eviction was required

34 Cameron McConnachie & Samantha Brener, *Litigating the Right to Basic Education, in* PUBLIC INTEREST LITIGATION IN SOUTH AFRICA 281, 299 (Jason Brickhill ed., 2018); following Linkside v. Minister of Basic Education [2015] ZAECGHC 36.

35 *Id.*

36 *Auctioning of Kopanong's Fleet Halted*, BLOEMFONTEIN COURANT, Feb. 10, 2021 (noting debts to Bloem Water).

37 *Bloem Water Heads to High Court in Battle against Mangaung Metro*, BLOEMFONTEIN COURANT, Sept. 20, 2019. See further *infra* note 57 (ordered prevention of electricity interruption). With thanks to Danie Brand for pointing out this corollary.

38 Gustav Muller & Sandra Liebenberg, *Developing the Law of Joinder in the Context of Evictions of People from their Homes*, 29 SAJHR 554 (2013).

39 This rule is now contained in practice directives of the various divisions of the High Court. Since the completion of this chapter, the government elected to suspend all evictions during the lockdowns required for suppression of COVID-19, Government Gazette, Mar. 26, 2020.

to be fourteen days after the City's obligation to provide accommodation – thus allowing the occupiers "some time and space" to be certain of their accommodation and to make arrangements for relocation. The private occupier was required to exercise "a degree of patience" in this respect, and (unlike in an earlier case involving a long-standing property owner and recent squatters[40]) no compensation was ordered for this time period. In finessing its order, the Court also delayed the date of eviction: it "should not follow too soon after the date of the judgment,"[41] according to the Court.

11.3.6 *Issuing Interim Relief*

Lower courts have also sought to relax the procedural rules on interim injunctions. For example, the North Gauteng High Court sought to prohibit the levying and collection of tolls pending further proceedings for final relief as to whether the government possessed the power to declare certain roads toll roads.[42] Although later reversed by the Constitutional Court, many local commentators had recommended that such an excessive intervention was justified according to a reordered conception of the separation of powers,[43] and the guarantee of economic and social rights.

11.3.7 *"Deeming"*

The right to education cases also involved complaints about the education department's failure to appoint teachers, despite earlier court orders. The courts then "deemed" teachers to have been formally appointed, if they had complied with a statutory and policy requirement in terms of qualification and hiring. The posture recalls a more peremptory form of review, beyond managerialism.[44] Early on, the Constitutional Court had engaged in peremptory review when it had "read in" rights-respecting words into otherwise rights-infringing legislation, thereby correcting it without further inter-branch involvement. In the remedial context involving positive duties, such peremptory review can involve an act of "amending" legislation (instead of overturning it) or "reading in" new words to "cure" legislation, rather than severing it.[45] Here, the deeming provisions were directed against the executive.

40 President of the Republic of South Africa v. Modderklip Boerdery (Pty) Ltd (2005) (5) SA 3 (CC) (ordering compensatory damages to the private landowner for the period before eviction could be carried out, with alternative land available).

41 City of Johannesburg Metropolitan Municipality v. Blue Moonlight Properties (Pty) Ltd [2011] ZACC 33, 2012 (2) SA 104 (CC).

42 National Treasury v. Opposition to Urban Tolling Alliance (OUTA) [2012] ZACC 18, 2012 (6) SA 223 (CC).

43 *See* Mia Swart and Thomas Coggin, *The Road Not Taken: Separation of Powers, Interim Interdicts, Rationality Review and E-Tolling in National Treasure v Opposition to Urban Tolling*, 5 CONST. CT. REV. 346 (2013).

44 YOUNG, *supra* note 7 (noting the features of peremptory review).

45 Khosa v. Minister of Social Development, 2004 (6) SA 505 (CC) (making "citizens *and permanent residents*" eligible for social security grants).

11.3.8 *Substantive Outcome Decrees*

As well as these structural interventions related to government actors, lower courts have, unsurprisingly, also issued a series of substantive outcome decrees. For example, the Supreme Court and the lower courts have ordered structural relief in relation to a number of discrete requirements for basic education, such as textbooks,[46] student chairs and desks,[47] teachers' salaries,[48] and school transport.[49] Yet such orders have revealed a basic incapability to comply, especially in the province of Limpopo, where litigation exposed "a deep rot in the provincial department, which . . . paralysed them in their attempts to deliver the building blocks of basic education . . . from textbook delivery . . . dilapidated school infrastructure, shortages of teachers, shortages of school furniture and the failure to provide adequate funding for schools' day-to-day needs."[50] In this context, after only scattered compliance, the court was forced to reorient its orders to the more basic competencies of public administration, such as data collection on schools or textbooks. After repeated failures of structural orders, complainants sought declaratory relief, in part in order to maintain their own control over the delivery, rather than rely on the court's schedule, as well as to limit further opportunities, on the part of the department, to seek extensions.[51] Such declaratory relief can avoid the unintended consequences, and rushed and ineffective action, that accompany structural orders, when planning systems are inadequate.[52]

11.4 DIALOGUE: INCREASING URGENCY AND INSTITUTIONAL ENGAGEMENT

An emphasis on dialogue occurs not when courts attempt to directly manage the correction of a rights dispute but, rather, when they invite an inter-branch response. This is done by a less detailed interpretation of the right and a less insistent (often declaratory) remedy. Yet the theorized tropes of dialogue – declarations of invalidity, suspended orders, the use of prelegislative parliamentary committees or legislative overrides – are complicated in respect of economic and social rights, particularly in relation to positive duties. From the early, famous displays of dialogue in the declaratory orders of *Grootboom* and *TAC*,[53] where the Court found no reason not to trust the

46 Minister of Basic Education v. Basic Education for All, 2016 (4) SA 63 (SCA).

47 Madzodzo v. Minister of Basic Education, 2014 (3) SA 441 (ECM).

48 Centre for Child Law v. Minister of Basic Education, 2013 (3) SA 183 (ECG).

49 Tripartite Steering Committee v. Minister of Basic Education, 2015 (5) SA 107 (ECG).

50 Stein, *supra* note 16, at 101.

51 Faranaaz Veriava, *The Limpopo Textbook Litigation: A Case Study into the Possibilities of Transformative Constitutionalism* (2016) 32 S. AFR. J. HUM. RTS. 321.

52 For the acknowledgment of such dangers, *see* McConnachie & Brener, *supra* note 34. Concerns of polycentricity are also raised. For broader analysis, *see* JEFF KING, JUDGING SOCIAL RIGHTS (2012); Kent Roach, *Polycentricity and Queue-Jumping in Public Law Remedies: A Two-Track Response* 66 U. TORONTO L. J. 3 (2016).

53 Government of the Republic of South Africa v. Grootboom [2000] ZACC 19; 2001 (1) SA 46 (CC).

government to comply with the standard of reasonableness in designing housing or healthcare policy, the Constitutional Court no longer assumes compliance.[54] It thus has engaged in forms of dialogue notable for their urgency and broader institutional engagement, seeking responses not only from the legislative and executive branches but also from a broader array of governmental actors and nongovernmental organizations (NGOs). This stance is demonstrated in a series of disputes related to housing and social security rights, and is indicated by four developments.

11.4.1 *Suspension of Declarations*

The suspension of declarations, that is, providing a timed delay before action is required by the order, which allows the government to design and deliver its own response to a constitutional infringement, has a long provenance in dialogue theory. Unlike managerialism, this form of review moves closer to the resolution of the representation problems of constitutional rights enforcement. In positive provisioning cases, however, the suspension has revealed a different justification: a suspension helps to ensure that rights-holders receiving an entitlement as part of a positive obligation are not subject to disruption or discontinuity. For example, in the social assistance cases described in Section 11.3, the Constitutional Court had to ensure that grant payments, although declared unconstitutional, could continue. This required a supervisory double-act: first declaring the original disbursement contract null and void, and then suspending this order of invalidity for a year in order to ensure the continuing disbursement of grants. Later, the original contract was reinstated in order to ensure the protection of the beneficiaries' personal data and to ensure the transparency and accountability of the payment process.

11.4.2 *Broader Institutional Involvement*

The Constitutional Court has also regularly called on other organs of state to assist in enforcing positive duties, through monitoring and other responsibilities. In this respect, auditors, treasury reporters, human rights commissions, health ombudspersons, and even private actors (such as law societies) have been named by the court in "unofficial" orders seeking particular action or accountability. Early on, in *Grootboom*, the Constitutional Court called on the South Africa Human Rights Commission to monitor the order.[55] But, in follow-up cases, an array of other actors have assisted, often in response to complainant requests.[56] In this respect, the

54 *See generally* CONSTITUTIONAL TRIUMPHS, CONSTITUTIONAL DISAPPOINTMENTS: A CRITICAL ASSESSMENT OF THE 1996 SOUTH AFRICAN CONSTITUTION'S LOCAL AND INTERNATIONAL INFLUENCE (Rosalind Dixon & Theunis Roux eds., 2018).

55 *Grootboom*, at para. 97.

56 *See, e.g.*, *Black Sash I*, *supra* note 31, at paras. 37, 71–74 (appointing the Auditor-General to review the interim contract, at the request of the Black Sash Trust).

Constitutional Court refers to the role obligations of each institutional actor – such as section 195(1) and the duties of public management, or duties on municipal authorities, duties of cooperative governance and the like. When electricity providers attempted to terminate supply to an entire municipality, for example, in order to extract payment from delinquent municipalities, the Supreme Court noted the duties of national and provincial governments to intervene, as well as those of the electricity provider itself to avert the disastrous consequences.[57]

11.4.3 *Duties to Budget and Plan*

Economic and social rights raise, of course, fiscal concerns, and yet the courts have been reluctant to order, by decree, that executive officials with taxing or borrowing authority exercise it in any general or specific way.[58] Instead, the posture of dialogue assumes that such response will follow. Yet even under this approach, the Constitutional Court has increasingly called on the functions and powers of local government, including those of budgeting and planning. In response to the city's argument that it was not obliged to go beyond its available resources to deal with emergency housing needs, the Court noted that "it is not good enough for the City to state that it has not budgeted for something, if it should indeed have planned and budgeted for it in the fulfilment of its obligations."[59] It ordered the alternative accommodation and the eviction, but also declared that the City's housing policy was unconstitutional insofar as it had excluded, when creating emergency accommodation, persons evicted by private property owners.[60]

11.4.4 *Common-Law Development*

Common-law development resembles a dialogic judicial stance insofar as the legislature is free to override such development in response. In one case, for example, the Constitutional Court suggested that the constitutional guarantee of economic and

57 Eskom Holdings SOC Ltd v. Resilient Properties (Pty) Ltd and Others [2020] ZASCA 185; [2021] 1 All SA 668 (SCA) (court holding that the interruption of electricity services to the entire municipality was inimical to constitutional obligations); *see also supra* note 37 (Bloem Water interruptions).

58 *Cf.* Missouri v. Jenkins, 495 U.S. 33 (1990) (holding that, as a remedy against school segregation, the court may order the defendant school board to increase taxes).

59 City of Johannesburg Metropolitan Municipality v. Blue Moonlight Properties, 39 *(Pty) Ltd* [2011] ZACC 33; 2012 (2) SA 104(CC) at para. 74.

60 While it is beyond the scope of this chapter, it is worth noting that a wider discourse of budgeting with respect to constitutional rights has developed: *see, e.g.*, Sandra Liebenberg, *Budget Must Take Human Rights into Account*, City Press (Mar. 21, 2021) (noting the submission of Michael Sachs, acting chairperson of the Financial and Fiscal Commission, detailing the obligations of the government to justify its decision "to reduce expenditure on socioeconomic rights-related budgetary items and to lower the tax burden on constitutionally mandated priorities").

social rights might provide a justification for departing from a prohibition against periodic payments in compensation in personal injury claims.[61]

11.5 EXPERIMENTALISM: LOCALISM AND MODELS OF ALTERNATIVE DISPUTE RESOLUTION

Managerialism and dialogue highlight different orientations for courts in enforcing positive duties, and can be situated along a spectrum of strong-form versus weak-form responses. A third model, experimentalist review, seeks to dislodge the inertia of inter-branch relations and inject a more directly democratic response, by requiring the participation and involvement of wider "stakeholders" in the interpretation and the discharge of the government's positive duties. This third model sees courts directing the parties to engage together to devise their own iterative solutions to ensure the realization of the claimed right. Many of the practical features of experimentalism draw on the insights of behavioral law and economics (i.e., nudging rather than prescribing) and the economic sociology of institutions (i.e., destabilizing public institutions from inertia and coordinating different actors in reflexive, problem-solving mode).[62] In South Africa, features of experimentalism have evolved in the context of an increasingly contentious politics and urban violence, putting pressure on its utility in securing rights to housing, health care and education.[63] This pressure may be observed in the following examples.

11.5.1 *Supervising Meaningful Engagement*

In South Africa, experimentalism is exemplified by the remedy of "meaningful engagement," in which the Court orders that the parties engage with each other to resolve their dispute. In an early evictions case, the order of meaningful engagement was issued in part so as to upend the adversarial postures of the occupiers and the city landlord seeking eviction, in a right to housing complaint. Since then, it has been utilized in additional evictions cases, finding appeal in its capacity to transform hostile parties into coordinated negotiators and to stimulate organizing around the complaint. More recent complaints involving the right to education have also resulted in the court's use of the meaningful engagement order, although the capacity to coordinate "engaged" parties has been limited when the complainants are unorganized.[64] In litigating the availability of school textbooks and other

61 Member of the Executive Council for Health and Social Development, Gauteng v. DZ obo WZ [2017] ZACC 37; 2018 (1) SA 335 (CC).

62 Influential commentators in the USA from each include Cass Sunstein and Richard Thaler, on the one hand, and Roberto Unger, Charles Sabel, William Simon, and Michael Dorf, on the other.

63 Irene de Vos and Dennis Webster, *No Place for the Poor: The Governance of Removal in Zulu and SAITF*, CONST. CT. REV. 321 (2018).

64 Governing Body of the Juma Musjid Parimary School v. Essay NO 2011, (8) NBCLR 761 (CC); *see* BRIAN RAY, ENGAGING WITH SOCIAL RIGHTS: PROCEDURE, PARTICIPATION AND DEMOCRACY IN SOUTH

resources, meaningful engagement has again been used, with greater organizing on behalf of parents' groups leading to greater compliance.[65] Further calls have been made for an "extrajudicial" (noncourt-centric) application of this model in bringing protest groups together to make demands of government.[66]

11.5.2 *Alternative Dispute Resolution (ADR)*

Finally, ADR, rather than litigation, has found renewed emphasis in large-scale institutional violations, particularly when a constitutional infringement has been conceded.[67] In the *Life Esidimeni* arbitration, the Gauteng health department had conceded its liability for violating the rights to health and other rights on the part of some 1,300 mental health care users, after it had terminated its contract with providers and moved rapidly to deinstitutionalize. In responding to an earlier interdict of the discharge, the health department had signed a settlement agreement undertaking to consult meaningfully with several mental health NGOs, such as the South African Depression and Anxiety Group and the South African Society of Psychiatrists, and to develop a reasonable plan for discharge and placement. It breached this agreement, as a later report by the Health Ombud revealed; that report recommended ADR, with the aim of providing redress and restoring trust in the leadership of the health department.[68] Deputy Chief Justice Moseneke was appointed and later delivered an innovative award (along with a stinging rebuke) that included constitutional damages, provision of counselling and support, construction of a monument within twelve months, and an order that the provincial government provide the Health Ombud with a recovery plan addressed to systemic change in the delivery of mental health care, within six months.[69]

AFRICA'S SECOND WAVE (2016); *see also* chapters by Sandra Liebenberg and Roberto Gargarella, *in* THE FUTURE OF ECONOMIC AND SOCIAL RIGHTS, *supra* note 3.

65 For general commentary on the importance of organized social movements in such claims, *see* SOCIAL RIGHTS JUDGMENTS AND THE POLITICS OF COMPLIANCE: MAKING IT STICK (Malcolm Langford, Cesar Rodriguez-Garavito & Julieta Rossi eds., 2017); T. Madlingozi, *Social Movements and the Constitutional Court of South Africa, in* TRANSFORMATIVE CONSTITUTIONALISM: COMPARING THE APEX COURTS OF BRAZIL, INDIA AND SOUTH AFRICA 537 (O.V. Vieira, U. Baxi & F. Viljoen eds., 2013).

66 Sameera Mahomedy, *Extra-judicial Engagement in Socio-economic Rights Realisation: Lessons from #FeesMustFall*, 36 S. AFR. J. HUM. RTS. 49–73 (2020).

67 For an examination of more community-centered and participatory alternatives to litigation, borrowing from a focus on organizing, conscientizing and mobilizing (OCMS) during the apartheid struggle, *see* Dhaya Pillay, *Moving Litigation from Dispute Resolution to Conflict Management, Problem Solving and Building Organisation* (Unpublished thesis, 2020, on file with author).

68 Health Ombud report, *see* Stein, *supra* note 16, at 109. Compare with observed retrenchments in court access and their implications: Judith Resnik, *Courts and Economic and Social Rights/Courts as Economic and Social Rights, in* THE FUTURE OF ECONOMIC AND SOCIAL RIGHTS, *supra* note 3.

69 For commentary, see Ebenezer Durojaye and Daphine Kabagambe Agaba, *Contribution of the Health Ombud to Accountability: The Life Esidimeni Tragedy in South Africa*, 20 HEALTH & HUM. RTS J. 161-8, 164 (2018).

11.6 CONCLUSION

This chapter has examined and updated my previous "catalytic" model of judicial review, which is a heuristic for understanding enforcement of the positive duties that arise from economic and social rights complaints, using the South African example. A clear trend toward a more personalized managerialism, more insistent dialogue, and a more contentious experimentalism can be observed, as well as judicial attempts to open up complaints to a broader net of governmental actors and stakeholders. One of the strengths of both earlier "catalytic" and "weak-form" models was the touted "representation-reinforcing" role of judicial review, which rested on the fact that courts had arrogated to themselves neither the final word on rights interpretation nor a peremptory remedial power. In the last decade, however, with further examples of governmental dysfunction, "weak-form" review has given way to a stronger, and particularly more managerial, function. Some dialogic remedies have become managerial once the declaration went unheeded; others went in the reverse direction, when supervisory jurisdiction failed and complainants sought greater potential leverage in declaratory orders. In interpreting what is "reasonable" in realizing economic and social rights, courts have emphasized the values of public administration, with explicit reference to the nonjusticiable, structural principles of section 195(1). It is notable that these, and not the constitutional values of dignity or equality,[70] have helped the courts define the duties in recent cases.

This is not to suggest that judicial enforcement will always proceed on these terms. While, in the case of South Africa, such managerialism has served to counter inept and corrupt government action, and various other forms of incompetence, comparative analysis reveals increased deference to government and even hostility toward economic and social rights claimants in some places. Moreover, it would be a mistake to view managerialism as a solely court-led intervention, as these forms of judicial review have developed in interaction with both recalcitrant governments and heavily involved nongovernmental actors in South Africa. Successful complainants in economic and social rights cases are often represented by sophisticated public interest organizations, who themselves coordinate with organized social movements and provide vital political pressure for compliance, and often draft their own preferred remedies for the court. This, we might conclude, has led to a form of governance that is highly reactive to litigation, and dependent on the premise that courts will not themselves be tainted by the features of dysfunction that they serve to guard against.

70 *Cf.* Dennis Davis, *The Scope of the Judicial Role in the Enforcement of Social and Economic Rights: Limits and Possibilities viewed from the South African Experience*, *in* SOCIAL AND ECONOMIC RIGHTS IN THEORY AND PRACTICE (Helena Alviar García et al. eds., 2015).

PART V

Executive and Administrative Constitutionalism in Effective Democratic Government

12

What Does Effective Government Have to Do With the Constitution?

Gillian E. Metzger[*]

12.1 INTRODUCTION

Nearly a million people dead and counting. More than 77 million infected, a little less than one-fifth of the total infections worldwide.[1] The United States has had more deaths than any other country, and its COVID-19 death rate of 276 per 100,000 people is the highest among the world's wealthiest nations.[2] Blacks, Hispanics, and Native Americans are hospitalized and die at significantly higher rates than whites.[3] Some bright lights exist too, one being the speedy development of vaccines and their deployment in 2021 – although there, too, both the national government and the states have sometimes stumbled.[4] Another is legislative enactment of major fiscal measures which sustained individuals and businesses in the face of economy calamity.[5] Still, by many public health measures, the United States' response to the COVID-19 pandemic has been a governmental failure.

Criticism of this response – whether from those attacking national and state measures as inadequate to protect public health, or those condemning these

[*] This chapter benefited greatly from conversations with Vicki Jackson and the conference on "Effective Government and the Constitution" she organized at Harvard Law School in May 2019. Many thanks to Brett Donaldson for excellent research assistance.

[1] Johns Hopkins Coronavirus Resource Center, https://coronavirus.jhu.edu/ (last visited Feb. 12, 2022).

[2] Johns Hopkins Coronavirus Resource Center, https://coronavirus.jhu.edu/data/mortality (last visited Feb. 12, 2022).

[3] Centers for Disease Control and Prevention, https://www.cdc.gov/coronavirus/2019-ncov/covid-data/investigations-discovery/hospitalization-death-by-race-ethnicity.html (data updated Feb. 1, 2022) (last visited Feb. 12, 2022) (listing Blacks as hospitalized at 2.5 times the rate of whites, and dying at 1.7 times the rate of whites; the comparable rates for Hispanics are 2.4 and 1.9, and for Native Americans 3.2 and 2.2).

[4] Lauren Leatherby & Amy Schoenfeld Walker, *After a Sluggish Start, Vaccine Rollout Is Improving in Every State*, N.Y. TIMES (Feb. 12, 2021), https://www.nytimes.com/interactive/2021/02/12/us/vaccine-doses-distribution.html.

[5] *See, e.g.*, Coronavirus Aid, Relief, and Economic Security (CARES) Act, Pub. L. No. 116–136, 134 Stat. 281 (2020).

measures as too restrictive and economically disastrous – has dominated political debate since the pandemic began. Views on how to handle the pandemic divide sharply on partisan grounds, and thus the pandemic became a central focal point of the country's polarized politics.[6] Yet, in these debates, one line of argument is largely absent: the suggestion that the national government's ineffective response violated the Constitution.[7] Instead, the Constitution has surfaced primarily as a barrier to governmental action, with multiple lawsuits challenging pandemic restrictions as a violation of constitutional rights. Some of these challenges have succeeded, in particular claims that certain restrictions on in-person religious services violate the Free Exercise Clause.[8] Commenters have also discussed the extent to which the Constitution's federalist structure limits the national government's ability to address the pandemic.[9] But other than a couple of passing references in legislative debate, silence has reigned on whether the national government has a constitutional obligation to respond effectively to the most severe public health threat in a century.[10]

This lack of discussion is hardly unusual. Consider another example: From December 2018 to January 2019, partisan fights over the budget led to a thirty-five-day national government shutdown, the longest in the United States' history. Much commentary decried the shutdown as a political failure, and some argued that shutdowns demonstrated the flaws in the US Constitution's separation of

6 Amelia Thomson-DeVeaux, *Republicans And Democrats See COVID-19 Very Differently: Is That Making People Sick?* FIVE-THIRTY-EIGHT (July 23, 2020), https://fivethirtyeight.com/features/republicans-and-democrats-see-covid-19-very-differently-is-that-making-people-sick/.

7 For example, most of the Senate debate over the CARES Act focused on policy disputes over specific features of the bill. There were occasional references to the Senate having a duty to act without referencing the Constitution per se. The comment most directly engaging the Constitution came from Minority Leader Chuck Schumer: "The oath we swear to the Constitution means we must protect the general welfare of the people. So let us marshal this government into action." 166 Cong. Rec. S2059 (daily ed. Mar. 25, 2020) (statement of Sen. Schumer); see also 166 CONG. REC. H1845 (daily ed. Mar. 27, 2020) (statement of Rep. Green) ("They want to know that we will promote the general welfare as extolled in the preamble to the Constitution."). For a rare article discussing the government's response to the pandemic in constitutional terms, *see* Ruth Robson, *Positive Constitutionalism and the Pandemic*, 12 CONLAWNOW 15 (2020).

8 South Bay United Pentecostal Church v. Newsom, 141 S.Ct. 716 (Mem) (2021); Roman Catholic Diocese of Brooklyn v. Cuomo, 141 S.Ct. 63 (2020). In other pandemic contexts, the Court has rejected constitutional claims. *See, e.g.*, Food and Drug Administration v. American College of Obstetricians & Gynecologists, 141 S.Ct. 578 (Mem) (2021) (staying a lower court order that had enjoined the requirement that women seeking medication abortions must pick up the required drug in person as a violation of their constitutional rights).

9 *See, e.g.*, Nicole Huberfeld, Sally H. Gordon & David K. Jones, *Federalism Complicates the Response to the COVID-19 Health and Economic Crisis: What Can Be Done?*, 45 J. HEALTH POL., POL'Y & LAW 951 (2020); Nancy J. Knauer, *The Covid-19 Pandemic and Federalism: Who Decides?*, 23 N.Y. U. J. LEGIS. & PUB. POL'Y 1 (2020); Dan Farber, *Federalism and the Pandemic*, CPRBLOG (Apr. 2, 2020), http://progressivereform.org/cpr-blog/federalism-and-pandemic/. Although litigation asserting federalism challenges is much rarer, at least one court has upheld such a claim. Terkel v. CDC, No. 6:20-cv-00564, 2021 WL 742877, at *1-*2 (E.D. Tex. Feb. 25, 2021).

10 *See supra* note 8.

powers structure, especially compared to parliamentary systems.[11] Others contended that the federal government violated the Thirteenth Amendment by requiring workers performing essential functions to keep working without pay until the shutdown ended.[12] But few suggested that a shutdown of national government itself raised constitutional concerns.[13] Surely, however, if securing effective government is an important constitutional goal, an over-one-month-long hiatus in the operation of national government has constitutional ramifications.

To be sure, in some contexts governmental failure is framed in constitutional terms. Courts have held that governmental failure to provide adequate medical care in prison or to adequately train their employees may violate the Constitution.[14] More unusually, advocates have started to challenge governmental failures to address climate change as constitutional violations.[15] Yet federal courts have rejected these climate change claims, in part on the grounds that individuals have no constitutional right to a life-sustaining climate.[16] Moreover, it is notoriously hard to succeed on systemic challenges to governmental functioning even when courts have acknowledged that constitutional rights are implicated.[17]

Put simply, effective government is today at best a sideshow in constitutional discourse, doctrine, and theory. In many ways, this situation is not surprising. It reflects the well-established doctrinal view that the US Constitution does not provide affirmative rights to governmental action and instead grants government powers subject to a variety of negative constraints, with questions about how those powers are wielded otherwise left to the political realm.[18] Nor is it at all clear how to

[11] *See, e.g.*, Dylan Matthews, *The Shutdown Is the Constitution's Fault*, WASH. POST, Oct. 2, 2013; Katharine G. Young, *American Exceptionalism and Government Shutdowns: A Comparative Constitutional Reflection on the 2013 Lapse in Appropriations*, 94 B.U. L. REV. 991, 992–93 (2014).

[12] Meagan Flynn, *Compelled to Work Without Pay, Federal Employees Sue Trump, Accusing Him of Violating 13th Amendment*, WASH. POST., Jan. 14, 2019.

[13] For rare discussions along these lines, *see* Alfred Hill, *Opinion: The Shutdowns and the Constitution*, 115 POL. SCI. Q. 273 (2000) (discussing the 1995–6 shutdown); Vicki C. Jackson, *Pro-constitutional Representation: Comparing the Role Obligations of Judges and Elected Representatives in Constitutional Democracy*, 57 WM. & MARY L. REV. 1717, 1775–76 (2013) (arguing that the 2013 shutdown was a failure of "pro-constitutional representation").

[14] Brown v. Plata, 563 U.S. 493, 511 (2011); City of Canton v. Harris, 489 U.S. 378, 388 (1989).

[15] *See* Juliana v. United States, 947 F.3d 1159, 1169 (9th Cir. 2020); Clean Air Council v. United States, 362 F.Supp.3d 237, 250 (EDPA 2019).

[16] Clean Air Council, 362 F.Supp.3d at 250–53 (no constitutional right implicated); Juliana, 947 F.3d at 1169–73 (noting the debate about whether a constitutional right exists, but concluding that, even if it does, federal courts cannot redress violations). State courts are more hospitable to such claims based on state law. *See, e.g.*, Robinson Twp. v. Commonwealth, 83 A.3d 901, 974 (Pa. 2013) (holding that the state constitutional obligation that Pennsylvania act as "trustee to conserve and maintain the public natural resources for the benefit of the people," including future generations, is enforceable in court).

[17] Gillian E. Metzger, *The Constitutional Duty to Supervise*, 124 YALE L. J. 1836, 1860–70 (2015).

[18] DeShaney v. Winnebago Cty. Dep't of Soc. Servs., 489 U.S. 189, 195 (1989). For a synopsis of this view and the scholarly criticism it has provoked, *see* Emily Zackin, *Positive Rights*, *in* THE OXFORD HANDBOOK ON THE CONSTITUTION (Mark Tushnet, Mark Graber & Sanford Levinson eds., 2015).

translate effective government concerns into a constitutional form or why we should do so. What does "effective government" mean – minimally adequate government or something more, and how much more? Would individuals have a constitutional right to effective government, or is effective government best understood as a collective obligation on the part of elected officials? Either way, would a constitutional concern with effective government be judicially enforceable, and how? The pandemic demonstrates the difficulty of trying to operationalize such an inquiry; even though the Trump Administration's response was deeply flawed, it was responding to an unfolding crisis not of its initial creation and marked by tremendous uncertainty. Does it make sense to think about that response as a constitutional failure of effective government, and what would such a framing add? Finally, perhaps most basically, what is the constitutional basis for bringing in effective government concerns and claims?

The difficulties in operationalizing effective government in constitutional terms are substantial. I touch on these issues, but my focus here is on highlighting effective governance's constitutional roots and justifying why recognizing these roots is valuable. Although conservatives claim that the Constitution sought to protect individual liberty by impeding governmental action rather than encouraging it,[19] in fact a commitment to effective government underlay the Constitution's creation and structure. Similarly, an active national state was evident in the nation's early years and decades, albeit a subject of some contestation and debate. Acknowledging effective government's constitutional basis matters in part to counter the conservative vision and constitutional attack on the administrative state that is now gaining judicial favor. It is additionally important for developing a fuller constitutional discourse, one that better embraces the idea that not all constitutional questions are for the courts to resolve.

12.2 EFFECTIVE GOVERNMENT'S CONSTITUTIONAL ROOTS

The Declaration of Independence is a testament to the value that the Founding generation put on effective government. At the core of the Declaration's justification of independence was a condemnation of King George III for failing to allow government in the colonies to function:

> He has refused his Assent to Laws[,] . . . forbidden his Governors to pass Laws of immediate and pressing importance, . . . dissolved Representative Houses repeatedly . . . [and] refused for a long time, after such dissolutions, to cause others to be elected . . . the State remaining in the mean time exposed to all the dangers of invasion from without, and convulsions within.[20]

19 Gundy v. United States, 139 S.Ct. 2116, 2133–34 (2019) (Gorsuch, J., dissenting).

20 The Declaration of Independence, paras. 3–4, 7–8 (U.S. 1776).

Moreover, the Declaration's identification of "the pursuit of happiness" as one of the "unalienable rights" that "Governments are instituted among Men" to "secure" is relevant as well.[21] William Novak and Stephen Pincus argue that to the signers of the Declaration "the pursuit of happiness ... mean[t] the promotion of the public good or welfare," and that they "believed passionately that states had a responsibility positively to promote the happiness of their populations."[22]

A concern to have government function better is equally evident in the Constitution's initial words. The goals set out in the Preamble – "to form a more perfect Union, establish Justice, insure domestic Tranquility, provide for the common defence, promote the general Welfare, and secure the Blessings of Liberty to ourselves and our Posterity" – all depend upon a functioning government for their realization.[23] Moreover, the Constitution then proceeds to "constitute" an expanded and empowered national government: reconfiguring Congress and expanding its authority, adding a new executive branch headed by a president, and creating the federal courts.[24] As others have noted, the constraints the Constitution imposes are inseparable from the government institutions it creates and the powers it grants.[25] Typically, the constitutional concern with securing effective government is associated with creation of the executive branch, with its "energy" and enforcement role. It is, after all, Alexander Hamilton's Federalist 70 on the executive branch that most overtly discusses the need for energetic and good government. Hamilton wrote: "Energy in the Executive is a leading character in the definition of good government. ... A feeble Executive implies a feeble execution of the government. A feeble execution is but another phrase for a bad execution; and a government ill executed, whatever it may be in theory, must be, in practice, a bad government."[26] Hamilton proceeded to list several structural factors leading to the US executive's energy, the chief of which was its unitarian structure compared to the numerosity of the legislature.[27] Although Hamilton was no doubt particularly enamored of the energetic executive, several others at the constitutional convention similarly spoke of such energy as an important feature.[28] The Constitution's

21 *Id.* para. 2; William J. Novak & Steven Pincus, *Revolutionary State Formation: The Origins of the Strong American State*, *in* State Formations: Global Histories and Cultures of Statehood 138, 143–45 (John L. Brooke et al. eds., 2018).

22 Novak & Pincus, *supra* note 21, at 146.

23 I am certainly not the first to invoke the Declaration and the Preamble as the basis for constitutional obligations on government. *See, e.g.*, Sotirios A. Barber, Welfare and the Constitution 29, 92, 100–06 (2003); Charles L. Black, Jr., *Further Reflections On The Constitutional Justice of Livelihood*, 86 Colum. L. Rev. 1103, 1105–08 (1986).

24 On the weakness of national government under the Articles of Confederation and the framers' commitment to providing additional powers, *see* Michael J. Klarman, The Framers' Coup 11–48 (2016).

25 *See* Richard H. Fallon, *Constitutional Constraints*, 97 Calif. L. Rev. 975, 987–89 (2009).

26 The Federalist No. 70, at 421–29 (Alexander Hamilton) (Clinton Rossiter ed., 2003).

27 *See id.*

28 *See* Jack N. Rakove, Original Meanings 43 (1996) (noting that Hamilton, Robert Morris, and James Wilson were enthusiastic on executive energy); Michael W. McConnell, The President Who Would Not Be King 33, 65 (2020).

text cements this connection of the executive and effective government with its imposition of a duty on the president to "take care that the laws be faithfully executed."[29]

Yet the creation of the executive was just one of several moves aimed at overcoming the deep dysfunctionalities of the Articles of Confederation system. Many of these moves involved empowering Congress, most notably by providing Congress with direct powers to tax, spend, and regulate, as well as military powers and such implied powers as were "necessary and proper for carrying into Execution" the powers granted by the Constitution.[30] Indeed, members of the constitutional "convention displayed a striking degree of consensus on substantially expanding Congress's powers."[31] And, not surprisingly, opposition to these grants of authority and the empowerment of the national government were central to the arguments of the Antifederalists, those who opposed the Constitution's ratification.[32]

Recent scholarship has sought to highlight the empowering efforts that underlay the Constitution. Historians such as Max Edling and Brian Balogh have emphasized the nation-state creation goals of the framers, as well as the substantial efforts to build out the new American state throughout the nineteenth century.[33] Edling revisits the Federalist–Antifederalist debate to argue that Federalists were more intent on creating a powerful central state, particularly when it came to fiscal and military matters, than often recognized.[34] Balogh underscores that these nation-state-building efforts often occurred out of sight – in the territories and at the border; through the army, courts, and the postal system; and through national subsidization of private and voluntary actors.[35] Both recognize the potent anti-statism that was also present at the Founding and in the years since, which heavily influenced how state power was wielded. Their point is that a commitment to a strong national government has existed alongside these anti-statist forces from the outset.

This is an important corrective. The anti-statist strain in the United States has often obscured the critical developmental and regulatory functions that national, state, and local governments have long played.[36] Battles over the proper role and size of government ran throughout the nineteenth century to the twentieth, from the early fights over the national bank and internal improvements, through the Civil War and Reconstruction, through progressivism to the New Deal to today. The desire to downplay government has spanned political parties – think President Bill Clinton's proclamation in 1996 that the era of big government was over, or neoliberalism's

[29] U.S. Const. art. II, §3.

[30] U.S. Const. art. I, §8.

[31] Klarman, *supra* note 24, at 154.

[32] *Id.* at 317–48.

[33] Several other historians have helped illuminate the extent of an early national administrative state. *See, e.g.*, Jerry Mashaw, Creation of the Administrative Constitution (2012); William J. Novak, *The Myth of the "Weak" American State*, 113 Am. Hist. Rev. 752, 757–62 (2008).

[34] Max Edling, A Revolution in Favor of Government (2003).

[35] Brian Balogh, A Government Out of Sight (2009).

[36] *See* Novak, *supra* note 33, at 753–57.

paeans to market-based regulatory tools over more "command-and-control" governmental demands. In the Reagan and post-Reagan era, calling for expanded, better resourced, more powerful government was thought a recipe for political failure. The Trump Administration's promise to "deconstruct" the administrative state was just the most recent manifestation of this conservative, anti-statist orientation.[37] Although not forestalling the development of a robust and active national government, this rhetoric has helped shape programs so that the state's involvement is often hidden and "submerged."[38]

In the face of such anti-statism and skepticism about regulation, with governmental heavy lifting happening outside of public view, it would not be surprising that the value of active and effective government dropped off our constitutional radar. Yet the country has also periodically and openly embraced active government, both in moments of national crisis and in ordinary times. More importantly, whatever its historical and cultural roots, the image of US anti-statism as an independent feature of our national landscape embedded in the Constitution is false. On the contrary, it is a constructed phenomenon, one that has always reflected particular political, economic, ideological, and regional interests.

The debate over internal improvements in the first half of the nineteenth century underscores this constructed character. Internal improvements – from lighthouses, to canals, roads, universities, and railways – are in many ways the epitome of an energetic, active state. Washington, Hamilton, and the Federalists were enamored of them, viewing internal improvements as a way to develop the new republic and keep its far-flung parts united. Jefferson was far more leery of such governmental endeavors and voiced concerns that internal improvements exceeded Congress's constitutional authority, as did Madison, Monroe, and Jackson.[39] Although these constitutional concerns often dominated debate in Congress, opposition to improvement projects was always animated by other factors as well, such as rival economic or regional interests. The South in particular feared the threat that an active national state might pose to slavery.[40] Perhaps more importantly, such constitutional doubts did not prevent improvements from occurring. It was Jefferson who made the Louisiana Purchase, it was under Jefferson that the Cumberland Road was built, and it was Albert Gallatin, Jefferson's Secretary of Treasury, who proposed a plan for a system of improvements.[41] And while Madison, Monroe, and Jackson all famously

37 *See* Gillian E. Metzger, *Supreme Court, 2016 Term–Foreword: 1930s Redux: The Administrative State Under Siege*, 131 Harv. L. Rev. 1, 9–17 (2017).

38 Suzanne Mettler, The Submerged State 4–6, 15–20 (2011).

39 John Lauritz Larson, Internal Improvement: National Public Works and the Promise of Popular Government in the Early United States 5, 18–20, 53–61 (2003); Ronald P. Formisano, *State Development in the Early Republic: Substance and Structure, 1780–1840*, *in* Contesting Democracy 7, 12–14, 16–21 (Byron E. Shafer & Anthony J. Badger eds., 2001).

40 Formisano, *supra* note 39, at 20–25; Steven Minicucci, *Internal Improvements and the Union, 1790–1860*, 18 Stud. in Am. Pol. Dev. 160, 163–65 & n.12 (2004).

41 Larson, *supra* note 39, at 40, 52–62.

vetoed some improvement bills, they allowed other measures to go forward and internal improvements represented a significant share of the national budget in the period 1825–38.[42]

The net result was anti-statist constitutional rhetoric that obscured the significant degree to which the state was fostering development and actively building out the nation. There were many who rejected this rhetoric and insisted that internal improvements were within Congress's constitutional powers. Such supporters of internal improvements justified these measures in terms straight from the Constitution's preamble, maintaining that Congress had an obligation to undertake internal improvements in order to advance the "general welfare" and help build "a more perfect union." Thus, for example, in his speech in Congress urging passage of the 1817 Bonus Bill, John Calhoun invoked the threat of "disunion" stemming from the nation's vast expanse and urged that the solution lay in internal improvements: "We are under the most imperious obligation to counteract every tendency to disunion. ... Let us ... bind the Republic together with a perfect system of roads and canals."[43] Henry Clay made similar arguments.[44] A strong defense of improvements as reflecting a governmental obligation also came from President John Quincy Adams in his First Annual Message to Congress. There he argued that "[t]he great object of the institution of civil government is the improvement in the condition of those who are parties to the social compact," including improvement in "communications and intercourse" through "roads and canals" as well as "moral, political, and intellectual improvement." Fostering such improvement was a central responsibility of government: "For the fulfillment of those duties governments are invested with power, and to the attainment of the end – the progressive improvement of the condition of the governed – the exercise of delegated powers is a duty as sacred and indispensable as the usurpation of powers not granted is criminal and odious."[45]

The internal improvements debate also highlights another reason for effective government's exclusion from contemporary constitutional discourse: These constitutional debates overwhelming occurred in the political sphere. Although the Supreme Court blessed nation-state building by taking a capacious view of Congress's powers in *McCulloch* v. *Maryland*, that decision hardly resolved the constitutional dispute over congressional authority.[46] This political dominance is a far cry from today's constitutional debates, which overwhelmingly take place in

42 Minicucci, *supra* note 40, at 162–67 (detailing the different constitutional views of these presidents and their willingness to support different types of improvement).

43 Internal Improvement, 30 ANNALS OF CONG. 854 (1817) (Calhoun); Michael J. Hostetler, *The Early American Quest for Internal Improvements: Distance and Debate*, 29 RHETORICA 53, 61, 64–65, 69–70 (2011).

44 LARSON, *supra* note 39, at 113–15.

45 John Quincy Adams, First Annual Message to Congress (Dec. 6, 1825). For an analysis of the constitutional arguments in the internal improvement debates, *see* Alison LaCroix, *The Interbellum Constitution: Federalism in the Long Founding Moment*, 67 STAN. L. REV. 397 (2015).

46 17 U.S. 316 (1819); Andrew Jackson Veto Message: Bank Veto, July 10, 1832.

courts accompanied by assertions of judicial constitutional supremacy.[47] Not only does political constitutionalism occur in a different venue but it often takes a different form than the judicial constitutional discourse with which we are now more familiar.[48] Thus, for example, Calhoun and Adams mixed arguments closely tied to the Constitution's text with broad policy and normative claims, as did improvements' opponents.[49]

Judicial constitutional involvement grew substantially after the Civil War, but increasingly took the form of judicial decisions invalidating or limiting legislative measures. Yet by the time of the New Deal era, defenders of active government succeeded in getting courts to uphold broad accounts of the scope of legislative power at the national and state levels.[50] To be sure, an emphasis on effective government often entails a broad view of legislative power, and thus arguments for an obligation to improve the country went hand-in-hand with claims that internal improvements fell within the scope of Congress's constitutional authority. At the same time, however, suggesting that governments have a constitutional obligation to act is at odds with claiming that the political branches enjoy broad discretion to set policy as they see fit. Critically, the latter framing leaves governmental inaction in the face of urgent problems as a perfectly valid constitutional option. As a result, contemporary judicial acceptance of broad congressional policy-setting discretion is simultaneously a prerequisite for and an obstacle to acknowledging a constitutional obligation to provide effective government.

Viewing effective government as a constitutional concern similarly appears somewhat in tension with the New Deal constitutional compromise, which treated economic and social policy as strictly political and limited judicial intervention to enforcing individual noneconomic rights or remedying blockages in the democratic process.[51] On the one hand, this compromise led to perhaps the most visible connection of effective government to the Constitution. In several contexts – prisons, schools, and mental hospitals are prime examples – federal courts came to hold that individuals' constitutional rights were violated when government institutions failed to function adequately, and as a result required systemic reform.[52] But these judicial efforts at systemic reform were attacked as illegitimately intruding on

47 *See* Shelby Cty v. Holder, 570 U.S. 529, 556 (2013) (invalidating the preclearance formula of the Voting Rights Act as outside Congress's enforcement power); United States v. Windsor, 570 U.S. 744, 760–62 (2013) (emphasizing "the separation-of-powers principle that 'when an Act of Congress is alleged to conflict with the Constitution, "[i]t is emphatically the province and duty of the judicial department to say what the law is."' Zivotofsky v. Clinton, 566 U.S. 189, 196 (2012) (quoting Marbury v. Madison, 1 Cranch 137, 177 (1803)).

48 *See* Keith E. Whittington, Constitutional Construction 1–15 (1999).

49 Adams, *supra* note 45; Internal Improvement, *supra* note 43.

50 Barry Friedman, The Will of the People 229–35 (2009).

51 *See, e.g.*, United States v. Carolene Prod. Co., 304 U.S. 144, 153 n.4 (1938); Bruce A. Ackerman, *Beyond Carolene Products*, 98 Harv. L. Rev. 713, 713–17 (1985).

52 Margo Schlanger, *Civil Rights Injunctions over Time: A Case Study of Jail and Prison Court Orders*, 81 N.Y.U. L. Rev. 550, 558–64, 605–12 (2006).

the political sphere by assuming control over resource allocation and policy-setting, decisions that the compromise assigned to democratically elected political leaders. Critics also argued that federal courts lacked the necessary institutional competency to undertake systemic reform successfully and were undercutting federalism by intruding in core state functions.[53] The net result was growing judicial reluctance to allow such systemic challenges on constitutional grounds, especially where governments do not exercise ongoing control over individuals.[54]

The idea of a constitutional commitment to effective government might seem to raise similar concerns of illegitimately intruding on democratic control and usurping the prerogatives of the political branches. Yet, if democracy is understood as necessitating governmental ability to act on public priorities and policy preferences, ensuring effective government becomes a requirement for democracy rather than a restriction upon it. A notable example of this view comes from the report by the President's Committee on Administration and Management created by President Franklin Delano Roosevelt. A repeated and central theme of the report was democracy's dependence on effective and capable government:

> By democracy we mean getting things done that we, the American people, want done in the general interest. Without results we know that democracy means nothing and ceases to be alive in the minds and hearts of men. . . . After the people's judgment has been expressed in due form, after the representatives of the Nation have made the necessary laws, we intend that these decisions shall be promptly, effectively, and economically put into action.[55]

The Committee went even further, insisting more contentiously that "[s]trong executive leadership is essential to democratic government today."[56] This statement is at the very least incomplete, as it fails to acknowledge the threat that a strong executive can pose to democracy. But that should not obscure the truth of the Committee's insight that democracy means much less – and is more vulnerable to authoritarian takeover – without effective implementation of the programs and policies that popularly elected representatives have chosen.[57]

At times, the Supreme Court has too blithely ignored this insight. Perhaps the paradigmatic example is its statement, when invalidating the line-item veto in *INS* v. *Chadha*, that "[t]he fact that a given law or procedure is efficient, convenient, and useful in facilitating functions of government, standing alone, will not save it if it is

53 *See* Missouri v. Jenkins, 515 U.S. 70, 131–33 (1994) (Thomas, J., concurring); *see also* Jason Parkin, *Aging Injunctions and the Legacy of Institutional Reform Litigation*, 70 Vand. L. Rev. 167, 182–89 (2017) (summarizing critiques).

54 *See, e.g.*, City of Los Angeles v. Lyons, 461 U.S. 95, 105–10 (1983); Bell v. Wolfish, 441 U.S. 520, 562 (1979).

55 President's Comm. on Admin. Mgmt., Administrative Management in the Government of the United States 1 (1937).

56 *Id.* at 47.

57 For a recent discussion of the Committee's report as a response to fascism, *see* Noah A. Rosenblum, *The Antifascist Roots of Presidential Administration*, 122 Colum. L. Rev. 1 (2022).

contrary to the Constitution. Convenience and efficiency are not the primary objectives – or the hallmarks – of democratic government."[58] On other occasions, however, the Court has acknowledged the constitutional emphasis on "workable government,"[59] recognizing that functionality is an important constitutional value as well.

The Court's broader point in *Chadha* was to underscore that the constitutional separation of powers system was set up to ensure checked and balanced power, not efficiency. Or, as Justice Alito recently put the point: "Our Constitution, by careful design, prescribes a process for making law, and within that process there are many accountability checkpoints. The Constitution's deliberative process was viewed by the Framers as a valuable feature, . . . not something to be lamented and evaded."[60] Plainly, this deliberative process can pose barriers to effective government by making it difficult for Congress to enact legislation and address pressing problems. But the Constitution can contain goals and commitments that are in tension. After all, exercises of government power can threaten individual rights, and vice versa. Perhaps more important, it is a mistake to view separation of powers and effective government as necessarily opposed. That was not the view of the framers, who separated out executive and legislative power, conjoined under the Articles of Confederation, and created the executive branch in order to have more effective government. And the framers viewed energetic government as serving the same goal as the deliberative process adopted for legislative enactments: as a means of protecting liberty. In *Federalist* 70, Hamilton listed energy in the executive as "essential to the steady administration of the laws; to the protection of property against those irregular and high-handed combinations which sometimes interrupt the ordinary course of justice; to the security of liberty against the enterprises and assaults of ambition, of faction, and of anarchy."[61]

Finally, the complaint that according effective government constitutional salience would trample on the prerogatives of the political branches presumes that a constitutional claim to effective government would be primarily judicially enforced. An alternative approach would understand effective government as a constitutional commitment largely left for the political branches to honor, as was the case with respect to internal improvements. For several reasons, such a political approach to enforcement is particularly appropriate here. One is the indeterminacy of what effective government requires for constitutional purposes. How should effectiveness be measured? Does effective government mean minimally effective, sufficiently effective, or maximally effective government? Should

58 INS v. Chadha, 462 U.S. 919, 944 (1983).

59 Mistretta v. US, 488 U.S. 361, 382 (1989) (quoting Youngstown Sheet & Tube v. Sawyer,343 U.S. 579, 635 (1952) (Jackson, J., concurring) ("While the Constitution diffuses power the better to secure liberty, it also contemplates that practice will integrate the dispersed powers into a workable government.").

60 Dept of Transp. v. Assn of Am. Railroads, 135 S.Ct. 1225, 1237 (2015) (Alito, J., concurring).

61 *See also* Balogh, *supra* note 35, at 54, 56.

effectiveness be assessed at a government-wide, program-wide, or more specific level? And so on. The Constitution offers no clear answers, and courts are ill-suited to make these determinations, all the more so when judicial involvement forces the political branches to take actions that they would not otherwise undertake. More specifically, securing effective government often involves committing resources, and the Constitution quite clearly gives control of the federal purse to Congress.[62] In addition, effective government is particularly systemic and collective in cast. This is not to say that individuals cannot have a right to effective government. But such a right would be so broadly shared as to feel more political than juridical. Even institutional reform litigation appears more cabined, both by being limited to those subject to the particular institution or program at issue and by asserting specific constitutional or statutory rights that are violated as a result of how poorly that institution or program is run.

Although direct judicial enforcement of a constitutional commitment to effective government is therefore problematic, indirect forms of judicial enforcement are more plausible. Courts could acknowledge the constitutional value accorded effective government when assessing separate constitutional or legal challenges that do take a determinate and individualized form. True, doing so would entail a more free-form constitutional analysis, but that is true of most structural constitutionalism today.[63]

12.3 WHY CONSTITUTIONALIZE EFFECTIVE GOVERNMENT?

In short, effective government has many roots in the US Constitution, making it fair to identify a constitutional commitment to effective government and an obligation on the part of Congress and the president to secure its realization. The question that remains is why do so. Particularly if this constitutional commitment and obligation are not directly judicially enforceable and thus will take shape in the political realm, what is gained by insisting on effective government's constitutional basis?

Put in more concrete terms, what does understanding the federal government's initial pandemic response as a constitutional failure add to our understanding of that event, already viewed by many as a collapse of political leadership and morally bankrupt given the unnecessary deaths and inequitable burdens that resulted? Given the constitutional concerns of federalism and individual liberty already at issue with the government's pandemic response, arguably adding yet another constitutional frame simply obscures more than it elucidates. Similar points could be made about government shutdowns. These result from intense political clashes and involve Congress and the president asserting their clear constitutional powers to reject legislation. Especially with the appropriations power increasingly becoming Congress's main lever in pushing back at executive branch unilateralism, shutdowns

[62] U.S. Const., art. I, §§ 8, 9 cl. 7.

[63] For a critique of free-form separation-of-powers analysis, *see* John F. Manning, *Separation of Powers as Ordinary Interpretation*, 124 Harv. L. Rev. 1939 (2011).

can be seen as serving important constitutional purposes even as they undermine effective government. It is therefore not clear that either of these examples is a case of constitutional failure, and effective governance concerns might be more powerfully asserted in a straight political and moral register.

This argument has a great deal of power. It underscores why recognizing effective government's constitutional significance must occur primarily within the political realm and not as a means for trumping political choices. Yet I believe that framing effective government in constitutional terms is valuable, precisely because of how this framing expands and complicates current constitutional understandings.

One way it does so is by challenging the dominant conception of the US Constitution in juriscentric, negative, and individualistic terms. The last few decades have witnessed a notable turn to judicial constitutional supremacy, with a concomitant restriction in legislative power.[64] As a result, simply identifying a constitutional commitment left primarily to political enforcement is a useful corrective. Similarly, identifying an affirmative and systemic constitutional obligation helps rebut an excessively narrow view of the Constitution as essentially negative and individualistic in scope.[65] It is also important to emphasize the connection between effective government and the legislative branch. As noted in Section 12.2, energetic and effective government has long been associated with the executive branch. But many of the powers most central to creating an effective government – powers to legislate, appropriate, and "make all laws which shall be necessary and proper for carrying into execution the foregoing powers, and all other powers vested by this Constitution in the government of the United States" – are constitutionally vested in Congress.[66] Given these authorities, a constitutional account that takes the idea of effective government seriously should put Congress center stage. And, connecting all three of these points, recognizing the constitutional basis of effective government is valuable in suggesting that *Congress* sometimes may have an affirmative constitutional obligation to act, even if that obligation is not one that courts can enforce or even articulate.

Even more significantly, perhaps, emphasizing the constitutional basis of effective government counters constitutional rhetoric that casts the national administrative state as at odds with the separation of powers principles and a threat to individual liberty. This rhetoric has grown at the Supreme Court with the conservative turn of the Roberts Court, but is equally present in nonjudicial spheres.[67] Nor is its impact

64 *See supra* note 47; LARRY D. KRAMER, THE PEOPLE THEMSELVES: POPULAR CONSTITUTIONALISM AND JUDICIAL REVIEW (2004) (critiquing contemporary judicial constitutional supremacy and contrasting it to popular constitutionalism at the Founding); Nikolas Bowie & Daphna Renan, *The Separation-of-Powers Counterrevolution*, 131 Yale L.J. (forthcoming 2022) (tracing historical development of judicial separation of powers enforcement).

65 *See* Metzger, *supra* note 17, at 1859–71 (critiquing the exclusion of systemic administration from constitutional doctrine); Zackin, *supra* note 18, at 724–30 (summarizing numerous arguments for affirmative rights in the U.S. Constitution).

66 U.S. Const., art. I, § 8.

67 *See* Metzger, *supra* note 37, at 9–38; *see also* David E. Lewis, *Deconstructing the Administrative State*, 81 J. POL. 767, 774–83 (2019).

limited to abstract constitutional analysis. On the contrary, this growing anti-statism is partially to blame for the failed pandemic response, with the Trump Administration's commitment to deconstructing the administrative state leading it to dismantle institutional structures aimed at countering pandemics and to resist advice from career government experts.[68] Similarly, although involving actions against state officials, recent decisions enjoining application of public health orders on free exercise grounds have been strikingly skeptical of governmental expertise and underscored the threat such orders pose to individual liberty.[69] And conservative rejection of big government – in part as unconstitutional – has played a role in government shutdowns going back to 1995.[70]

This constitutional anti-statism is deeply contested in politics, the courts, and academe. Numerous scholars have challenged the historical basis of constitutional attacks on modern administrative government, and judges have argued powerfully that challenged measures fall within the scope of congressional power.[71] Less common, however, are accounts that seek to develop a positive constitutional mandate in favor of active government.[72] Identifying the constitutional importance of effective government helps provide that fuller constitutional picture.

68 Paul E. Rutledge, *Trump, COVID-19, and the War on Expertise*, 50 AM. REV. PUB. ADMIN. 505, 506–09 (2020).

69 *See, e.g.*, South Bay United Pentecostal Church v. Newsom, 141 S.Ct. 716, 717–20 (2021) (Gorsuch, J., concurring in part and dissenting in part).

70 Young, *supra* note 11, at 994–98; David Scott Louk & David Gamage, *Preventing Government Shutdowns: Designing Default Rules for Budgets*, 86 U. COLO. L. REV. 181, 217–19 (2015).

71 *See, e.g.*, Gundy v. United States, 139 S.Ct. 2116, 2129–30 (2019); Julian Davis Mortensen & Nicholas Bagley, *Delegation at the Founding*, 121 COLUM. L. REV. 277 (2021); sources cited *supra* in notes 33–35.

72 For a prior effort in this direction, see Metzger, *supra* note 37, at 87–95.

13

The President's Two Bodies

Daphna Renan[*]

For the King has in him two bodies, viz., a body natural, and a body politic. His Body natural (if it be considered in itself) is a body mortal, subject to all infirmities that come by nature or accident . . .. But his body politic is a body that cannot be seen or handled, consisting of policy and government . . ..[1]

13.1 INTRODUCTION

American constitutionalism consists of two quite foundational, conflictual, but ultimately interdependent understandings of the presidency – what we might think of as the president's "two bodies." On one view, the presidency is an *individual* – a "he" (maybe one day "she"). Presidential power is individualistic along three dimensions: it is singular, temporary, and personal. On the other view, the presidency is an *institution*. It is composite, permanent (or at least indefinite), and impersonal. Ever since George Washington embodied the idea of an institution still in the making, we've had this deep tension – these competing impulses between a personal or charismatic president and a more impersonal and deliberative institutional presidency. Public law reveals different perspectives on how to manage this duality. But public law cannot resolve it. Rather, the president's "two bodies" is the defining ambiguity of the constitutional office. It is the conception on which our understandings of presidential power rest.[2]

[*] The content of this chapter is excerpted from Daphna Renan, *The President's Two Bodies*, 120 COLUM. L. REV. 1119 (2020). For terrific research and editorial assistance on that larger project and in creating this excerpt, I thank Ben Miller-Gootnick.

[1] Case of the Duchy of Lancaster (1561) 75 Eng. Rep. 325, 326; 1 Plowd. 212, 213; *see also* ERNST H. KANTOROWICZ, THE KING'S TWO BODIES: A STUDY IN MEDIAEVAL POLITICAL THEOLOGY 7–9 (Princeton Classics ed. 2016).

[2] *Cf.* Martin Loughlin, *The Constitutional Imagination*, 78 MOD. L. REV. 1, 12 (2015) ("[I]deology not only has a distortive or legitimatory role: it also has a constitutive function . . .. Ideology becomes the central concept of the constitutional imagination, the concept on which our understanding of the constitution rests.").

This chapter, an excerpt from a larger project, briefly develops the president's duality along each dimension. In so doing, it shows how our disagreements over presidential power are elucidated through the two-bodies prism. The chapter concludes by synthesizing some of the patterns and themes that emerge.

13.2 SINGULAR/COMPOSITE: THE NATURE OF PRESIDENTIAL INTENT

Consider, first, the question of "presidential intent": Is presidential intent a unitary construct rooted in the purpose and motives of one individual? Or is it instead a composite institution that produces presidential policy through regularized process and inter-agency input? The question has implications both for how courts and executive branch actors interpret presidential orders and for the frameworks that jurists and lawyers use to address constitutionally impermissible animus.

A purely institutional approach to the presidency – one that ignores the intentions of the incumbent – sits uneasily with a "unitary" understanding of the office, which usually focuses on the will of the individual and understands the executive branch as there to do his bidding. Meanwhile, if the institutional presidency *is* central to governance – if its deliberative processes regularize and discipline presidential decision-making – then public law needs some way to decide when or at what point the incumbent's personal motives have become sufficiently attenuated from the decisions of the institutional presidency.

These issues were at the heart of *Trump* v. *Hawaii*.[3] The case concerned a proclamation by President Trump, issued under the Immigration and Nationality Act, to restrict the entry of nationals of eight countries into the United States. Two prior iterations of the policy – what became known as the "travel ban" – were struck down on Establishment Clause and statutory grounds in the lower courts.[4] In disposing of the case, a fractured Supreme Court issued several opinions. Each opinion assumes a different body of the president controls. And its implicitly chosen frame then in effect decides the question presented. What results are three different understandings of the relationship between the individual president and the composite presidency. Yet the work that each is doing in the logic of the opinions is almost entirely implicit. As a result, the opinions seem to talk past each other on the pivotal issues of the case.

13.2.1 *President- versus Presidency-Based Doctrine*

The majority opinion, authored by Chief Justice Roberts, embraces an impersonal, thoroughly institutional presidency. Any anti-Muslim animus of the sitting president is nearly irrelevant to the doctrinal question of whether the presidential

3 138 S. Ct. 2392 (2018).
4 *Id.* at 2403–04.

proclamation violated the First Amendment. So long as the institutional presidency has put forward a national security purpose, and in light of what the majority perceived to be a rigorous inter-agency process, the Court need not assess whether the president himself intended to ban Muslims. Though plaintiffs in the case, along with their amici curiae,[5] established an extensive record of statements from President Trump avowing interest in a Muslim ban and expressing anti-Muslim animus, directing his subordinates to implement such an anti-Muslim policy, and connecting earlier iterations of the presidential proclamation to that objective, the majority did not find those statements probative. At stake was not the conduct of a "particular President," the majority reasoned, but the "authority of the Presidency itself."[6]

The opinion is striking in part because it is written by Chief Justice Roberts, author of *Free Enterprise Fund* v. *Public Co. Accounting Oversight Board*,[7] and joined by the Court's fiercest unitarists.[8] It is widely understood that the Constitution's choice to establish a single chief executive was designed to enable energetic and effective governance, but US scholars and judges are divided on the further implications of this choice for how constrained the president may be by statutes. "Unitary executive" theory typically embraces a construction of the presidency in which implementing the will of the incumbent is central to the proper functioning of Article II of the US Constitution. And yet, the presidency of *Trump* v. *Hawaii* is neither charged with, nor expected to implement, the incumbent's will. It is an institutional infrastructure, seemingly autonomous from presidential interference or at least insulated from the sitting president's impermissible animus.

Recognition of executive "unitariness" – at least insofar as the incumbent has informal powers to direct his subordinates – comes instead from Justice Sotomayor's dissent. Because the sitting president in practice controls the goals and objectives of the presidency, in part by directing his senior aides and his Cabinet, the person of the president cannot – as a legal matter – hide behind the façade of an orderly office. If presidential governance promotes accountability through the incumbent, then his avowed animus has legal consequence: Deference ordinarily afforded to the institution of the presidency is inappropriate when its current inhabitant has expressly repudiated constitutional commitments of religious freedom. For Justice Sotomayor, then, the presidential proclamation was "contaminated" by the incumbent's "impermissible discriminatory animus against Islam and its followers."[9]

5 *See, e.g.*, Brief of Constitutional Law Scholars as Amici Curiae in Support of Respondents at 19–23, *Hawaii*, 138 S. Ct. 2392 (2018) (No. 17–965).

6 *Hawaii*, 138 S. Ct. at 2416–23.

7 561 U.S. 477 (2010).

8 *See, e.g.*, Richard H. Pildes, *Free Enterprise Fund, Boundary-Enforcing Decisions, and the Unitary Executive Branch Theory of Government Administration*, 6 Duke J. Const. L. & Pub. Pol'y 1, 1–2 (2011) (emphasizing the starkly unitary vision of the executive branch in *Free Enterprise Fund*).

9 *Hawaii*, 138 S. Ct. at 2440–45 (Sotomayor, J., dissenting).

Justice Breyer's dissent (joined by Justice Kagan) suggests a middle approach between these presidency- and president-based perspectives: The institutional presidency can operate as a check on the animus-driven objectives of a sitting president. But the question is *has it here?* This is a question for courts to resolve. And the implementation of the proclamation's "elaborate system of exemptions and waivers," by other actors of a composite presidency, provides relevant evidence.[10] "For one thing," Justice Breyer reasons, "the relevant precedents – those of Presidents Carter and Reagan – would bear far less resemblance to the present Proclamation" if the government were not meaningfully implementing these "case-by-case exemption[s]."[11] And, if the government is not implementing the exemption and waiver system specified in the proclamation, then the argument that the proclamation *is* in fact the incumbent's desired "'Muslim ban' . . . becomes much stronger."[12] As Justice Breyer suggests, there is both an individual and an institution at the crux of Article II. The challenge, in adjudicating presidential authority, is to give conceptual and doctrinal content to their interconnection.

13.2.2 *Accommodating the Two Bodies*

Judicial review of presidential instruments requires theories of both decision-making inside the presidency and adjudication or the role of courts in reviewing presidential action.[13] With respect to presidential decision-making, Chief Justice Roberts's focus on the institution makes good sense *absent indicia of an un-institutional decision.* Roberts's opinion valuably reorients questions of presidential decision-making to a more institutional understanding – one that sees inter-agency consultation and the distinctive fact-finding capacities of the executive branch as relevant to an assessment of presidential power.

The problem, however, is that Roberts sees an institution all the way down. Absent from his framework is any consideration of when the incumbent might exercise un-institutional power or why this could matter to our public law understandings of the presidency. This legal and conceptual gap seems to be what Justice Breyer is getting at. Breyer's dissent can be read to suggest something of a burden-shifting model under which evidence of the incumbent's impermissible animus alters the burden of proof, the discovery and evidence available to those challenging the presidency, or some combination of the two. Put differently, it recognizes the possibility of an un-institutional decision, one rooted in the incumbent's personal animus.

10 *Id.* at 2429 (Breyer, J., dissenting).

11 *Id.* at 2430.

12 *Id.*

13 *Cf.* John F. Manning, *Without the Pretense of Legislative Intent*, 130 Harv. L. Rev. 2397, 2431 (2017) ("[E]very theory of [statutory] interpretation involves a question of legislation and a question of adjudication . . . .").

With respect to adjudication, an intermediate approach – that is, an approach primarily focused on the institution but sensitive to the possibility that the individual president could be legally salient – requires further elaboration of why the incumbent's role matters in the first place. Is the court engaged in routine legal interpretation – discerning the legal purpose of a legal instrument, such as a presidential proclamation or executive order? If so, courts might want to assume that the order was developed through the regular, institutional process and that institutional sources (including Department of Justice briefs) are more probative of legal meaning than unfiltered presidential speech.[14]

If the court is trying to sniff out a constitutionally impermissible purpose, however, then adjudication should not ignore clues of an irregular process or an un-institutional decision. A president who acts on unconstitutional animus to effectuate policy through the presidency is not executing institutional power. Rather, he is laundering personal animus through the composite institution of the presidency. In such circumstances, Chief Justice Roberts has it backwards: The question is *not* the "authority of the presidency itself" but the potentially unconstitutional conduct of "a particular president."[15]

A theory of adjudication should also ask whether it is desirable for courts to play some role in regulating the incumbent's rhetoric. Under Chief Justice Roberts's approach, the incumbent's expressed desire for and commitment to effectuating a "Muslim ban" is legally irrelevant. The dissents, by contrast, interpret the incumbent's rhetoric as relevant to a legal accounting of the presidential policy at issue. If avowed animus from the person of the president is uniquely pernicious in our constitutional culture, in part because of the outsized role that the person of the president has come to play in American politics, then we might think that courts should play some role – perhaps especially an indirect one – in checking presidential rhetoric that threatens substantive constitutional commitments. By heightening judicial scrutiny of the policy outputs that follow anti-Muslim speech by the president himself, courts could do two things. They could recognize the possibility of a legal connection between avowed animus on the part of the incumbent and the policies of his presidency. At least as important, courts could serve an expressive function; they could recognize that avowed animus on the part of the incumbent *is* a basis for vigilance from courts to protect religious minorities – not in spite of but because he is president.

13.3 TEMPORARY/CONTINUOUS: INSTITUTIONAL CONSISTENCY AND THE INCUMBENT'S MANDATE FOR CHANGE

If presidential intent highlights what we might think of as the singular/composite dimension of the president's duality, then presidential precedent illustrates its

[14] *See* Katherine Shaw, *Beyond the Bully Pulpit: Presidential Speech in the Courts*, 96 Tex. L. Rev. 71, 100–03 (2017).

[15] *See Hawaii*, 138 S. Ct. at 2418.

temporary/continuous dimension. Consider this threshold question: Why should the decisions of a particular president survive his administration? On an exclusively president-centered view, it is not clear that they should. In contrast to judicial opinions or statutes that, by design, survive their makers, the Article II authority underlying presidential decisions ceases with the end of his term.

Notwithstanding the incumbent's temporary status, however, the presidency needs some way to integrate the decisions of prior presidents. These decisions generate invaluable information about how the presidency has been conducted and the consequences of the choices made. They also affect innumerable individuals, both inside the government and beyond. This means that some presidential decisions create hugely consequential reliance interests, both domestically and abroad. Following the practice of prior presidents can have political advantages for the incumbent as well, and it can provide a source (though not an unqualified source) of legitimacy or acceptability for conduct that the incumbent desires to continue.

Presidential practice is thus a core component of presidential power. It supplies the incumbent with institutional continuity and the capacity to govern in a manner that others in the system deem "respect-worthy."[16] It creates a source of precedent crucial for (though not legally binding on) individual presidents. And it provides a *legal* precedent through which jurists and executive branch lawyers have augmented the scope of presidential power over time.

And yet, if elections matter, if representative democracy means something for the presidency, then a new president must be able to revisit, refine, or repudiate some of the decisions of his predecessors. He needs to have some say, maybe substantial say, in the law and policy of his administration. This is the challenge of presidential precedent: Make it too entrenched through the institution and you inhibit the authority of the current president. Make it too unstable, too focused on the person, and the presidency cannot execute the powers of an indefinite institution. Even as the institutional presidency provides a source of precedent foundational to current understandings of presidential power, the role of the institution as a means of consistency and entrenchment – that is, as a restraint on the incumbent's "presentist" impulses – is a source of recurring tension.

Jurists and administrative law scholars have long debated the conflicting public law goal of stability in executive branch law and policy commitments, on the one hand, and, on the other, democratic responsiveness through the incumbent. This conflict is at the crux of enduring disagreements about the role of administrative law in constraining administrative policy change and the special solicitude that the case law and theory sometimes afford those decisions with the personal imprimatur

16 *See generally* Frank I. Michelman, *Ida's Way: Constructing the Respect-Worthy Governmental System*, 72 Fordham L. Rev. 345 (2003) (exploring what "respect-worthiness" means in a system of constitutional government).

of the president.[17] At its core, the debate concerns the capacity of presidential elections to imbue individual presidents with a mandate for programmatic and ideological change, and the legal implications of such a mandate in the context of national administrative governance. Does something about the distinctive political character of the incumbent give him a unique authority to advance his particular policy and moral vision through the administrative state?[18] Or must policy change be justified on more rational and technocratic grounds? Framing this tension as one of presidential versus administrative government (as is often debated) somewhat obscures the issue, for technocracy exists inside the presidency as well.

Instead, a defining ambivalence of the modern state concerns the charismatic legitimacy of administration *through* the individual of the president, notwithstanding the apparatus of a more rational bureaucracy – both inside the White House and in the agencies – that is capable of producing stable policy and consistent legal interpretations. The danger, increasingly realized, is that the charismatic presidency "can, as it grows stronger, cancel itself out across administrations."[19] As Jerry Mashaw and David Berke observe, the individual president's "ability to control administration has become sufficiently powerful that erasing a prior Administration requires little more than determination – and perhaps a dash of ruthlessness."[20] The "regulatory whiplash" of recent years is not simply a threat to values of regularity or predictability in governance; it is a challenge to the idea of popular sovereignty itself.[21] These erratic swings in American public policy and national commitments underscore the costs of presidential direction even as they call into question the resilience of anything resembling a durable presidential mandate.

And yet, the president *is* the means through which American public law has recognized some connection between administration and sovereignty in a system of policymaking and remaking that increasingly operates without Congress.[22] It is also public law's response to the concern that administrative problems often require *some* value judgment and persistent unease about unelected bureaucrats exercising such moral authority over American life. If technocracy all the way down is either unappealing or

17 *See* Jide Nzelibe, *The Fable of the Nationalist President and the Parochial Congress*, 53 UCLA L. Rev. 1217, 1260–67 (2006) (observing and critiquing this practice).

18 *Cf.* Motor Vehicle Mfrs. Ass'n v. State Farm Mut. Auto. Ins. Co., 463 U.S. 29, 59 (1983) (Rehnquist, J., concurring in part and dissenting in part) ("A change in administration brought about by the people casting their votes is a perfectly reasonable basis for an executive agency's reappraisal of the costs and benefits of its programs and regulations.").

19 Jerry L. Mashaw & David Berke, *Presidential Administration in a Regime of Separated Powers: An Analysis of Recent American Experience*, 35 Yale J. on Regul. 549, 607 (2018).

20 *Id.*

21 *See* Jessica Bulman-Pozen, *Administrative States: Beyond Presidential Administration*, 98 Tex. L. Rev. 265, 280–81, 316–18 (2019).

22 On the early foundations of the relationship between administration and sovereignty, *see generally* Richard Tuck, The Sleeping Sovereign (2016). On the challenges that agencies face in designing policy solutions without Congress, *see generally* Jody Freeman & David B. Spence, *Old Statutes, New Problems*, 163 U. Pa. L. Rev. 1 (2014).

unachievable, then we cannot entirely write out the charismatic president. The challenge for public law is to recognize and hold both commitments at once. How public law manages this duality decides the capacity of the administrative state to make durable national commitments, grounded in science and data, even as it retains some conceptual and legal space for a more transient presidential judgment.

13.4 PERSONAL/IMPERSONAL: DISENTANGLING THE PRESIDENT'S PRIVATE AND PUBLIC CHARACTER

These disagreements point to a further problem: Are the president's official and personal identities fully severable? In contrast to Congress or the courts, "the President never adjourns."[23] The duties and functions of the presidential office are ongoing, underspecified, and, in a fundamental sense, inextricably linked to the persona of its occupant. The boundary of the constitutional office, and the extent to which it overlaps with the personal identity of the incumbent, is a question that cuts across a range of legal frameworks.

The Supreme Court, for example, has recognized an absolute immunity from civil liability for conduct within "the 'outer perimeter' of [the president's] official responsibility."[24] But when does the president's conduct fall beyond this "outer perimeter"? As to the behavior itself, *Clinton* v. *Jones*[25] presented the easy case because the allegations of sexual misconduct involved the person prior to his term as president. Though it recognized that any legal proceedings would need to be structured to accommodate the incumbent's schedule and duties of office, the Court declined to adopt a presidential immunity from damages actions pertaining to the president's "unofficial" conduct.[26] Yet the sexual misconduct claims led to related allegations of defamation that may have occurred after Clinton took office, demonstrating how quickly the legal difficulties emerge. The Court declined to weigh in on the question of whether that separate claim, concerning alleged misconduct by President Clinton after he took office, would be justiciable.[27]

Impeachment presents the same question from the other side. If the sitting president cannot be sued civilly for alleged abuses of office, he *can* be impeached for them.[28] With respect to the presidency, a long-standing debate concerns the question of whether personal misconduct can amount to an abuse of office actionable under the Impeachment Clause.[29] This question was deeply contested during

23 Clinton v. Jones, 520 U.S. 681, 713 (1997) (Breyer, J., concurring).
24 Nixon v. Fitzgerald, 457 U.S. 731, 756 (1982).
25 520 U.S. 681.
26 *See id.* at 691–93.
27 *See id.*
28 Indeed, the availability of impeachment is one of the main arguments in favor of absolute immunity from civil damages in *Fitzgerald*. *See* 457 U.S. at 757.
29 *See* Charles L. Black, Impeachment: A Handbook 24–30 (1998); Cass R. Sunstein, Impeachment: A Citizen's Guide 134 (2017); Laurence Tribe & Joshua Matz, To End a Presidency 43–58 (2018).

the proceedings to impeach President Clinton for sexual misconduct with a White House intern, and his lies under oath to cover it up. Commentators debated whether President Clinton's behavior amounted to personal indiscretions, perhaps "disgraceful" but not impeachable,[30] or whether his misconduct "gravely damage[d] the capacity of the President to lead," and thereby undermined his fitness for office.[31] In a post-Me Too legal and political culture, it might be that the president's sexual indiscretions with a White House intern inside the Oval Office become more recognizable as an abuse of the powers of the office – an argument that did not gain much traction during the Clinton controversy.

If impeachment makes it possible to sever the sitting president from the presidency, however, the national "trauma" that it is said would result only underscores the two bodies' interconnection – the charismatic pull of the person of the president in American constitutional culture.[32] The debate over a presidential "self-pardon" underscores their legal interconnection as well.[33] The self-pardon raises profound rule-of-law concerns precisely because the office and the "flesh-and-blood human occupying [it]" are, in a sense, so inextricable.[34] The Office of Legal Counsel has concluded that a presidential self-pardon would run afoul of the basic premise "that no one may be a judge in his own case."[35] Though the legal question remains contested,[36] President Ford's pardon of Nixon (however politically fraught) is different from a President Nixon pardon of Nixon. It is different in constitutionally meaningful terms; we cannot fully pry apart the office and the person occupying it.

30 *See, e.g.*, Background and History of Impeachment, Hearing Before the Subcomm. on the Constitution of the H. Comm. on the Judiciary, 105th Cong. 98 (1998) (statement of Arthur M. Schlesinger, Jr., Professor of History, City University of New York).

31 *Id.* at 95 (statement of Richard D. Parker, Williams Professor of Law, Harvard University School of Law).

32 Laurence H. Tribe, *The Three Key Questions of Impeachment*, Slate (Sept. 30, 2019), https://slate.com/news-and-politics/2019/09/impeachment-ukraine-and-its-costs-three-key-questions.html; *see also* James Bryce, The American Commonwealth 190 (1888) (observing that "[i]mpeachment ... is the heaviest piece of artillery in the congressional arsenal, but because it is so heavy it is unfit for ordinary use," and emphasizing that it is exceptionally difficult for Congress to remove a sitting president through impeachment).

33 The Constitution prohibits a pardon "in cases of impeachment." U.S. Const. art. II, § 2, cl. 1.

34 *Cf.* Trump v. Mazars USA, LLP, 940 F.3d 710, 725–26 (D.C. Cir. 2019) (observing that a challenged subpoena to a third party seeking financial documents related to Donald Trump in his pre-presidential, private capacity "presents no direct inter-branch dispute [but] separation-of-powers concerns still linger in the air").

35 Presidential or Legislative Pardon of the President, 1 Op. O.L.C. 370 (1974).

36 *Compare, e.g.*, Robert Nida & Rebecca L. Spiro, *The President as His Own Judge and Jury: A Legal Analysis of the Presidential Self-Pardon Power*, 52 Okla. L. Rev. 197, 198–201 (1999) (arguing that text and history support self-pardons and proposing a constitutional amendment), *and* Saikrishna Bangalore Prakash, Imperial from the Beginning: The Constitution of the Original Executive 108 (2015) (defending self-pardon on originalist grounds), *with* Andrew Kent, Ethan J. Leib & Jed Handelsman Shugerman, *Faithful Execution and Article II*, 132 Harv. L. Rev. 2111, 2189–90 (2019) (arguing against self-pardons on originalist grounds), *and* Brian C. Kalt, Note, *Pardon Me: The Constitutional Case Against Presidential Self-Pardons*, 106 Yale L. J. 779, 781 (1996) (arguing that constitutional text, structure, history, and policy proscribe self-pardons).

Indeed, perceptions of the person as head of state create confusions of another sort. A long-standing debate concerns the president's authority to empower "personal" representatives in the conduct of foreign affairs.[37] Ever since President Washington dispatched Gouverneur Morris to serve as his "private Agent" in discussions with the British, such agents have been part of the tapestry of presidential leadership.[38] Yet these agents occupy a constitutionally ambiguous posture as the personal representative of the president charged with advancing the nation's foreign policy interests.[39] Such representatives often lack any official status and do not undergo advice and consent in the Senate, even as they exercise significant informal power to effectuate US policy as a result of their perceived intimacy with or proximity to the incumbent. Scholars and lawyers debate whether this use of "ad hoc diplomats" is permitted under the Appointments Clause, and also whether it can be statutorily restricted.[40]

Finally, a spate of recent cases challenge President Trump's receipt of payments by foreign, federal, and state governments in connection with the Trump International Hotel in Washington as a violation of the Emoluments Clauses.[41] Defending the president, the Justice Department has argued that an emolument "must be predicated on services rendered in an official capacity."[42] The plaintiffs in these cases argue that the term should be interpreted more broadly but that, in any event, the distinction simply collapses as applied to the president: "When the President interacts with domestic governments or foreign nations, he does not do so as an 'ordinary citizen,' but as a head of state whom they have a powerful incentive to influence in any way possible."[43]

Ultimately, the legal lines demarcating a presidential or "public" character are insoluble in their own terms. Rather, those lines must be constructed in reference to the substantive values at stake, such as the norm against self-dealing or the

[37] *See* Maurice Waters, *Special Diplomatic Agents of the President*, 307 Annals Am. Acad. Pol. & Soc. Sci. 124, 125 (1956).

[38] Ryan M. Scoville, *Ad Hoc Diplomats*, 68 Duke L. J. 907, 980–81 (2019); *see also* Maurice Waters, The Ad Hoc Diplomat: A Study in Municipal and International Law 7 (1963).

[39] Maurice Waters, *The Ad Hoc Diplomat: A Legal and Historical Analysis*, 6 Wayne L. Rev. 380, 392 (1960) ("If the agent were exploring a matter pertinent to the executive's personal life . . . it might be maintained that [the action is without] bearing upon the State. But in each mission known to this writer the objective had some bearing, at times significant . . .[,] upon United States' policy.").

[40] *See* Scoville, *supra* note 38, at 913, 915–16 (contesting on originalist grounds the "orthodox" view that ad hoc diplomatic appointments are constitutional without Senate confirmation); *see also* Cory R. Gill & Susan B. Epstein, Cong. Research Serv., R44946, State Department Special Envoy, Representative, and Coordinator Positions: Background and Congressional Actions 2–4 (2017) (discussing S. 1631, a bill that would have limited the use of ad hoc diplomats and expanded advice-and-consent requirements).

[41] *See, e.g.*, Bobby Allyn, *Trump Still Faces 3 Lawsuits over His Business Empire*, NPR (Dec. 12, 2019, 5:00 AM), https://www.npr.org/2019/12/12/787167408/trump-still-faces-3-lawsuits-over-his-business-empire.

[42] Memorandum in Support of Defendant's Motion to Dismiss at 32, District of Columbia v. Trump, 315 F. Supp. 3d 875 (D. Md. 2018) (17-cv-1596).

[43] Memorandum of Law in Support of Plaintiffs' Opposition to Motion to Dismiss at 38, *District of Columbia*, 315 F. Supp. 3d 875 (17-cv-1596).

commitment to effective governance. Those substantive commitments are contained not *within* the duality but in the substantive constitutional order in which the presidency exists.

13.5 CONCLUSION: UNDERSTANDING THE CONSTITUTIONAL PRESIDENCY

The duality plays a role in how we understand the legitimacy of presidential power by equivocating on the idea of "the president." The president means two different things; it has two distinct bundles of attributes. This enables constitutional and political argument to obscure the ways in which each body creates constitutional unease by emphasizing attributes that inhere in the other – and by suggesting or implying that those attributes pertain to the president as a whole.

Failing to ask which body is being relied upon in a particular context (and why) creates some incoherence in our law, but, more importantly, it opens the door to opportunism. Jurists and executive branch lawyers can rely on whichever body expands (or, if this is one's preference, contracts) presidential power in a particular decisional domain.[44] The conflictual accounts of presidential power in *Free Enterprise Fund* and *Trump* v. *Hawaii* are suggestive of this dynamic. If public law requires the president to be personally responsible for the decisions of the presidency, then the animus of the incumbent is salient, even central to the constitutional analysis of impermissible discriminatory intent. If, on the other hand, the individual president does not fully control the decisions of the institution, then a central (and growing) critique of the administrative state – that limits on the sitting president's control over administration render aspects of the administrative state unconstitutional – is overdrawn. Power sharing between the elected president and unelected bureaucrats occurs at the center of the presidency as well; it is a facet of, not a threat to, presidential power.

Even as it obfuscates political and legal disagreements, however, the duality is also constitutive of "the president" that exists. The two-bodies conception orients practice toward certain fundamental, though conflicting, ideas about what the exercise of presidential power should actually entail. In this sense, the "two bodies" play a role in legitimating presidential power by shaping what the office is. That we have a presidency distinct from any individual incumbent is an organizing tenet of American constitutional practice. It structures patterns of behavior across the institution of the presidency and among those who interact with it. Presidential lawyers interpret law and establish precedent with the understanding that they are creating rules to govern not just "their guy" but future occupants. This has the effect of both constraining and empowering the constitutional office. Lawyers may look for limiting principles that will restrain the exercise of presidential judgment when it is

[44] *Cf.* Karl N. Llewellyn, *Remarks on the Theory of Appellate Decision and the Rules or Canons About How Statutes Are to Be Construed*, 3 VAND. L. REV. 395, 395–400 (1950).

exercised by someone else. But they also develop precedent sensitive to and wary of unduly constraining the office when future presidents confront new challenges. Because these actors understand their role as being to serve an institution, not just a person, there is greater continuity across administrations.

There is no final answer between the two bodies. Public law cannot solve or somehow move beyond the duality. But it can get the nature of the problems right. Recognizing the duality provides analytical coherence to the structure of presidential power. It elucidates both our contestations over and the constituted reality of the constitutional presidency. And it suggests that presidential charisma is both inseparable from American constitutionalism and itself governed – albeit incompletely and provisionally – by choices that jurists and lawyers make about how to construct the president's duality.

PART VI

Legislatures, Representation, and Duties of Effective Self-Government

14

Legislatures and Effective Government: Raising Expectations for Representatives

Vicki C. Jackson[*]

14.1 INTRODUCTION

Effective governance is necessary in a successful constitutional democracy. This is not to deny that a central animating force in a democracy must be respect for the human individual. But a government that is not effective and seen as such is not likely to be able to protect individual rights. It is thus a mistake to conceptualize individual rights simply as in conflict with the collective goals of a democratic government: those goals are effective governance and rights preservation, and – in a democracy – these two are connected.

The framers of the US Constitution well understood that a constitutional state must act for public-regarding purposes – to "establish Justice, ensure domestic Tranquility, provide for the common defence, promote the general Welfare, and secure the Blessings of Liberty." To the extent that it fails to move in these directions, government will lose the confidence of the people. Effective government in constitutional democracies requires effective legislatures to promote all of these purposes. Whether effective government is viewed as a right, or a duty, or a principle, or a value of a constitutional state, it is a constitutional necessity.

US constitutional law and scholarship tend to focus on the Constitution's restraining force in ways that obscure the *constitutional* requirement that governments act to promote affirmative goals – justice, domestic tranquility, defense, welfare, and liberty. It is common in US doctrine to speak of governments as having "interests" that may justify limitations on the scope of individual or group rights; but "interests" (e.g., in effective delivery of basic government services, or regulation of markets to

[*] With thanks to Yasmin Dawood, participants in the Yale Macmillan Center Workshop on Representative Institutions and the Structure of American Government, and participants in law faculty workshops at Harvard and Oxford who read prior versions of this chapter, for comments, and to Sam Weinstock, Youzhihang Deng, Nolan Brickwood, Maseed Moradi, and Lauren O'Brien for research assistance.

ensure their honest operation) are viewed as *optional* matters of "policy," belonging not to the realm of constitutionalism but to the realm of ordinary politics.[1]

This view confuses the scope of constitutional obligations with their justiciability. What is the purpose of having a government, a state, under a constitution, if not to promote the public well-being?[2] Governments have obligations to act in accordance with their purposes – in the USA, the goals identified in the Constitution's Preamble. How governments do so may indeed involve a large realm of discretionary policy judgments, but *aiming* to serve those goals is a nondiscretionary duty falling into the realm of political, if not legal, constitutionalism.

Some statutory "duties" to act to promote effective governance are justiciable – for example, to deliver commissions to properly appointed public servants, or to determine whether greenhouse gases contribute to global warming.[3] Some constitutional duties might not be justiciable, as with "directive principles" that establish goals, stated to be nonjusticiable, toward which government must work.[4] But constitutional discourse and theory are diminished if they fail to recognize the obligation of constitutional governments to act toward fulfilling the goals of their existence.

14.2 LEGISLATURES AND REPRESENTATION

Much constitutional study focuses on restraints on government action enforced by courts, with resultant neglect of the positive duties of governments and their legislatures.[5] But effective constitutional self-government requires an effective legislative branch.

In a democracy, popularly elected representatives must play some role in meeting the demands of effective governance, by setting policy at least in broad strokes and providing for government funding and spending.[6] Popularly elected legislative representatives

[1] *See, e.g.*, Stephen E. Gottlieb, *Compelling Governmental Interests*, 68 B.U. L. Rev. 917, 938 (1998).

[2] *See generally* N.W. Barber, The Principles of Constitutionalism (2018). Cf. Restatement (2d) of Contracts §205 Comment d (American Law Institute 1981) (treating action undermining the spirit of a contract as breach of implied duty of good faith performance).

[3] Marbury v. Madison, 5 U.S. (1 Cranch) 137 (1803); Massachusetts v. EPA, 549 U.S. 497 (2007).

[4] For examples of "directive principles" stating goals but expressly declared to be nonjusticiable, see Const. India, art. 37; Const. Ireland, art. 45. Directive principles may be used to uphold legislation when challenged and to interpret judicially enforceable constitutional provisions. *See* Chapter 15, this volume (explaining that directive principles may create state duties implemented through political rather than legal constitutionalism). Even if one declares a "right" to effective government – see Chapter 6, this volume – such a right need not be conceived of as primarily one for judicial enforcement.

[5] *See generally* Vicki C. Jackson, *Pro-constitutional Representation and Constitutional Democracy: Comparing the Role Obligations of Judges and Elected Officials*, 57 Wm. & Mary L. Rev. 1717 (2016) (describing glorification of judging and neglect of legislating); *see also* Neil S. Siegel, *After the Trump Era: A Constitutional Role Morality for Presidents and Members of Congress*, 107 Geo. L. J. 109 (2018).

[6] On challenges to representation, *see* Nadia Urbinati & Mark Warren, *The Concept of Representation in Contemporary Democratic Theory*, 11 Ann. Rev. Pol. Sci. (2008). Elected legislatures, however, can benefit from innovative democratic fora, e.g., deliberative minipublics chosen by lot.

cannot be entirely replaced by direct voting on referenda. Why? Normatively, too much power would lie in whoever formulates referenda questions, without the participatory transparency of representative deliberation. Practically, complex trade-offs are required in funding and running a general government; it is hard to imagine how the hard work of organizing those trade-offs could be done in the population at large. Other limitations would apply to reliance on randomly chosen assemblies, although recent experience suggests their utility for helpful deliberation on discrete questions.

That legislatures are obligated to act for the polity should require no argument. As political theorists have insisted, "the capacity to act is an integral part of the meaning of democracy. When legislatures deadlock because of their inability to negotiate, their inaction undermines key democratic values."[7] The US Constitution contemplates members of Congress having "pro-constitutional" obligations to take legislative action and engage in oversight across a range of jurisdictional responsibilities.[8]

Representation as "acting for" is the most important perspective introduced by Pitkin on the "activity of representing"; it implies a relationship with constituents requiring, for example, representatives to justify acting in disagreement with their constituents.[9] Being a representative entails a special set of what we might call public virtues: private persons can act on impulse, but representatives "are expected to act as if [they] would eventually have to account for our actions."[10] But elected representatives cannot "account for" or justify their actions in the ways courts do. The "acting for" obligations of elected representatives are different, and more complex, entailing obligations to constituents (both those who support and those who oppose the representative), to the whole polity, to other members of the legislature, to their party, and to their own conception of the good. They are distinctive in several other ways.

First, they are members of a body that for the most part can act effectively only if it acts in some way collectively. (Here my emphasis is on the verb "acting" rather than on the preposition "for.") This point is underdeveloped in much of the literature on representation.[11] Pitkin does note the collective character of the legislature as a reason to reject strong versions of the "delegate" theory: "if each representative were pledged to and instructed by his constituency, political compromise would become impossible. It is necessary to leave room for the crucial activities of the legislature itself – formulating issues, the deliberation and compromise on which decisions should be based."[12]

7 Mark Warren & Jane Mansbridge, *Deliberative Negotiation*, in APSA Task Force Report: Negotiating Agreement in Politics 86, 86 (Jane Mansbridge & Cathie Jo Martin eds., 2013).

8 Jackson, *supra* note 5.

9 Hanna Fenichel Pitkin, The Concept of Representation 112 (1972).

10 *Id.* at 118–19. Voters who cast anonymous ballots do not have expectations to account for their votes.

11 Exceptions exist. *See, e.g.*, Neomi Rao, *Administrative Collusion: How Delegation Diminishes the Collective Congress*, 90 N.Y.U. L. Rev. 1463 (2015) (arguing that delegations of rulemaking authority are inconsistent with the requirement that Congress act as a collective body).

12 Pitkin, *supra* note 9, at 147. *See also id.* at 213 ("[The representative] works with other representatives in an institutionalized context at a specific task – the governing of a nation or a state.").

But why must *compromise* (sometimes) be a basis for decision? Pitkin suggests that "one of the most important features of representative government is its capacity for resolving the conflicting claims of the parts, on the basis of their common interest in the welfare of the whole."[13] In reconciling the particular interests of different parts of the nation, she argues, a creative process of accommodation must occur: "the harmony of final-objective-interest must be *created*," a task performed in the legislature. A representative's duty, then, is to pursue "both local and national interest."[14] Whether the legislature is reconciling local or partisan differences, if no one compromises then no version of the good may be implemented.

A member of a body that can act only in concert with other members will find it necessary, in order to advance their constituency's interests, to prioritize goals and make deals with others to accomplish at least some of those goals.[15] More "Burkean" representatives may view the collegial nature of legislative action as a deliberation-enhancing benefit of hearing from others in deciding on the good of the nation as a whole. But even for representatives who see themselves as something closer to a delegate, it may be necessary to work with others, to find compromises, to determine what is most intensely important and what is less so in order to be able to make deals and facilitate governance.

A legislature is a multi-member collegial body; its purpose entails some degree of communication among its members, to substitute for discussion among all the members of a polity too large and complex to converse directly, and to act. The obligation to consider the interests advanced by other representatives, and sometimes to compromise, may be implied from the nature of a legislative assembly and from the more specific requirements of the US Constitution.

The US Constitution contemplates that the Congress will actually assemble. Article 1, section 4 provides: "The Congress shall assemble at least once in every year, and such Meeting shall be on the first Monday in December, unless they shall by Law appoint a different Day." Why require representatives to assemble, a physical act in a physical place – or why adhere to that requirement in an era when teleconferencing or electronic voting is possible?

The reasons include the need for developing, and bringing to bear, knowledge, practical wisdom, and then law to resolve common challenges on behalf of an entire community. A deliberative obligation is implied in being a member of a body that is required actually to convene together and that for the most part can act only collectively. The idea of being a political representative in a collective body,

[13] *Id.* at 217.
[14] *Id.* at 218.
[15] On John Stuart Mill and legislative compromise, *see* Dennis F. Thompson, *Mill in Parliament: When Should a Philosopher Compromise?*, *in* J.S. MILL'S POLITICAL THOUGHT (Nadia Urbinati & Alex Zakaras eds., 2007). On compromise and liberal tolerance, *see* AVISHAI MARGALIT, ON COMPROMISE AND ROTTEN COMPROMISES 168 (2009).

empowered to act on those outside the body only through some form of collective action, necessarily implies dealings and relationships with other representatives.

This brings me to my second point. Not only is the representative chosen to sit in a multi-member body that can act only collectively, but each of those other representatives sits in the body by virtue of a presumably equivalent authorization to act. That is, other members of that body are equally authorized and equally legitimate in representing other members of the body collectively represented in the legislature.[16] Representatives are dealing with others, in the House of Representatives, from roughly comparably sized constituencies; the equal legitimacy of the members of the Senate derives from a combination of their election and the Constitution's requirement that senators be equally allocated per state.[17] Recognition of this equivalent normative status, in the context of a body that can act in law-making only collegially, imposes some presumptive obligations of equal respect among members.[18]

Third, elected legislators exercise powers to make laws that bind all, from which "exit" is not possible for most people without enormous disruption. And, in a rule-of-law state, legislation will typically outlast the terms of some members of the legislature; one of the distinct characteristics of a "rule-of law" regime is stability in the law.[19] That laws outlast their enacting legislative session also may reflect on the legitimacy of the legislature as an institution, whose members benefit from its ongoing character. Given the coercive effect of the laws they enact, over time and over persons who disagree, representatives who hold the law-making power should be held to have obligations of good faith in considering different views of the public interest in the law-making process, to enhance the representativeness of the legislative product – which can be achieved in part by learning from other representatives.[20]

16 *Cf.* JEREMY WALDRON, DIGNITY OF LEGISLATION 28–29 (1999) (noting the equality of members of Parliament in discussing the challenges of defining a single legislative intent).

17 This is not to deny the challenges to democratic legitimacy from gerrymandering and inequitable distribution of senators. On the latter, *see* Vicki C. Jackson, *The Democratic Deficit of U.S. Federalism? Red State, Blue State, Purple*, 46 FED. L. REV. 645 (2018) (comparing the democratic legitimacy of the state legislatures favorably to that of Congress).

18 *Cf.* John Rawls, *The Idea of Public Reason Revisited*, 64 U. CHI. L. REV. 765, 767, 769 (1997) (noting the "criterion of reciprocity" in defining the idea of public reason).

19 *See* LON L. FULLER, THE MORALITY OF LAW 33–39, 79–81 (rev'd ed. 1969) (1964) (identifying eight characteristics of the rule of law, including law's stability or "Constancy . . . through Time").

20 For an empirical finding that laws passed on a partisan basis are somewhat more likely to be repealed than other laws, *see* JORDAN M. RAGUSA & NATHANIEL A. BIRKHEAD, REPEALS FROM RECONSTRUCTION TO THE PRESENT 127–28 (2020). Being a good "pro-constitutional" legislator is a complex challenge because of competing pulls of accountability, including to one's institution in government and one's political party. *See* Jackson, *supra* note 5, at 1735–37. Party loyalty can conflict with broader public interests and limit the possibilities of deliberative exchange; but party loyalty can also play a salutary role, including by promoting competition, teeing up clearer choices to the public, and encouraging beneficial intraparty compromises. *See* Yasmin Dawood, *Democracy and the Problem of the Partisan State*, 54 NOMOS 257 (2013); NANCY ROSENBLUM, ON THE SIDE OF THE ANGELS: AN APPRECIATION OF PARTIES AND PARTISANSHIP (2008).

Thus, our understanding of the normative obligations of elected representatives in legislative bodies must take account of both the collective character of "acting" by legislatures and the equal legitimacy of all representatives in the body in representing the heterogeneous views of the self-governing people, in the context of a political body exercising coercive law-making power that binds intertemporally.

14.3 RAISING EXPECTATIONS

Party polarization, private campaign-financing, and other structural changes have made legislatures, including the US Congress, decreasingly functional.[21] Civility and reciprocity across party lines have broken down; public trust in legislatures has declined.[22] Losing legislatures as a principal location for meaningful representation, policy oversight, and major policy decisions – a possibility foreshadowed by the decline in functionality and respect for legislatures and political representation – is likely to have adverse consequences for constitutionalism and democracy, including what Carl Friedrich described as the worrisome rise of "nonrational" leadership.[23] Institutional incentives can and should be restructured. But so too should the lack of normative attention given to legislators by constitutionalists. Taking seriously normative expectations of legislators and valorizing legislators who perform their roles well would serve important public ends.

A survey of twenty countries' legislative codes of conduct identified one – the UK – that identified ethical aspirations for legislators of "selflessness, integrity, objectivity, accountability, openness, honesty, and leadership."[24] In the USA, awards recognize legislative "profiles in courage."[25] More discussion of such normative expectations should matter. Why?

[21] *See* Chapters 17 and 18, this volume.

[22] *See* Gallup, Confidence in Institutions, http://www.gallup.com/poll/1597/confidence-institutions.aspx (reporting in 2016 that only 9 percent of respondents had either a "great deal" or "quite a lot" of confidence in Congress, compared with the Presidency (36 percent) and the Supreme Court (36 percent), with similar differences in later years).

[23] Carl Friedrich, Constitutional Government and Democracy 283 (4th ed. 1968) (1950); *see also* Siegel, *supra* note 5, at 113–15 (arguing that dysfunctionality in the "convictions and conduct of the public and the political branches," even if not illegal, raises "concerns that are properly denominated *constitutional*"). But *cf.* Adrian Vermeule, "Imagine There's No Congress," Wash. Post, Jan. 11, 2016, https://www.washingtonpost.com/news/in-theory/wp/2016/01/11/imagine-theres-no-congress/?utm_term=.50a7664979fd (suggesting that a system without Congress might be an improvement over the current system); A. King & I. Crewe, The Blunders of Our Governments 361 (2013) ("As a legislative assembly the parliament of the UK is, much of the time, either peripheral or totally irrelevant. It might as well not exist.").

[24] National Democratic Institute for International Affairs, Legislative Research Series, Paper #4, Legislative Ethics (1999).

[25] *See* JFK Library, Profiles in Courage Awards, https://www.jfklibrary.org/events-and-awards/profile-in-courage-award/award-recipients (recipients include Republican and Democratic senators who cosponsored campaign finance reform and ex-president George H.W. Bush for negotiating budget compromise with Democrats).

It is reasonable to assume that political culture plays some role in sustaining democratic constitutionalism. Institutions alone do not necessarily determine major constitutional outcomes, including the rate of amendment.[26] It seems implausible to think that the currents of ideas that are in play around the work of government, including the aspirations for elected representatives, will have no effect on their behavior. This is so, even if the principal determinants of the behavior of legislators connect more to how to win reelection under the current campaign-finance system, or increased use of gerrymandered districts that may be diminishing the incentives for cross-party moderation in electoral campaigns.[27] At the margins, aspirational expectations matter, even if heightened expectations influence only a small number of members in a small number of interactions. Given the nature of collective bodies, it may take only a few members willing to work across party lines – or significant intraparty divisions – to make a difference.[28]

There is some basis in scholarship to think that raising publicly discussed expectations might have such effects. Though not entirely analogous, the "Pygmalion" effect, first identified as such in a study of children's performance and teacher expectations in classrooms, might be brought into play through heightened expectations for public-spirited performance. Positive expectations of how someone will perform in classrooms have positive effects on performance;[29] negative expectations, similarly, tend to produce negative results, a result sometimes called the "Golem" effect.[30]

These effects have generally been discussed in contexts involving the relationship of a leader or authority figure and their followers, such as employees, students, or soldiers,[31] and may not extend to more diffuse contexts, such as those involving public discourse about the role of representatives. It is uncertain, at best, whether

26 *See* Tom Ginsburg & James Melton, *Does the Constitutional Amendment Rule Matter At All? Amendment Cultures and the Challenge of Measuring Amendment Difficulty*, 13 I.CON 686 (2015). On the effects of the general civic culture on democracy, *see* Russell J. Dalton & Christian Welzel, *Political Culture and Value Change*, *in* THE CIVIC CULTURE TRANSFORMED 3–11 (Russell J. Dalton & Christian Welzel eds., 2013).

27 For an argument that the polarization of Congress is the result of long-term, unlikely-to-change historical trends, *see* Richard Pildes, *Why the Center Does Not Hold*, 99 CALIF. L. REV. 273 (2011); see also Chapter 18, this volume.

28 Consider past efforts in the Senate, e.g., by the "gang of 14" on judicial nominations, *see* https://www.nytimes.com/2005/06/12/opinion/the-center-can-hold.html, or the "gang of 8" on immigration reform, *see* https://www.politico.com/story/2016/07/immigration-reform-gang-eight-225028.

29 *See* ROBERT ROSENTHAL & LENORE JACOBSON, PYGMALION IN THE CLASSROOM: TEACHER EXPECTATION AND PUPILS' INTELLECTUAL DEVELOPMENT (1968).

30 *See* Dov Eden, *Self-Fulfilling Prophecy and the Pygmalion Effect in Management* (Oct. 28, 2014), http://www.oxfordbibliographies.com/view/document/obo-9780199846740/obo-9780199846740-0014.xml; *cf.* W. Glenn Rowe & James O'Brien, *The Role of Golem, Pygmalion, and Galatea Effects on Opportunistic Behavior in the Classroom*, 26 J. MGMT. EDUC. 612, 615–16 (2002) (worrying that graduate students taught to expect opportunistic behavior may fail to develop helpful trust among working teams in business management).

31 *See* Eden, *supra* note 30; Paul Whiteley et al., *Leaders' Conceptions of Followers: Implications for Naturally Occurring Pygmalion Effects*, 23 LEADERSHIP Q. 822, 822 (2012).

such effects exist with respect to the expectations of followers vis-à-vis their leaders.[32] Pygmalion effects are most noticeable when those subject to the possible influence of heightened or lowered expectations first enter the arena of performance;[33] a "Galatea" effect, referring to the effect of enhanced self-expectations, has also been observed.[34] But again, whether such effects would translate from high-intensity situations of hierarchical human relations (or ones where there are clear and objective markers of success) to more diffuse societal levels and the performance of elected representatives is uncertain.[35] However, it is hard to imagine that developing higher expectations for legislators' performance in office and greater public appreciation for those who perform well would have negative effects, and it might have some marginal positive effects.[36]

Political and economic theorists have also hypothesized another, possibly related phenomenon in the design of institutions. Although the idea that constitutions should be designed on the assumption that "enlightened statesmen will not always be at the helm" is quite long-standing,[37] more recent work has argued that there are risks that systems designed too much on the assumption that those who fill government positions are badly intentioned actors will produce badly intentioned behavior. Professor Bruno Frey entitled an essay "A constitution for knaves

32 *Compare* Whitely et al., *supra* note 31, at 831 (stating that "little research has examined [or supports] … 'role reversed Pygmalion effects,'" but urging further research on the "intriguing possibilities") *with* R. Hezkiau-Ludwig & D. Eden, *Bottom-Up Pygmalion: A Field Experimental Test of the Effects of Follower Expectations on Leader Performance* (Working Paper No. 11/2010, Oct. 2010) (reporting that the experiment did not confirm the bottom-up Pygmalion hypothesis while noting the limitations of the study). On the theoretical possibilities of followers' expectations impacting leaders, *see* Morela Hernandez & Sim B. Sitkin, *Who Is Leading the Leader? Follower Influence on Leader Ethicality*, *in* Behavioral Business Ethics: Shaping an Emerging Field 81, 87–88 (David De Cremer & Ann E. Tenbrunsel eds., 2012) (proposing, within an organizational context, ways in which the "leader-follower relationship is fundamentally affected by upward influence strategies on the part of followers, which tend to either promote or prohibit certain types of morally relevant leadership behavior"); *see also* Jane M. Howell & Boas Shamir, *The Role of Followers in the Charismatic Leadership Process: Relationships and Their Consequences*, 30 Acad. Mgmt. Rev. 96, 107 (2005).

33 *See* J. Sterling Livingston, *Pygmalion in Management*, 81 Harv. Bus. Rev. 97, 102 (2003); *see also* Rosenthal & Jacobson, *supra* note 29, at 74–75 (finding a greater effect from higher teacher expectations for first graders than for sixth graders).

34 A "Galatea" effect is one in which a person's expectations of their own future success have a self-fulfilling effect; higher self-expectations may be created, for example, by prior successful experience, or by seeing someone similar to yourself succeed. *See* Dov Eden & Joseph Kinnar, *Modeling Galatea: Boosting Self-Efficacy to Increase Volunteering*, 76 J. Applied Psych. 770, 770–72 (1991).

35 Monitoring and measuring "good" pro-constitutional legislative behavior is likely more difficult than measuring pupil achievement, or business successes.

36 These effects may be enhanced for relative newcomers to political office, *see supra* note 33, and, perhaps, in electoral districts where there is effective monitoring of representatives' performance and some degree of competitiveness in the election. (With thanks to Youzhihang Deng for this point.)

37 Federalist No. 10; *see also* Adrian Vermeule, *Precautionary Principles in Constitutional Law*, 4 J. Legal Analysis 181, 185 (2012) (noting Hume's suggestion that constitutions should be designed on the assumption that the government will be filled with knaves, while explaining why this principle should not be the sole guide to constitutional design).

drives out civic virtue,"[38] suggesting that external incentives supplied by prohibitory rules may tend to drive out or replace internal incentives based on a sense of virtue or civic duty. On this account, too stringent an effort to control bad behavior in advance by legal rules may be counterproductive, inducing shifts in attitudes from wanting to do the right thing because it is right to seeing what can be gotten away with within the rules; in other words, the message conveyed by the incentives undermines internal attitudes promoting virtuous behavior.

Evidence suggests that the messages given by institutional rules can change attitudes toward desirable or undesirable behavior, sometimes in unexpected ways. Positive incentives may produce *less* of the desired conduct if it leads actors to derive less satisfaction from behaving in ways previously seen, internally, as normatively desirable, but which come to be seen as a service to be paid for.[39] Sanctions can produce *more* of an undesired conduct if the sanctions are low enough that actors come to see them as simply pricing the behavior, rather than condemning it.[40] This scholarship thus suggests that too much emphasis on institutional design in preventing "knavery" may have this counterproductive effect, for at least two reasons: First, the performance of some in public office may tend to meet the expectations for knavery suggested by the rules, as their internal normative sense of what is expected shifts; second, as an institution becomes known for the self-interested behavior of its occupants, persons who are not knaves will not seek those positions.[41]

This work suggests that messages given by rule- or compensation-based approaches matter; they support the possibility that conveying expectations of higher aspirations may have some value in discouraging undesired conduct and encouraging desired conduct.

Moreover, as Dan Kahan has argued, there is a "logic of reciprocity," motivated by emotions of trust, that can be disrupted by incentives through the expectations

38 Bruno Frey, *A Constitution for Knaves Drives Out Civic Virtue*, 107 Econ. J. 1043 (1997).

39 *See id.* at 1047–48 (reporting on an experiment comparing willingness to accept the nearby siting of a nuclear plant by those who were offered and those who were not offered payment to agree); Uri Gneezy & Aldo Rustichini, *Pay Enough or Don't Pay at All*, 115 Quart. J. Econ. 791 (2000) (describing an experiment in which charitable collections by high school students declined when they were offered a payment incentive).

40 *See* Uri Gneezy & Aldo Rustichini, *A Fine Is a Price*, 29(1) J. Leg. Stud. 1 (2000) (describing how a change in pickup policies at a Haifa daycare center, to charging monetary penalties for delays, came to be seen as legitimizing (and increasing) late pickups (rather than discouraging them) because they were being paid for); Bruno S. Frey & Felix Oberholzer-Gee, *The Cost of Price Incentives: An Empirical Analysis of Motivation Crowding-Out*, 87 Am. Econ. Rev. 746 (1997) (describing the above-noted (*supra* note 39) experiment concerning willingness to accept nearby nuclear plants and concluding that the "public spirit" declined in response to offers of compensation).

41 *See* Lewis A. Kornhauser, *Virtue and Self-Interest in the Design of Constitutional Institutions*, 3 Theor. Inq. L. 15–16 (2002); Adrian Vermeule, *Hume's Second-Best Constitutionalism*, 70 U. Chi. L. Rev. 421, 424–25 (2003); Vermeule, *supra* note 37, at 207 (explaining that "[c]onstitutional sanctions . . . might undermine social norms that would constrain the same behavior . . . [or] might (unintentionally) convey a signal that many other officials are engaged in the behavior that the sanctions aim to eliminate," leading to diminished compliance, or that too many rules may filter in "self-interested" actors while filtering out "public-spirited actors").

they communicate.[42] For Kahan, one such mechanism of disruption is the message sent by rules designed to constrain rent-seeking, which, he says, conveys that "we expect political actors to engage in rent-seeking behavior whenever it is in their interest to do so."[43] To the extent that the "message" matters, devoting more attention to articulating aspirations for being a good representative and identifying examples of good representatives may be helpful in overcoming what in recent years appears as a spiraling downward of norms of cooperation in getting the public's business done in Congress. As Bill Marshall has argued,

> instructing Congress that it has a constitutional duty to act in certain circumstances might serve to change political culture. The position that congressional action is optional sends the message that there is no need for members to work together because there are no common responsibilities. The notion that Congress has a duty to act, on the other hand, tells the members that they have common goals and common obligations.[44]

Robin West has explained that law schools in the United States tend to valorize judges much more than legislators:

> We stud our "casebooks" with portraits and photographs and short biographies of judges – of Oliver Wendell Holmes, Learned Hand, and Benjamin Cardozo – whose "thoughtful countenance" portrayed in a portrait ... is the window to an admirable judicial sensibility. We do not teach students to respect, admire, or emulate the heroic legislator, ... from Cicero to Ted Kennedy, from Daniel Webster to Orrin Hatch.[45]

Examples of people who served in Congress with integrity and effectiveness, helping to produce public-regarding legislation, include Senator Philip A. Hart[46] and Senator Paul Douglas.[47] Law school classrooms could, but generally do not,

42 *See* Dan M. Kahan, *The Logic of Reciprocity: Trust, Collective Action, and Law*, 102 MICH. L. REV. 71, 75–77 (2003). *Cf.* Vermeule, *supra* note 37, at 207 (noting the possibility of office-holders who are "reciprocal altruists," willing to "comply with public-regarding norms if others" do, but "afraid of being chumps and are thus unwilling to comply unilaterally").

43 Kahan, *supra* note 42, at 100.

44 William P. Marshall, *The Limits on Congress's Power to Do Nothing: A Preliminary Inquiry*, 93 IND. L. J. 159, 171 (2018). He argues for defining a constitutionally unacceptable level of congressional inaction – for example, failures to act on appropriations or nominations that threaten the government's ability to function – to help counteract "the pressures of polarization" that deter "even members of Congress who might otherwise work across the aisle ... from doing so"; "where politicians need excuses to work with each other, setting a constitutional standard for congressional behavior might provide some political cover for bipartisan action." *Id.* at 167. On the importance of positive expectations for public officials, see Chapter 6, this volume.

45 Robin West, *Toward the Study of the Legislated Constitution*, 72 OHIO ST. L. J. 1343, 1347 (2011).

46 *See* MICHAEL O'BRIEN, PHILIP HART: THE CONSCIENCE OF THE SENATE (1995).

47 *See* Edward Rubin, *Legislative Methodology: Some Lesson from the Truth in Lending Act*, 80 GEO. L. J. 223, 263, 306 (1991) (praising Douglas as "the guiding force behind the Truth in Lending Act ... not ... motivated by political or vote maximizing considerations at all ... virtually a living refutation of microeconomic pessimism ... honest, independent, conscientious, and, most important, totally committed to those who are in greatest need of the services that the government can provide"). Rubin

consider Lyndon Johnson, in Robert Caro's words, "Master of the Senate," who may have manifested a smaller range of human virtues than the unusual Senator Hart, but won compromises for legislation that improved the lives of constituents and the nation, with great energy and command of the legislative process.[48]

Many factors have contributed to political polarization, to the "breakdown of bipartisan norms" that previously had enabled Congress to do its legislative work,[49] and to seeing the other party as the enemy.[50] Yet advancing a positive understanding of deliberative negotiation in Congress "may help us to construct collective social identities and to change our perceptions of ourselves vis-à-vis the larger society . . . [to understand that] politics is not only about struggle over resources [but] also about the search for value-creating opportunities and social solidarity."[51] That is, it may be possible to promote change to "bring citizens to view political discourse in more positive terms. We Americans preach cooperation and sharing to our children, but in the political sphere, we have forgotten the lessons of our childhood."[52] Some evidence suggests that politicians in the United States are more polarized and less moderate than voters;[53] there is still the possibility of repair.

Words and ideas matter. Law itself is sometimes said to have an important "expressive" function;[54] on this account, *Brown* v. *Board of Education* was important in manifesting and promoting a norm shift, even if its legally operative consequences were delayed.[55] Words matter in conveying normative meaning, and especially when embraced by those who hold power in the development of opinion – representatives themselves, the media, possibly even scholars.[56] Words of praise for legislative courage

is critical of the legislative product as having insufficiently considered the connection between the legislative goal and the legislative means.

48 *See generally* ROBERT CARO, THE YEARS OF LYNDON JOHNSON: MASTER OF THE SENATE (2002); *see also* AMY GUTMANN & DENNIS THOMPSON, THE SPIRIT OF COMPROMISE: WHY GOVERNING DEMANDS IT AND CAMPAIGNING UNDERMINES IT Loc. 1452 (Kindle, 2012) (discussing Johnson's compromises to obtain passage of the 1964 Civil Rights Act). To be sure, it is easier to identify public-spirited judges, virtuous in their role, because being a good legislator may often occur in private discussions, and is less visible.

49 *See e.g.* Michael Barber & Nolan McCarty, *Causes and Consequences of Polarization*, *in* APSA TASK FORCE REPORT, *supra* note 7, at 35 (noting weaker "social fabric" from commuting back to home districts rather than socializing in DC).

50 *Cf.* MARGALIT, *supra* note 15, at 43–44 (describing compromises that turn "enem[ies]" into "rival[s]").

51 Cathie Jo Martin, *Negotiating Political Agreements*, *in* APSA TASK FORCE REPORT, *supra* note 7, at 15.

52 *Id.* at 15.

53 *Id.* at 25–26. There are disagreements on the degree to which voters are as polarized as elites and, to the extent that voters are growing polarized, the role of elites in causing this. See GUTMANN & THOMPSON, *supra* note 48, at 432 n.20.

54 *See e.g.*, Cass Sunstein, *On the Expressive Function of Law*, 144 U. PA. L. REV. 2021 (1996). *Cf.* LAWRENCE FRIEDMAN, IMPACT: HOW LAW AFFECTS BEHAVIOR 153–216 (2016) (discussing peer pressure, internal conscience, and morality as factors influencing compliance with law).

55 *See* Walter Dellinger, *How Brown v Bd of Education Changed the South Forever*, SLATE (June 28, 2007), https://slate.com/news-and-politics/2007/06/how-brown-v-board-of-education-changed-the-south-forever.html.

56 *Cf.* N.W. Barber, *Why Entrench?* 14(2) INT'L J. CONST. L. 325, 331 (2016) (rejecting arguments that entrenchment through requirements of express form is no barrier to change, insofar as a required "framing," or requirements of clarity, may impede changing the underlying rule).

have inspired careers in elected office;[57] examples of admirable behavior by legislators may inspire others. Even if words trigger primarily hypocritical assertion of allegiances to normative roles,[58] such action helps reinforce that there is a norm to which actions can be held to account. And words spoken in the constitutional register of being a good elected representative may have more power to resist wrongful behavior by constitutional actors than the language of pure self-interest that so many now use.[59]

57 *See* Senator Russ Feingold, Acceptance Speech, 1999 Profile in Courage Award Recipient (May 24, 1999) ("I'm holding in my hand my own original 35-cent copy of Profiles in Courage that I read as a young teenager. I loved it. It fueled my not very well hidden interest in going into politics and maybe even becoming a U.S. Senator. But its influence was not simply to make me want to be a senator. Rather, this thin little book spoke volumes about what kind of a senator it is worthwhile to be.").

58 Even if hypocrisy is only the homage vice pays to virtue, per Francois de La Rochefoucauld, public praise of virtue may help reinforce what is virtuous; the possibility of public critique of nonvirtuous self-interested statements may produce a "civilizing effect," even if the internal spirit of a representative is not accurately reflected by that representative's external statements. *See* Jon Elster, *Deliberation and Constitution-Making, in* DELIBERATIVE DEMOCRACY 97, 104 (Jon Elster ed., 1998) (discussing the "civilizing force of hypocrisy").

59 *See* Siegel, *supra* note 5, at 117 (emphasizing the significance of "the language of *constitutional illegitimacy*").

15

Constitutional Directives and the Duty to Govern Well

Tarunabh Khaitan[*]

15.1 INTRODUCTION

Liberal constitutional discourse has been dominated by a proceduralist, acontextual, universalising worldview. This Rawlsian vision of constitutionalism castigates thick, substantive, moral commitments (other than fundamental rights) in constitutions as illiberal and unwise, at best to be tolerated as minor deviations only when absolutely unavoidable. In practice, however, the ideal of proceduralist constitutionalism is approximated only by a handful of liberal democratic states, arguably the United States and Australia.[1] Many other (sufficiently or aspirationally) liberal-democratic states not only include thick moral commitments in their constitutions, tasking their governments with the duty to govern well, but also specify various facets of (what they believe to be required by) good governance.

Jeff King has characterised such thick moral commitments as constitutional 'mission statements'.[2] An important, but much-ignored, form of these thick commitments is a set of provisions I will call 'constitutional directives' or simply 'directives'. One honourable exception to this academic silence is the developing scholarship of Lael Weis, which has significantly informed my thinking on the topic.[3] Directives give substantive constitutional guidance on how the state ought to be governed by future politicians. Constitutional texts variously describe them as 'directive principles of

* This chapter is a lightly edited excerpt from Tarunabh Khaitan, *Constitutional Directives*, 82 MOD. L. REV. 603 (2019).

1 I understand a liberal state to be one that aspires to some conception of the ideology identified as 'liberal' in political theory. This includes free-market libertarianism at the one end of the liberal spectrum to liberal socialism or a 'property owning democracy' at the other. Constitutional theory, unlike political theory, has traditionally had a narrower conception of what a 'liberal' state might be. *See generally* Tarunabh Khaitan, *Political Insurance for the Relative Poor*, 8 GLOB. CONST. 536 (2019).

2 Jeff King, *Constitutions as Mission Statements*, *in* COMPARATIVE CONSTITUTIONAL LAW AND POLICY: SOCIAL AND POLITICAL FOUNDATIONS OF CONSTITUTIONS 73 (Denis J. Galligan and Mila Versteeg eds., 2013).

3 *See especially* Lael K. Weis, *Constitutional Directive Principles*, 37 OXFORD J. LEG. STUD. 916 (2017).

social policy', 'directive principles of state policy', 'goals and principles of state action', 'principles governing economic and social policy', 'fundamental objectives', 'fundamental obligations of government', 'principles of state policy', 'state tasks',[4] 'fundamental tasks', and so on. On a conservative count, thirty-six-odd state constitutions around the world – starting with that of Ireland in 1937 – feature such constitutional directives.[5] While the Irish provisions are treated as pioneering, it has been suggested that they were themselves inspired by proto-directives in Republican Spanish[6] and Weimar constitutions.[7]

All thirty-six of these constitutions contain at least some directives that seek to secure access to a social minimum (in relation to health care, education, nutrition, or such like). About fifteen of these constitutions also contain an egalitarian directive requiring redistribution of income and wealth.[8] Environment protection also features prominently.[9] So do provisions relating to national unity and identity, especially in relation to language, religion, and culture. Many directives concern themselves with economic organisation of the state, usually favouring a 'balanced' system between state socialism and unfettered market capitalism. Here are a few sample directives:

– 'The State shall endeavour to ensure that the strength and health of workers, men and women, and the tender age of children shall not be abused and that

4 On 'state tasks,' *see generally* KARL-PETER SOMMERMANN, STAATSZIELE UND STAATSZIELBESTIMMUNGEN (1997).

5 These include the constitutions of: Ireland (1937), India (1950), Qatar (provisional constitution, 1970), Bangladesh (1972), Panama (1972), Pakistan (1973), Papua New Guinea (1975), Portugal (1976), Spain (1978), Sri Lanka (1978), Nigeria (1979), Tanzania (added in 1984 by amendment to the 1977 Constitution), Zanzibar (1984), Nepal (1990), Namibia (1990), Sierra Leone (1991), Zambia (1991), Tibet (constitution of the government in exile, 1991), Ghana (1992), Andorra (1993), Lesotho (1993), Uganda (1995), Ethiopia (1995), Gambia (1996), Eritrea (1997), Thailand (1997), Sudan (1998), Nigeria (1999), Somaliland (2001), Swaziland (2005), Thailand (2007), Nepal (interim constitution, 2007), Bhutan (2008), Angola (2010), South Sudan (2011), and Nepal (2015). This count does not include constitutions of federal units (such as Jammu and Kashmir, Lower Austria, Basel City, and Western Cape) which also contain such directives. Also excluded are 'positive rights' provisions in communist constitutions – such as the right to work under the Constitution of the Union of Soviet Socialist Republics 1977, art. 40 – which were also typically non-justiciable. The list also excludes provisions such as the Canadian Constitution Act 1982, § 36, which are *probably* best understood as directives, even though they do not characterise themselves as such.

6 IVOR JENNINGS, THE APPROACH TO SELF-GOVERNMENT 19 (1956). *See* Constitution of the Spanish Republic 1931, arts. 42–50.

7 Rachael Walsh, *Private Property Rights in the Drafting of the Irish Constitution: A Communitarian Compromise*, 33 DUBLIN U. L. J. 86, 95 (2011). Weimar [Constitution], art. 151: 'The economy has to be organized based on the principles of justice, with the goal of achieving life in dignity for everyone. Within these limits the economic liberty of the individual is to be secured.' On social provisions in post-World War I European constitutions generally, *see* AGNES HEADLAM-MORLEY, THE NEW DEMOCRATIC CONSTITUTIONS OF EUROPE 264f (1928).

8 On a constitutional duty to achieve material equality, *see* Khaitan, *supra* note 1.

9 On environmental 'directive principles' generally, *see* DAVID RICHARD BOYD, THE ENVIRONMENTAL RIGHTS REVOLUTION: A GLOBAL STUDY OF CONSTITUTIONS, HUMAN RIGHTS, AND THE ENVIRONMENT 45 (2012); Lael K. Weis, *Environmental Constitutionalism: Aspiration or Transformation?*, 16 INT'L J. CONST. L. 836 (2018).

citizens shall not be forced by economic necessity to enter avocations unsuited to their sex, age or strength.'[10]

- 'Government shall direct its policy towards ensuring that there are equal and adequate educational opportunities at all levels.'[11]
- 'The State shall strive to promote the welfare of the people by securing and protecting as effectively as it may a social order in which justice, social, economic and political, shall inform all the institutions of the national life.'[12]

Constitutional directives were enthusiastically embraced by post-colonial constitutions of the New Commonwealth (i.e., former non-settler British colonies) coming to terms with the legacy of divisive and impoverishing colonial policies, which included ethnocultural identity wars and deep material inequalities. They were popularised by early post-colonial adopters such as India (1950) and Nigeria (1979), and have remained popular with drafters ever since. In this chapter, I will give a conceptual account of constitutional directives. In a previous paper, from which this chapter is excerpted, this account has been supplemented with a functional account of what these directives can do.[13]

The chapter has two parts. In Section 15.2, I will show that constitutional directives are *obligatory* in a special way: they are telic norms that identify (typically specific) moral objectives whose full realisation is deferred to a future date. Their telic character gives them a temporal dimension, facilitating partial deferral of their obligatory burdens. I will also argue that these directives impose two distinct duties: (i) a *duty to endeavour* to realise the directed goal, which kicks in immediately, and (ii) a *duty to fully realise* that goal by some (specified or unspecified) future date. Although framers can seek to fine-tune the degree of expressive salience that directives have, this salience tends to be lower than that of preambular values. Directives also tend to be more precise and contained, in relation to preambular values.

In Section 15.3, I will argue that although directives are *contrajudicative* – in that the duties they impose are not accompanied by reflex rights and therefore their breaches are not corrected by courts – they are only *weakly* contrajudicative. Limited forms of judicial engagement with directives are frequent and legitimate. The combination of partial deferral and contrajudicative character allows them to be used as fine-grained tools of constitutional incrementalism. Finally, I will argue that whether a norm is a directive or a right depends not on the structure of the provision containing it but on the manner in which the constitutional practice of a jurisdiction treats a provision. This implies that directives and rights are mutable – a former directive can become a right and vice versa. Newer constitutions have begun

10 Constitution of Ireland, art. 45(4)(2).

11 Constitution of the Federal Republic of Nigeria 1999, art. 18(1).

12 Constitution of India, art. 38(1).

13 Tarunabh Khaitan, *Constitutional Directives*, 82 Mod. L. Rev. 603 (2019).

experimenting with constitutional design tools that might make the political enforcement of directives more effective.

15.2 ON OBLIGATORINESS

15.2.1 *Directives as Obligatory Constitutional Norms*

The directives that this chapter is concerned with are *constitutional* norms. There are no doubt comparable directives contained in legislation, which may or may not have a constitutional character,[14] but in this chapter I am particularly interested in directives found in big-C constitutional codes. This feature also distinguishes them from purely *moral* norms, at least in the sense that they are *posited* social facts that are found in constitutional documents. It is a moral norm that the state ought to further the welfare of its people. It applies whether or not the constitution of that state says so. But it becomes a *constitutional* norm only if posited in its constitution, whether explicitly or by implication. No doubt, a constitutional norm can *also* be a moral norm when there are moral reasons to discharge the obligations it imposes.

As Weis has written, constitutional directives 'place binding constitutional obligations on the state'.[15] This feature distinguishes directives from non-obligatory provisions of a constitution, such as provisions that are merely permissive or power-conferring. For example, permissive 'by law' clauses, such as § 22 of the 1996 South African constitution stating that the 'practice of a trade, occupation or profession *may* be regulated by law', tend not to be obligatory.[16] Directives, on the other hand, impose binding obligations on state institutions. Directives are also different from constitutional provisions that, although obligatory, are indifferent to the substantive purpose to be achieved. Mandatory 'by law' clauses – such as Article 18(6) of the 2005 Iraqi Constitution requiring that '[c]itizenship provisions *shall* be regulated by law' – tend to be obligatory for the legislature.[17] However, this provision does not, at least on its own, appear to care about the nature of the citizenship regime the legislature establishes. It seems to be compatible with a restrictive or liberal regime, and equally at home with a *jus soli* regime as with a *jus sanguinis* regime.

Constitutional directives, on the other hand, are 'directive' in two different senses: in the first sense they are *directions* or obligations addressed to the government of the state. In the second sense, they also determine the *direction of travel* for the state's policy, although – depending on the level of abstraction in which the directive is specified – this can leave very broad or relatively little discretion for the future

14 *See generally* Child Poverty Act 2010.

15 Weis, *supra* note 3, at 920.

16 On 'by law' clauses generally, *see* Rosalind Dixon & Tom Ginsburg, *Deciding Not to Decide: Deferral in Constitutional Design*, 9 Int. J. Const. L. 636 (2011).

17 The words 'may' and 'shall' are indicative of whether the provision is permissive or obligatory, but they do not determine the issue conclusively. More contextual information is needed to know for certain.

policymaker. Section 18(3) of the Constitution of the Federal Republic of Nigeria 1999, for example, obliging the government to 'strive to eradicate illiteracy, and to this end . . . provide (a) free, compulsory and universal primary education; (b) free secondary education; (c) free university education; and (d) free adult literacy programme' not only imposes an obligation on the state but also specifies the goal towards and even some means[18] by which it must act to fulfil its obligation. This is rather different from the permissive § 93 of the Canadian Constitution Act 1867, which states that '[i]n and for each Province the Legislature may exclusively make Laws in relation to Education'. Directives are, therefore, distinct not only from constitutional provisions that are non-obligatory but also from provisions that oblige the state to act but are indifferent to the objective it might seek to achieve.

15.2.2 *Directives as Telic Norms*

While constitutional directives are obligatory for the state, so are a host of other 'mission statements'.[19] As with all constitutional obligations, they apply irrespective of the ideology or policy-orientation of the governing party or coalition, and are mandatory. This does not mean, however, that there is no conceptual distinction between directives and other mission statements. Constitutional directives necessarily impose *telic* (teleological) duties, whereas other constitutional obligations may be telic or *deontic* (deontological). Telic and deontic norms differ in the nature of the duties they impose with regard to their subject-matter (say, 'X'). Deontic norms speak to the character of the action being considered; telic norms are concerned about its goals. A deontic norm requires us to honour/respect/recognise/venerate/consider X. A telic norm, on the other hand, is purposive, and seeks to promote/seek/secure/achieve/realise X. Intense debates on the legitimacy of affirmative action to favour disadvantaged groups can be understood in terms of the distinction between telic and deontic norms: opposition to affirmative action is often articulated in terms of its failure to *honour* the value of equality (since affirmative action requires unequal treatment); however, those who support affirmative action often do so because it will help *promote* equality.

Preambular values are sometimes expressed in telic form ('to secure to all its citizens justice'),[20] at other times in deontic form ('commit ourselves to . . . respect for human dignity').[21] Constitutional directives, however, almost always take the form of a telic norm, requiring the state to secure/realise/achieve/provide, etc., the stated objective. The distinction is clearly brought out while comparing the language in Articles 44 and 45 of the Constitution of Ireland. Article 44(1) imposes a deontic duty on the state to '*respect* and *honour* religion'. This article immediately

18 Section 93 has other, non-permissive provisions too.
19 King, *supra* note 2.
20 Constitution of India, preamble.
21 Constitution of the Republic of Fiji, preamble.

precedes Article 45, containing directive principles, which uses telic verbs like *promote* and *secure*. In fact, whether or not a constitution explicitly characterises them as 'directives', telic obligatory norms which also satisfy the contrajudicative feature discussed in Section 15.3 are best treated as constitutional directives in substance.

Deontic and telic norms are differently sensitive to time. Deontic norms do not have a temporal dimension: if they apply, they apply immediately. Deontic norms do not require the state to 'start respecting the value of equality in ten years' time' or 'progressively honour the rule of law over time'. Of course, a deontic norm may be 'brought into force' at a later date. But once it is operationalised, it applies with its full force, without reference to time. Telic norms are different – they *can be* made sensitive to time. A duty to secure X may or may not come with a deadline ('within ten years').[22] It may impose a duty to 'gradually implement corresponding policies' designed to achieve the stated objective.[23] Thus, even though a telic norm is operational, the duty to realise its objective may unravel over time.

It is precisely this temporal possibility with telic norms that facilitates the use of constitutional directives as deferral tools. This is why directives can help reduce decisional costs at the time of framing a constitution by shifting the decisional weight on a controversial issue from now to the future (and from entrenched constitutional solutions to reversible political ones).[24] They are able to perform this function of deferring controversial decisions only because of their telic character. No doubt, 'by law' clauses also perform a similar deferral role.[25] Directives, however, entail *partial*, rather than *full*, deferral of a given decision. To understand the distinction, consider some of the possible questions one could ask in relation to a practical decision:

i. *Whether* to act on the relevant issue at all?
ii. If yes, *what* should the action seek to achieve?
iii. Once we know that, *how* should one go about achieving it?
iv. And, finally, *when* would be a good time to act?

Because these stages in decision-making are conceptually separable, it is open to a constitution-maker to defer some, but not all, of these questions to a future decision-maker. A full deferral entails the deferral of all of these questions to the future, whereas a partial deferral settles some of these questions constitutionally but leaves others for politics to sort out later. Directives do not postpone all decisions relating to their subject matter: we have already noted that they are 'directives' both in the sense of being *directions* to the state as well as in the sense of being *directional*,

22 Constitution of India, art. 45.
23 Constitution of Nepal 2015, art. 52.
24 Tarunabh Khaitan, *Directive Principles and the Expressive Accommodation of Ideological Dissenters*, 16 Int'l J. Const. L. 389 (2018).
25 Dixon & Ginsburg, *supra* note 16.

that is, charting the direction of travel. The *when* question is clearly deferred; usually so is the *how* question. On the other hand, the *whether* and the *what* questions are usually settled by the constitution in the form of binding obligations on the state.

It is the telic character of directives which allows them to be simultaneously obligatory and deferred. The best way to capture this temporal simultaneity is by noticing that they entail two distinct duties: (i) a *duty to endeavour* to realise the directed goal, which kicks in immediately, and (ii) a *duty to fully realise* that goal by some (specified or unspecified) future date. Compare this with the duty of 'progressive realisation' entailed in some social rights guarantees (e.g., in the South African constitution). Progressive realisation, in the context of social rights, is different partly because it makes these duties justiciable, and partly because it sometimes includes an additional duty to immediately guarantee the minimum core of the right in question.[26] Given that the mobilisation of contemporaneous political will is essential to the realisation of any constitutional directive, democratic objections to thick moral norms in the constitution ought to be muted – while the past continues to oblige, it needs the present's permission to manifest itself.

15.2.3 *Expressive Salience of Directives*

The necessarily telic character of directives distinguishes them from preambular value statements which may or may not be telic. There is another, non-conceptual distinction between them – as *moral* commitments of the state (whether telic or deontic), these provisions typically have differing levels of expressive salience. Our moral values and goals indicate who we are. Their *constitutional* status makes them symbolically weighty in determining the moral and ethnocultural identity of the state in question. Expressive salience is a characteristic that admits to degrees – a provision can be more or less salient. This degree of salience can depend on a number of factors, including its anteriority, its abstraction, and its controversiality.

On two of these three counts, preambular provisions are likely to have features that tend to garner greater expressive salience than constitutional directives. Firstly, with respect to *anteriority*, preambles and fundamental value statements appear at or closer to the start of a constitutional text, which tends to have higher salience than provisions buried somewhere in the middle of the document, which is where directives usually find a home. There are exceptions, of course: the directives in the Ugandan Constitution of 1995, for example, are incorporated as part of the preambular text, and precede the substantive provisions of the constitution. The Bangladeshi Constitution of 1972 places constitutional directives in Part II, right after the state-constituting Part I, signalling their relative importance in the constitutional scheme. These approaches, however, are rare; it is far more common for

26 *See generally* David Bilchitz, *Giving Socio-economic Rights Teeth: The Minimum Core and Its Importance*, 19 S. African L. J. 1 (2003).

constitutional directives to find mention somewhere in the subsequent parts of a constitutional text. Of course, anteriority in a constitutional scheme is not the sole determinant of salience. Political discourse on a given provision is ultimately the key determinant of its expressive importance at any given point in time. Salience of a constitutional norm cannot be fixed in time, nor can its authors do more than merely try to influence it. Like much else in constitutionalism, constitution-makers frame and influence the discourse, but politics ultimately takes the final call. Anterior placement is, at best, indicative, of the potential salience of a provision.

Secondly, the level of *abstraction* of a provision is likely to matter. Abstract moral goals and values are likely to be more salient than their specific policy articulations often found in directives. Public commitments to liberty, equality, or justice, in general, will usually have greater symbolic weight than an agenda for guaranteed annual leave, unemployment benefit, or free legal aid. If Mario Cuomo's famous dictum – 'You campaign in poetry. You govern in prose' – has any truth to it,[27] it should be unsurprising that poetic preambular values tend to be more inspirational than typically prosaic directives. No doubt there are exceptions, but these exceptional specific goals have more salience than general ones despite their specificity rather than because of it, usually for one of the other reasons identified in this subsection.

Finally, when it comes to *controversiality*, the tables might be turned. Precisely because of their high-level abstraction, preambular values tend not to be especially controversial. Directives, because of their relative specificity, invite greater discontent. What is more, deferring controversial decisions to a future date is one of the reasons why framers sometimes use directives as a tool of constitutional incrementalism.[28] A controversial provision, like the cow slaughter directive or the uniform civil code directive in the Indian Constitution, tends to be more salient than uncontroversial ones.

15.2.4 *The Contained Normativity of Directives*

The relatively more specific character of directives also allows drafters to police their scope a lot more effectively than the more abstract – and therefore more expandable – fundamental values. The indeterminacy of value statements tends to originate from their vagueness, generality, or ambiguity. These indeterminacies can be distinguished by a simple example: the word 'child' is vague because there is no sharp dividing line that separates a child from an adult; 'child' is general because it under-specifies the gender of a child who could be a boy or a girl; 'child' is also ambiguous inasmuch as it could mean one's offspring or a person of a young age. Broad values such as liberty, equality, justice, secularism, dignity typically suffer from indeterminacies of all three

27 Jon F. Barnes, *Meet Mario the Moderate: Is He the Last Liberal or a Lost Liberal?*, 110 New Republic 207 (1995).

28 Khaitan, *supra* note 24.

sorts. This is precisely what makes them relatively uncontroversial – at a broad level of abstraction, people can read them to endorse their particular conception of the relevant value. This very attribute, however, also puts expansionist pressures on these values – their meaning is malleable, so that while they cannot mean anything one wants them to mean, they can mean quite a few different things.

More precise directives, on the other hand, can be more determinate and resist expansionist pressures better than abstract values. Being more specific, they also admit to further containment strategies such as qualification, instantiation, and contradiction. *Qualification* can moderate the goal outlined by a directive – a duty on the state to strive to provide 'free *primary* education' or 'reduce *extreme* inequalities of wealth' limits the normative force of a directive in a manner that is usually difficult to achieve with fundamental values. One need only consider the implausibility of provisions that declare 'moderate liberty', 'due dignity', or 'measured equality' to be a cherished value to appreciate the difficulty. Of course, qualification can happen with fundamental values as well: equality *of opportunity* is an example. But the qualified value should be a celebrated value in its own right (like 'equality of opportunity') for this to work. Rights provisions giving effect to these fundamental values do often temper their force ('no deprivation of liberty without due process', for example). But when expressed as a fundamental or preambular value, qualification is difficult to enshrine.

Instantiation works by making a specific directive an instance of a controlling, more general directive. This was used to great effect by the Indian framers to moderate some of the more illiberal directives requiring the state to seek to prohibit cow slaughter (made subservient to a general directive to organise agriculture on scientific lines) and alcohol consumption (again, made an instance of a general directive to improve health and nutrition).[29] Framers can also introduce *contradiction*, either between directives or between a directive and another constitutional provision, in order to contain its scope. The alcohol prohibition and cow slaughter directives in India were clearly in conflict with several fundamental rights, which would necessitate a fine balancing act by the state trying to implement the directives.[30]

15.3 ON CONTRAJUDICATIVE CHARACTER

The second feature of constitutional directives is, to borrow Weis's term, their *contrajudicative* character: 'they are not designed to be given effect by direct judicial enforcement'.[31] It is true that constitutional directives, although addressed to the state as a whole, are meant to be enforced primarily by the political organs of the

29 *Id.*

30 *Id.* at 410.

31 Weis, *supra* note 3, at 920.

state, viz. the executive and the legislature.[32] In most constitutions that contain them, this non-justiciability is expressly provided for in the text.[33] In other constitutions, such exclusion may be through implication or convention.[34] Some constitutions even go to the extent of providing the mode of their political enforcement: § 162 of the Thai Constitution of 2017 requires that '[t]he Council of Ministers which will assume the administration of State affairs must, within fifteen days as from the date it takes office, state its policies to the National Assembly, which must be consistent with ... directive principles'. Similarly, Articles 53 and 54 of the Constitution of Nepal 2015 require the government to present an annual report on the progressive implementation of the directives, which is to be monitored by a parliamentary committee.[35] Their contrajudicative character is a key reason for the controversy surrounding directive principles, and for their ostensible rejection in the South African Constitution.[36] When contrasted with the Nepali and Thai innovations, the South African scepticism about their effectiveness suggests a limited constitutional imagination. Whatever we might make normatively of their contrajudicative character, it remains the defining feature of constitutional directives, making them an important tool for political constitutionalism.

15.3.1 *Weakly Contrajudicative Character*

This is not to suggest that directives are, or are meant to be, irrelevant to adjudication. Judges can, and have, used them in several ways. These uses are illegitimate only if one understands their contrajudicative feature too strongly. Take, for example, a court trying to determine whether the fundamental right to property was proportionately restricted by a land redistribution legislation. A constitutional directive requiring the state to 'endeavour to promote material equality' is surely relevant to determining whether the objective of the redistribution legislation was legitimate. This might, in turn, depend on the scope of this directive, and especially whether it required the promotion of equality of opportunity or of resources. Surely, in a case such as this, the court will rightly see its role as encompassing determination of the scope of the directive. Therefore, a more precise understanding of its contrajudicative character is necessary. This is where our discussion in Section 15.2.2 on the telic obligatoriness of directives is helpful. We concluded that section by

[32] I do not deny that courts, too, are, or can be, political. But, usually, they are political in a different – attenuated – sense.

[33] *See, e.g.*, Constitution of India, art. 37; Constitution of Spain, § 53(3); Constitution of Ireland, art. 45.

[34] On the status of the Ghanaian and Ethiopian Constitutions, which do not have a non-justiciability clause, *see* Abdi Jibril Ali and K. Appiagyei-Atua, *Justiciability of Directive Principles of State Policy in Africa: The Experiences of Ethiopia and Ghana*, 1 ETH. J. HUM. RTS. 1 (2013).

[35] *See also* Constitution of the Republic of Ghana, art. 34. Dedicated guarantor institutions can be another mechanism for enforcing specific directives. See generally, T. Khaitan, *Guarantor Institutions*, ASIAN J. COMP. L. (2022 forthcoming).

[36] D.M. Davis, *The Case against the Inclusion of Socioeconomic Demands in a Bill of Rights Except as Directive Principles*, 8 S. AFRICAN J. HUM. RTS. 475 (1992).

discovering that directives impose two duties on the state: (i) a *duty to endeavour* to realise the directed goal, which kicks in immediately, and (ii) a *duty to fully realise* that goal by some (specified or unspecified) future date. What is key to the contrajudicative character of constitutional directives is that a breach of either of the two duties may not, on its own, give rise to a cause of action in courts. It is this contrajudicative feature of the nature of the obligations that directives impose that distinguishes them from rights. Unlike rights, directives do not match the obligations they impose with corresponding rights vested in any person. In Kelsen's terms, directives lack corresponding 'reflex rights' – when their duties are breached, their intended beneficiaries do not have any correlative legal claims against the breach.[37] Kelsen gives the example of the duty to perform military service, which is not accompanied by any reflex right vested in any person.[38] Constitutional directives are similar – they are not accompanied by reflex rights either.

Nothing in this subsection should be read to imply that rights are the *sole* domain of the judiciary. Rights impose obligations on politicians as well as judges and, to that extent, they may also be seen as 'directives'.[39] The difference is simply that breaches of rights give rise to a cause of action in courts; breaches of directives do not.

15.3.2 *A Right or a Directive? Practice, Not Structure*

Although they are both obligatory norms, we know that the key distinction between rights and directives is the contrajudicative character of the latter. What makes constitutional directives contrajudicative? Typically, the constitutional text itself bars judicial enforcement of these directives.[40] But a textual prohibition is not necessary for a constitutional provision to be treated as contrajudicative. Section 24(b) of the South African Constitution, which guarantees the 'right to have the environment protected, through legislative and other measures', is treated as a contrajudicative directive principle even though it appears in the fundamental rights chapter.[41] Constitutional text is an important factor, but it is not determinative of whether a provision is a right or a directive.

Weis claims that 'it is the structural features of a provision – and *not* its practical operation – that determines whether it is a directive principle'. It is no doubt true that a provision needs to satisfy certain structural features in order to qualify as a directive – in particular, it has to be an obligatory normative provision. But its contrajudicative character cannot be settled by its structure. Whether a provision is

37 Hans Kelsen, The Pure Theory of Law 127–28 (1967).
38 *Id.* at 128.
39 *See generally* Grégoire Webber et al., Legislated Rights: Securing Human Rights through Legislation (2018).
40 *See, e.g.*, Constitution of India, art. 3; Constitution of Ireland, art. 45.
41 Weis, *supra* note 3, at 921.

a *right* or a *directive* is settled not by its structure but by how the practice of a given jurisdiction treats it.

Let us recall the two duties that directives typically impose: (i) a *duty to endeavour* to realise the directed goal, which kicks in immediately, and (ii) a *duty to fully realise* that goal by some (specified or unspecified) future date. However, there is no general conceptual difficulty in enshrining accompanying reflex rights alongside either of the two duties that directives impose. There are several ways in which a government may breach the first duty 'to endeavour to realise' the stated objective – by failing to do anything at all in regard to the objective, by doing something that clearly detracts from that objective, and so on. The South African social rights jurisprudence has been instructive in demonstrating how such duties can indeed be enforced judicially.[42] Of course, there will be cases in the grey zone, but that is true of almost every constitutional right. Furthermore, with regard to the second duty, at least for some objectives – say the objective to enact a uniform civil code in the Indian Constitution[43] or the objective to provide workers with adequate rest in the Gambian Constitution[44] – it is possible to determine whether 'full realisation' has been (broadly) achieved.

Admittedly, there exists interpretive latitude in determining their scope, but, again, that is true of rights, too. Interpretive latitude is not a bar to justiciability – at most it calls for greater judicial deference in hard cases. If the level of interpretive latitude is a difference between rights and directives, it is at best one of degree. There is nothing in the *structure* of § 24(b) of the South African Constitution, concerning environmental rights, that prevents a court from enforcing its duties, even if it might defer to the will of the political branches in most cases of alleged breaches. It may be that South African courts have so far treated it as a directive principle and refused to legally enforce its duties, but nothing in its *structure* stops them from changing their stance in the future.

What emerges then is that whether a constitutional duty is a 'right' or a 'directive' is a positive doctrinal choice, to be made by the practitioners (framers, enforcers, revisers, and interpreters) of a constitution. The same duty can be a right in one jurisdiction and a directive in another. Even within a given jurisdiction, a directive can, at a subsequent time, be translated into a right, or a right be treated as a directive. Several directives in the Indian constitution, concerning social minimum guarantees, have been translated into rights by the judiciary (by being read as implied by the right to life and personal liberty under Article 21).[45] A constitutional amendment in India converted the primary education directive into a fundamental

42 David Bilchitz, Poverty and Fundamental Rights chs. 4–6 (2007).

43 Constitution of India, art. 44.

44 Constitution of the Republic of the Gambia 1997, art. 216(6).

45 Gautam Bhatia, *Directive Principles of State Policy*, *in* The Oxford Handbook of the Indian Constitution (Sujit Choudhry, Madhav Khosla & Pratap Bhanu Mehta eds., 2016); Farrah Ahmed & Tarunabh Khaitan, *Constitutional Avoidance*, 35 Oxford J. Leg. Stud. 607 (2015).

right.[46] Ultimately, it is not the structure or the content of a norm that determines its contrajudicative character, but whether the practice of that jurisdiction treats its duties as judicially enforceable or not.

15.4 CONCLUSION

Constitutional directives are norms of good governance that contain the possibility of a morally committed liberal democratic constitutionalism. Conceptually, constitutional directives are obligatory telic norms that identify thick moral objectives whose full realisation is deferred to a future date. These directives impose two duties: (i) a *duty to endeavour* to realise the directed goal, which kicks in immediately, and (ii) a *duty to fully realise* that goal by some (specified or unspecified) future date. The telic character of these duties facilitates the use of directives as an incrementalist tool, where current constitutional controversies are passed on for future resolution through ordinary politics. They tend to have a lower, if variable, expressive salience than value statements and are more amenable to containment strategies. Directives are weakly contrajudicative in that these duties are not directly enforced by courts. Ultimately, the characterisation of a norm as a directive depends on the constitutional practice in a given jurisdiction, rather than on the constitutional text or the structure of the norm in question.

With these conceptual and functional features, constitutional directives hold the promise for a morally committed political constitutionalism. Greater scholarly attention to their functioning in different jurisdictions, including the effectiveness of the innovative political enforcement mechanisms being adopted by some constitutions, will enrich our understanding of constitutionalism. It will also widen our understanding of the range of possibilities that exists within liberal democratic constitutionalism. The scope of this chapter has been analytic; many normative issues concerning constitutional directives' desirability, content, efficacy, and enforceability await further scholarly attention.

46 *See* Constitution of India, art. 21A. *See also* Unni Krishnan v. State of Andhra Pradesh, (1993) AIR 2178 (India).

16

Recursive Representation

The Basic Idea

Jane Mansbridge

16.1 INTRODUCTION: ADD RECURSIVITY TO OUR IDEALS OF REPRESENTATION

Today we face a long-run crisis of democratic legitimacy. Our increasing human interdependence is steadily increasing the numbers of "collective action," or "free-rider" problems. Those problems in turn require increasing amounts of state coercion. Yet, in part precisely because state coercion is growing, that coercion is becoming less legitimate. As the demand for legitimacy increases and the supply decreases, every ounce of legitimacy becomes more precious.

A long-run response to this crisis requires many changes, including major restructuring to decrease inequality.

A relatively modest, but perhaps practicable and far-reaching, change in our thinking would make recursivity, meaning mutually responsive and iterated communication between representatives and constituents, more central to both the ideals and the practices of the representative system. In the aspirational ideal of recursive representation, representatives in the legislative, administrative, and societal realms engage in ongoing back-and-forth communication with their constituents. That recursivity allows each party to listen and learn, facilitating mutual influence and mutual adjustment. Because the process is more respectful of each citizen than the current system, the outcomes are more likely to reflect citizens' needs. The resulting coercion should be both more defensible normatively and experienced as more legitimate.

16.2 INCREASING NEEDS FOR STATE COERCION HAVE CAUSED A CRISIS IN LEGITIMACY

Over the course of human history, human beings have slowly become more interdependent, despite massive and smaller moves in the other direction at times.

Through the division of labor and economies of scale, such increasing interdependence brings most human beings increased capacity to fulfill their individual and collective goals. That interdependence is not all to the good, however, as it usually makes the already vulnerable even more heavily reliant on the already powerful.

Increasing interdependence usually also entails a greater need for "free-use goods" – goods that, once produced, anyone can use, including those who do not pay to produce them. Free-use goods include all the goods that materialist political theorists have advanced as reasons for government: defense of the realm, law and order, toll-free roads, open harbors. In the mid-twentieth century, several thinkers finally pieced together the underlying logic: the need for a free-use good creates a free-rider problem because the users of free-use goods do not have to pay for them; the goods are thus underproduced relative to need.[1] Humans have typically addressed these problems with a two-part strategy. First, we encourage the motives of empathy, solidarity, and duty, nurturing innate empathy and solidarity while teaching the importance of duty. These motives lead people to cooperate to produce free-use goods even though they could use those goods without contributing to their production. Second, we make up for what those normative motives do not accomplish by instituting sufficient coercion on the noncooperators to get them to contribute adequately. That coercion usually ensures that the noncooperators do not unduly exploit the cooperators. Smaller societies can use informal coercion, through scorn, ostracism, or tit-for-tat retaliation, because in smaller societies each member may know the reputations of others and find ways of informally punishing deviation from collective norms. Larger societies of strangers need coercion by superordinate actors, notably government. In short, human beings need state coercion because we need free-use goods. The more free-use goods we need and the more important those free-use goods are to us, the more we need state coercion. A stable climate, clean air, and clean water are important free-use goods. In the past, these goods often seemed to be in infinite supply. Today, because we must actively produce them, they pose the biggest free-rider problem ever.[2]

As our need for state coercion increases, we need more legitimacy for that coercion than we did in an era when it could make sense to say that a government is best which governs least. Yet the legitimacy-producing mechanisms of most democracies, designed in and for the eighteenth century, cannot produce sufficient legitimacy for today. Indeed, as our needs for state coercion have increased, citizens

[1] For citations, see Jane Mansbridge, *Recursive Representation*, *in* CREATING POLITICAL PRESENCE (Dario Castiglione & Johannes Pollak eds., 2019). The classic argument against government, ROBERT NOZICK 's ANARCHY, STATE AND UTOPIA (1974), puzzlingly made no mention of the free-rider/collective action logic, discovered between 1950 and 1965.

[2] For a longer exposition of this logic, e.g., explaining that the standard nomenclature of "public goods" and "nonexcludable goods" is technically incorrect in this context, see Mansbridge (2019), *supra* note 1, and Jane Mansbridge, *Recursive Representation in the Representative System*, with Appendices A and B, paper presented at Annual Meeting, American Political Science Association, San Francisco (2017), https://ssrn.com/abstract=3040139.

in many democracies have come to perceive that coercion as increasingly illegitimate for many reasons. One reason derives from the very increase in coercion that citizens now experience. Another reason, in some democracies, may derive from the number of years since World War II, when national appeals to solidarity and duty combined with increases in state coercion, perceived as legitimate, to fight a clear external enemy. In many democracies, a broader decline of trust in other people has accompanied, and probably played a causal role in, the decline of trust in government. Growing inequality across many democracies has undoubtedly played a role in this decline of trust in others and in the state. Growing heterogeneity in populations may also play a role.[3] For these and other causes, in many developed democracies the legitimacy of state coercion has declined just as the need for that coercion has increased.

In other ways, too, our world is not the world that laid the foundations of today's democratic practice and democratic theory. Eighteenth-century democracies managed to withstand relatively high levels of corruption in both the lowest and the highest layers of government precisely because that government was comparatively minimal. In addition, elected representatives in the eighteenth century drove away to capitals in their stagecoaches and were reachable only with difficulty for months thereafter, leading some to advocate tying those representatives to their constituents with "instructions" while others advocated that the representatives should act independently – a choice later formulated as "delegate" versus "trustee." In this era, legislatures could also adhere fairly easily, both in principle and to some significant degree in practice, to the "nondelegation principle," forbidding them to delegate their law-making power to the administrative/executive branch. All this has changed. As each increment in legitimacy has become more valuable, corruption can now threaten the very life of democracies. Increased communication has made the concepts of delegate and trustee almost obsolete. The sheer volume of necessary law-making undermines the nondelegation principle.

Recursivity, in the form of iterated mutually responsive communication between representatives of all kinds and their constituents, addresses these problems. Recursivity can reduce corruption. Recursivity makes interactive communication central to representation, in contrast to the passivity of the "delegate" or the loner independence of the "trustee." Recursivity allows government administrations, along with societal bodies such as nongovernmental organizations (NGOs) and unions, to play more legitimate law-making roles and thus enhance effective governance.

[3] For the large literature on declining trust in government, including causes other than these, *see, e.g.*, Jack Citrin & Laura Stokes, *Political Trust in a Cynical Age*, 21 ANN. REV. POL. SCI. 49 (2018); Russell J. Dalton, *The Social Transformation of Trust in Government*, 15 INT'L REV. SOCIO. 133 (2005); MARC J. HETHERINGTON, WHY TRUST MATTERS (2005); Robert D. Putnam, *Diversity and Community in the Twenty-First Century*, 30 SCAND. POL. STUD. 137 (2007).

16.3 RECURSIVITY CREATES GREATER LEGITIMACY IN THE LEGISLATIVE REALM

In a polity where, as Rousseau had it, "the common good is everywhere apparent, and only good sense is needed to perceive it,"[4] elected representatives would have an easy job. The small and relatively homogeneous polities that Rousseau considered fit for democracy generally have a relatively high proportion of common interests. Not so in the larger polities characteristic of today's nation-state. In larger polities, a representative system must not only identify and forge common interests when possible but also clarify conflict and find ways to manage it in the many instances where a first-level common good is not apparent.[5]

Yet representation breeds distrust. Whether elected representatives make their decisions through straight majority rule or through negotiated majorities or super-majorities, opportunities abound for both corruption and genuine misunderstanding. In some democracies, straightforward illegal corruption is commonplace. Other democracies are undermined by the legal "wining and dining of bureaucrats" or, far worse, legal systemic corruption through the significant power of money in politics. Both illegal and legal forms of corruption in representation delegitimate the democratic process.

Representation also generates genuine misunderstanding. Elected representatives may simply misunderstand the needs and preferences of their constituencies. In the United States, both Democratic and Republican representatives often think their constituencies are more conservative than they are.[6] Constituents in turn often misunderstand their elected representatives, partly because those representatives act with information that only a few of their constituents have. Particularly after a complex negotiation, the full rationale for the representative's vote is not immediately apparent. Advertising and social media can also distort what the constituent perceives. After one major advertising blitz, an elected representative in the US House of Representatives told political scientist John Kingdon:

> Very frankly, if I had a chance to sit down with all of my constituents for 15 minutes and talk to them, I'd have voted against the whole thing. But I didn't have that chance. They wanted [x]. If I voted against it, it would appear to them that I was against [x], and I wouldn't have had a chance to explain myself.[7]

Distrust arises in any model of representation. In one model, based on monitoring and sanctioning, representatives act "anticipatorily," thinking ahead to probable voter reactions to their records in office at the next election and changing their

[4] Jean-Jacques Rousseau, *The Social Contract, in* THE SECOND CONTRACT AND OTHER LATER POLITICAL WRITINGS x (Victor Gourevitch trans., 1997) (1762).

[5] JANE MANSBRIDGE, BEYOND ADVERSARY DEMOCRACY (1980).

[6] David E. Broockman & Christopher Skovron, *Bias in Perceptions of Public Opinion among Political Elites*, 112 AM. POL. SCI. REV. 542 (2018).

[7] JOHN W. KINGDON, CONGRESSMEN'S VOTING DECISIONS 48 (1981).

behavior accordingly in order to be reelected. In another model, based on selection, voters choose representatives whom they believe will act "gyroscopically" on their own convictions and interests, which the voters have reason to believe match relatively closely their own convictions and interests.[8] Neither model matches the old "delegate" or "trustee" model of representation. Unlike the "trustee" model, the selection model need carry no implication of the representative's greater wisdom or knowledge. Rather, voters often want to select "someone like me." Although voters may be more likely to trust gyroscopic representatives, neither model of representation guarantees trust. Both are open to both illegal and legal corruption as well as misunderstanding.

Recursive representation would probably increase legitimacy in each of these instances. Frequent interactions with voters should help curb both illegal and legal corruption by facilitating voter questioning and requiring the representative's response. Recursive practices should also make it clearer to representatives what constituents want and help constituents refine their understandings of the constraints the representatives face in their deliberations, negotiations, and votes with other representatives. If recursive representational practices bring representatives and citizens closer together, they can approach more nearly the deeper aspirational ideal of citizens making the laws for themselves.[9]

16.4 RECURSIVITY IN PRACTICE: THE LEGISLATIVE REALM

What do constituents want from their elected representatives? Communication. In the only study I know to ask this open-ended question, constituents in the USA said that they wanted their representative to listen to and be available to them.[10] As Richard Fenno summarized the insight: "Access and the assurance of access, communication and the assurance of communication – these are the *irreducible underpinnings of representation*."[11] Since Fenno wrote, the demand for

[8] Jane Mansbridge, *Rethinking Representation*, 97 AM. POL. SCI. REV. 515 (2003); Jane Mansbridge, A "*Selection Model" of Political Representation*, 17 J. POL. PHIL. 369 (2009).

[9] Jane Mansbridge, *Representation Failure*, *in* DEMOCRATIC FAILURE 101–40 (Melissa Schwartzberg & Daniel Viehoff eds., 2020).

[10] CHRISTOPHER J. GRILL, THE PUBLIC SIDE OF REPRESENTATION: A STUDY OF CITIZENS' VIEWS ABOUT REPRESENTATIVES AND THE REPRESENTATIVE PROCESS (2007).

[11] RICHARD FENNO, JR., HOME STYLE: HOUSE MEMBERS IN THEIR DISTRICTS 239–40 (1978) (emphasis in original). *See also* David Plotke, *Representation Is Democracy*, 4 CONSTELLATIONS 19, 22 (1997); MELISSA WILLIAMS, VOICE, TRUST, AND MEMORY: MARGINALIZED GROUPS AND THE FAILINGS OF LIBERAL REPRESENTATION 231–32 (1998); IRIS MARION YOUNG, DEMOCRACY AND INCLUSION 128, 130 (2000); CAROLYN M. HENDRIKS ET AL., DEMOCRATIC MENDING: DEMOCRATIC REPAIR IN DISCONNECTED TIMES (2020). John Lapinski et al., *What Do Citizens Want from Their Member of Congress?*, 69 POL. RSCH. Q. 535, 537 (2016), show that 76 percent of US respondents in a 2013 survey ranked "keeping in touch with constituents" as "very important," compared to 57 percent (the next highest ranking) for "working on national issues."

communication has increased exponentially, prompting new technologies and shifts in resources to provide at least rudimentary recursivity.

Many reforms and novel institutions could increase the amount and quality of mutually responsive communication between elected representatives and their constituents.

One easy reform would simply give elected representatives more staff. Members of the US Congress have already shifted many of their staff into "communications," depleting their other capabilities. With the increasing use of relatively cost-free email, by 2004 the representatives were getting more than 200 million messages a year from their constituents, up almost 100 percent from only four years before. Many of these were "identical form communications" that could rightly be answered with a form reply.[12] More recursively, for more individual communications, instead of sending out the standard form letter, staff with even a little expertise in several issue areas could reply to constituents' correspondence on policy questions with some responsive content. At the same time, they could screen that correspondence for useful suggestions and information, passing that up to the staff with greater expertise in the relevant issue areas. In the most recursive and most aspirational form of the ideal, the representative's staff could even contact the constituents later to report the outcome.

Another easy reform in the US system would restructure the current in-person "townhall" meetings of citizens with their representatives, which can degenerate into shouting sessions. One model allows a representative to choose from the sea of raised hands first five citizens, and then three more who say they have different points, to speak for a full five minutes to explain their positions clearly, then respond and bring in other citizens in a structured encounter that encourages listening and more varied citizen voices.[13] A new telephone townhall technology uses robocalls to contact all reachable constituents or simply allows constituents to phone in, producing some interaction between representatives and those constituents who choose to participate over the phone, with the representatives' staff screening and choosing the questions (e.g., http://teletownhall.com/ or https://www.broadnet.com/products/accesslive/). These sessions now consist almost entirely of two-way communications – a constituent's question and a representative's answer – but could become more recursive if constituents were allowed to respond and if the representative were to ask constituents questions and particularly follow-up questions, a powerful signal of listening.[14]

A more complex response uses the newly developed vehicle of a randomized selection of citizens in recursive deliberation with an elected representative. In the

12 Brad Fitch et al., *Communicating with Congress: How Capitol Hill Is Coping with the Surge in Citizen Advocacy*, Congr. Mgmt. Found. (2005), https://www.congressfoundation.org/storage/documents/CMF_Pubs/cwc_capitolhillcoping.pdf.

13 For detail, *see* Lawrence Susskind, *How Should You Respond to the Noisy Health Reform Critics?* (Aug. 2009), https://www.mediate.com/articles/SusskindLbl20090817.cfm.

14 Alison Wood Brooks & Leslie K. John, *The Surprising Power of Questions*, 96 Harv. Bus. Rev. 60 (2018).

USA, Michael Neblo, David Lazer, and Kevin Esterling have designed an inexpensive way for elected representatives to talk interactively over the Internet for an hour on a single important topic, such as immigration, with a group of 175 eligible voters chosen randomly from among their constituents.[15] At the Congressional level, their randomized selection process, with concerted follow-up for less interested constituents, produced in its first iterations a genuinely representative sample, including the appropriate proportions of traditionally marginalized groups. The constituents learn, feel enthusiastic about the experience, discuss the conversation with their friends, and seem more likely to vote in the next election. Further study suggests that the elected representatives also learn. If every member of the US House and Senate held such a conversation twice a week, in six years they could have covered a quarter of the eligible voters in their districts. If this practice became a standard part of the representative system, each eligible voter could expect to take part once, or perhaps several times, over their lifetime. Citizens would talk about these mutual consultations with their friends. Schools would teach their students how to prepare for these conversations. This model has spread to Australia.[16] In Germany, in a slightly different model, Constituency Councils allow members of Parliament from any of Germany's 299 electoral districts to invite 30 or more randomly selected, unpaid constituents together in-person for a day to discuss a current political issue and develop solutions.[17]

More broadly, the democratic mechanism of representation by lot in randomly selected citizens' assemblies is now being deployed in every continent, and particularly in Europe, to supplement and be integrated into legislative representation.[18] Practitioners and theorists currently disagree among themselves as to whether, when, and how such assemblies should involve legislators directly in their deliberations, as opposed to the assemblies serving as independent sources of information and political pressure. In Iceland, the citizens' assembly was fiercely independent, on the assumption that the presence of legislators might prove intimidating and that the legislators' facility with language and their greater information on issues might

15 Michael Neblo et al., Politics with the People: Building a Directly Representative Democracy (2018).

16 With the Centre for Deliberative Democracy and Global Governance at the University of Canberra, one member of the Australian House of Parliament, Andrew Leigh, has already held online and in-person sessions with randomly selected constituents on the controversial and technical subject of legislating the use of mitochondrial DNA, asking constituents questions and even follow-up questions to help him understand their thoughts and feelings about facets of the policy (https://connect2parliament.com/townhalls).

17 See Der Wahlkreisrat: Vorstellung eines Konzepts zur Stärkung der repräsentativen Demokratie (2021), https://www.esgehtlos.org/site/assets/files/1505/egl_wahlkreisrat_konzept.pdf. I thank Katharina Liesenberg of *Es Geht LOS!* (private communication) for these details. *See also* the Columbian "Concejo a la Casa." Sebastian Camilo Guanumen-Parra & David Leonardo Núñez-Amórtegui, *Innovacion politica y participacion por sorteo: "Concejo a la casa," el primer caso de democracia por aleatoriedad en Colombia*, 8 Opera 111 (2021).

18 For a list of examples and analysis of types, *see* OECD, *Innovative Citizen Participation and New Democratic Institutions: Catching the Deliberative Wave* (June 10, 2020).

allow them to dominate. In Ireland, the citizens' assembly built in an active role for legislators, on the assumption that they would eventually have to argue for and pass the assembly's recommendations in the legislature, and should therefore have an intimate experience of the evolution of the dialogue and the reasons the citizens in the assembly gave for their conclusions. In the Ireland case, for perhaps idiosyncratic reasons, the elected representatives who participated in the deliberations did not dominate but acted deferentially, as learners, in the assembly.[19]

In the German-speaking Community of East Belgium, citizens' assemblies have a highly integrated relationship with the legislature. A permanent Citizens' Council of twenty-four citizens, whose members are now randomly drawn from former citizen assembly participants and serve on a rotating basis for eighteen months, selects the topics on which broader Citizens' Assemblies, who are randomly drawn from the public, deliberate one to three times a year. The Citizens' Council then meets with members of parliament to discuss the Citizens' Assemblies' proposals, and monitors the parliament's implementation of the assemblies' recommendations. The parliament must provide a formal justification for any decision not to implement a recommendation.[20] The process provides considerable recursivity among the Citizens' Council, the Citizens' Assemblies, the parliamentarians, and the public.

In a more common model, legislatures mandate ad hoc citizens' assemblies, usually committing to implement their recommendations or provide formal public justification for not doing so. These ad hoc assemblies vary greatly in their degree of recursivity with both the legislature and the public. Whenever citizens' assemblies also evaluate later the effects of the legislation, as in Colombia,[21] they enforce a kind of institutional responsiveness.

The increased interaction of individual elected representatives with constituents, whether individually or collectively in a citizens' assembly, necessarily detracts from the time those representatives can spend learning the details of policy and deliberating with other elected representatives to reach negotiated decisions. The recursive ideal, however, harnesses the communicative skills that many representatives have already developed as prerequisites for seeking electoral office. The ideal envisions the representative primarily as *interlocutor* with constituents, other representatives, and administrators – listening to the situated experiences and stated needs of all parties, informing each about the heterogeneity, needs, and constraints of the others, listening again to their responses, and interpreting each to the other, while leaving more of the specifics of policy-making to high-level staff and administration. In this

19 Hélène Landemore, Open Democracy: Reinventing Popular Rule for the Twenty-First Century (2020).

20 Christoph Niessen & Min Reuchamps, *Institutionalising Citizen Deliberation in Parliament: The Permanent Citizens' Dialogue in the German-Speaking Community of Belgium*, Parliam. Aff., Sept. 5, 2020.

21 Indira Latorre & Felipe Rey, *Sequencing Deliberation: The Itinerant Citizens' Assembly Model*, NewDemocracy (2021), https://www.newdemocracy.com.au/research-and-development-notes/.

ideal, which leaves more power to administrators, it is important that administrative representation be recursive.

16.5 ADMINISTRATIONS NEED MORE RECURSIVITY

Administrative law-making is both pervasive and a democratically legitimate creator of state coercion in most advanced democracies. Yet almost all administrations could easily use more normative and perceived legitimacy. Greater recursivity could provide both.

At the policy-making level, the normative legitimacy of administrators derives primarily from formal delegation of powers by the legislature and the legislature's continuing decision not to withdraw those powers. It requires the absence of corruption as the legislature chooses the administrators and delegates powers. It should also derive from balanced and equitable inputs from affected sectors. In addition, the normative and perceived legitimacy of administrative law-making derives in great part from the quality of the justifications or reasons the administrators can give for their decisions and actions. Yet citizens often experience a democratic deficit even when the formal processes of delegation and selection meet high standards of normative legitimacy and the justifications meet high rational standards for accuracy and relevance. The great volume and importance of administrative policy-making, the long lines of delegation and consequent distance from the original legislative authorization, and, most importantly, the difficulty that relevant publics often have in understanding the justifications all undermine perceived legitimacy. In modern democracies, administrative representatives have thus often instituted both formal and informal procedures for communication with the public both to improve the quality of the outcome and to increase the perceived and normative legitimacy of the decision. Formally, many administrations have developed ways of consulting the organized societal entities that represent affected interests.[22] These fledgling recursive procedures deserve more empirical and normative attention.

In the traditional democratic account, legislatures cannot delegate their law-making power.[23] Yet current conditions of interdependence and complexity often make this traditional stance untenable and undesirable. Administrators at both the higher policy-making levels and the street level must make law.[24] At either level,

22 *See, e.g.*, Charles F. Sabel & Jonathan Zeitlin, *Learning from Difference: The New Architecture of Experimentalist Governance in the EU*, 14 EUR. L. J. 271 (2008).

23 For nondelegation, see JOHN LOCKE, TWO TREATISES OF GOVERNMENT (Peter Laslett ed., 1963) (1679–89); JÜRGEN HABERMAS, THE STRUCTURAL TRANSFORMATION OF THE PUBLIC SPHERE (Thomas Burger & Frederick Lawrence trans., 1989) (1962); THEODORE J. LOWI, THE END OF LIBERALISM: THE SECOND REPUBLIC OF THE UNITED STATES (1979) (1969); and, more recently, *e.g.*, DAVID SCHOENBROD, POWER WITHOUT RESPONSIBILITY (1993). I am more persuaded by, *e.g.*, Cass Sunstein, *Is the Clean Air Act Unconstitutional?*, 98 MICH. L. REV. 305 (1999).

24 Some analysts would not consider a one-off discretionary administrative decision "making law" because such a decision does not legally bind others to similar results. At the risk of concept-stretching, I would argue that when a duly empowered actor habitually interprets and implements

however, if state officials do not consult with the public in their policy-making, the resulting policies will be of lower quality and have less normative and perceived legitimacy.

In practice, therefore, policy-making administrators frequently consult recursively with major stakeholders. Yet consultation with ordinary citizens, through notice and comment, for example, tends to be only one-way, from the citizen to the administration, and sometimes one-way from the citizen to the void. The consultation process is thus deeply unequal. Administrators have recently begun to consult with various versions of randomly drawn citizens' assemblies, such as the Deliberative Polls that legitimated building massive numbers of windmills in Texas,[25] or the consultations on infrastructure in Ghana or Mongolia[26] and China.[27] Yet even these institutions, while deliberative among the citizens, rarely contain recursive interactions between citizens and administrators – often to preserve the citizens' independence.

What I will call a Citizens' Initiative for Administrative Accountability (CIAA) might produce more recursivity.[28] In such an initiative, some number of citizen signatures might mandate that a lower-level official appear before a group of citizens to explain and discuss an administrative policy, a higher number of signatures might mandate a discussion with a higher-level official, and a still higher number mandate a discussion with the highest-level official on that policy in the relevant polity. In line with the recursive ideal, such processes would require administrators to explain the reasons for their actions, listen well to citizens' disagreements or suggestions, respond iteratively, and, when appropriate, ask their own questions and follow-up questions about citizens' experiences. Administrators need to understand how what they do affects the lives of the citizens on the ground, and sometimes need to get depth by hearing from the citizens themselves in situations that facilitate recursive interaction. For their part, citizens need to hear the ideas of the administrators in situations where the citizens can pursue their questions, pressing deeply and interactively into the responses.

the law in a predictable way, those acts of interpretation and implementation constitute "making law" for many practical purposes. Even when a single individual actor interprets and implements the law in a one-off and unpredictable way, that actor is, through that act, "making law" for the person affected. From the perspective of the coerced, what has happened (if not challenged successfully in a court of law) "is" the law. That law, as experienced by the coerced, rests on varying degrees of normative legitimacy. This interpretation of making law is important for understanding the fragility of the legitimacy of state coercion and the need for creating, maintaining, and reinforcing that legitimacy all the way down.

25 James S. Fishkin, When the People Speak (2009).

26 James S. Fishkin, Democracy When the People Are Thinking (2018).

27 Baogang He & Mark E. Warren, *Authoritarian Deliberation: The Deliberative Turn in Chinese Political Development*, 9 Persp. on Pol. 269 (2011).

28 Jane Mansbridge, *The Fallacy of Tightening the Reins*, 34 Österreichische Zeitschrift für Politikwissenschaf 233 (2005); Jane Mansbridge, A *Contingency Theory of Accountability*, *in* The Oxford Handbook of Public Accountability 55–68 (Mark Bowens et al. eds., 2014).

At the street level, bureaucrats in all countries also make law. The police, teachers, social workers, customs inspectors, and clerks at the motor vehicles registry usually have some, sometimes considerable, discretion.[29] When they use that discretion, they are making law. For reasons much like those of administrators at the policy level, these street-level administrators sometimes engage the public in coproducing these laws. The police may institute community policing measures to bring the public into the decisions they make on how to pursue their broader mandate.[30] The schools may rely on Parent-Teacher Associations or their equivalents to inform decisions. A broader normative mandate for greater recursive communication would encourage other street-level bureaucracies to devise institutions to allow them to consult citizens deliberatively and regularly. Even printed explanations on a sign in a waiting room for problems that citizens typically experience, such as a long wait, would help. Easy ways for citizens to suggest how to ameliorate these problems would be another step, if someone actually responded to the suggestions. A mandate to create recursivity might also mean restructuring administrative representation to make street-level bureaucrats more descriptively, and therefore communicatively, representative of the population for whom they make law, to give them incentives for recursive interaction, and to give citizens more power to initiate that interaction from below.

Recalibrating our understanding of administrative representation could allow us to accept, from a normative democratic perspective, some autonomy for administrators selected for their competence and public-interest motivation. We could then provide deliberative counterweights to that autonomy by adding incentives and institutions for greater responsiveness to informed public desires, greater respect for public knowledge and perceptions, greater and more equal public voice in decisions, and greater recursive capacity for mutual education, communication, and deliberation between administrative representatives and the public. In many such instances, the arrows of control and communication may rightly bypass the electoral system to go directly from the citizens to the responsible administrators.

In the ideal model of recursive administrative representation, power and persuasion would travel in both directions and affect the next moves of all the communicative partners. This democratic ideal is deliberative as well as aggregative. It is also educative rather than static. It respects all three crucial sets of actors in the official political world: citizens, elected representatives, and administrative representatives. It asks what settings will encourage all of these actors to develop both their personal and their institutional capacities in ways that foster critical intelligence, concern for the public good, and the ability to listen and communicate across the lines of class, ethnicity, gender, and culture.

29 *See, e.g.*, Michael Lipsky, Street-Level Bureaucracy: Dilemmas of the Individual in Public Services (2010) (1980).

30 *E.g.*, Archon Fung, Empowered Participation: Reinventing Urban Democracy (2004).

16.6 SOCIETAL REPRESENTATION NEEDS MORE RECURSIVITY

Today the social, private, or societal realm, consisting of NGOs and other associations, occasionally makes law and more often plays an integral part in how the legislative and administrative realms make law. Both legislatures and administrations need the information and the connection with constituencies that societal associations can provide. Societal sector actors often have significant perceived legitimacy, although less normative legitimacy. Recursive and more egalitarian representation of their constituents would increase their normative legitimacy and perhaps even their perceived legitimacy.

Many associations, for example, derive both perceived and normative legitimacy from their voluntary character. They are nominally free, like markets responding to supply and demand, with accountability derived, when plausible, from their dependence on members' voluntary entry and exit. Yet their normative democratic legitimacy may be low – sometimes because the societal representatives do not speak accurately for, or are not authorized by or accountable to, the groups for whom they speak (e.g., entry and exit from the groups is not fully voluntary), or because the larger system of societal representation is biased, with only some groups robustly represented.

As a crucial piece of the larger representative system, the societal realm deserves normative attention. Yet normative democratic standards for associations in that realm are only beginning to be developed and are often strongly contested. Two sets of distinctions are relevant. The first is a two-part distinction between internal and external. Some developing standards apply to the *internal* legitimacy problems of misrepresentation, authorization, and accountability. These are problems within the representative-represented relationship. Other standards apply to *external* questions of bias within the system in which the representative relationship is embedded. Our norms regarding external, or systemic, bias are usually stronger and clearer than our norms regarding the internal governance of organizations.

The second involves three degrees of societal organizations' closeness to the state. Some societal organizations have powers *directly delegated* by the state. Other organizations *consult formally* with state agencies. Still other organizations and individuals aim only at *informal influence* on the state. Many organizations play several of these roles. The content and level of the standards required for the democratic legitimacy of these organizations and individuals should vary with their closeness of connection to the state. Public perceptions of legitimacy sometimes follow this pattern, but not always.

The official *delegation* of state powers provides the strongest connection with the state. This closeness legitimates some public regulation of both the relevant associations' internal organization and their place in the external context. Legislatures, for example, explicitly delegate considerable power to political parties. Although political parties are strictly speaking private entities, the state legally regulates those parties in most nations. In the European Union (EU), political parties receive state funding. The connection of the state with political parties is so tight that the public has a strong legitimate interest in both the internal representative processes of the parties and their external systemic biases. Regarding internal party procedures for selecting candidates, in the United States the public has favored, but not legally mandated, primaries over more informal methods of candidate selection. In Europe the public has favored, and occasionally even legally mandated, party gender quotas. Regarding external systemic norms, states, rather than the parties themselves, decide on the electoral systems. When the public considers moving from one electoral system to another, it rightly considers seriously issues of systemic bias.

Administrations also directly delegate many powers to the societal sector, from multinational for-profit corporations to municipal nonprofits. The administrative nexus with the societal sector has received less public scrutiny than the electoral nexus, and the norms are correspondingly less well developed. Yet direct delegation is pervasive. Sometimes governments even create private organizations in order to give them policy and enforcement responsibilities. Sometimes administrations delegate their powers to existing private entities and simply enforce the rules those entities make. Sometimes administrations formally adopt as law the codes developed by private entities. In the United States, the federal government adopts the accounting standards of one private nonprofit group, the Financial Accounting Standards Board, and gives another private group, the Financial Industry Regulating Authority, the legal power to discipline the firms and individuals who violate those standards.[31] Counting both administrative law-making and the many administrative delegations to the private sector, some analysts estimate that "[t]aken together, agency rulemaking and the policy decisions of private groups account for most policy-making in advanced societies."[32] Usually these private groups have their own internal mechanisms for selecting their officers, unregulated by the state and almost entirely ignored by the public. Scholars are only beginning to develop norms for *internal* governance, recursive and otherwise, to apply when administrators delegate powers to societal organizations.[33] Nor is there much public scrutiny of the biasing roles that the administrative selection of some private groups rather than others plays *externally* in the larger representative system.

Moving from direct delegation to *formal consultation* with societal organizations, the normative issues become even more complex. Regarding *external* inequalities, both legislative committees and administrators often consult formally with a biased selection of interest groups and other NGOs. Regarding *internal* relationships with members, although many associations of stakeholders, including unions, engage in

31 Catherine E. Rudder et al., Public Policy-Making by Private Organizations 61–62 & ch. 4 (2016).

32 *Id.* at 1.

33 *E.g.*, Graham Smith & Simon Teasdale, *Associative Democracy and the Social Economy: Exploring the Regulatory Challenge*, 41 Econ. & Soc'y 151 (2012); Paul Hirst, Associative Democracy: New Forms of Economic and Social Governance (1994).

formal consultative processes with governments (as in the EU), those associations rarely consult their own members during the process. Nor do they typically even explain to their members the rationales behind the ensuing regulations. In the EU, for example, even when construction unions have participated significantly in creating the regulations that their members must obey, they rarely make an effort to explain the reasons behind those regulations to their members, let alone institute recursive forums to find out how their members experience those regulations on the ground. At the moment, even normative theory on the democratic legitimacy of these associations is in its infancy. As that theory develops, external equality and internal equality as well as recursivity will become legitimating features.

Finally, at the level of *informal influence* on the state, societal organizations that represent the public almost always fall far short of existing normative democratic standards on both internal and external dimensions. Much recent work in democratic theory has focused on the *internal* dimension, the relationship between the representatives in these associations and those they represent. On the grounds of freedom of association and freedom to organize one's association as one wants, Nancy Rosenblum warns against "government intervention in the lives of associations." In her analysis, choice and exit, the processes of "shifting involvements," and pluralism give the public all the democracy and accountability it needs.[34] I argue here, however, that the closer the formal relationship with the state, the greater the normative justification for states requiring internal associational democracy.[35]

We may conclude that, in societal representation, our aspirational democratic norms regarding the *external* representative system seem relatively clear: individuals should be represented societally either proportionally to their numbers within an existing democratic polity or proportionally to the degree to which they are affected. Yet, in practice, societal representation rarely approaches this standard, even when the state bodies explicitly delegate powers to societal organizations, let alone when the state merely consults or is influenced by them.[36] Our norms regarding *internal* governance are in flux, but we may agree that the closer a societal organization comes to influencing the state definitively, the more the public has a legitimate normative claim that the organization organize itself democratically, along egalitarian and recursively communicative lines.

34 Nancy L. Rosenblum, Membership and Morals: The Personal Uses of Pluralism in America 6, 17, 20, 25, 27 (1998).

35 For a model giving all citizens a limited number of vouchers to "spend" on the representative associations of their choice, see Phillipe C. Schmitter, *The Irony of Modern Democracy and Efforts to Improve Its Practice*, 20 Pol. & Soc'y 507 (1992). This process would then generate both state subsidies in proportion to the vouchers allocated and consultative rights with the appropriate administrations. This scheme would to some degree rectify the external bias in the existing interest group system and improve internal democracy, since every association so chosen would be required to be internally democratic.

36 On the USA, *see* Kay Lehman Schlozman et al., The Unheavenly Chorus: Unequal Political Voice and the Broken Promise of American Democracy (2012); Kay Lehman Schlozman & John T. Tierney, Organized Interests and American Democracy (1986).

16.7 NOT YOUR GRANDMOTHER'S DEMOCRACY

The twenty-first century is not the eighteenth. Today we require more state coercion, and we will need still more in the future. Today the choice between "trustees" and "delegates" is obsolete. Legislators can and should consult the public recursively throughout the law-making process. Today the nondelegation doctrine is also obsolete. Administrations must make law – a great deal of law – and must therefore both institute recursive processes and make those processes as egalitarian as possible. Today, the societal sector, with both its for-profit and its nonprofit associations, is increasingly involved in law-making, and for good reason. The closer these associations come in their relations with the state, the more the public should demand both equal representation of interests externally and more democratic practices internally, including recursive representation with their "constituents."

It is not an accident caused by distance from the last unifying war or the confrontational incentives in social media that most democracies across the world are experiencing democratic deficits. Our increasingly interdependent lives require more state coercion to handle increasing numbers of free-rider problems, but our democratic systems cannot yet generate sufficient legitimacy to sustain that degree of coercion. Creating more recursivity throughout our representational systems should help increase that legitimacy.

PART VII

Politics, Sociology, Media, and Corruption as Contexts for Constitutionalism and Governance

17

Can Constitutions Fix Party System Breakdowns?

A Skeptical View

David Landau

17.1 INTRODUCTION

Parties have emerged as a central concern of comparative constitutional law, and for good reason. Parties should be at the forefront of descriptive analyses of how constitutions function. In practice, for instance, the separation of powers depends heavily on the shape of the party system, as do many other aspects of constitutional performance.[1] Moreover, breakdowns of party systems have been a significant factor in explaining recent episodes of democratic erosion or breakdown.[2] In other words, crises of liberal democratic constitutionalism are often caused by crises in party systems.

But what is more challenging is developing a *normative* theory linking constitutions and parties. In other words, to what extent can constitutions (or comparative constitutional law) prevent or fix breakdowns in party systems? On that question, this chapter offers some skepticism, or at least outlines a series of challenges.

Section 17.2 develops a brief map of the different ways in which party systems break down. It makes a point that is fairly obvious, but still worth fleshing out: party systems can go bad in a number of different ways. That is, while analysts focusing on a single context (such as the USA) tend to emphasize only one pathology, comparative work clarifies that there are many different, serious problems faced by party systems around the world: deinstitutionalized party systems, where parties tend to be extremely fragmented, volatile, ideologically incoherent, and lack stable connections to society; collapsing party systems, where institutionalized and well-functioning parties implode because of a crisis or series of crises, leaving a vacuum; dominant party systems, where a single party consistently wins elections

[1] *See* Daryl J. Levinson & Richard H. Pildes, *Separation of Parties, Not Powers*, 119 HARV. L. REV. 2311 (2006); Stephen Gardbaum, *Parties, Voting Systems, and the Separation of Powers*, 65 AM. J. COMPAR. L. 229 (2017).

[2] *See* Kim Lane Scheppele, *The Party's Over*, *in* CONSTITUTIONAL DEMOCRACY IN CRISIS? 495 (Mark A. Graber, Sanford Levinson & Mark Tushnet eds., 2018).

and controls institutional and patronage resources; and, finally, polarized systems, where parties mobilize competition along increasingly intense and destabilizing cleavages.

Section 17.3 argues that the multiplicity of pathways through which party systems can fail suggests that it will be difficult to develop a persuasive normative theory of how constitutions can develop and protect healthy party systems. This is for three interrelated reasons. First, institutional design choices embody a series of trade-offs, and choices that protect against one pathway of failure may make others more likely. Second, electoral rules and other regulations of parties embody a very strong form of the endogeneity problem, where existing parties can use their power to stymie productive reforms. Third, and perhaps most fundamentally, constitutions and state institutions simply have a limited influence over parties, which themselves act as a kind of intermediary between the state and civil society. Many of the things that have the most significant effect on constitutional performance are things over which constitutions themselves have only limited control.

17.2 PATHOLOGIES IN PARTY SYSTEMS: A BRIEF TOUR

This section seeks to develop a typology of the major ways in which party systems around the world have been said to fail. A couple of caveats are in order. The first is that this brief tour is not an attempt to develop a comprehensive typology of characteristics of party systems, or even of all of their possible dysfunctions. It is rather a partial sketch, focusing on some of the most prevalent problems in modern democracies. The second caveat is that this section sketches pathways through which party systems break down; it does not attempt the (even more difficult) question of *why* key changes occur. The complexity of that second question, of course, makes the challenge that parties pose for constitutional law even more difficult to meet.

Still, constructing even a rough and surface-level roadmap like the one in this section has some utility. It may act as a corrective to lines of work that focus too narrowly on only one pathway to democratic dysfunction or breakdown, for example the rise of "populists." More generally, it suggests that party systems are fragile institutions that can fail through many different routes.

17.2.1 *Deinstitutionalized Party Systems*

For a long while now, analysts have identified a set of problems identified with "deinstitutionalized" party systems.[3] Institutionalization is a complex concept, but it

[3] *See* BUILDING DEMOCRATIC INSTITUTIONS: PARTY SYSTEMS IN LATIN AMERICA (Scott Mainwaring & Timothy Scully eds., 1995); PARTY SYSTEMS IN LATIN AMERICA: INSTITUTIONALIZATION, DECAY, AND COLLAPSE (Scott Mainwaring ed., 2018); Staffan Lindberg, *Institutionalization of Party Systems? Stability and Fluidity Among Legislative Parties in Africa's Democracies*, 42 GOV'T & OPPOS. 215 (2007).

essentially measures the roots that parties have among the public and civil society groups. Institutionalized party systems are composed of parties with deep and stable ties. As a result, parties have clear platforms and do not frequently appear or disappear. Furthermore, electoral volatility is relatively low, since parties have stable bases of support. So patterns of electoral competition fall into predictable patterns, along familiar ideological cleavages. Major ideological or party system realignments are rare. In contrast, deinstitutionalized parties lack stable roots in society. Thus, they appear and disappear with great frequency, and electoral volatility is much higher. Further, parties themselves are often organized around ambiguous platforms or personalistic ties, rather than reflecting clear ideologies. Party discipline will usually be low, and defections common, since parties lack clear organizing principles.

Deinstitutionalized party systems are not typically identified with a good performance record and may even threaten the survival of democracy. Legislatures in such systems will tend to be very weak bodies, beset by a range of problems including fragmentation, corruption, and a lack of party discipline. These problems will make it difficult for legislatures to form stable coalitions in order to carry out tasks such as passing legislation and exercising oversight of other branches of government.[4] Moreover, because parties are organized around personal interests rather than stable policy platforms, it will be difficult for voters to know what they are voting for, and thus the link between votes and outcomes will be weak. In other words, parties cannot carry out their core function as links between political institutions and citizens.

In these situations, "populist" outsiders or similar actors may win elections by promising to save the country, and the weak party system will allow them plenty of avenues to achieve their goals, whether commandeering an existing party as a personalist vehicle or simply creating a new movement. This describes some recent cases of democratic threat well. Consider Latin America, for example, with Alvaro Uribe in Colombia, Rafael Correa in Ecuador, and Jair Bolsonaro in Brazil (also, less recently, Alberto Fujimori in Peru).

The election of Bolsonaro is particularly noteworthy because it occurred after the strongest and best-institutionalized Brazilian party, the Worker's Party or PT, was gravely weakened through a number of measures, including by the impeachment of a sitting PT president Dilma Rousseff and imprisonment of its past president, Luiz Inácio Lula da Silva, on corruption charges.[5] More than a decade of consistent PT rule produced a coherent set of left-leaning policy measures that reduced poverty while maintaining stable and effective economic governance. But the destruction of the PT left a vacuum, with the remainder of the party system dominated by a series of

4 *See* Gary W. Cox & Scott Morgenstern, *Epilogue: Latin America's Reactive Assemblies and Proactive Presidents*, *in* Legislative Politics in Latin America 446 (Scott Morgenstern ed., 2002).

5 *See, e.g.*, Marcelo Lopes de Souza, *The Land of the Past? Neo-populism, Neo-fascism, and the Failure of the Left in Brazil*, 83 Pol. Geog. (2020).

weak, clientelistic traditional parties with high levels of corruption and ambiguous ideological platforms. In such an environment, the authoritarian pitch of an outsider like Jair Bolsonaro to fix problems and impose order had great resonance.

I have focused here on institutionalization, which measures the rootedness of parties, rather than on fragmentation, which measures their sheer number.[6] The relationship between fragmentation and democratic instability or quality seems less clear (at least in cases where fragmentation is not so extreme as to essentially imply deinstitutionalization). In presidential systems, for example, some historical work argued that multiparty systems were incompatible with presidentialism because presidents will have a hard time constructing coalitions to pass legislation, but recent experience in regions like Latin America has challenged that view.[7] Even in parliamentary systems, of course, extreme forms of fragmentation may cause instability and unpredictability in coalition formation. Some important instances of electoral engineering, such as the creation of a minimum threshold of votes for representation and the constructive vote of no confidence in the post-war German Basic Law, were designed to guard against this risk.[8]

17.2.2 *Collapsing Party Systems*

There is a related series of cases where parties are initially strong and well-institutionalized, but become gravely weakened by a crisis or series of crises.[9] This crisis might be an economic collapse, significant corruption scandal, or national security crisis. Once the party system has been seriously weakened, these cases proceed much like the deinstitutionalized party systems noted in Section 17.2.1. Established patterns of party competition break down but are often not replaced by new strong parties. Legislatures and other representative institutions thus cease to function as effective conveyors of popular preferences. Moreover, the collapse of the existing party system opens up space for outsiders who can run as saviors, who again can pose a threat to democratic governance.[10]

Venezuela offers an interesting example. The two-party system in Venezuela was once so strong that analysts called it a "partyarchy."[11] The two major parties offered

6 *See* Markku Laakso & Rein Taagepera, *"Effective" Number of Parties: A Measure with Application to Western Europe*, 12 COMPAR. POL. STUD. 3 (1979).

7 *See* Carlos Pereira & Marcus Andre Melo, *The Surprising Success of Multiparty Presidentialism*, 23 J. DEMOCRACY 156 (2012).

8 *See* Thomas Saalfeld, *Institutions, Chances, and Choices: The Dynamics of Cabinet Survival*, *in* CABINETS AND COALITION BARGAINING: THE DEMOCRATIC LIFE CYCLE IN WESTERN EUROPE 327 (Kaare Strøm et al. eds., 2010).

9 *See, e.g.*, JASON SEAWRIGHT, PARTY-SYSTEM COLLAPSE: THE ROOTS OF CRISIS IN PERU AND VENEZUELA (2012).

10 *See id.*

11 *See* Michael Coppedge, *Brazil: The Rise and Fall of Partyarchy*, *in* CONSTRUCTING DEMOCRATIC GOVERNANCE: SOUTH AMERICA IN THE 1990S 3 (Jorge I. Dominguez & Abraham F. Lowenthal eds., 1996).

a moderate set of policy differences and were strongly identified with civil society institutions such as labor unions and business organizations. Indeed, they penetrated virtually all areas of Venezuelan life. But by 1998 the system had been rocked by a series of deep economic crises, large-scale corruption, and escalating political violence and chaos, most notably the 1989 *Caracazo*, a series of violent street protests that led to hundreds of deaths. In that context, the traditional two parties lost virtually all legitimacy and support, and Chavez won the 1998 election after having led a failed coup attempt against the elected government only six years earlier.[12] Scheppele argues that there are similar dynamics in other recent collapses of democracy, for example in the 2010 election that brought the right-wing populist party Fidesz to power in Hungary.[13]

17.2.3 *Dominant-Party Systems*

In a great many cases, of course, the main problem is not that party systems are too weak but that they are controlled by a single dominant actor, which wins election after election.[14] Even where the party represents the authentic choice of a very high proportion of the population at a given point in time (e.g., South Africa's African National Congress, or ANC, after the end of apartheid), they pose well-known risks to democracy.[15] The dominant party can use its control of state institutions to further entrench itself, while weakening or repressing opposition movements. For example, the dominant party will likely be able to capture institutions designed to check state power, such as courts, electoral commissions, media watchdogs, and ombudspersons. Once captured, these institutions may be deployed to help the dominant party consolidate more power, rather than protecting constitutional democracy. Dominant parties may also be able to undertake a series of legal and constitutional changes that effectively change the rules in favor of the incumbents. Take Turkey, where the ruling Justice and Development party has amended the constitution repeatedly since taking power in 2002, making a series of changes including packing the judiciary and switching to a presidential form of government, that it perceived as furthering its interests.[16] Thus, dominant party systems raise a very significant risk that the electoral playing field will become heavily tilted over time.

12 *See, e.g.*, Damarys Camache, *From Bullets to Ballots: The Emergence of Popular Support for Hugo Chavez*, 44 LATIN AM. POL. & SOC'Y 69 (2002).

13 *See* Scheppele, *supra* note 2, at 495.

14 *See, e.g.*, DOMINANT POLITICAL PARTIES AND DEMOCRACY: CONCEPTS, MEASURES, CASES AND COMPARISONS (Matthijs Bogaards & Françoise Boucek eds., 2010).

15 *See, e.g.*, Sujit Choudhry, *"He Had a Mandate": The South African Constitutional Court and the African National Congress in a Dominant Party Democracy*, 2 CONST. CT. REV. 1 (2010); Samuel Issacharoff, *The Democratic Risk to Democratic Transitions*, 5 CONST. CT. REV. 1 (2013).

16 *See* Ahmet Erdi Ozturk & Istar Gozaydin, *Turkey's Constitutional Amendments: A Critical Perspective*, 2 RSCH. & POL'Y ON TURKEY 210 (2017).

Apart from the risks of democratic erosion posed by dominant-party systems, there are also concerns about performance. The dominant party may be able to retain power despite a relative lack of responsiveness to popular will, given the absence of credible alternatives.[17] Dominant parties are often riven with factions that differ on ideological or personalistic lines, but the existence of these factions may be far less clear to ordinary citizens than competing parties with clear ideological platforms. Thus, the link between popular preferences and outcomes may become attenuated, in a similar way as occurs in deinstitutionalized systems. Dominant-party democracies are also sometimes associated with other maladies, including higher levels of corruption, perhaps because of the lack of responsiveness noted already, or because of their considerable ability to wield patronage resources in order to deepen their hold on power.[18]

17.2.4 *Polarized Party Systems*

Even where parties are relatively strong and the system is competitive, serious problems can arise. Recent literature on developed democracies has focused heavily on the supposed ills of strong but increasingly polarized parties. Polarization is said to involve the sorting of parties into multiple distinct groups that are far apart. Using Poole and Rosenthal's influential definition, polarized parties are far apart in policy space, and members of each party are tightly clustered around the mean ideological position of the party.[19]

The USA has become a paradigm case for this concern: using several different methodologies, scholars have found greatly increased polarization in the USA in recent decades.[20] Outside of the USA, it is unclear whether there is any trend toward greater polarization; indeed, some recent work found a reduction in polarization across much of Western Europe, during the same period in which it exploded in the USA.[21] However, polarization is a concern across a number of different contexts. Across parts of Europe, for example, analysts have pointed to the rise of far-right or populist-right parties and observed a corresponding rise in polarization.[22]

The impact of polarization on democratic functioning is a complex topic, but it does seem to have a number of negative impacts. In the USA, for example, scholars have argued that polarization makes it harder to legislate in order to change the

17 *See* Hermann Giliomee & Charles Simkins, *The Dominant Party Regimes of South Africa, Mexico, Taiwan, and Malaysia: A Comparative Assessment*, *in* THE AWKWARD EMBRACE: ONE-PARTY DOMINATION AND DEMOCRACY 1 (Hermann Giliomee & Charles Simkins eds., 1999).

18 *See, e.g.*, Petra Schleiter & Alisa M. Voznaya, *Party System Competitiveness and Corruption*, 20 PARTY POL. 675 (2012).

19 *See* Keith T. Poole & Howard Rosenthal, *The Polarization of American Politics*, 46 J. POL. 1061 (1984).

20 *See, e.g.*, Levi Boxell et al., *Cross-Country Trends in Affective Polarization* (NBER Working Paper 26669, Jan. 2020).

21 *See id.*

22 *See, e.g.*, Milana Anna Vachudova, *From Competition to Polarization in Central Europe: How Populists Change Party Systems and the European Union*, 51 POLITY 689 (2019).

status quo, because presidents cannot build coalitions with opposition figures.[23] These dynamics may be especially marked in presidential systems, where they make it more difficult for politics to reflect popular sentiment, and in the extreme may even lead to democratic breakdown.[24] But, even in parliamentary systems, polarization may be costly by making it harder to construct and maintain coalition governments, leading to gridlock and instability. Polarization, where accompanied by higher party discipline, may also have the effect of transferring power from the legislative to the executive branch, with proposals coming down from party leaders who then whip votes to ensure that they are passed.

One of the peculiarities of the polarization literature is that focusing on polarization as such may seem incomplete without understanding *what* parties are increasingly polarized about. In other words, the relevant axes of polarization may be at least as important as its extent. Some of the recent comparative work makes this point. For example, it suggests that increasing polarization around ethnic or religious issues, as in India, Israel, and Turkey, may be especially destabilizing because of their tendencies to inflame conflict and the difficulties of forging compromise around such issues.[25] Similarly, Scheppele has recently argued that in the United States, a key problem is not just the rightward drift of the Republican party but the fact that a good chunk of its voters and elected officials seem to have increasing attachment to authoritarianism.[26] Enyedi suggests, similarly, that the rise of authoritarian actors in Hungary and elsewhere in Eastern Europe is related to a "populist" form of polarization where competing forces adopt a Manichean distinction between themselves and their opponents, as opposed to more typical forms of policy polarization.[27]

Finally, related to the dynamic of polarization is that existing parties or movements can be captured by new actors or factions that push the party in a radically different, and problematic, direction. There has been much attention to this phenomenon in the United States with the rise of Trump, and a corresponding body of

23 *See, e.g.*, Thomas E. Mann & Norman Ornstein, It's Even Worse Than It Looks: How the American Constitutional System Collided with the New Politics of Extremism (2012); Michael Barber & Nolan McCarty, *Causes and Consequences of Polarization*, in *Negotiating Agreement in Politics: Report of the Task Force on Negotiating Agreement in Politics* 19, American Political Science Association (Dec. 2013).

24 A classic case study is Chile in 1973, where Salvador Allende's government was overthrown in a coup in a context of a highly polarized, three-party system. *See* Arturo Valenzuela, The Breakdown of Democratic Regimes: Chile (1978).

25 *See* Madhav Khosla & Milan Vaishnav, *The Three Faces of the Indian State*, 32 J. Democracy 111 (2021); Sultan Tepe, *The Perils of Polarization and Religious Parties: The Democratic Challenges of Political Fragmentation in Israel and Turkey*, 20 Democratization 831 (2013).

26 *See* Kim Lane Scheppele, *Symposium on the Legacies of Trumpism and Constitutional Democracy in the United States – The Life of the Party*, Int'l J. Const. L. Blog (Jan. 23, 2021), http://www.iconnectblog.com/2021/01/symposium-on-the-legacies-of-trumpism-and-constitutional-democracy-in-the-united-states-part-iv-the-life-of-the-party/.

27 *See* Zsolt Enyedi, *Populist Polarization and Party System Institutionalization: The Role of Party Politics in De-Democratization*, 63 Probs. Post-Communism 210 (2016).

work looking at how candidates are selected. One argument of much of this work is that the US primary system has inadvertently become too open in the modern period – mass voters, rather than party leaders, play too big a role in selecting candidates, thus undermining the screening function that parties can otherwise play in protecting democracy and ensuring ideological continuity.[28] This narrative is interesting because it suggests that polarization can in some aspects be a product of party weakness rather than strength – the disempowerment of party elites in favor of a more polarized set of grassroots actors, via changes in candidate selection rules and also related areas like campaign finance.[29]

17.3 WHITHER A THEORY OF PARTIES AND CONSTITUTIONAL DESIGN?

The revival of interest among comparative constitutionalists in parties is a welcome development since it recognizes their centrality to the way that constitutions actually work, and why they fail. But the many ways in which parties break down seems to illustrate the challenges of putting them at the center of a normative agenda for comparative constitutional law.

Building a normative theory of how constitutions should engage parties is challenging. In the postwar period, some comparative constitutional law scholarship focused on the conception of militant democracy that arose out of the German Basic Law, and which imbued the judiciary (or some other actor) with the power to ban anti-constitutional or anti-democratic parties.[30] The core insight of militant democracy is that democracy is not inherently self-regulating, and thus constitutional democracies cannot afford to tolerate anti-democratic movements just because they win votes. But much recent scholarship has been critical of party-banning as a tool, for several reasons. There is a risk of abuse, of course; moreover, modern parties that pose an authoritarian threat often carry ambiguous ideologies that make them difficult to ban.[31] At any rate, party banning is a rarely used and extreme tool that may say relatively little about the most common circumstances in which party systems fail.

The renaissance has focused in part on finding other ways in which constitutions can engage productively with political parties. Scheppele,[32] for example, looks at other aspects of the militant democracy provision in the German Basic Law

[28] *See* Stephen Gardbaum & Richard H. Pildes, *Populism and Institutional Design: Methods of Selecting Candidates for Chief Executive*, 93 N.Y.U. L. Rev. 647 (2018); Steven Levitsky & Daniel Ziblatt, How Democracies Die (2018).

[29] *See* Samuel Issacharoff, *Outsourcing Politics: The Hostile Takeovers of our Hollowed Out Political Parties*, 54 Hous. L. Rev. 845 (2017); Frances McCall Rosenbluth & Ian Shapiro, Responsible Parties: Saving Democracy from Itself (2018).

[30] *See* Samuel Issacharoff, *Fragile Democracies*, 120 Harv. L. Rev. 1406 (2007).

[31] *See* David Landau & Rosalind Dixon, *Abusive Judicial Review: Courts Against Democracy*, 53 UC Davis L. Rev. 1313 (2020); Tom Gerald Daly & Christopher Jones, *Parties Versus Democracy: Addressing Today's Political-Party Threats to Democratic Rule*, 18 Int'l J. Const. L. 509 (2020).

[32] *See* Scheppele, *supra* note 2.

regulating parties, among other things by requiring that their "internal organization … conform to democratic principles" and that they be funded transparently.[33] Daly and Jones focus on strengthening the rights of the opposition, and on limiting the ability of incumbents to change electoral rules in order to self-entrench.[34]

These are attractive ideas, but some of their effects on party systems may be more uncertain than one might expect. They may tend to resolve some problems, while tending to cause others. For example, insisting on democratic partisan organization may avoid certain ways of hijacking parties, but may actually make them more vulnerable to other methods, such as the Trump takeover of the Republican party in the USA, already noted. Strengthening the rights of the opposition may help to avoid democratic erosion by majoritarian movements but may also frustrate governance. Even a prohibition on "self-dealing" in electoral matters may be a double-edged sword since it could have trouble distinguishing between interventions to tilt the electoral playing field and those designed to "untilt" it. The more fundamental point, though, is that these proposals, while important, still seem to work closer to the periphery rather than the center of those factors that influence day-to-day party behavior.

One might make a similar point about the emergent comparative literature on courts and parties.[35] Of course, the shape of the party system has a major influence on how courts operate descriptively, and potentially on normative conceptions of judicial role. But the ability of courts (and other accountability institutions) to "fix" deficiencies in party systems may in fact be quite limited. Sometimes the problem may be a lack of adequate political breathing room – Roux, for example, finds that the Constitutional Court of South Africa has been weakest when working on electoral issues, because these are at the core of the dominant ANC party's interests.[36] Other kinds of problem may simply be beyond the capacity of courts or constitutional doctrine to resolve. For instance, it would be extremely challenging for courts to institutionalize a deinstitutionalized party system by giving it stronger roots in society, or to make the resulting legislature a stronger or more deliberative body. Again, courts should without question pay attention to parties in developing theories of judicial role.[37] But they may need to take them largely as givens, rather than being able to repair significant problems.

More central is a subdiscipline that is quite well travelled, albeit much more heavily identified with political science than with law: electoral engineering, or changes in electoral laws that aim to shape the nature of the party

33 German Basic Law, art. 21.

34 *See* Daly & Jones, *supra* note 31.

35 *See, e.g.*, Samuel Issacharoff, Fragile Democracies: Contested Power in the Era of Constitutional Courts (2015); Choudhry, *supra* note 15.

36 *See* Theunis Roux, The Politics of Principle: The First South African Constitutional Court, 1995–2005 334 (2013).

37 *See, e.g.*, David Landau, A *Dynamic Theory of Judicial Role*, 55 B.C. L. Rev. 1501 (2014); Stephen Gardbaum, *Comparative Political Process Theory*, 18 Int'l J. Const. L. 1483 (2020).

system.[38] Sometimes, of course, these rules are found in ordinary legislation rather than the constitutional text itself, but they are always constitutional in the broader sense of their impact on the constitutional structure. That is, they are at least always part of the "small c" constitution.[39]

The most basic insights, like the division between plurality and proportional representation and their effects on the number of parties, are of course well known by comparative constitutional lawyers. But there are a number of issues that have perhaps not been as thoroughly mined. Electoral rules, for example those dealing with the nature of party lists and district magnitude, also have a significant impact on the strength of parties, or their internal level of discipline.[40] As well, electoral rules may have some influence over the levels and types of polarization that emerge in a party system, although the evidence here is more disputed.[41]

The ongoing renaissance of interest in parties within comparative constitutional law would benefit from more direct engagement with electoral rules themselves, and with the political science literature on the topic. Constitutional lawyers can contribute to these debates by linking designs of electoral rules to causes of constitutional failure, and by thinking more normatively than political scientists about the desirability of different electoral designs. Dixon and Gauja, for example, argue that Australia's unusual mix of mandatory and preferential voting (in the lower house) has been one of the key structural safeguards in limiting polarization and populist movements, and thus in stabilizing democracy in that country.[42] No aspect of design is likely to have nearly as direct, or significant, an impact on the nature of the party system as electoral rules.

Nonetheless, important cautions remain. Drawing on the analysis in Section 17.2, I would suggest three major challenges that inevitably complicate any normative program of parties and constitutions. The first is about trade-offs. Since there are many different ways in which party systems can deteriorate, electoral engineering generally involves a series of trade-offs, which can lessen some risks but at the same time increase others. There are a number of tools available to strengthen parties by increasing levels of party discipline. These can help to "institutionalize" the party system. But, of course, increases in party discipline may not be an unmitigated good: strong parties may vote en bloc, which may also impede governance, especially in presidential systems. Also, the impact of any intervention will depend heavily on the

38 *See, e.g.*, Arend Lijphart, Patterns of Democracy: Government Forms and Performance in Thirty-Six Democracies (2d ed. 2012); Giovanni Sartori, Comparative Constitutional Engineering: An Inquiry into Structures, Incentives, and Outcomes (2d ed. 1997); Pippa Norris, Electoral Engineering: Voting Rules and Political Behavior (2004).

39 *See* Rosalind Dixon & Anika Gauja, *Australia's Non-populist Democracy? The Role of Structure and Policy*, *in* Constitutional Democracy in Crisis? 395 (Mark A. Graber et al. eds., 2018).

40 *See, e.g.*, John M. Carey & Matthew Soberg Shugart, *Incentives to Cultivate a Personal Vote: A Rank Ordering of Electoral Formulas*, 14 Elec. Stud. 417 (1995).

41 *See* James F. Adams & Nathan J. Rexford, *Electoral Systems and Issue Polarization*, *in* The Oxford Handbook of Electoral Systems 247 (Erik S. Herron, Robert J. Pekkanen & Matthew S. Shugart eds., 2018).

42 *See* Dixon & Gauja, *supra* note 39.

context in which it is employed. Take again debates on party discipline. Some of the work on dominant-party systems shows that decreases in party discipline (e.g., by relaxing floor-crossing rules) will empower the dominant party and impede the construction of a competitive system because the dominant party has so many patronage resources to lure defectors.[43] Of course, the impact of party discipline rules will be very different in other kinds of party systems.

This brings us to the second problem: endogeneity. Electoral systems are often selected not because they are the "best" fit from a democratic stability or performance perspective but because they serve the interests of the existing parties. Negretto, for instance, presents strong evidence through a historical analysis of Latin American constitutions that parties select electoral rules to maximize their own perceived interests.[44] Endogeneity is a problem within the entire field of constitutional design, so should not be viewed as an invitation to despair. But it seems to be especially strong with respect to issues like electoral rules, precisely because they are so obviously central to patterns of partisan competition. Parties and politicians have strong incentives to develop sophisticated knowledge about how changes in these rules will impact them, and to use that knowledge to shape outcomes. Debates are unlikely to approximate the kind of veil of uncertainty that might aid constitutional design on other kinds of question. Unexpected deviations may be most likely to occur when incumbent parties lose control over the reform agenda, at least partially.[45]

But it is a third problem that I think is the most fundamental one: parties occupy a kind of halfway position between state institutions and civil society. That is, they are both inside and outside the state. Despite the centrality of parties to modern constitutionalism, there are limits on the ability of constitutional design or jurisprudence to influence them.

Consider an interesting example from Colombia. For a variety of reasons, some rooted in electoral changes made in the 1991 Constitution, and some in broader social, political, and historical factors, the Colombian party system deinstitutionalized in the 1990s and early 2000s.[46] Analysts recognized that these problems

43 *See, e.g.*, Nkopodi Patrick Kanego Masemola, Floor-Crossing and Its Political Consequences in South Africa (EISA Occasional Paper Series 44, June 2007), https://www.eisa.org/pdf/OP44.pdf.

44 *See* Gabriel Negretto, *Choosing How to Choose Presidents: Parties, Military Rulers, and Presidential Elections in Latin America*, 68 J. Pol. 421 (2006). *See also* Gabriel L. Negretto, *From Duverger to Rokkan and Back: Progress and Challenges in the Study of Electoral Systems, in* The Routledge Handbook of Comparative Political Institutions 113, 120–22 (Jennifer Gandhi & Ruben Ruiz-Rufino eds., 2015) (surveying literature and evaluating its persuasiveness).

45 *See* Negretto, *From Duverger to Rokkan, supra* note 44, at 122. Consider Arizona, where voters worked around parties by ballot initiative to establish an independent redistricting commission, a move that the US Supreme Court upheld against a challenge by the Republican-dominated state legislature. *See* Arizona State Legislature v. Arizona Independent Redistricting Commission, 576 U.S. 787 (2015).

46 *See* Eduardo Dargent & Paula Munoz, *Democracy Against Parties? Party System Deinstitutionalization in Colombia*, 3 J. Pol. Latin Am. 43, 53–56 (2011); Juan Albarracin et al., *Deinstitutionalization without Collapse: Colombia's Party System, in* Party Systems in Latin America 227 (Scott Mainwaring ed., 2018).

impeded governance, creating a crisis, and Congress was able to push through a sweeping reform to the party system in 2003. The reform ended the prior practice of allowing more than one party list, introduced a new minimum threshold of 2 percent for party representation, allowed parties to choose either open or closed lists, and changed the formula for apportionment toward one that favored larger parties.[47] The reforms were perhaps more modest than they needed to be, hindered in part by the endogeneity problem noted already. But they were still quite significant. Yet analyses of their impact have generally found that they only partially succeeded in their goals. They reduced fragmentation in Congress by at least modestly bringing down the effective number of parties.[48] But analysts are more skeptical that they significantly reversed the trend toward deinstitutionalization. The broad confluence of factors that created the deinstitutionalization trend in Colombia – such as the delegitimization of parties, their loss of control over formal and informal resources, and fiscal decentralization – has proven sticky and difficult to reverse.[49] Changed rules alone could not create stronger ties among parties, the public, and civil society. Formal rules have thus had only a limited influence on the problem.

Of course, the point is more general. Many of those features of the political and social landscape that have the most significant impact on constitutional performance are partially or largely outside of constitutional (or even legal) control – consider recent debates about economic inequality as a vivid example. This should not lead us to give up on an agenda of the ways in which constitutions can defend a vibrant party system, but it does counsel humility in the effort.

47 *See* Albarracin et al., *supra* note 46, at 250.

48 *See id.* at 251.

49 *See id.* at 250–51; Dargent & Munoz, *supra* note 46, at 57 (noting that changes to electoral rules "cannot by themselves increase party institutionalization and aggregation").

18

Political Fragmentation and the Decline of Effective Government

Richard H. Pildes

18.1 INTRODUCTION

What is the most fundamental challenge facing democracies today? One major concern is democratic backsliding, regression, or the rise of "illiberal democracies." Another concern, closely related, is the rise of "populism," at least in certain forms, such as those that are fundamentally anti-pluralist and view the "people" as a "moral, homogenous entity whose will cannot err,"[1] or, in less virulent form, those that express impatience with institutional structures and norms – such as judicial review, independent institutions, or separation of powers – that stand in the way of direct, unmediated expression of the "popular will." Good reasons exist for these concerns across many democracies today. But, in my view, the deepest and perhaps most enduring challenge to democratic governments across the West that has emerged in recent years is what I call "political fragmentation."[2] Put briefly, political fragmentation is the dispersion of political power into so many different hands and power centers that it becomes extremely difficult to marshal enough political power and authority for governments to function effectively.

To take the United States as one example, there is little question that recent decades have seen a dramatic decline in the effectiveness of government, whether that is measured in the number of important bills Congress is able to enact, the proportion of all issues people identity as most important that Congress manages to address, or the number of enacted bills that update old policies enacted many decades earlier.[3] Social scientists now write books with titles like *Can America Govern Itself?* The inability of democratic governments to deliver on the issues their populations care most about poses enormous dangers. At a minimum, it can

[1] JAN-WERNER MÜLLER, WHAT IS POPULISM? 101 (2016).

[2] See Richard H. Pildes, *Romanticizing Democracy, Political Fragmentation, and the Decline of American Government*, 124 YALE L. J. 804 (2014).

[3] Suzanne Mettler & Claire Leavitt, *Public Policy and Political Dysfunction*, *in* CAN AMERICA GOVERN ITSELF? (Frances E. Lee & Nolan McCarty eds., 2019).

lead to alienation, resignation, distrust, and withdrawal among many citizens. Even worse, it can spawn demands for authoritarian leaders who promise to cut through the dysfunction of the political process. And, at an even greater extreme, it can lead people to question the efficacy of democracy itself and become open to antidemocratic systems of government. The rise of a more prosperous China, and its model of one-party, authoritarian capitalism, increases the risk that some citizens in democratic states might become tempted to look to nondemocratic systems in search of effective governance.

Analysis of modern democracies has not begun to recognize the emergence of political fragmentation as a major challenge, or to grasp the range of implications it has for the possible future of democratic processes, institutions, and governance. Political fragmentation is related to polarization, populism, and reversion to authoritarianism. But the most profound question it poses to democracies – both for those that seem precarious and those that currently seem stable – is whether the ability to sustain legitimate democratic authority is coming into question.

In Section 18.2, I define political fragmentation more fully and describe its various manifestations, including the different forms that fragmentation takes today in proportional-representation (PR) political systems and in first-past-the-post (FPTP) ones.

Section 18.3 then explores the causes of political fragmentation, with an eye to whether the fragmentation we are currently experiencing across democracies reflects temporary, contingent forces or more enduring ones. In particular, I focus on the communications revolution, which I argue is a central driver of political fragmentation. This section argues that the challenge the communications revolution poses to democracy goes beyond concerns with intentional manipulation, fake news, "hate speech," or anonymous speech funded through "dark" (undisclosed) money. Even apart from those issues, the communications revolution enhances the ability to undermine the authority of many institutions, both public and private. In the political sphere, this revolution propels political fragmentation and the undermining of sustainable political authority.

Democratic governments must be able to function effectively. Yet the rise of political fragmentation makes this increasingly difficult – and no simple fixes for this emerging challenge loom on the horizon. Are we becoming destined to experience temporarily successful forces of disruption, which are then soon undermined in turn by other new disruptive forces, in an endless cycle that makes effective governance far more difficult to sustain?

18.2 POLITICAL FRAGMENTATION

An image for our age: French President Emmanuel Macron, the great disruptor of the traditional two-party structure that had dominated French politics for six decades – elected in 2017 with two-thirds of the final-round vote – one year later effectively trapped in his office, trying to remain "invisible," because any public appearance would lead to the nearly instant mobilization of spontaneous, yet somehow organized, large street crowds of Yellow Vest protestors.[4] A year after Macron had swept aside the long-dominant structures of traditional political authority, his own legitimacy and authority were in turn being eroded and undermined – not by the return of those traditional structures or conventional partisan opposition – but by leaderless, popular political forces. The disruptor was disrupted overnight: a particularly dramatic example of both the fragmentation of political authority and the resulting difficulty of sustaining legitimate authority.

Political fragmentation takes many different forms. But in general I mean the myriad ways in which political power today is effectively dispersed among so many political parties, organized groups, nonorganized groups, and independent political figures, including both governmental actors and nongovernmental actors. No longer is political power, in most democracies, effectively controlled by, or contained within, the centralized, major institutions that had long been perceived to be the legitimate vehicles for organizing and exercising that authority (the leadership of the executive and legislative branches, the traditional political parties and their leaders, the governing majority coalition). We do not appreciate fully how pervasive are these developments, or the depth of the challenge they pose to democracies.

18.2.1 *PR Systems and Fragmentation*

In the proportional-representation democracies, the most obvious and familiar expression of political fragmentation is the unraveling of the traditionally dominant, center-left and center-right major political parties or coalitions that had governed in most democracies since World War II. These parties and coalitions were largely organized along class lines; higher-income voters and those with higher levels of education gave most of their votes to the parties of the right, while middle-income and working-class voters cast most of their votes for the party of the left. The unknitting of this fundamental structure of political competition, in both attitudes and voting behavior, is both cause and effect of the ensuing political fragmentation that now characterizes many of the European democracies.

The most consequential, direct manifestation of that fragmentation is the decline of the vote share and hence the political power of the traditional two major parties across various European democracies. Overall, the mean vote share for the traditional major parties declined from 86 percent to 72 percent between 2004 and 2015; emerging new parties doubled their vote share during this time to 23 percent.[5] This

4 Sylvie Corbet, *As Protest Rages in France, Macron Remains Invisible*, Associated Press (Dec. 7, 2018), https://www.apnews.com/3b7d4a322df34823b448dabd46e2e03a; *see also* Sophie Pedder, Revolution Française: Emmanuel Macron and the Quest to Reinvent a Nation (2018).

5 Roger Eatwell & Matthew Goodwin, National Populism: The Revolt Against Liberal Democracy (2018).

fracturing of power across more and smaller parties not only makes putting together effective governing coalitions more difficult but also makes the political sphere more volatile, as new parties pop up almost overnight and grab slices of power, including parties that style themselves as "anti-parties," reflecting a view that politics should somehow do away with parties altogether.[6] In various individual countries, the details of this general story are particularly dramatic.

In the most recent national elections in Germany, voters in 2017 abandoned the traditionally dominant large parties of the center-left (the Social Democrats) and the center-right (the Christian Democrats) in droves. In the 1970s, these parties regularly combined to receive more than 90 percent of the vote; in 2017, they combined for only 53 percent.[7] The Christian Democrats received their lowest vote share since 1949; the votes the major parties hemorrhaged were grabbed by smaller parties of the right and the left, including the Alternative for German (AfD), the Free Democrats, the Greens, and the Left. Not surprisingly, it then took six months to put together a governing coalition, longer than at any time since Germany's post-World War II democracy was created.

In France, the shock of the 2017 election was that neither of the main center-left (the Socialists) or center-right (the Republicans) parties that between them had governed France since World War II was able to garner sufficient support even to get a candidate into the final round of the election. Disaffection from these long-dominant parties was so great that Emmanuel Macron was able to create a new party virtually overnight, which then vaulted him into the presidency and captured majority control of Parliament.

Fragmentation is also reflected in political attitudes that reveal a sharp decline in those who strongly identify with any political party. This decline, too, has been developing over a long period of time. The percentage of those in Western European democracies who strongly identify with a political party declined between the 1960s and the 1990s in Austria by 66 percent; in Italy and Ireland by 77 percent; in Sweden and Norway by 54 percent and 45 percent, respectively; in France by 32 percent.[8] Put another way, in earlier decades in countries such as Sweden, two-thirds of people felt loyal to a particular party, but by 2010 that had fallen to 28 percent. So too with formal membership in the parties: between 1980 and 2009, party membership declined dramatically in nearly all European countries, with a fall-off of more than 30 percent in the UK, Norway, France, Sweden, Ireland, Switzerland, Finland, Denmark, Italy, and Belgium.[9] The magnitude of these declines, the consistency of their direction, and the fact that they have occurred in nearly all Western democracies for which data are available suggests that general structural forces are at work fracturing all these democracies.

6 Nadia Urbinati, *A Revolt Against Intermediary Bodies*, 22 CONSTELLATIONS 477, 480 (2015).

7 Stefan Wagstyl, Guy Chazan & Tobias Buck, *Merkel Wins Fourth Term but Far-Right Populists Make Gains*, FIN. TIMES, Sept. 24, 2017, https://www.ft.com/content/12de72a0-a11c-11e7-9e4f-7f5e6a7c98a2.

8 RUSSELL J. DALTON, DEMOCRATIC CHALLENGES, DEMOCRATIC CHOICES: THE EROSION OF POLITICAL SUPPORT IN ADVANCED INDUSTRIAL DEMOCRACIES 33 (2004).

9 PETER MAIER, RULING THE VOID 41 (2013).

Using one standard measure of volatility, frequency in Western Europe of high-volatility elections soared in the 1990s and 2000s.[10] In the 1990s and 2000s, the percentage of high volatility elections was 33 percent and 27 percent, respectively; in each of the four decades before then, it had ranged from only 4 percent to 11 percent.[11] As Peter Maier, one of the first and most astute analysts of the unraveling of strong political parties in postwar Europe, put it, "in contemporary politics, in other words, it has become less and less easy for any one party or bloc of parties to monopolize power, with the result that shared government has become more common."[12] But amidst increasing political fragmentation, even putting together coalitions capable of governing has become much more difficult, leading to considerably longer delays in the time it takes actually to form a government.

After the 2017 elections in the Netherlands, it took a record 225 days to form a government.[13] In earlier years, the three largest political parties were able to forge a government among themselves. But just as in many other European countries, between 1986 and 2012, the proportion of parliament that those long-dominant (three) parties won plunged from 89 percent to around 60 percent. The proliferation of small, successful fringe parties doesn't only make it more difficult to form governments; it also makes those governments more precarious, for when more small parties are needed to form a government, the withdrawal of any of them can bring down the government and force new elections. Belgium and Israel have their own unique polities, but they represent these developments in their most extreme forms. After its most recent elections, in 2019, Belgium took nearly 500 days to form a government; Israel was forced to hold 4 national elections between 2019 and 2021 in the effort to form a governing coalition.

18.2.2 *First-Past-the-Post Systems and Fragmentation*

In FPTP countries, political fragmentation has also emerged as a significant obstacle to effective governance, though fragmentation gets expressed differently than in PR countries. Minor parties face significant structural barriers in FPTP systems. Yet, despite this, the UK has been experiencing the same long-term party fragmentation as in the PR countries. Indeed, "[o]ne of the biggest long-term stories in British politics [over the last several decades] is that of declining [voting] support for the two largest parties."[14] In 1970, around 90 percent of people voted for either Labour or the

[10] This measure calculates the level of volatility by summing the (total) electoral gains of all the winning parties in an election. *Id.* at 31. This measure reveals the extent to which party strength shifts from one election to the next between winning and losing parties. *See* Mogens N. Pederson, *The Dynamics of European Party Systems: Changing Patterns of Electoral Volatility*, 7 Eur. J. Pol. Rsch. 1 (1979).

[11] *Id.*

[12] *See* Maier, *supra* note 9, at 52.

[13] Aamna Mohdin, *It Took a Record 225 Days for the Dutch to Get a Government*, Quartz (Oct. 26, 2017), https://qz.com/1112509/the-dutch-took-a-record-long-225-days-to-form-a-government/.

[14] Simon Kaye, *2015 and the State of Two-Party Politics in the UK*, British Democracy Blog (Sept. 6, 2015), https://britishdemocracy.com/2015/06/09/2015-and-the-state-of-two-party-politics-in-the-uk/.

Conservatives; by 2010, that had fallen to 65 percent.[15] Some of this reflects the rise of regional parties in Northern Ireland, Scotland, and Wales, but even in England alone, the vote share for the two major parties declined from a peak of 97.6 percent in 1950 to 67.6 percent in 2010.[16]

This political fragmentation culminated in the UK being forced to hold three elections between 2015 and 2019. The minority government elected in 2017 quickly fell, requiring a new election just two years later.[17] Effective governing majorities were put back together in the 2019 election, at least temporarily, when the election was clearly based on a single, overriding issue: who to put in charge of managing Brexit. The Conservative Party won a landslide, enabling decisive action finally to be taken regarding Brexit. But whether this recent election put only a temporary pause on the splintering of the political sphere remains to be seen. Even this victory exposed the underlying ferment and turmoil of the political dynamics at work in the UK, as elsewhere; it was the unscrambling of traditional party alliances, with the Conservative Party winning over traditional Labour Party working-class voters in the North, that generated this electoral mandate. Whether these voters remain with the Conservatives, switch back to Labour, support other parties, or withdraw from politics will shape how strong and durable a governing coalition is capable of being these days in the UK.

Public opinion certainly suggests that fragmentation will resurface, now that the clarifying nature of "the Brexit election" has passed. In terms of public attitudes, the percentage of those in the UK who strongly identify with a party declined by 15 percentage points between the 1960s and the mid-2000s;[18] from 1980 to 2009, political-party membership in the UK declined by 66 percent.[19] Similarly, in the most recent UK elections for the European Parliament, where voting can be more purely expressive and less directed toward the need to form a workable government, the two major parties received only a *combined* vote share of 23.2 percent.[20] The rest of the vote was splintered among the Brexit Party (31.6 percent); the Liberal Democrats (20.3 percent); the Greens (12.1 percent); and other parties.

In the United States, the extraordinary polarization of the two political parties[21] can easily obscure the extent to which the USA is experiencing its own form of political fragmentation. Indeed, we see the same declines in public attitudes toward the two major political parties. In the early 1960s, 70–75 percent of people identified

15 *Id.*

16 Peter Riddell, *No Longer Just Big Party Dominance*, INST. FOR GOV'T BLOG (Aug. 28, 2014), https://www.instituteforgovernment.org.uk/blog/no-longer-just-big-party-dominance.

17 Gavin Freeguard, *The 2017 General Election, in Seven Charts*, INST. FOR GOV'T BLOG (June 9, 2017), https://www.instituteforgovernment.org.uk/blog/2017-general-election-seven-charts.

18 Russell J. Dalton, *Party Identification and Its Implications*, under "Politics" in OXFORD RESEARCH ENCYCLOPEDIA (2016).

19 MAIER, *supra* note 9, at 41.

20 *European Election 2019: UK Results in Maps and Charts*, BBC NEWS (May 27, 2019), https://www.bbc.com/news/uk-politics-48403131.

21 *See* Richard H. Pildes, *Why the Center Does Not Hold: The Causes of Hyperpolarized Democracy in America*, 99 CALIF. L. REV. 273 (2011).

with either the Democratic or the Republican Party; by 2014, that figure had fallen to 56 percent. Asked whether the main parties were doing an "adequate job," 56 percent said yes in 2003 but only 34 percent said the same by 2017.[22] Reflecting this alienation from the major parties, the desire for a new third party rose from 40 percent in 2003 to a significant majority of 62 percent by 2021.[23] Well before the 2016 election (in January of that year), Gallup reported that American's attachment to the two major parties was the weakest since polling on this issue had begun.[24]

Within the domain of governance, the way that political fragmentation takes shape in the United States, given its FPTP system, is through internal fragmentation *within* the two major parties. This fragmentation makes forging and implementing unified party agendas difficult, which makes effective governance even more difficult. Examples are abundant. In recent years, when the Republican Party has controlled the House, the party's internal factions have devoured its own Speakers of the House and forced them out. Similarly, the party's second-in-command, the House Majority Leader, was defeated in his party's *primary* in 2014, the first time that had happened in the 115 years since that leadership position had been created.

In the area of legislation, the most vivid recent example of the effects of internal party fragmentation was the Republican Party's inability to enact legislation on one of its signature issues over the last decade – health-care – even with unified Republican control of the House, Senate, and White House. Despite the conviction of party leaders in both the White House and Congress that the party's credibility with its voters hinged on this issue, the factional divisions within a fragmented Republican Party made it impossible for the party – even under unified party government – to deliver on one of its key issues. Indeed, the central theme of former House Speaker John Boehner's recent memoir is precisely how ungovernable his own party caucus was, because it had come to include a sizable contingent of what he calls "insurgents" and "the chaos caucus" which, in today's circumstances, he simply lacked the power to bring together to enable unified party positions on policy.[25]

As is widely recognized, the Democratic Party is always factionally riven between its more moderate and progressive wings. During the 2020 presidential primaries, these differences might have exploded in major ruptures, but the need to defeat Donald Trump was perceived as such an overwhelming imperative that the progressives reluctantly surrendered to unifying behind Joe Biden. Those differences remained suppressed in the first months after Biden took office, given the urgent need to address the ongoing pandemic and its economic fallout. As policy turns to other issues, whether the Democratic Party will be able to govern effectively, even

22 Eatwell & Goodwin, *supra* note 5, at 237.

23 *Id.*

24 Jeffrey M. Jones, *Democratic, Republican Identification Near Historical Lows* (Jan. 11, 2016), https://news.gallup.com/poll/188096/democratic-republican-identification-near-historical-lows.aspx.

25 John Boehner, On the House: A Washington Memoir (2021).

with unified control of government, or will be too internally fragmented, remains to be seen. President Biden clearly recognizes that the overarching role that has fallen to him is to show both democratic and nondemocratic states that democratic systems are still capable of delivering effective governance.[26]

18.3 FRAGMENTATION AND THE COMMUNICATIONS REVOLUTION

Democratic politics have become far more fragmented in recent decades across Western democracies, which weakens the capacity to deliver effective governance. The question then becomes whether this fragmentation is best understood as a temporary, contingent state of affairs or is likely to define the nature of democracy in a more enduring way for some time. The answer depends on the causes that have driven political fragmentation.

In a simple sense, it is easy to say that this fragmentation has been spawned by the seeming inability of democratic governments to exercise effective control over the major economic and cultural issues similarly roiling all these polities. On the economic front, stagnant incomes over many decades, globalization, the 2008 financial meltdown, and the economic effects of the pandemic have led many disaffected citizens to search for alternatives to the traditional political elites and parties. On the cultural front, anxieties over the specter of rapid cultural change due to historically high rates of immigration have, rightly or wrongly, been the second major force that has led to the splintering of traditional politics and parties. In theory, if governments could come to exercise more effective control along these two fronts, in ways that satisfy enough of their citizens, the forces generating fragmentation might conceivably be put back in a bottle. But political fragmentation also contains its own paradox: it comes about from the failures of governments to deliver on these issues and yet it makes it that much harder for governments to do so.

My view, however, is that the communications revolution is also one of the major forces that has generated the remarkable fragmentation of the political sphere. If that is so, it also suggests that this fragmentation is likely to be a more permanent feature of democratic politics, since there is no way to go back to an earlier era of political communication.

The early days of assessing the political ramifications of the communications revolution celebrated the democratization of influence and information, and the way these transformations would undermine authoritarian regimes. No longer could such governments easily control the spread of information and ideas, or the ability of groups to organize, mobilize, and occupy public space almost spontaneously. But it turns out that the information revolution poses a challenge to all forms of political authority, including democratic ones. The challenge is much deeper than is

26 David Brooks, *The Heart and Soul of the Biden Project*, N.Y. Times, Apr. 8, 2021, https://www.nytimes.com/2021/04/08/opinion/biden-economic-plan.html.

generally recognized because it goes beyond the now familiar issues of disinformation and conspiracy spreading (though these are serious problems). But the communications revolution might be thought almost inherently to undermine the capacity for legitimate, broadly accepted political authority – the authority necessary to be able to govern effectively in democratic systems. As Lincoln famously said, in democracies, "public sentiment is everything. With it, nothing can fail; against it, nothing can succeed."[27]

The information revolution might well make it impossible for public sentiment to be anything but highly fractured. The great cultural historians Robert Darnton and Lynn Hunt, in an acclaimed series of works, have described how, in the years leading up to the French Revolution, the print medium was used to spread (illegal) pornographic images of the monarchy that, in their view, became the principal agent of the monarchy's delegitimation[28] and cleared the path to the Revolution. Those images had an appropriate target and purpose. But today, the information revolution functions like that with respect to *all* forms of constituted political authority.

As Nancy Rosenblum and Russell Muirhead put it in their recent book on communications platforms today, "[w]e are learning what delegitimation looks like. Authorities are cast as hostile elements – worms in the bowels of the nation. Officials are 'so-called' officials."[29] France's philosophically inclined president recognizes this; as Emmanuel Macron has observed, democracies are undergoing a "leveling that destroys the principle of authority," without which they cannot function effectively.[30]

With so many sources of possible authority, marshaling concerted authority to support major governmental action becomes considerably more difficult. Political power now can be mobilized so immediately and effectively through the instruments of the communications revolution that we should expect democratic governments of all political ideologies to find it far more difficult to act. No major policies exist without resistance, but resistance today can be organized with astonishing rapidity, at least in the information domain, and at times in actual physical public spaces. The Yellow Vests in France, the *Podemos* in Spain, the Gezi Park protests in

27 David Zarefsky, *"Public Sentiment Is Everything": Lincoln's View of Political Persuasion*, 15 JALA 23–40 (1994), https://quod.lib.umich.edu/j/jala/2629860.0015.204/–public-sentiment-is-everything-lincolns-view-of-political?rgn=main;view=fulltext.

28 *See, e.g.*, ROBERT DARNTON, THE FORBIDDEN BEST-SELLERS OF PRE-REVOLUTIONARY FRANCE (1995); Lynn Hunt, *Pornography and the French Revolution, in* THE INVENTION OF PORNOGRAPHY, OBSCENITY AND THE ORIGINS OF MODERNITY, 1500–1800 301–40 (Lynn Hunt ed., 1993) ("Politically motivated pornography [which peaked in 1790] helped to bring about the Revolution by undermining the legitimacy of the ancient regime as a social and political system.").

29 RUSSELL MUIRHEAD & NANCY L. ROSENBLUM, A LOT OF PEOPLE ARE SAYING 35 (2019). While Muirhead and Rosenblum are concerned with the spreading of rumors and conspiracies, my concern goes beyond that: even if that problem could somehow be contained, social media would still be a major source for undermining the ability to establish legitimate, sustained political authority.

30 Roger Cohen, *Macron Tells Biden That Cooperation With U.S. Cannot Be Dependence*, N.Y. TIMES, Jan. 29, 2021, https://www.nytimes.com/2021/01/29/world/europe/macron-biden.html.

Turkey all exemplify this. Violent political mobs are mobilized through encrypted means such as WhatsApp groups.[31] Even after free and fair elections, the legitimacy of political authority is now under continual attack, an assault that is easy to muster. Many of these groups are leaderless as well, which can leave their political demands opaque and hinder any effort to accommodate or negotiate them.[32]

In the United States, one way the communications revolution facilitates political fragmentation is in the ability of individual legislators to exist as political free agents, independent of a need to adhere to party positions. Traditionally, legislators elected to the United States House or Senate had to work within the party structure and hierarchy, and wait many years, before they became nationally known and carried substantial political weight. Their success and stature depended on building support over time within the party. Now, it is possible – and, indeed, is happening regularly – for legislators in their very first years in the United States House or Senate to act as independent political entrepreneurs. Social media enables them to find and build their own national constituency, and to raise large amounts of money to fund their elections, all independently of their political party and its leadership. As a result, these newly elected figures can essentially bypass the party hierarchy and structure; political "leadership" becomes less effective. In America's system of bicameralism and separation of powers, the existence of many independent free agents in Congress makes putting together effective governing coalitions all that much more difficult.

When I first made this point seven years ago, I offered the examples of Senators Ted Cruz, on the right, and Elizabeth Warren on the left, both of whom in their first year or two in the Senate were able to exercise levels of power that would have been unheard of at such early stages of a political career for senators in the past.

Now, the most striking example is Representative Alexandria Ocasio-Cortez (known as AOC), who won the primary that launched her with just under 16,000 votes (and then easily won general elections in her overwhelmingly Democratic district). Yet, as a master of social media, she had nearly 9 million followers on various social media platforms; other than Nancy Pelosi (3.6 million), the next most for a Democrat in the House at the time was Steny Hoyer, with an anemic 220,000 followers. Thus, a few months into her first term in the House, AOC was one of the most nationally known Democrats. Never before was this possible. On the Republican side, John Boehner describes the moment he knew that effective power had shifted from the Speaker of the House to the fragmenting power of outside forces. When he refused to give a young Michelle Bachman a powerful committee seat she wanted (he notes that in earlier decades, no one so new to Congress would even have dared to have made the request), she threatened to go around him by taking to the platforms she could access on Fox News. The House

31 *Mob Violence Against Palestinians in Israel Is Fueled by Groups on WhatsApp*, DNYUZ (May 19, 2021), https://dnyuz.com/2021/05/19/mob-violence-against-palestinians-in-israel-is-fueled-by-groups-on-whatsapp/.

32 Zeynep Tufekci, Twitter and Tear Gas 49–83 (2017).

Speaker describes his realization: "I wasn't the one with power, she was saying. I just thought I was. She had the power now. She was right, of course."[33]

But one does not even have to be a new member of government to wield a level of disruptive power previously unimaginable. In the week before Germany's 2019 elections for the European Parliament, a twenty-six-year-old YouTuber named Rezo produced, from his parents' basement, a scathing fifty-five-minute mash-up video that relentlessly attacked Angela Merkel's ruling Christian Democratic Union of Germany (CDU).[34] Before the election, the video was seen a staggering 9 million or so times. The Christian Democrats, whose candidates started being asked regularly about the claims in the video, struggled unsuccessfully to figure out how to respond to what they believed were many misrepresentations. In the last week, the CDU lost about 7 percent of its support, for which CDU party figures blamed the Rezo video.

This same splintering of political authority applies in still further ways to the effort to forge complex political compromises on tough issues. The combination of the communications revolution with modern transparency requirements enables potential deals to be undermined before they get very far off the ground. Take immigration, one of the most important and difficult policy problems in the United States for many years now. In 2013, a seemingly powerful, bipartisan group of eight senators negotiated a comprehensive immigration bill, which the Senate passed sixty-eight to thirty-two. But grassroots conservative opposition was so effectively mobilized through cable television, radio, and the Internet that it caused that bipartisan deal to collapse.[35] The United States has not come as close to major immigration legislation since then. Brexit affords a similar example of how the communications revolution has made it easier to mobilize effective opposition. As Nigel Farage said, the existence of the Breitbart News website gave euroskeptic voices a power they would not otherwise have had, given that the major media and much of the political establishment strongly opposed Brexit.[36]

One can agree or disagree with some of the ends to which the newfound power that the communications revolution creates is put. But, as sources of information and persuasion have proliferated, or fragmented, there is little question that so too has political power. Perhaps the limitless ability to challenge and contest political authority is inherently good in a democracy. But when political authority becomes

33 BOEHNER, *supra* note 25, at 21.

34 Peter Kuras, *German Politics Discovers YouTube*, FOREIGN POLICY (June 4, 2019), https://foreignpolicy.com/2019/06/04/german-politics-discovers-youtube/; Christopher F. Schuetze, *Youth's Video Takes Aim at Merkel's Party in Run-Up to European Elections*, N.Y. TIMES, May 25, 2019, https://www.nytimes.com/2019/05/25/world/europe/rezo-cdu-youtube-germany.html.

35 Molly Ball, *The Little Group Behind the Big Fight to Stop Immigration*, THE ATLANTIC, Aug. 1, 2013, https://www.theatlantic.com/politics/archive/2013/08/the-little-group-behind-the-big-fight-to-stop-immigration-reform/278252/.

36 *Watch Deleted Video of Nigel Farage Thanking Steve Bannon and Breitbart for Brexit*, THE NEW EUROPEAN, Apr. 6, 2018, https://www.theneweuropean.co.uk/brexit-news/breitbart-video-nigel-farage-25806.

so fragmented that governments of all political ideologies are simply unable to marshal concerted, sustained power to deliver policies, democracies are more likely to become paralyzed and unable to deliver.

18.4 CONCLUSION

Political fragmentation is one of the major challenges and defining features of democracies today. In PR systems, this fragmentation takes the form of fracturing the long-dominant major parties into numerous smaller parties, which makes putting together effective, sustainable governing coalitions far more difficult. In the United States, the political parties are more internally splintered, with many politicians now independent free agents unconstrained by the need to follow party leaders and party positions. In all democracies, outside actors now have far greater power than ever before to destabilize political authority.

Most Western democracies are perceived by many of their members as having failed to address the major issues of the day. Yet this political fragmentation makes it all the more difficult to do just that. The communications revolution is one of the major forces driving this fragmentation and, because that genie cannot be put back into its bottle, political fragmentation will be an enduring challenge to the ability of democratic governments to provide effective governance. Democracies must figure out how to meet this challenge, lest their inability to deliver effectively on the issues their citizens find most urgent leads to even greater threats to democratic politics.

19

Constitutionalism and Public Corruption

An Introductory Sketch

Matthew C. Stephenson[*]

19.1 INTRODUCTION

The theme of this volume – constitutionalism and the right to effective governance – has important connections with the fight against public corruption.[1] This short contribution to the volume will briefly introduce three aspects of this topic: (1) How might corruption pose a threat to effective constitutional governance? (2) How might anticorruption efforts also put strain on the constitutional system? (3) In what ways might constitutional design choices affect the scope, prevalence, or type of corruption? The hope is that, by sketching out these relationships, this discussion can help to stimulate more dialogue and engagement between constitutional theorists and anticorruption specialists, who sometimes occupy separate intellectual and professional universes despite the close connections between their subject areas.

19.2 CORRUPTION AS A THREAT TO EFFECTIVE CONSTITUTIONAL GOVERNANCE

The threat that corruption poses to effective governance is sufficiently obvious that it is probably not worth dwelling on. Almost by definition, corruption renders governance less effective because the agents of the state are not doing what they are supposed to do.[2] In extreme cases, corruption can lead to what is sometimes called "state capture," a situation in which, notwithstanding the formal institutional rules,

* This chapter is adapted from a presentation prepared for the Harvard Law School Workshop on Effective Governance and Constitutionalism (May 2–3, 2019).

1 "Corruption" is a term that has many meanings. For purposes of this discussion, I use the term "corruption" to mean the abuse of entrusted power for private gain, particularly things like bribery, embezzlement, nepotism, and (unlawful/unethical) conflict of interest, rather than concerns regarding (legal) lobbying or campaign contributions, or the broader worry that "the system is rigged."

2 I say "almost" because under some circumstances corruption can actually improve governance if corruption facilitates the circumvention of inefficient or unjust official rules. *See* SAMUEL P. HUNTINGTON, POLITICAL ORDER IN CHANGING SOCIETIES 64–70 (1968); Nathaniel H. Leff,

the apparatus of government is exercised for the benefit of a relatively narrow clique, usually a combination of high-level politicians and their private-sector cronies.[3]

In addition to that direct threat, corruption also threatens the legitimacy, and hence the sustainability, of the constitutional order. The root cause of this problem is simple but important: People do not like corruption. Notwithstanding persistent tropes about how "corruption" is a culturally relative concept fashioned by and for wealthy Western countries, in fact both quantitative survey data and qualitative case studies demonstrate that, while in some countries people grudgingly tolerate corruption, or participate in corrupt systems because they feel that they have no choice, overwhelming majorities of surveyed citizens in every country intensely dislike corrupt practices.[4] Moreover, exposure to corruption breeds resentment, distrust of the government, and (in democracies) lower confidence that democracy is a good system of government.[5]

In addition to this direct negative effect of corruption on public confidence in both the government of the day and the constitutional system, corruption correlates strongly with other factors that might threaten the legitimacy of the constitutional order. For example, widespread corruption correlates with lower incomes, greater economic inequality, worse health and education levels, poorer infrastructure, and a host of other social ills that may undermine confidence in the institutions of government, whether or not people ascribe these ills to government corruption.

In addition to the general and diffuse threat that corruption poses to the legitimacy of the constitutional system, public anger and frustration over corruption can be exploited by demagogues to advance an agenda that is hostile to liberal-democratic constitutionalism. We have seen many examples of this now, including Rodrigo Duterte in the Philippines,[6] Viktor Orban in Hungary,[7]

Economic Development through Bureaucratic Corruption, 8 Am. Behav. Sci. 8 (1964). But the empirical work on the topic suggests that this is not usually the case. *See, e.g.*, Matthew C. Stephenson, *Yes, Corruption Is Bad for Development. No, Corruption Is Not a Western Obsession*, Global Anticorruption Blog (Apr. 29, 2014), https://globalanticorruptionblog.com/2014/04/29/yes-corruption-is-bad-for-development-no-corruption-is-not-a-western-obsession-2/ (collecting and linking to sources).

3 *See, e.g.*, Joel S. Hellman et al., *Seize the State, Seize the Day: State Capture and Influence in Transition Economies*, 31 J. Compar. Econ. 751 (2003); Bob Rijkers et al., *All in the Family: State Capture in Tunisia*, 124 J. Dev. Econ. 41 (2017).

4 *See* Stephenson, *supra* note 2 (collecting and linking to sources).

5 *See, e.g.*, Alessandro Pellegata & Vincenzo Memoli, *Can Corruption Erode Confidence in Political Institutions among European Countries? Comparing the Effect of Different Measures of Perceived Corruption*, 128 Soc. Indic. Rsch. 391 (2016); Tom van der Meer & Armen Hakhverdian, *Political Trust as the Evaluation of Process and Performance: A Cross-National Study of 42 European Countries*, 65 Pol. Stud. 81 (2017).

6 *See* Beatriz Paterno, *What Does Rodrigo Duterte's Victory Say About the Philippines' Experience with Corruption?*, Global Anticorruption Blog (May 20, 2016), https://globalanticorruptionblog.com/2016/05/20/what-does-rodrigo-dutertes-victory-say-about-the-philippines-experience-with-corruption/.

7 *See* Katie King, *How Corruption Politics Facilitated Hungary's Response to the Refugee Crisis*, Global Anticorruption Blog (Nov. 13, 2015), https://globalanticorruptionblog.com/2015/11/13/how-corruption-politics-facilitated-hungarys-response-to-the-refugee-crisis/.

Jimmy Morales in Guatemala,[8] and Jair Bolsonaro in Brazil.[9] Furthermore, anger about corruption can boil over into mass protests that destabilize the existing order, for better or worse. The 1989 Tiananmen Square protests were originally triggered in large measure by anger about corruption,[10] as were the more recent Arab Spring protests.[11] Sometimes these developments produce positive end results, but sometimes they do not. In some cases, corruption has been invoked as the pretext for an antidemocratic coup or authoritarian takeover, with large segments of the population tolerating or even welcoming the ousting of the civilian government largely because of frustration over widespread, unchecked corruption.[12] And even when anger over corruption does not prompt a regime change, this anger can make the government more vulnerable to internal security threats, such as terrorism and separatist violence. In Afghanistan, for example, the Taliban insurgency, which ultimately toppled the Western-backed government in 2021, likely benefitted from the widespread perception among many ordinary citizens that the Taliban was less corrupt than the incumbent government. In some cases government corruption may have pushed Afghans to embrace the Taliban, or at least to have viewed the government and the Taliban as equally bad, which reduced citizens' inclination to assist the government's counter-insurgency efforts.[13]

8 *See* Rathna Ramamurthi, *Not Corrupt, Not a Thief, But Not the Answer: Jimmy Morales and Corruption in Guatemala*, Global Anticorruption Blog (Nov. 16, 2015), https://globalanticorruptionblog.com/2015/11/16/not-corrupt-not-a-thief-but-not-the-answer-jimmy-morales-and-corruption-in-guatemala/.

9 *See* Matthew C. Stephenson, *Brazil's Electoral Dilemma: Which Outcome Will Be Better for Anticorruption?*, Global Anticorruption Blog (Oct. 16, 2018), https://globalanticorruptionblog.com/2018/10/16/brazils-electoral-dilemma-which-outcome-will-be-better-for-anticorruption/. Donald Trump is a more complicated case, as I do not think his alleged anticorruption rhetoric – "drain the swamp" and all that – was really about "corruption" in the sense in which I am defining it here; I think that was more coded racism and anti-elitism. *See* Matthew C. Stephenson, *Why Did Trump's Anticorruption Rhetoric Resonate? Three Hypotheses*, Global Anticorruption Blog (Dec. 13, 2016), https://globalanticorruptionblog.com/2016/12/13/why-did-trumps-anticorruption-rhetoric-resonate-three-hypotheses/. But in many other countries, including the ones mentioned above, more traditional anticorruption was an explicit and prominent part of these politicians' platforms.

10 *See* David Daokui Li & Yujiang Wang, *Political Conditions for Reform: China vs. Eastern Europe Revisited*, 4 J. Eur. Econ. Assoc. 342, 349 (2006); Stanley Vittoz, *Confucianism and the Spirit of Democracy in China: The Beijing Uprising of* 1989, 7 Int'l J. Pol., Cult., & Soc'y 329, 350 (1993).

11 *See* Chonghyun Christie Byun & Ethan J. Hollander, *Explaining the Intensity of the Arab Spring*, 24 Dig. Middle East Stud. 26 (2015); Juliet Sorensen, *Ideals Without Illusions: Corruption and the Future of a Democratic North Africa*, 10 Nw. J. Int'l Hum. Rts. 202 (2012).

12 This seems to have been the case, for example, in the Thai coup of 2014. *See* Claudio Sopranzetti, *Thailand's Relapse: The Implications of the May 2014 Coup*, 75 J. Asian Stud. 299, 309–11 (2016); Pavin Chachavalpongpun, *The Politics of International Sanctions: The 2014 Coup in Thailand*, 68 J. Int'l Aff. 169, 176 (2014).

13 *See* Sarah Chayes, Thieves of State: Why Corruption Threatens Global Security (2015); Josh VonTrapp, *Will Afghanistan's New Taliban Rulers Govern Corruptly?*, Global Anticorruption Blog (Nov. 1, 2021), https://globalanticorruptionblog.com/2021/11/01/will-afghanistans-new-taliban-rulers-govern-corruptly/.

19.3 ANTICORRUPTION AS A THREAT TO EFFECTIVE CONSTITUTIONAL GOVERNANCE

For the reasons sketched already, corruption, if left unchecked, may threaten the liberal-democratic constitutional order. Paradoxically, however, the fight *against* corruption might also strain or challenge liberal-democratic constitutionalism. There are two principal concerns in this vein.

The first concern follows directly from the previous discussion of how much people dislike corruption. Given the seriousness of the corruption problem in many countries, and the pressure on the government to do something about it, the fight against corruption can sometimes involve stretching or overstepping constitutional limits, especially with respect to things like the power of the executive to act unilaterally and the rights of criminal suspects and defendants. Troublingly, many of the most familiar modern anticorruption "success stories" seem to involve autocratic or semi-autocratic chief executives initiating widespread crackdowns that make use of aggressive law enforcement techniques. Hong Kong and Singapore are the most familiar examples, but we see something of a similar pattern even in democracies like Georgia and Botswana.[14] Even milder anticorruption measures, such as the creation of specialized court systems, have triggered constitutional challenges in places like Indonesia and Slovakia.[15]

The second issue is related but distinct: Although anticorruption typically has broad cross-party support when framed as an abstract issue, whenever there is a specific case involving specific individuals or parties, anticorruption can become hyperpoliticized. The targets of anticorruption investigations inevitably complain that they are the victims of politically motivated "witch hunts" – and sometimes they have a point. Those complaining of "witch hunts" sometimes make sweeping claims that the institutions of justice (the investigators, prosecutors, and judges) are acting out of an improper partisan agenda. (Here, too, this claim, while clearly self-serving, is not always wrong.) This sort of conflict poses important challenges to the constitutional order. One obvious challenge concerns how to design institutions that will not, in fact, be politically biased – or that will at least reduce and constrain such bias. But even if we assume for the moment that the institutions of justice are operating tolerably well, the plausibility of the accusation of bias, coupled with the natural human tendency to believe charges against those we dislike – and to minimize, ignore, or dismiss

[14] *See* Matthew C. Stephenson, *Corruption and Democratic Institutions: A Review and Synthesis, in* CORRUPTION: GLOBAL INFLUENCES, POLITICS AND THE MARKET 92, 100 (Susan Rose-Ackerman & Paul Lagunes eds., 2015); David Sebudubudu, *Corruption and Its Control in Botswana*, 35 BOTS. NOTES & REC. 125, 130–31 (2003).

[15] *See* Sofie Arjon Schütte, Specialised Anti-corruption Courts: Indonesia, U4 Brief 2016:4, CHR. MICHELSEN INSTITUTE (2016), https://www.cmi.no/publications/5886-specialised-anti-corruption-courts-indonesia; Matthew C. Stephenson, Specialised Anti-corruption Courts: Slovakia, U4 Brief 2016:2, CHR. MICHELSEN INSTITUTE (2016), https://www.cmi.no/publications/5882-specialised-anti-corruption-courts-slovakia.

allegations against our allies – means that a significant anticorruption investigation can provoke a broad-based attack on the legitimacy of core institutions.

19.4 CORRUPTION PREVENTION THROUGH CONSTITUTIONAL DESIGN

While both corruption and aggressive anticorruption efforts may pose challenges to effective constitutional governance, the right sort of constitutional design might help mitigate or constrain corruption. After all, while constitutions have multiple purposes, many constitutional drafters and their advisors are concerned with designing a system that will be less susceptible to corruption.[16] How might constitutional provisions help or hinder anticorruption efforts?

This short chapter is not the right place for a thorough consideration of this important and complex issue, but, in the interest of provoking further conversation and inquiry along these lines, here is a preliminary list of some of the ways in which constitutions might try to address the public corruption problem:

- First, a constitution might embed certain anticorruption requirements directly into the constitutional text. The US Constitution's Emoluments Clauses are an example.[17]
- Second, some constitutions provide for the independence and authority of key anticorruption bodies – such as specialized anticorruption investigators, prosecutors, and courts – by giving such bodies constitutional status, with independence guarantees similar to those provided to judges.[18]
- On a related note, the extent to which the prosecution service falls under the control of the chief executive, and the extent to which line prosecutors are subject to control by the prosecutor general/minister of justice/attorney general, are important constitutional design choices that may be especially significant for anticorruption.[19]
- Federalism may be important here, too. Despite much theorizing, there is not a lot of strong evidence that, when comparing across countries, federal systems

16 *See* Zephyr Teachout, *The Anti-Corruption Principle*, 94 CORNELL L. REV. 341 (2009); Center for Constitutional Transitions et al., *Combating Corruption – Institutional Frameworks for the Middle East and North Africa* (2014), http://www.constitutionaltransitions.org/publications/combating-corruption/.

17 The Foreign Emoluments Clause states that no officer of the United States "shall, without the Consent of the Congress, accept of any present, Emolument, Office, or Title, of any kind whatever, from any King, Prince, or foreign State." U.S. CONST. Art. I, Sec. 9, cl. 8. The Domestic Emoluments Clause states that "[t]he President shall, at stated Times, receive for his services, a Compensation, ... and he shall not receive within [his term] any other Emolument from the United States, or any of them." U.S. CONST. Art. II, Sec. 1, cl. 7.

18 *See* Mark Tushnet, *Institutions Protecting Constitutional Democracy: Some Conceptual and Methodological Preliminaries*, 70(2) U. TORONTO L. J. 95 (2020); OECD, *Specialised Anti-corruption Institutions – Review of Models* (2013).

19 See Anne van Aaken et al., *Do Independent Prosecutors Deter Political Corruption? An Empirical Evaluation across Seventy-Eight Countries*, 12 AM. L. & ECON. REV. 204 (2010).

are notably more or less corrupt than unitary systems.[20] But in individual countries, the existence of parallel systems of courts and prosecutors seems to have been quite important. In the US experience, for example, federal enforcement played a key role in breaking corrupt political machines at the state and local level.[21]

- The design of electoral systems may play a role in shaping the level or type of corruption. Likewise, the separation of powers (presidential v. parliamentary systems, unicameral v. bicameral legislators, etc.) might matter also. The cross-country evidence does not suggest major differences with respect to overall perceived corruption level across different types of democratic system when controlling for other factors (such as income and region), but there is some suggestive evidence that at least the form of corruption may differ across different sorts of constitutional system.[22]
- Constitutional guarantees regarding press freedom, civil society associations, and transparency may be important, given that external monitoring has consistently been shown to be important in disclosing corruption and promoting accountability.[23]

This is, to be sure, an incomplete list, and the extent to which these or other aspects of constitutional design actually have a substantial impact on corruption remains the subject of ongoing research and considerable controversy. The larger message here is that while unchecked corruption can threaten the legitimacy and sustainability of the constitutional system, the design and implementation of constitutions can have an important influence on the efficacy of the fight to contain corruption – and, thus, to maintain the liberal-democratic constitutional order.

20 *See* Danila Serra, *Empirical Determinants of Corruption: A Sensitivity Analysis*, 126 PUB.C CHOICE 225 (2006); Sebastian Freille et al., *Federalism, Decentralisation and Corruption* (2008) (unpublished manuscript on file with author).

21 *See* Richard Messick, *Borrowing Integrity in the United States: Federal Prosecution of State and Local Corruption*, GLOBAL ANTICORRUPTION BLOG (July 22, 2015), https://globalanticorruptionblog.com/2015/07/22/borrowing-integrity-in-the-united-states-federal-prosecution-of-state-and-local-corruption/.

22 *See* Stephenson, *supra* note 14, at 111–25.

23 *See* Aymo Brunetti & Beatrice Weder, *A Free Press Is Bad News for Corruption*, 87 J. PUB. ECON. 1801 (2003); Piero Stanig, *Regulation of Speech and Media Coverage of Corruption: An Empirical Analysis of the Mexican Press*, 59 AM. J. POL. SCI. 175 (2015).

Index

Printed in the USA
CPSIA information can be obtained
at www.ICGtesting.com
CBHW050053151124
17337CB00015B/109

9 781009 158534